# TYING AND FISHING
# THE NYMPH

# TYING AND FISHING THE NYMPH

TAFF PRICE

BLANDFORD

**A BLANDFORD BOOK**
First published in the UK 1995
by Blandford
(a Cassell imprint)
Wellington House
125 Strand
LONDON
WC2R 0BB
© Taff Price 1995

Distributed in Australia
by Capricorn Link (Australia) Pty Ltd
2/13 Carrington Road, Castle Hill, NSW 2154

**British Library Cataloguing-in-Publication Data**
A catalogue record for this book is available from the British Library.

ISBN 0-7137-2374-2 (Hardback)
0-7137-2595-8 (Paperback)

Typeset by Litho Link Ltd, Welshpool, Powys, Wales
Printed and bound in Great Britain
by The Bath Press, Avon

# CONTENTS

# Part III   ADDITIONAL ARTIFICIALS

# INTRODUCTION

The term 'nymph', as used in fly-fishing today, encompasses a wide range of aquatic creatures. In the past it was only the larval stages of the mayflies (Ephemeroptera) and the dragonflies and damsel-flies (Odonata) that were referred to as nymphs. Today it is a different story because any insect that lives in the water and forms part of the diet of the trout is, for the purposes of fly-fishing, broadly termed a nymph. Using imitations of such creatures falls into the category of 'nymph-fishing'.

Among the many other aquatic insects that are both imitated by flies and used in modern nymph-fishing are:

(a) The larval and pupal stages of caddisflies (Trichoptera).

(b) The larval stages of stoneflies (Plecoptera), found in swiftly flowing rivers and considered in many parts of the fly-fishing world to be of prime importance. Such stonefly nymphs were once used as livebait by many anglers and, in the UK, were called 'creepers'.

(c) Chironomid midges, the phantom midge (*Chaoborus*) and even those flies that can be a problem with their annoying bites, the mosquitoes, in their larval and pupal stages.

(d) Aquatic genera of the Hemiptera, such as *Corixa* spp., the small beetle-like bugs that dart up to the surface to clothe their thoraxes with life-giving air.

(e) Aquatic beetles (Coleoptera), of which both adults and larvae are taken by trout.

(f) Crustacea, such as freshwater shrimps (*Gammarus* spp.), and the closely allied water lice.

It is probably true to say that, in the early days of fly-fishing, only the adult insects were copied by the old-time fly-tiers; they imitated what they could see. With few exceptions, their knowledge of what went on under the water was extremely scant to say the least, so naturally they tied up flies only after observing the insects that were found on the surface of the water. I am of the opinion, however, that many of the traditional spider-dressed, wet-fly patterns would certainly be taken by the trout in mistake for nymphal forms of aquatic flies, even though the fisherman may have been ignorant of this fact.

The flies of the north of England, Italy and northern Spain can all fall into this category, even though there are subtle differences in the style of dressing and in the materials used in the make-up of the flies. (It is an interesting side-note that, in the flies used in these mountain and moorland rivers, the tiers dispensed with the wing. Was the wingless fly developed independently in the various countries or was there a missing link?) Flies such as those used for over 200 years in the Piedmont region of northern Italy, and called 'Valasesiana' and 'Ossolina' after the Rivers Sesia and Ossola respectively, are very nymph-like in their construction and conception, as are the Cocchetto nymph flies from the area close to Milan that were tied with silk dubbing from the cocoons of wild silkmoths. The Spanish flies in Juan de Bergera's *Manuscrito de Astorgas* (1624) are again all spider-dressed flies from the Province of Léon in Spain, unlike the earlier flies referred to in the Basurto manuscript of 1520. These flies from Navarre were almost streamer-like in appearance. I have no doubt that, in all these sparsely dressed spider patterns, from around the world, we are looking at the ancestors of today's nymphs.

In the rest of the fly-fishing world, from the fly described by Aelian in AD 240, to the flies given by Dame Juliana Berners in the *Boke of St Albans*, and even those described by Cotton in Walton's *Compleat Angler*, all had wings, presumably in imitation of the adult insects. Skues noted, during a fishing trip to Bosnia in the late 1890s, that the flies used by the Moslem fishermen of that area were identical in style to those described by Dame Juliana. Although links were tenuously made between these and early English flies, it is believed that the crude Bosnian patterns were copies of flies used by visiting fly-fishing officers of the Austro-Hungarian Empire. The local peasants noted the effectiveness of fly-fishing and probably copied flies that they found caught up in bushes and lost on the bankside by the visitors.

In the USA, New Zealand, Australia and South Africa, and many other fly-fishing countries, traditional wet-winged patterns were standard fare for many years; most of the flies used in these countries could only be classed as fancy attractor flies. In truth, few, if any, of these winged flies emulated the nymph as we know it, either by design or in the way they were originally fished. When fished wet, they could, at best, only represent a drowned winged insect and, when dapped in the surface film, they may have resembled an adult winged insect or, with a stretch of imagination, an emerging fly caught in the surface film.

It is possible, however, to believe that some traditional winged wet flies could be mistaken by the trout for emerging caddisflies. I mooted this theory as a possibility in my last book, *The Angler's Sedge*. The live larvae of the stoneflies (creepers) and, in some areas, caddis larvae were collected by anglers and used as livebait for trout but, although it was obvious to the angler that trout fed upon such creatures, very little if anything was done to imitate them by means of fur or feather. I suppose, as there was no restriction on the use of livebait, that there was simply no need to use artificials, and the ethics of using the artificial fly only was not a consideration.

Pre-occupation with dry fly on the rivers of southern England also depressed the use of nymphal patterns for some considerable time. It was left to anglers such as Skues, Mottram and a few others to penetrate this Victorian dry-fly dogma by tying nymph flies to be fished beneath the surface. The snobbish look-down-the-nose attitude of the dry-fly purists was not, as many have thought, a doctrine of Halford; he was only of the opinion that the wet fly was not as effective as the dry fly on the clear chalkstreams. It must also be said in Halford's defence that he did in fact tie imitations of such 'nymph' flies; his imitation of the grannom larva is one such pattern. Skues was strongly influenced by northern fly fishermen and the way they fished with their traditional wet-spider patterns, often upstream. He adopted their

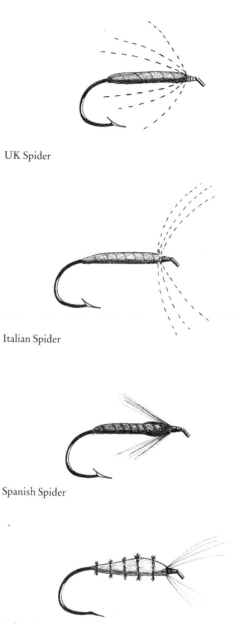

UK Spider

Italian Spider

Spanish Spider

Italian Cocchetto Nymph

methods and adapted their flies to suit the more tranquil-flowing chalkstreams of Hampshire. The nymph as we know it today was born.

In his book, *The Way of a Trout with a Fly* (1921), Skues refers to a fly, the Half Stone, a wet-spider pattern popular in Devon and other parts of the west of England, as a form of nymph. Today the nymph is now firmly accepted on all rivers and stillwaters as an important weapon in the armoury of the fly-fisherman. On very few stretches of the

Hampshire chalkstreams dry fly is still mandatory, but this is now the exception rather than the rule and the upstream nymph is allowed on most waters.

The knowledge that the trout does most of its feeding below the surface encourages today's angler to make use of the 'nymph' in its broadest sense for most of his or her fishing. In the UK the development of stillwater fisheries has gone a long way to making the nymph the most important of artificial flies and, at the same time, it has made the fly-fishermen of the UK probably the most expert at fishing stillwaters. All over the continent of Europe anglers fish the rivers with the nymph, for both trout and grayling. Some of the aficionados of the nymph from France and countries as far away as Poland, the Czech Republic and the former republics of Yugoslavia – Slovenia and Croatia – have proved themselves to be highly skilled in the use of the weighted nymph.

In the USA the use of nymphs on rivers has reached a peak of efficiency and patterns are tied to represent many of the varied creatures found in the rivers of that country. A large number of their killing patterns have travelled across the Atlantic to take fish in the UK and Europe, but this is not a one-way route, for many European patterns are now finding their way to the rivers of North America. Today the fly-fisherman of the Antipodes has started to relinquish the large lure-type flies for more exquisite small nymphs, and this is true also in South Africa, where the once fancy large flies are being ousted by more subtle imitations of natural creatures.

# ACKNOWLEDGEMENTS

To all the fly tiers, fly fishermen, guides and writers mentioned in the book, my thanks. Without their efforts there would be no book. My thanks also to Harry Ranger who helped me with some of the flies depicted in the colour section.

# PART I

# INTRODUCING THE NYMPH

# CHAPTER ONE

# THE NATURAL NYMPH

When a fish takes its food from the surface it is possible, more often than not, to recognize and, in many cases, identify what that fish is feeding upon; even though the angler may not be able to identify the fly precisely, at least he will be able to match the natural for size and colour from the flies he carries in his box. No such help is available if the trout is feeding beneath the surface, unless it is in very slow-moving, crystal-clear water, when it may be possible to observe trout take a particular nymph or other aquatic creature.

How does the angler know what is going on beneath the surface? Knowledge of the life-forms in the water can be obtained by regular examination of the stomach contents of caught fish but this, of course, is not possible if one fishes to catch-and-release principles. I am of the opinion that fish can be harmed by using stomach pumps and similar items of equipment. Fish should be subjected to as little stress as possible and should always be returned quickly and carefully to the water.

Examination, by sifting with seine nets, can reveal the nymphs and other creatures that swim in the main body of the water. Such periodic examination of good, fish-holding riffle water increases the successful angler's knowledge. Investigation of stones and small boulders often shows nymphs and caddis forms, and gravel-sifting with a sturdy scoop-type net will also reveal those insects that hide in the safety of the silt. A close look at the aquatic weeds will reveal the small, and sometimes not so small, creatures that use this greenery as a browsing pasture and a safe haven.

The recognition and identification of winged adult insects obviously tells the fisherman what nymphs the trout could possibly be feeding upon beneath the surface. Some keen anglers even go to the extent of studying nymphs and other aquatic fauna in home aquaria. The knowledge they gain about the behaviour of the insects can, when they are fishing, have a direct bearing on the resultant behaviour of the trout. Fly-fishing is a continual

learning process, and it is an extremely ignorant person who states that he knows it all. Every day spent at the waterside is usually one of learning as well as of sport and enjoyment. At least, every time I go fishing, I feel I learn something; usually it is from my own stupid mistakes.

The purpose of this chapter is to give the reader some means of broadly identifying the particular family of the creatures that make up the sub-aquatic diet of the trout. Specific insects will be dealt with in subsequent chapters. In many instances the type of tail can give a rough-and-ready guide as to which group of insects an individual nymph belongs. I have found this tail feature helpful for the beginner, who can have difficulty in absorbing all the disciplines and information that constitute the sport of fly-fishing. Entomology need not be the mystery that many anglers believe it to be.

## TAILS OF NYMPHS

### MAYFLIES (Ephemeroptera)
As nymphs, most species possess three tails (cerci), although the adult insects may have only two. The tails are generally long and thin and approximately the same size. In other parts of the world – the USA and the Antipodes – there are a number of species that possess two tails only as nymphs and, elsewhere, there are some species that have two longish outer cerci and a much smaller, almost non-existent, middle tail.

### STONEFLIES (Plecoptera)
Stonefly nymphs always have two robust tails, usually spread quite wide apart.

### CADDISFLIES (Trichoptera)
The cased caddis larva is easily recognized by most anglers. The only confusion could be with larvae of certain aquatic moths, but this is unlikely. A large number of caddis larvae make no cases at all,

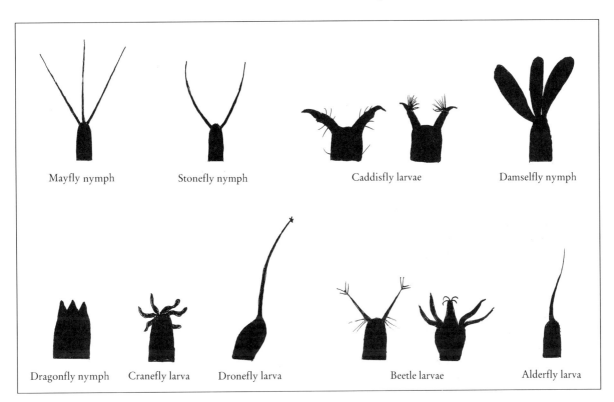

Mayfly nymph          Stonefly nymph          Caddisfly larvae          Damselfly nymph

Dragonfly nymph   Cranefly larva   Dronefly larva          Beetle larvae          Alderfly larva

so I thought it reasonable to depict the rear of two such larvae.

### DAMSELFLIES (Odonata)
Three broad, flat tails form the breathing organs, which absorb oxygen from the water.

### DRAGONFLIES (Odonata)
These have no 'tails' as such, but most species appear to have three sharp projections sticking out of the final segment of the abdomen.

### TRUE FLY LARVAE (Diptera)
The larvae of the aquatic Diptera are wide and varied. The two illustrated are of the aquatic crane fly and the drone fly or rat-tailed maggot. As a generalization, if the creature has no legs as such, you can be almost certain that it is the larva of an aquatic dipteran.

### BEETLES (Coleoptera)
The aquatic beetles show a wide variety of tail configuration. All I can say is that, if the nymph does not fit into the categories already mentioned and if it possesses legs, you can be pretty certain that it is a beetle larvae.

### ALDERFLIES (Megaloptera)
The breathing appendage at the rear of the alder larva's body looks like a single tail.

### GENERAL IDENTIFICATION

### MAYFLIES (Ephemeroptera)
The life-cycle of the mayfly is as follows: egg; nymph; sub-imago; imago. Both the last two stages are winged and are known by anglers as the dun and the spinner. The nymphs of the mayfly vary greatly in size, shape, colour and habitat. Some are broad and flat and appear to be built for clinging to stones in fast water; others are to be found in the aquatic weed. Some are fast-moving, slim creatures designed for swimming, and yet others spend their life as crawlers. A number of the larger species dig into the gravel and silt and have robust legs for this purpose. As a general rule, the time spent as a nymph can vary between 1 and 2 years (some say 3), depending on the species; the larger species require a greater length of time.

### STONEFLIES (Plecoptera)
Like the mayflies these insects are to be found in a wide variety of sizes, again depending on the

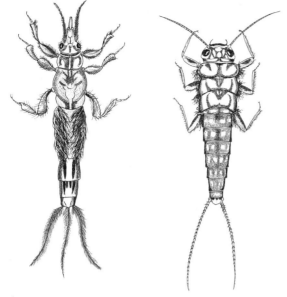

*Ephemera* sp.                    *Perla* sp.

## DRAGONFLIES AND DAMSELF

These are very important cre
stillwaters; the winged adu
fishing and add a flash of colc
and dart above the water surfa
on the larval forms. Some slc
their share of these predato
reaches of faster streams. T
known; there is no pupal
migrate from the water an
vegetation, laboriously breaking out of the old
nymphal skin.

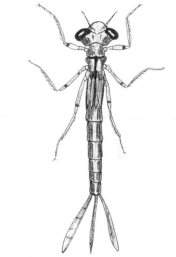

Damselfly nymph

species. Stoneflies are found only in the purest of water because they have a low pollution tolerance. Unlike the mayflies, there is no intermediate winged sub-imago stage, nor is there a pupal stage. Like the damselflies, the nymphs hatch directly into the adult insects.

## CADDISFLIES (Trichoptera)

Most of the larvae of the sedge- or caddisfly are easily recognized by the cases which they construct for themselves. A number of species do not construct such mobile shelters but utilize webs and silken tubes to trap their prey. The caddis has a quiescent pupal stage like the butterflies and moths, to which they are closely related.

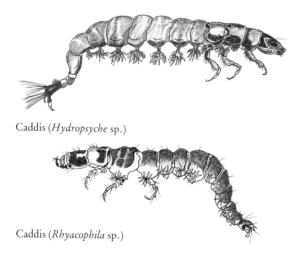

Caddis (*Hydropsyche* sp.)

Caddis (*Rhyacophila* sp.)

## TRUE FLIES (Diptera)

Some of the members of this wide and divergent group must be considered very important insects as far as the diet of the trout is concerned. The chironomid midges are found in large numbers on stillwater and perforce must be one of the prime insects that trout feed upon. In recent years their importance has been emphasized for river-dwelling game-fish. The life-cycle is egg, larva, pupa – all are aquatic – and a winged adult stage. The phantom midges (*Chaoborus* spp.) can also be of prime importance on many stillwaters. Mosquitos are also taken by trout, especially in the larval and pupal stages. Other midges, such as the *Simulium* biting midges, may well be a source of trout food on some trout rivers. Larger members of the Diptera also figure on the trout's menu; such creatures as the aquatic crane flies, the daddy-long-legs (Tipulidae), some of the horse flies (Tabanidae) and hover flies (Syrphidae) have all been imitated by fly-tiers.

## WATER BUGS (Hemiptera)

The lesser water boatman (Corixidae) and the water boatman or back swimmer (Notonectidae) are the two most important of the Hemiptera that are often taken by the trout. The Corixidae has many species, 33 in the UK compared with four species of Notonectidae. There is, however, a traditional fly tied to represent the water cricket *Velia caprai*, (Velidae), but I have never found the naturals in the stomach contents of caught fish nor seen a trout take them off the surface as they skate across the film. Water bugs have no pupal stage; the infant larvae, or instars, develop by moulting at least five times until the adult insect is formed.

## WATER BEETLES (Coleoptera)

There are many different species of water beetles, and both larvae and adults could end up in the stomach of the voracious trout. There are a number of nymphal fly patterns tied to imitate both stages, especially of the larger species, such as the *Dytiscus* beetle. The pupae of the beetles are generally quiescent and are not taken by the trout.

## ALDERFLIES (Megaloptera/Neuroptera)

The larva of the alderfly (*Sialis* spp.) is an important early-season nymph in British stillwaters. The larva migrates to dry land in order to pupate. In other parts of the world, close relatives of the alder, the Dobson flies, are imitated by artificial flies.

## CRUSTACEA

Non-insect adult Crustacea can, in terms of fly-fishing, be called 'nymphs'. Perhaps the most important is the freshwater shrimp or scud, as it is known in the USA. There are a number of different species in the UK, the most common being *Gammarus pulex*. These shrimps belong to

*Gammarus* sp.

the family Amphipoda. The water lice belong to the family Isopoda and have also received the attention of fly-tiers. The largest crustacean likely to be encountered in the UK is the crayfish, and there are a large number of patterns worldwide to imitate this and other members of the Decapoda. In places such as South Africa and South America freshwater crabs are taken by large trout. The smallest crustaceans we are likely to try to imitate are the water fleas, or daphnia, of the family Cladocera (but with patterns a little larger than the actual creature).

## LEECHES (Hirudinea)

Trout often feed on these rather unattractive creatures, and there are many patterns tied to imitate these worm-like members of the Hirudinea.

*Erpobdella* sp.

## SPIDERS (Arachnida)

The aquatic spiders could be taken by the trout if they existed in the same habitat but, as those spiders that build themselves sub-aquatic webs and fill them with air tend to live in weedy ponds, the likelihood of their becoming the prey of trout is remote. Many times, when doing an autopsy on the stomach contents of caught fish, I have found many small aquatic mites. There is at least one pattern in existence, the Large Red Mite, tied to represent the largest of these mites.

\*    \*    \*

With such a tempting variety of food, it is little wonder that the trout chooses to do most of its feeding beneath the surface. Of course, it does venture off the bottom to sip a winged fly off the surface – thank goodness or there would be no dry fly fishing – but surface-feeding requires a greater expenditure of energy by the trout and, throughout nature, all predators usually take the easiest option. Although the grayling rises to the surface to take a dry fly, its mouthparts are most definitely designed for bottom-feeding.

# CHAPTER TWO

# THE ARTIFICIAL NYMPH

The secret of a successful nymph pattern lies in the simple fact that the quarry must view the imitation as a live creature. To the fish it must not only appear to be food but must also seem to be alive. Integral life can be given to the artificial fly by the use of mobile materials in its make-up and also by the way the fly is fished. It is the method of retrieve, along with the speed and type of retrieve, that causes the fly at the end of the leader to work in a natural and enticing way. It must provoke the trout into taking it by triggering a response, be it one of feeding, curiosity, perhaps even anger, or, in some cases, what might be called play.

A fish has no hands; it cannot pick up something, look at it and then discard if it if does not like what it sees. A fish can only look at something and, if it wants to investigate further, for any of the reasons given, take it into its mouth; from there, it either accepts the object as food or rejects it. That is the 'take' of the trout and it can happen so quickly that the fisherman does not even know that his fly has been seized and subsequently rejected. Quite often a take registers with the angler and he tightens, only to strike at nothing. You will often hear anglers say that the fish are 'coming short', or 'nipping the tail'. Of course, this may be true but, more often than not, the fly has been well and truly taken and ejected from the trout's mouth before the so-called take has registered with the angler.

Materials used in the manufacture of nymphs should emulate as closely as possible the texture of the natural creatures, so that the artificial not only looks and behaves as if it were alive but also feels alive. It goes without saying that size can also be an important factor in nymph imitation, especially with extremely selective trout, those fish that are preoccupied with feeding on a specific creature. On the other hand, there are times when a slightly larger, or even a slightly smaller, fly may well tempt a trout, whereas a more correctly sized imitation could well be ignored. So one can conclude that size can be important most of the time, but there are exceptions.

What about colour? Well, as with size, the right colour is also important but, again, there are occasions when, for one reason or another, a trout does not seem to differentiate between one colour and another. Yet, on other days, it becomes hyperselective and will only take a fly of a particular shade. Perhaps the best advice is initially to match the colour of your artificial as closely as possible to the natutral; if this is not succesful, then ring the changes. In nature, there is always a degree of variation in size and colour within a single species. If the predominant colour of the nymphs found in the water that you are fishing is brown, then it would be prudent to fish artificials of the colour.

On one water that I fish, the damsel larvae are nearly always the shade of brown that matches the muddy bottom of the lake – a natural camouflage. Because of this, I generally fish artificials approximating the shade of brown of the naturals and, for most of the time, this is highly acceptable to the trout. Sometimes, however, the trout seem to go off the brown-coloured nymphs and then a damsel nymph imitation in olive-green seems to work. In these circumstances I believe that the trout may well be tempted to take because the fly is different, a curiosity, as well as because a feeding response is triggered. It is also possible that caught and returned fish may have become wary of the original brown-coloured fly. We can never know for certain why a trout will take a fly on one occasion and ignore it on another; we can only speculate. One point to remember is that some materials darken considerably when wet, so bear this in mind when matching against the natural.

## IMITATING THE NATURAL

All imitations of natural creatures, in this case the larval and pupal forms that make up the angler's nymph box, as well as the crustaceans, etc. menioned in the previous chapter, can be divided into two basic types: the realistic and the impressionistic.

## REALISTIC IMITATIONS

This type of fly can also be called *exact imitation* or, sometimes, *naturalistic imitation*. There are those who say that there are differences between these three terms, but they are so slight that I think it would be splitting hairs to try to define them. It must be admitted, however, that there are degrees of realism. This type of fly is a very modern concept in fly design and in many cases can be described as only an exercise in fly-dressing, albeit a satisfying one. The resulting flies are true marvels of the fly-dresser's art, virtually exact models of the real thing.

The biggest problem I have found with this type of fly is that, for me, they are not as effective as the more impressionistic fly when it comes to tempting trout. In the tying vice they look so real that you would think no trout would refuse such a perfect specimen, but perhaps in their very perfection they lack something essential, they have become too real. Throughout nature it is often the slight imperfection that attracts. Perhaps because the fly is so realistic it needs to be fished with the same sort of perfection in order to give it a natural life, something I am probably not doing. The fault may rest with my presentation and not with the type of fly.

## IMPRESSIONISTIC IMITATIONS

Under this category we may also find suggestive patterns and, at the furthest point from a natural creature, the type of fly I would term as *broad spectrum*. An *impressionistic fly*, as the words suggest, is one that has certain features in common with the real insect but is not exact enough to be a perfect copy. The size, colour and shape will be the same but that is where the resemblance ends. A soft hackle may be used instead of more realistic legs constructed from a variety of materials. Segmentation may well be left to a tinsel rib instead of a more realistic plastic body material. A broad-spectrum nymph imitates no specific aquatic creature and, in its shape, may well imitate more than one insect type. Its success lies in the fact that it appears to be edible; it looks like some sort of food, and the trout take it as such. At the bottom end of the scale of imitation we find a group of flies that can best be described as *attractor nymphs*, which owe nothing to nature in their conception, except the generic term 'nymph'. Some are heavily tinsellated; some have rubber legs or polystyrene eyes; most look like nothing that swims in the trout's environment. Nevertheless, this type of fly has seen the downfall of many a fish.

## PARTS AND PROPORTIONS OF THE NYMPH

Along with all the considerationas given above as to what makes a good, effective nymph, we should add balance and proportion. I have always tried to work to the 'thirds' principle in trying to achieve a well-balanced nymph, i.e. one should divide the hook into three and allow two-thirds of the shank for the abdomen and one-third for the thoracic area. This, of course, does not apply to those flies that imitate non-insect food, e.g. shrimps. As far as the tail is concerned, for many nymphs the length should be the same as that of the thorax. However, for some nymphs, a larger or smaller tail will be required.

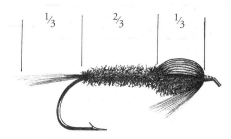

Proportions of the nymph

## SHELL-BACK NYMPHS

This style of nymph is used mainly to tie shrimp patterns. The back material is tied at the tail end of the hook and subsequently taken right across the back, where it is then tied down at the head. A few non-shrimp flies are tied in this manner; these are of the broad-spectrum variety.

## WEIGHTED NYMPHS

It is necessary to weight many of our nymphal patterns. Sometimes the weight is applied throughout the length of the shank; at other times it is confined to one part of the hook (the front, sometimes the back end or sometimes to the sides). Where and how you place your lead ultimately dictates the position that the nymph adopts in the water: upside-down, right side up or even on its side. It will sink headfirst or tailfirst depending on where the weight is placed; a weight in the head of the fly can activate a mobile tail into a loping movement when retrieved, which will prove very enticing to fish.

Weight is usually achieved by adding lead or copper wire, and some flies call for strips of flat lead. It is obvious that the more lead that is applied, the faster the flies will sink; some patterns call for heavy weight and others for much lighter weight. There are a number of modern French grayling nymphs whose bodies are made of painted solid lead. Some patterns utilize weighty gold beads, while others use bead-chain eyes to achieve the same effect. Buoyant tying materials, such as foam or clipped deer hair, are sometimes used in conjunction with lead weight to create flies that sink very slowly. This sometimes occurs by design but, generally weight will be required to overcome the buoyancy of the materials used in the fly's construction. Sometimes weight is achieved in a pattern by ribbing with heavy wire, giving the resultant fly, in one operation, weight, imitation of the natural insect's segments and a degree of flash and glitter.

## FLOATING NYMPHS

Sometimes a floating nymph is required to imitate either an emergent insect struggling in the barrier of the surface film or a dead or dying larva. Some natural larvae come to the surface in order to take in air; a number of the aquatic Diptera do this. Buoyancy can be achieved by the materials used in the construction of the fly. Foam bodies and wing pads, clipped deer hair, polystyrene beads, balls of polypropylene enmeshed in nylon stockings and, in recent years, *cul de canard* feathers have all been used to keep our nymphal patterns close to or on the surface.

\*      \*      \*

The nymph is the prime weapon in the armoury of the fly-fisherman. It is a fly for all seasons and all waters.

# CHAPTER THREE

# THE NYMPH-TIER'S PALETTE

In this age of conservation, preservation and green issues the protection of many of the world's birds and animals is, and must be, the paramount concern of us all. In some countries the very fish we seek with our feathered lures are under threat. This enlightenment about the protection of species means that some of the materials used by fly-tiers in the past are no longer available. If the ban on these furs and feathers helps to protect endangered species then that is all to the good. Fly-tiers have always used what was readily available, and effective substitutes for the now-banned materials can be found. The modern nymph-tier has a wealth of man-made products with which to construct his or her patterns.

There are some pundits who preach the gospel of 'Purity of Breed', i.e. if a fly once called for a small feather from the rump of a blackbird or the fur from the throat of a civet cat, then that is what should be used if the fly is to be the same. This is, of course, nonsense, for less esoteric materials can be used to the same effect without altering the ultimate effectiveness of the fly. The very popularity of our sport in recent years is to an extent self-destructive because, as more and more people take up fly-fishing and tying their own flies, good-quality materials become scarcer and certainly more expensive. Man-made materials, I am sure, will be the saviour of our consuming interest.

## FEATHERS

Use can be made of a wide variety of bird plumage; that of coot, moorhen, crow, jackdaw, magpie, guinea fowl and starling have all figured in traditional fly-dressing. The most commonly used feathers are described below.

## POULTRY

Whereas good-quality cock hackles are of prime importance for the tying of dry flies, softer hen hackles are better for nymphs because they pulsate and kick in the water and move in an enticing way. These feathers can come from the neck or saddle patches of the hen. They are readily available in a wide variety of natural plain, mottled or dyed colours. Some patterns, however, do call for a stiffer cock hackle fibre, usually for tails or antennae. Stripped cock hackle quills are used as bodies or antennae on some patterns.

## PEACOCK

The bronze-green herl of the eyed feather is a popular material for the bodies, etc. of many patterns. Peacock feathers are not on a banned list, provided that they are shed plumage. There is, however, a ban on the import and export from India of all other peacock plumage, such as the blue body feathers and the mottled and cinnamon wing quills. Only home-grown plumage can be offered for sale and that only under licence. A few patterns call for the use of the green sword feathers, usually for tails.

## STRIPPED PEACOCK

This material is obtained by removing the soft herl from the quill. This can be achieved using a razor blade or an eraser, or by dipping the quill into a weak solution of household bleach. The herl can also be removed by dipping the quill in a bath of hot paraffin wax, but care must be taken that the wax is melted in a bain-marie. The dipped herl is cooled under cold water and the wax scraped off. The stripped quills are used for the bodies of some traditional nymphs.

## PARTRIDGE

The feathers from the grey (Hungarian) partridge are, to my mind, one of the most important sources of hackles for many of my own nymphs. The brown back and grey breast feathers are used; the grey feathers can often be purchased dyed in a number of natural-looking colours. The tail feathers are sometimes used for wing pads and thorax covers. The feathers of the French (red-legged) partridge are not used to the same extent on established nymphal patterns but there is nothing to stop the tier using them, for they are an interesting feather. In countries where partridges are not indigenous, other small game-birds are used, e.g. the Cape francolin in South Africa; most other countries have similar game-birds.

## PHEASANT

Plumage from the ring-necked pheasant is used extensively for many flies, and nymphs are no exception. The cock centre tails are the main component in the ubiquitous Pheasant Tail Nymph and the popular Teeny Nymph. The wide variety of feathers found on the cock bird can be used for many patterns; they have great potential. Hen pheasant plumage also provides the fly-tier with a wealth of feathers with which to experiment. The hen centre tails have always been used on British traditional wet flies; some tiers use them as thoracic covers.

## GOLDEN PHEASANT

This elegant, beautiful bird has always figured in the palette of the fly-tier. The golden crest feathers are used in some nymphs, as are the orange-and-black neck feathers. The red-and-gold body feathers can have many uses and the tails provide excellent mottled nymph bodies.

## OTHER PHEASANTS

Plumage from the silver, argus, Lady Amherst's and other pheasants is sometimes used but it is not that common. Some of the species are on the endangered list and only locally bred plumage is available to the fly-dresser, and then only at a premium.

## GROUSE

The body plumage is used for hackles or to provide legs on some patterns. The tail or wing feathers can be used for wing cases. In traditional wet flies, the feathers of the grouse are used for the Grouse series of lake or sea-trout patterns and hackles taken from the inside wing of a young grouse were used in the Poult spider pattern.

## WOODCOCK

Like the pheasant, partridge and grouse, this bird is available through the courtesy of the sporting gun. The barred wing feathers and the body plumage can be used to provide hackles for some flies.

## DUCK

Again the shooting fraternity provides a number of ducks whose plumage is used by fly-dressers. The mallard is probably the most common of British ducks to be used. As far as nymph flies are concerned, both the bronze and grey plumage can be used in a variety of ways, e.g. for the backs of some nymphs and for the antennae and tail of others. The wing feathers, although used mainly for dry- and wet-fly wings, are sometimes used as wing cases for nymphs. Plumage from teal and widgeon can be utilized in the same way. While discussing ducks, mention must be made of the preen-gland feathers surrounding the uropygial gland, which are now universally known by their French name *culs de canard* (abbreviated to CDC). These feathers are used in continental Europe for many dry-fly patterns and, in recent years, have become firmly established in the UK and the USA. Some tiers dye them and use them for weighted nymph flies. They are commonly used in a number of emergent-nymph patterns.

## GOOSE

White plumage from the domestic goose is used for many patterns; usually dyed, the feathers are sold and used as a substitute for condor in herl-bodied flies. Wing cases and pads are also devised using goose feathers. Wild-goose feathers can also be used.

## GOOSE BIOTS

These are the short, spiky feathers found on the slim, 'bad' side of a goose quill. They are used to form legs, tails and also the antennae of some nymphs.

## HERON

This bird is a protected species and there is a ban on the sale of plumage; the only feathers available are those which have been shed or those from road-kills. The herl is used for nymph bodies and the body plumage is used for hackling some types of salmon and steelhead flies. In other countries, the plumage of similar birds is used, e.g. the blue crane in South Africa.

## MARABOU

The soft, mobile plumes of turkey marabou are

used in many patterns, usually for tails and breathing filaments. In the UK only the 6in (15cm) plumes are sold, but I believe the smaller immature feathers known as *marabou bloods*, or *shorts*, to be far better; they are generally fuller and nicely tapered. The plumes are obtainable in a wide variety of dyed colours. The smallest marabou plumes are known as *slipper marabou*; these are between 1 and 3in (2.5 and 7.5cm) long and are ideal for nymph patterns. They used to come from the legs of the turkey. Other feathers from wing and tail quills of the wild or domestic turkey are used for wing pads, etc. When dyed, they act as a reasonable substitute for condor herl.

## GRIZZLE MARABOU
In recent years, the soft, fluffy feathers found at the base of grizzle-cock or hensaddle skins has been used for tails and hackling of a number of patterns. Most fly-shops now stock this feather in a variety of dyed colours.

## OSTRICH
Ostrich herl, both natural and dyed, is used on many nymphal patterns for body, thorax and head.

## FURS

### SEAL
This fur is now probably a thing of the past because the ban in Europe of the sale of all seal products includes the fur used for many years in fly-dressing. There may be a few outlets which have old stock, but they must by now be limited. The emotive issue of seal-culling often hit the headlines in the world's newspapers and the methods employed in such culls left a lot to be desired. Having said that, there now appear to be imbalances in some parts of the world, where too many seals are hunting too few fish, to the sad detriment of both and to the livelihood of fisher-men. Seal fur used in fly-tying, dyed as it was in a rich variety of colours, was probably one of the finest natural furs used for the bodies of flies. Substitutes are now available and will be dealt with specifically later in this chapter.

### MOLE
The velvet fur of the mole is used on a number of nymphs. It can be treated with picric acid to give a subtle olive shade and has also been dyed in other colours.

## HARE
The fur from the ears and mask of the hare is a popular fly-tying medium. A number of traditional patterns require this fur and, likewise, many modern nymphs. The body fur, both the underfur and the guard hairs, is also used. The dubbing made with such fur was known as *hare's flax* by the fly-tiers of the last century.

## RABBIT
The body fur of wild rabbit and the tanned skins of the domestic rabbit are both used in fly-tying. The wild skins are more often than not used as dubbing while the dyed domestic skins are used in strip form.

## SNOW-SHOE RABBIT FOOT
Who would have thought that we could find a material on the soles of rabbit's feet. The fur from the feet of the snow-shoe rabbit is extremely water-repellent and has been used in recent years for emerger patterns.

## SQUIRREL
The body fur of different species of squirrel makes excellent dubbing for nymphs. In many ways I prefer this squirrel fur to hare's ear. The tail hair is also used on some patterns.

## MINK
A number of patterns call for this fur. The skins are usually obtained from those animals culled as pests or from furrier's trimmings.

## OTTER
This fur is obtainable in the USA where it is incorporated into a number of fly-dressings. Like all aquatic mammal furs, it has water-repellent properties.

## BEAVER
A good water-repelling fur, beaver, when used on weighted nymphs, retains little air bubbles.

## OPOSSUM
The fur of the Australian (but not the American) opossum is used as body dubbing for a number of patterns.

## WOODCHUCK
This fur is excellent for nymphs and has a good mottled coloration.

## DORMOUSE

Not a common material but, in eastern Europe, where the edible dormouse is a pest of fruit crops, this fur is used on a number of flies. That from the tail is the most used; it possesses a natural grease.

## MUSKRAT

Like the beaver, this aquatic mammal has good water-repelling fur and makes excellent dubbing. This fur can also be used in lieu of water-rat fur.

## WILD PIG (Pecarry)

The stiff bristle hair is used for legs, tails and antennae in some patterns. Hair from the European wild boar is also used in some countries.

## DEER HAIR

The body hair from the many species of deer and, in some countries, antelope, is used extensively, usually clipped to form shaped bodies, heads, etc. Moose, elk, caribou, reindeer, antelope and, in southern Africa, klipspringer and duiker have all been used to this end. The finer hair from these animals is used extensively for e.g. dry-fly wings. A few nymphs call for the tail hair.

## HORSEHAIR

This hair is sometimes used to form the bodies of some pupae and also the legs and antennae of other flies.

\*       \*       \*

While most fly-tiers obtain their supplies of feathers and furs from fly-tying supply houses, others are finding a wealth of useful materials from charity shops and car-boot or garage sales. Old fur coats, stoles and hats can often be found and will yield a supply of material to last a lifetime.

## SYNTHETICS

Synthetics, or man-made products, are playing an ever-increasing role in modern fly-tying. They are more than just a substitute for natural products and deserve to be treated as such. They are readily available and pose no threat to any wildlife. Many fly-tiers today use nothing but synthetic products to tie their flies. Natural and man-made products can be combined to form interesting dubbing mixtures; hare fur combined with Antron is such a medium. But each year new blends come onto the scene and last a while, before being superseded by yet more subtle mixtures.

## SYNTHETIC LIVING FIBRE (SLF)

This new form of dubbing was developed by the British tier, Davy Wotton. It is the most perfect substitute for seal fur yet devised. It comes in two dubbing grades: normal and a finer blend called Finesse. It can also be obtained in hank form.

## POLYPROPYLENE

Sold either as dubbing, in a wide variety of colours, or as flat sheet and yarn, this material is very easy to use and dubs exceptionally well. To my mind, however, it lacks sparkle.

## ANTRON

Sometimes called 'sparkle yarn' because of its shiny, light-reflecting properties, this product can be used on its own as dubbing or mixed with natural fur fibres. It can also be used as a substitute for seal fur. There is a proprietary blend on the market, Haretron, which comes in a wide range of good natural colours.

## Z-LON

Similar to Antron, this product has the same glistening effect. Like Antron the fibres are trilobic.

## NYLON

Nylon wools are often used for the bodies of many flies and nylon monofilament can be used for ribbing.

## EXPANDED POLYSTYRENE

In sheet form this can be used as underbody for some floating nymphs. Balls of polystyrene are also used to keep nymphs and pupae at the surface. Sometimes a buoyant fly is used with a sinking line and short leader in order to fish close to the bottom, with the fly hovering just above the bed of the lake or reservoir.

## POLYURETHANE

Another expanded foam, this is used to form the bodies, etc. of emergent nymphs.

## PVC

This material, polythene sheet and Tyvac can all be used as an overbody or as wing pads on some nymphs. Coloured strip is also available for making realistic segmented bodies. Swannundaze and Larva Lace are two such products in common use. Speckle Flake consists of flexible strips with in-built specks of glitter and is used for legs on poppers and/or exotic nymphs.

## SPECTRAFLASH
This shiny, light-reflecting material, supplied by Traun River Products, is used for the backs of shrimps. There are a number of pearly-coloured sheets and tinsels available on the market.

## PLASTAZOTE
A close-celled foam, this is used mainly for shaped bodies, especially buoyant nymphs.

## FURRY FOAM
A thin foam, backed with a fur nap, this product is excellent for both nymph and pupal imitations.

## LATEX
Thin rubber sheet, sometimes sold as Dental Dam, is a popular material for some nymphs and pupa. It is used to form realistic segmented bodies.

## RAFFENE (Swiss Straw)
An artificial raffia, this is available in many colours and is used for the backs of nymphs and shrimps. When treated with a fixative, it can be used for wings on dry flies. Untreated, it becomes very soft and limp when wet, making it suitable for the wings of emergent nymphs.

## DUBBING WICK
This product originally came from the Czech Republic. It consists of a twist of copper wire combined with various fur dubbings and has the advantage of providing quick and easy bodies for nymphs. The body, weight and rib are all applied in one operation. It may also be found under the name of 'Dubbing Brushes'.

## TYING THREAD
In the past pure silk was the only thread used in the construction of flies. Today nylons in various diameters and strengths are the most popular. Most are supplied ready waxed. Polyester thread and ultra-strong Kevlar threads are also now common. I use Canadian Uni-thread in gauges 6/0 and 8/0, and also the American threads from the Danville company.

## FLOSS SILKS
Natural and/or rayon floss is still required for some traditional nymphs but its use is on the wane.

## GLITTER MATERIALS
Flashbou, Crystal Hair and Twinkle are all modern glitter materials usually incorporated in the tails of some nymphs. Other glitter or 'pearly' materials are available in sheet or strip form and are used as wing cases, etc. (See also Spectraflash.) There is one material of this pearly type that can be applied as a dubbing; this goes under the name of 'Lite Brite'.

## FLUORESCENT MATERIALS
Various yarns and silk, as well as some dubbing products, are being increasingly used to provide extra attraction in the nymphs.

## TINSELS
Silver and gold, in flats, ovals and rounds are available. Copper and bronze, and others in a wide range of colours, are used to provide ribbing for many patterns. Modern Mylar tinsel, which is gold on one side and silver on the other, is one such non-tarnishable product now in common use. In recent years, pearl tinsels have been used to good effect on some flies.

## CHENILLE
A very popular product, chenille is available in a wide range of thicknesses, colours and materials. A number of imitations call for chenille, e.g. the Montana and Ted's Stonefly Nymph. Suede chenille, or ultra-chenille, is a very tight, smooth chenille, suitable for many patterns; it has been used in woven-body flies. Crystal and other plastic chenilles are now in common use for some attractor patterns. Micro-chenille is a superfine chenille now used on bodies of very small flies and also as legs on some nymph patterns.

## WATERPROOF MARKER PENS
These are used to provide the body markings on some patterns, especially stonefly nymphs. Acrylic paints can be used in the same way.

## BEADS AND EYES
In recent years the use of gold beads on a number of nymphs and pupae has become universal. In other patterns painted lead-shot and dumb-bell shaped eyes are used. Eyes on some of the larger

nymph patterns are created with plastic or metallic bead chain. Burnt nylon is also used.

\*      \*      \*

New materials are continually coming on the market, a few of them have been developed specifically for the fly-tier but most are usually not – they are materials used for other purposes. Some of the modern knitting wools, combinations of natural wools and man-made fibres, have proved to be a boon to the fly-tier. Some of the up-to-date chenilles used in knitting incorporate flecks of tinsel, etc. which can be very useful.

# CHAPTER FOUR

# EARLY BEGINNINGS

Mention has already been made of the spider-style of fly with its mobile game-bird hackle. With a little imagination, one can visualize, in these traditional soft-hackled flies, the nymphal form. It could be that, when retrieved through the water, the soft hackles sweep back and envelop the body, creating a very life-like nymph shape, although some experts doubt this theory. Many of these spider patterns can be reconciled with the natural creature because they have been given names of the true insect, e.g. February Red, Early Brown, Needle Fly, etc. All these are stonefly imitations and, if you think about it, the larva, or creeper, closely resembles the final adult insect; the change in appearance is not so great as that found in, say, the caddisflies.

Skues was of the opinion that these spider-dressed flies could be taken for nymphs. Two flies

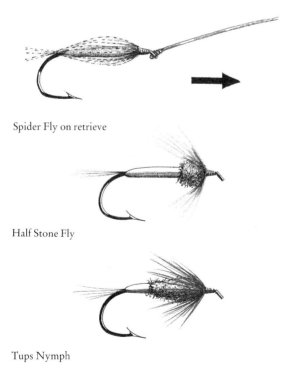

Spider Fly on retrieve

Half Stone Fly

Tups Nymph

he specifically mentions are the Half Stone and the Tups, both created by the Devon fly-dresser, R.S. Austin. The Tups Fly did, in fact, become the Tups Nymph; the yellow abdomen became more of a tip and the button of tups wool and other furs became extended further down the body. Skues went on to devise his own series of nymph flies, using dubbed fur bodies, because he believed the fur-bodied flies were more realistic in the water, having more life. He also maintained that they landed more softly on the water and did not disturb the trout. Skues used two methods of tying his nymphs both of which are summarized below. The first method is as follows:

*Step 1* Wrap a few turns of tying thread onto the shank to the point shown.
*Step 2* Take a bunch of feather fibres and tie in at this point.
*Step 3* Take the thread down the shank, trapping the feather fibres as you go along.
*Step 4* Lift up the feather fibres and continue the thread down the shank.
*Step 5* At the tail end, tie in a couple of cock hackle fibres and a length of ribbing wire and dub some fur onto the hook.
*Step 6* Return the fur-laden thread down the shank to form the body and the thorax. Follow this with the ribbing wire.
*Step 7* Clip off the waste fibres at the front of the hook, then take the feather fibres over the thorax and tie in. Sweep the ends of the feather fibres backwards and downwards to form the legs. Finish with a whip finish and varnish.

The second method begins in the same way.

*Step 1* Take the tying thread to the same point as in method one.
*Step 2* Tie in a bunch of feather fibres with the long ends pointing over the eye of the hook.

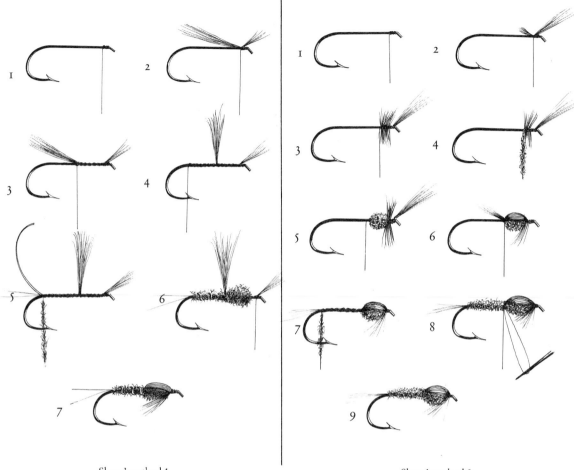

Skues' method 1

Skues' method 2

*Step 3* Splay out the ends of the feather fibres; these will ultimately form the legs.

*Step 4* Dub the tying thread, which is now behind the feather fibres, with fur dubbing.

*Step 5* Wind the fur-laden thread around the hook to form the thorax.

*Step 6* Take the projecting feather fibres over the thorax and tie down. The thorax and wing case is now complete.

*Step 7* Take the tying thread down the shank, tie in a few hackle fibres for the tail and dub a further amount of fur onto the thread.

*Step 8* Take the fur-laden thread up the shank to form the body of the fly and finish the fly with half-hitches behind the thorax.

*Step 9* This shows the completed fly.

**Iron-blue Nymph** · Skues · UK

| | |
|---|---|
| *Hook* | Sizes 14–16 |
| *Thread* | Crimson |
| *Tail* | Two or three soft, white hackle fibres |
| *Body* | Mole fur with two or three turns of tying thread left exposed at the tail |
| *Hackle* | Jackdaw throat hackle, two or three turns |

Skues' Iron-blue Nymph

### Large Dark Olive Nymph · Skues · UK

*Hook*   Sizes 12–14
*Thread*   Yellow waxed with brown wax
*Tail*   Short unspotted olive guinea-fowl fibres
*Body*   Dark olive-green seal fur
*Rib*   Gold wire
*Hackle*   Short-fibred dark blue dun cock

Skues' Dark Olive Nymph

### Medium Olive Nymph · Skues · UK

*Hook*   Sizes 14–16
*Thread*   Primrose waxed with clear wax
*Tail*   Three pale blue dun cock hackle fibres
*Body*   Olive heron herl
*Thorax*   Blue squirrel body underfur
*Hackle*   Short fibred dark blue dun cock hackle

### Grannom Nymph · Skues · UK

*Hook*   Sizes 12–14
*Thread*   Bright green waxed with clear wax
*Body*   Bright green lamb's wool
*Hackle*   Brown partridge

Skues' Grannom Nymph

### Freshwater Shrimp · Skues · UK

*Hook*   Sizes 12–14
*Thread*   Pale olive
*Body*   Pale orange and olive seal fur, mixed
*Ribt*   Gold wire
*Hackle*   Palmered brown hackle dyed olive, the hackle and fur trimmed off the top of the hook

Skues' Freshwater Shrimp

This last fly is probably one of the earliest shrimp imitations, and it is interesting to note the use of orange combined with olive in the body fur. This mixture of colours has been used more recently on some modern damsel nymph patterns. Skues did not appear to add extra weight to his flies so one must assume that, in the clear waters of the chalk rivers in southern England, he fished to bulging trout that he could see feeding on nymphs just below the surface.

As far as the grannom nymph is concerned, even Halford noted, I suspect with a little pain, that trout early in the season became preoccupied with these small caddis, so he too felt obliged to create an imitation, copying a natural larva taken from the stomach contents of a caught fish in 1884.

### Grannom Larva · Halford · UK

*Hook*   Sizes 12–14
*Thread*   Green
*Body*   Pea-green floss silk
*Rib*   Grannom green stripped peacock quill
*Wing*   Point of a brown partridge hackle
*Hackle*   Rusty dun

Halford's Grannom Larva

It would appear that both Skues and Halford ignored the fact that the natural grannom larva had a case. Could they have imitated the pupal stage and not the larva? Or did they find the larva in the stomach contents of caught fish, out of their cases?

In *A Book of Angling* (1867) Francis Francis depicts a number of grub-type flies used for grayling, one of which was called the Grasshopper. This pattern looks nothing like a grasshopper; Francis admits to this, describing it as being more like a gooseberry. The fact that it was heavily weighted meant that it was devised to take fish feeding on the bottom. Apart from the colour there is not a great deal of difference between this fly, together with the depth at which it was fished, and the more up-to-date pattern devised by Frank

Francis' Grasshopper

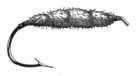

Sawyer's Grayling Bug

Sawyer, the Grayling Bug. Patterns such as those depicted by Francis Francis go back to the days of Charles I and Oliver Cromwell. Robert Venables, a colonel in the Commonwealth army, in his book *The Experienced Angler*, published patterns weighted with lead and covered in chamois leather to imitate caddis larvae or pupae. In 1914, the year of Halford's death, Dr J.C. Mottram's book, *Fly Fishing, Some New Arts and Mysteries* was published. Among the 'new' flies that Mottram invented was a pattern to imitate a midge larva. This fly is probably one of the first to use marabou as a mobile tail to give an in-built life to the fly.

**Midge Larva** · Mottram · UK

| | |
|---|---|
| *Hook* | Smallest possible (as Mottram advised) |
| *Thread* | Black |
| *Tail* | Turkey down |
| *Body* | White silk |
| *Rib* | Black silk |
| *Thorax* | As rib |

Mottram's Midge Larva

In France anglers had for some time been using nymphs of sorts to catch their fish. One such nymph was the fly Nymphe Jeannot, perfected in 1873 by Jean Lysik of Brion-sur-Ource. This fly, unlike the Skues' nymphs, was designed to be fished near the bottom and, as you can see from the date, is earlier than many British lightly weighted nymphs.

**Nymphe Jeannot** · Lysik · France

| | |
|---|---|
| *Hook* | Sizes 11–13 (10–14 nowadays) |
| *Thread* | Black silk |
| *Tail* | Cock-pheasant tail fibres |
| *Body* | Peacock or heron herl |
| *Underbody* | Purple-coloured copper wire |
| *Wing case* | As body |
| *Thorax* | Exposed purple-coloured copper wire |

Nymphe Jeannot

This fly, using pheasant tail and copper wire, is similar in many respects to Sawyer's famous Pheasant-tail Nymph but very much earlier.

Perhaps the best-known of American nymph-fishing pioneers was James E. Leisenring, who has lent his name to the method of nymph-fishing known as the Leisenring Lift. He was born in 1878 and died in 1951. He corresponded with his British counterparts over a number of years.

**July Dun Nymph** · Leisenring · USA

| | |
|---|---|
| *Hook* | Size 14–16 |
| *Thread* | Orange silk |
| *Tail* | Ginger hen hackle fibres |
| *Body* | Brown-olive seal fur |
| *Rib* | Gold wire |
| *Thorax* | Medium-brown mole |
| *Hackle* | Short-fibred rusty dun, one turn only |

July Dun Nymph (Leisenring)

**Pale Watery Nymph** · Leisenring · USA

| | |
|---|---|
| *Hook* | Size 14–16 |
| *Thread* | Primrose silk |
| *Tail* | None |
| *Body* | Thin, of Australian opossum or Chinese mole |

Pale Waltery Nymph (Leisenring)

| | |
|---|---|
| *Rib* | Fine gold wire |
| *Thorax* | As body but well pronounced |
| *Hackle* | Short-fibred dark blue dun cock, two turns |

**Dark Olive Nymph** · Leisenring · USA

| | |
|---|---|
| *Hook* | Size 14 |
| *Thread* | Primrose silk |
| *Tail* | Short blue dun cock hackle fibres |
| *Body* | Greenish-olive seal and brown-bear hair, mixed |
| *Rib* | Fine gold wire |
| *Thorax* | As body but well pronounced |
| *Hackle* | Short blue dun hen, two turns |

The period between the two World Wars showed no great advances in the fishing of the nymph. In fact, it is possibly true to say that, with the exception of one or two individuals, most anglers persisted with the traditional wet fly and those that fished the verdant chalkstreams concerned themselves with the cult of the dry.

In the USA in 1938, Ray Bergman published his highly popular book *Trout*, in which he devoted some time to fishing the nymph, although what nymphal patterns he depicts are lost amid a sea of fancy wet flies. A number of flat, hard-bodied nymphs from a contemporary of Bergman, E.R. Hewitt, are included and depicted in Bergman's book.

**Ray Bergman Nymph** · Bergman · USA

| | |
|---|---|
| *Hook* | Medium longshank (2x), sizes 10–12 |
| *Thread* | Black |
| *Tail* | Black-and-white guinea fowl |

Ray Bergman Nymph

| | |
|---|---|
| *Body* | Buff wool, brown lacquer on the back |
| *Rib* | Black linen thread |
| *Hackle* | As tail |
| *Antennae* | As tail |

The R.B. nymph is one of a series of different natural-coloured nymphs, as are the Hewitt series of nymphs numbers 1 to 3.

**Hewitt Nymph No. 1** · Hewitt · USA

| | |
|---|---|
| *Hook* | Regular shank, sizes 8–12 |
| *Thread* | Black |
| *Tail* | Black hackle fibres |
| *Body* | White with a brown back |
| *Rib* | Black silk |
| *Hackle* | Black cock hackle fibres |

Hewitt Nymph No. 1

In the UK Dr Bell produced a number of 'nymph' artificials, namely his Amber Nymphs (caddis-pupa imitations) and chironomid-pupa imitations, the Blagdon Buzzer being one of them. He tied these flies after investigating the stomach contents of trout which he had caught from Blagdon Reservoir in the west of England.

**Amber Nymph** · Bell · UK

| | |
|---|---|
| *Hook* | Mustad 3904, sizes 8–12 |
| *Thread* | Yellow |
| *Body* | Amber seal fur or silk (rear half) |
| *Thorax* | Brown seal fur or silk (front half) (smaller sizes used orange instead of brown fur later in the season) |
| *Back* | Brown-speckled turkey or similar feather |
| *Hackle* | Honey hackle fibres |

Bell's Amber Nymph

**Blagdon Buzzer** · Bell · UK

| | |
|---|---|
| *Hook* | Mustad 3904, sizes 10–12 |
| *Thread* | Black |
| *Body* | Tapered black wool |
| *Rib* | Flat gold tinsel |
| *Breathing appendages* | White floss-silk tuft |

Bell's Blagdon Buzzer

After World War Two, as the world returned to a degree of sanity, a plethora of fly-fishing and fly-tying books was published on both sides of the Atlantic and I will mention a few that were of importance to me and apologize to those who may consider I have left out other books of equal or more importance and standing. W.H. Lawrie's small work, *The Rough Stream Nymph*, is perhaps the earliest of the post-war books to give exclusivity to the nymph and, furthermore, as far as I can see, he is perhaps the first writer in the UK to emphasize the importance of the emerging nymph and to give patterns to imitate them. On the other hand, Courtney Williams, in his famous *Dictionary of Trout Flies*, hardly gives the nymph a mention, although he admits to their growing importance.

Two favourite books of mine from the USA in this post-war period are *Fishing Flies and Fly Tying* by William F. Blades and *How to Fish from Top to Bottom* by Sidney W. Gordon. The first gives a wealth of naturalistic nymphal patterns far ahead of its time. Without doubt, the books of C.F. Walker on both chalkstream and stillwater flies are important reading. The book by Colonel

Joscelyn Lane, *Lake and Loch Fishing* emphasizes the importance of nymphs and gives a number of attractive imitations that are still of use today. The late Tom Ivens was one of the most influential British pioneers of reservoir trout-fishing; most of his flies are still in use today and some of the dressings will appear in later chapters, along with those of C.F. Walker and Joscelyn Lane.

Perhaps the best known of Britain's post-war nymph fishermen was Frank Sawyer, who perfected his 'induced-take' method of fishing for trout on his beloved Hampshire Avon. His contemporary, Oliver Kite, also influenced many of today's anglers, although his greatest contribution to fly patterns was his famous dry fly, the Imperial (this fly was very similar to flies already established on rivers of the Welsh Borders). His best-known nymph fly does nothing for the art of fly-tying because it was a simple, unadorned, bare hook with a thorax of copper wire.

Bare-hook Nymph

The last 25 years have seen nymph and nymph-fishing reach new heights. In Europe and the USA the use of the nymph in fishing all types of rivers is now common practice, while the development of reservoirs and smaller put-and-take fisheries in the UK has seen the British fly-fisherman lead the world in the techniques of fishing stillwater with the nymph.

For every fly-fisherman who wrote and published his patterns, there must have been many more who did not, and their patterns may well have been used long before those flies that have been described in print.

# PART II

# NATURALS AND THEIR IMITATIONS

# CHAPTER FIVE

# MAYFLIES

Of all the groups of aquatic insects that make up the diet of the trout it is the Ephemeroptera that has received the most attention from anglers, writers and, of course, fly-tiers.

Mayflies are part of the magic of fly-fishing. These delicate insects are to be found on most waters; chalkstreams, karst rivers, rain-fed, free-stone and limestone rivers all have their share of mayfly species. Lakes and reservoirs and the most insignificant of ponds can also provide a habitat for certain species. On large expanses of water other insect groups, such as the Chironomidae, may well be more important from a fishing point of view, but it is still the mayfly that captures the romance of fly-fishing. Artificial nymphs tied to represent the larval stage of the mayfly are now legion and in this chapter I shall give examples of such nymphs tied to represent particular mayfly species. In later chapters, other patterns will be given that can also be used for this purpose, although they are tied to represent either no particular species or a number of different insect larvae, including mayflies.

## NATURALS

Depending on species, the natural nymph is found in many different forms and habitats. Some cling to stones, burrow into the bottom or crawl on the bottom or among weed and moss; others are much more active and swim in the water column. In the following lists I have included representative species from different parts of the world because today's fly-fisherman is less conservative than his or her forebears and more fishermen are going to foreign countries to seek their sport. Many fly patterns from other countries are being used in the UK and, likewise, British flies are finding themselves in the fly-boxes of Continental and American anglers. The insects listed are those that have achieved some importance. Of course, not all nymphs will behave as categorized: some agile darters will cling to stones; silt-crawlers can be found amid the weeds; and those described as poor swimmers may well appear to be making a good account of themselves as they swim to the surface. Some species of *Siphlonurus* could well be described under the more active swimming nymphs, but I have listed all of them together as Laboured Swimmers. The following classifications are very general and are intended as a rough-and-ready guide.

### STONE-CLINGING MAYFLY NYMPHS (Ecdyonuridae, Heptageniidae)

In fast-moving water and turbulent streams, most species cling to stones and rocks. They are easily recognized by their strong, crab-like legs and flattened bodies. Their large heads are as wide as their bodies.

## Stone-clinging Mayfly Nymphs

| Scientific Name | Common Name | Distribution |
|---|---|---|
| Deleatidium lilli | | NZ |
| D. myzobranchia | | NZ |
| D. vernale | | NZ |
| Ecdyonurus dispar | Autumn Dun | UK & Europe |
| Ec. insignis | Large Green Dun | UK & Europe |
| Ec. torrentis | Large Brook Dun | UK & Europe |
| Ec. yoshidae | | Japan |
| Ec. venosus | Late March Brown | UK & Europe |
| Epeorus aesculus* | | Japan |
| Ep. assimilis* | | Spain & Europe |
| Ep. latifolium* | | Japan |
| Ep. pleuralis* | Quill Gordon | USA |
| Heptagenia lateralis | Dusky Yellow Streak | UK & Europe |
| H. sulphurea | Yellow May Dun | UK & Europe |
| Rithrogena germanica | March Brown | UK & Europe |
| R. hageni | Red Quill | USA |
| R. iberica | | Spain |
| R. japonica | | Japan |
| R. morrisoni | Western March Brown | USA |
| R. semicolorata | Olive Upright | UK & Europe |
| R. undulata | Small Red Quill | USA |
| Stenonema fuscum | Gray Fox (Light Cahill) | USA |
| S. guttulata | Green Drake | USA |
| S. vicarium | American March Brown | USA |

*These nymphs have only two tails.

## LARGE BURROWERS (Ephemeridae)

These nymphs live down in the silt, gravel or mud. They include the largest of the British mayflies and possess strong digging legs. Many have pronounced horn- or tusk-like appendages on their heads.

## Large Burrowing Mayfly Nymphs

| Scientific Name | Common Name | Distribution |
|---|---|---|
| Ephemera danica | Mayfly Nymph | UK & Europe |
| E. guttulata | Green Drake | USA |
| E. glaucops | | Spain |
| E. japonica | | Japan |
| E. simulans | Brown Drake | USA |
| E. strigata | | Japan |
| E. varia | Yellow Drake | USA |
| E. vulgata | Mayfly Nymph | UK & Europe |
| Hexagenia atrocaudata | Great Lead-wing Drake | USA |
| H. bilineata | Great Brown Drake | USA |
| H. limbata | Burrowing Mayfly | USA |
| Ichthybotus hudsoni | Mayfly Nymph | NZ |

*Heptagenia* sp.

*Rithrogena* sp.

*Stenomena* sp.

*Ephemera* sp.

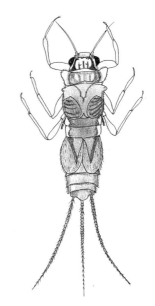

*Caenis* sp.

Worldwide and especially in the USA, there are many more species of large burrowing nymphs.

### SMALL BURROWERS OR BOTTOM-CRAWLERS (Caenidae)

In the USA the small *Tricorythodes* would appear to be more important than *Caenis*, judging from the number of articles that appear in American fly-fishing magazines. There are very few imitations of either species as nymphs.

### WEED- AND MOSS-CRAWLERS (Ephemerellidae)

This group includes some of the most important mayflies for the fly-fisherman. Their habitat is the aquatic weeds and bottom mosses over which they crawl or scuttle.

**Small Burrowing or Bottom-crawling Mayfly Nymphs**

| Scientific Name | Common Name | Distribution |
|---|---|---|
| Caenis amica | Tiny Gray-winged Blue Dun | USA |
| C. hilaris | Tiny White-wing Curse | USA |
| C. horaria | Caenis Nymph | UK & Europe |
| C. jocosa | Tiny Gray-wing Sulphur | USA |
| C. macrura | Caenis Nymph | UK & Europe |
| C. moesta | Caenis Nymph | UK & Europe |
| C. rivularum | Caenis Nymph | UK & Europe |
| C. robusta | Caenis Nymph | UK & Europe |
| C. simulans | Tiny White-wing Sulphur | USA |
| Tricorythodes explicatus | Trico | USA |
| T. minutus | Trico | USA |

**Weed- and Moss-crawling Mayfly Nymphs**

| Scientific Name | Common Name | Distribution |
|---|---|---|
| Ephemerella coloradensis | Slate-winged Olive | USA |
| E. cornuta | Large Blue-winged Olive | USA |
| E. doddsi | Western Green Drake | USA |
| E. dorothea | Pale Evening Dun | USA |
| E. ignita | Blue-winged Olive | UK & Europe |
| E. inermis | Pale Morning Dun | USA |
| E. infrequens | Pale Morning Dun | USA |
| E. lata | Small Blue-winged Olive | USA |
| E. nigra | | Japan |
| E. notata | Yellow Evening Dun | UK & Europe |
| E. okumai | | Japan |
| E. rotunda | Light Hendrikson | USA |
| E. rufa | | Japan |
| E. subvaria | Dark Hendrikson | USA |

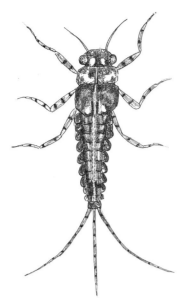

*Ephemerella* sp.

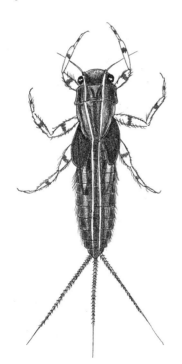

*Ephemerella rufa*

In the USA, as well as *E. lata*, there are many other species of *Ephemerella* that are also called blue-winged olives (or green drakes in the western states). Most, if not all, can be imitated by the same artificial nymphs. Today, in Japan, there is a great interest in fly-fishing and fly-tying. The two excellent books by Nori Tashiro prove this, and it is to be hoped that one day they will be translated into English so that they can be appreciated fully by a wider audience. The species listed above are important mayflies in Japan.

### AGILE DARTERS (mainly Baetidae)

These are the most accomplished swimmers of the Ephemeroptera. Streamlined in appearance, they can be found in large numbers in waters where there is a lot of weed. This family contains some of the most important anglers' flies.

**Agile-darting Mayfly Nymphs**

| Scientific Name | Common Name | Distribution |
|---|---|---|
| *Baetis atrebatinus* | Dark Olive | Ireland & Spain |
| *B. buceratus* | Medium Olive | UK & Europe |
| *B. fuscatus* | Pale Watery | UK & Europe |
| *B. muticus* | Iron Blue | UK & Europe |
| *B. niger* | Iron Blue | UK & Europe |
| *B. parvus* | Iron-blue Quill | USA |
| *B. rhodani* | Large Dark Olive | UK & Europe |
| *B. scambus* | Small Dark Olive | UK & Europe |
| *B. tenax* | Medium Olive | UK & Europe |
| *B. thermicus* | — | Japan |
| *B. vagans* | Iron-blue Quill | USA |
| *B. vernus* | Medium Olive | UK & Europe |
| *Calibaetis americanus* | Speckle-wing Dun | USA |
| *Ca. coloradensis* | Speckled Dun | USA |
| *Ca. fluctuans* | Pale Speckle Wing | USA |
| *Ca. nigritus* | Speckled Dun | USA |
| *Ca. pacificus* | Medium Speckled Dun | USA |
| *Ca. pallidus* | Pale Speckle Wing Sulphur | USA |
| *Centroptilum luteolum* | Small Spurwing | UK & Europe |
| *Ce. pennulatum* | Large Spurwing | UK & Europe |
| *Cloëon dipterum* | Pond Olive | UK & Europe |
| *Cl. simile* | Lake Olive | UK & Europe |
| *Nesameletus ornatus* | Grey Darter | NZ |
| *Procloëon pseudorufulum* | Pale Evening Dun | UK & Europe |
| *Pseudocloëon edmundsi* | Tiny Western Olive | USA |
| *Ps. japonica* | — | Japan |

### Laboured-swimming Mayfly Nymphs

| Scientific Name | Common Name | Distribution |
| --- | --- | --- |
| Habrophlebia fusca | Ditch Dun | UK & Europe |
| Isonychia bicolor | Lead-wing Coachman | USA |
| I. japonica | — | Japan |
| I. velma | Great Western Lead-wing | USA |
| Leptophlebia marginata | Sepia Nymph | UK & Europe |
| L. vespertina | Claret Dun | UK & Europe |
| Paraleptophlebia chocorata | — | Japan |
| P. cincta | Purple Dun | UK & Europe |
| P. submarginata | — | Spain |
| Siphlonurus alternatus | Summer Dun | UK & Europe |
| S. armatus | Summer Dun | UK & Europe |
| S. binotatus | — | Japan |
| S. croaticus | Summer Dun | Europe |
| S. lacustris | Summer Dun | UK & Europe |
| S. mirus | Large Summer Olive | USA |
| S. occidentalis | Black (or Gray) Drake | USA |
| S. quebecensis | Eastern Brown Quill | N. America |
| S. rapidus | Little Dark Olive | USA |
| S. spectabilis | Western Yellow Drake | USA |
| Zephlebia cruentata | Orange Nymph | NZ |
| Z. dentata | Brown Nymph | NZ |
| Z. nodularis | Sepia Nymph | NZ |
| Z. versicolor | Striped Nymph | NZ |

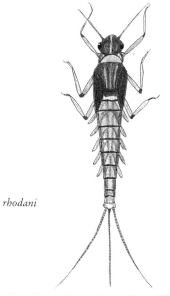

*Baetis rhodani*

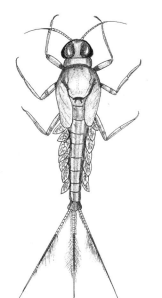

*Calibaetis* sp.

## LABOURED SWIMMERS
### (Leptophlebiidae, Siphlonuridae)

The remaining group includes the bottom-crawlers and poor swimmers, many of which are important fly-fishing nymphs. Oliver Kite referred to them as 'laboured swimmers', although I have included one or two species that may be a little better at swimming than the majority.

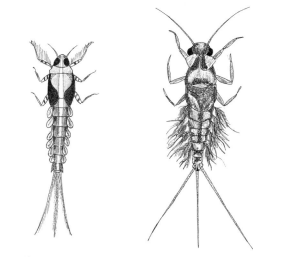

*Isonychia* sp.                    *Leptophlebia* sp.

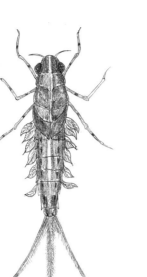

*Siphlonurus* sp.

## SOUTH AFRICAN MAYFLIES

There has been little published work on South African fly-fishing entomology, but the new breed of angler is going a long way to remedy this. Work done in the late 1920s by Dr Keppel H. Barnard on some of the rivers, including the Dwars, yielded a number of species, many of which are stone-clingers.

### Mayflies of South Africa

| Scientific Name | Common Name |
| --- | --- |
| Afronus harisoni | Dwarf Tawny Yellow |
| A. peterseni | Pied Dun |
| Apionyx tabularis | April Dun |
| Austrocaenis capensis | Cape Cain Fly |
| Baetis harrisoni | Yellow Dun |
| Centroptilum exicsum | Rusty Dun |
| Lithogloea harrisoni | Blue-winged Orange |
| Neurocaenis discolor | Worcester Dark Blue |
| Oligoneuriopsis lawrenci | Mooi Moth |

Barnard stated that all the species found on the Dwars River belonged to the sub-orders Baetoidea and Heptagenoidea, and that there was no evidence of any of the larger burrowing species. This information was published in the journal of the Cape Piscatorial Club magazine, *Piscator*, in Autumn 1967, and was passed on to me by Ed Herbst of Cape Town.

## ARTIFICIALS

The fish lay in a chalk-white channel between the trailing tresses of weed, it moved a little to the left and then dropped back, obviously feeding on nymphs. I kept well away from the water, not wishing to disturb the first fish in the river that I had seen actually feeding. I had spent the morning in a fruitless search for feeding fish. It is not often that you get a chance to fish the hallowed Test and, when such days occur, it is rather nice to catch at least one fish. I had walked up the velvet lawns in front of the big house, which was once owned by Disraeli, and had spotted this active rainbow beyond the quaint fishing-lodge that graced the lordly river's bank.

A little earlier I had put on a largish mayfly nymph in the hope of tempting a fish. Because all smaller flies had been totally ignored, I decided not to change the fly and, without much more ado, I knelt as though in supplication to the water and cast my fly well in front of the trout. The fly swept down over the green weed and into the clear channel; the trout turned and I saw the whiteness of its mouth; I tightened and the fish was on. I landed this, my only fish of the day, after a spirited fight that lasted about 5 minutes (an eternity to an angler); it weighed about 3lb (1.4kg) but, more importantly, I had christened my new fly.

Earlier in the day, it had been raining and I had not seen fin nor scale of a fish. I desperately needed a call of nature but there was just nowhere to go. I decided to gain some relief by the old fishing-lodge, out of view from the windows of the big house. I was just finishing when I heard female voices from the opposite bank and hastily pulled at my zip. It was not one of my days because the zip, with an inbuilt malevolence, caught a part of me which it should not have, drawing tears to my eyes. I quickly freed myself and pretended I was lighting my pipe. As I turned towards the river, the lady with her guest called out: 'Have you caught anything?' 'Just a small one,' I replied, with tears still flowing down my cheeks. I will always remember that day, the day I christened my new nymph, and the pain. The thought still makes my eyes water.

\* \* \*

In the following pages I describe some of the many mayfly nymph dressings and their origins. It is not the purpose of this book to give every possible nymph for every possible ephemerid; a line must be drawn. What I have endeavoured to do is give the reader and tier a sampling of just some of the mayflies that could be of value to the fisherman.

### BRITISH AND IRISH PATTERNS

Some professional fly-dressers in a number of European countries do not, as a general rule, publish their fly patterns. Spain and France are two such countries. I have it on good authority from the eminent French fishing-writer, Raymond Rocher, that some dressers have even resorted to the law courts to protect the integrity of their patterns. Flies illustrated in some books from the Continent are depicted with reference numbers so that the reader can purchase the flies from the fly-tying house concerned. Nevertheless a number of patterns from these and other European countries will be given in subsequent chapters.

The following fly, and all others described in this chapter, can be tied weighted or not, as desired. I usually weight it with one turn of lead wire along the length of the shank. The tuft of marabou behind the thorax simulates the breathing appendages of the natural nymph. I now tie this fly upside-down on a swimming-nymph hook and have found it to be very effective.

### Mayfly Nymph (*Ephemera danica, E. vulgata*) · UK

| | |
|---|---|
| *Hook* | Mustad 79580, sizes 12–8 |
| *Thread* | Brown |
| *Tail* | Cock-pheasant tail fibres |
| *Body* | Cream wool or fur |
| *Rib* | Brown silk |
| *Thorax* | Cream wool or fur |
| *Breathing appendages* | Tuft of brown marabou |
| *Wing case* | Cock-pheasant tail fibres |
| *Legs* | Ends of wing-case fibres divided and swept back |

Mayfly Nymph

One of the late Richard Walker's patterns, this next fly is perhaps the most popular, as well as the one that is most sold commercially in the UK. I have often said that it has a higher lead content that the roof of St Paul's Cathedral but that is a slight exaggeration.

### Mayfly Nymph · R. Walker · UK

| | |
|---|---|
| *Hook* | Mustad 79580, sizes 12–8 |
| *Thread* | Brown |
| *Tail* | Cock-pheasant tail fibres |
| *Body* | Yellowish-cream angora |
| *Rib* | Brown silk |
| *Thorax* | As body |
| *Wing case* | As body |
| *Legs* | Ends of wing-case fibres divided and swept backwards |

To tie the fly, proceed as follows:

*Step 1*   Weight the hook with a double layer of lead wire and take the tying thread down to the bend of the hook. There, tie in a few fibres of cock-pheasant tail and a length of brown ribbing silk.

*Step 2*   Return the tying thread back along the shank and there tie in a length of yellowish-cream angora wool.

*Step 3*   Wind the angora down the shank and back again to form the abdomen. Follow this with the rib; apply the first few turns close together to form two distinct bands. Tie off the body and the ribbing materials and remove any surplus ribbing silk. Tie in a strip of cock-pheasant tail fibres on top of the hook for the wing case.

*Step 4*   Take the thread to the eye, then form the thorax with the remaining angora wool. Take the cock-pheasant tail fibres over the back of the thorax and tie down. Divide the fibres either side of the hook and tie backwards to form the legs. Finish the fly in the usual way with a whip finish and a dab of varnish. Treat the wing case and back of the abdomen with a flexible cement. The fly is now complete.

The original Walker pattern used cock-pheasant tail fibres for the two bands at the rear of the abdomen; using silk is much easier. His first Mayfly Nymph used ostrich herl, and there are many who still prefer this pattern. There are many other so-called 'Mayfly Nymphs', but the two given above cater for most anglers' needs.

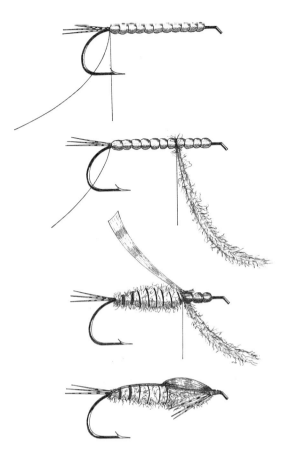

Large Dark Olive Nymph

This pattern, in smaller sizes, serves for most of the olive nymphs without any alteration to the dressing.

The Large Dark Olive was sometimes referred to as the Early Olive, for obvious reasons; the following nymph is thus entitled.

### Early Olive Nymph *(Baetis rhodani)* · UK

| | |
|---|---|
| *Hook* | Mustad 94840, sizes 12–14 |
| *Thread* | Olive |
| *Tail* | Dark olive hen strands |
| *Body* | Dark olive seal fur |
| *Rib* | Gold wire |
| *Thorax* | As body |
| *Wing case* | Dark starkling wing or grey duck |
| *Legs* | Dark olive hen hackle, one turn |

Mayfly Nymph

The nymph of the large dark olive can be imitated by many of the broad-spectrum nymphs found in the fly-boxes of most anglers. I devised the first of the following patterns many years ago and, on its day, it still catches fish. The insect is fairly well distributed throughout Europe and, in the UK, makes its first appearance in late February, often appearing in the autumn.

### Large Dark Olive Nymph
### *(Baetis rhodani)* · UK

| | |
|---|---|
| *Hook* | Mustad 94840, sizes 12–16 |
| *Thread* | Yellow |
| *Tail* | Dark olive cock hackle fibres |
| *Body* | Dark olive fur |
| *Rib* | Gold wire |
| *Thorax* | Brown seal fur |
| *Wing case* | Dark olive goose quill |
| *Legs* | Fibres from wing case divided and turned backwards either side of the thorax, or brown partridge hackle |

Early Olive Nymph

The slightly smaller medium olive (*Baetis tenax*, *B. buceratus*, *B. vernus*) is widely distrubuted throughout Europe, and there are many patterns devised to imitate the larval stage. The insect can be seen on the water as early as April and as late as October on British rivers. It can be imitated by any of the Olive Nymph patterns given but should be smaller.

### Olive Dun Nymph *(Baetis vernus)*

| | |
|---|---|
| *Hook* | Mustad 94840, sizes 14–16 |
| *Thread* | Olive |
| *Tail* | Medium olive hen hackle fibres |
| *Body* | Medium olive seal fur |
| *Rib* | Gold wire |
| *Thorax* | As body |
| *Wing case* | Starling wing or grey duck-wing quill |
| *Legs* | Short-fibred medium olive hen, one turn |

After the large mayfly (*Ephemera danica*), the blue-winged olive (*Ephemerella ignita*) must be considered as one of the most important angler's flies. As an adult it is easily recognized because, unlike other olives, it possesses three tails (the others have only two, although the nymphs have three). The adult fly is usually found on the water from May onwards and can hatch at any time during the season right through to late October. It is widely distributed throughout Europe. Trout forage for this nymph off the bottom or intercept the hatching nymph on its journey to the surface. It is probably true to say that the adult is more important than the nymph; nevertheless there are a number of patterns devised to imitate the larva.

### Blue-winged Olive Nymph (*Ephemerella ignita*) · UK

| | |
|---|---|
| *Hook* | Mustad 94840, size 14 |
| *Thread* | Olive or yellow |
| *Tail* | Dirty yellow grizzle hackle fibres |
| *Body* | Greenish-olive heron herl |
| *Rib* | Fine gold wire |
| *Thorax* | Dark olive seal fur |
| *Wing case* | Pale olive goose breast |
| *Legs* | Dirty yellow, grizzle-hen, one turn only |

Blue-winged Olive Nymph

The next pattern, which I devised, makes use of more modern materials, such as Swannundaze.

### Blue-winged Olive Nymph (*Ephemerella ignita*) · Price · UK

| | |
|---|---|
| *Hook* | Mustad 9671, sizes 12–14 |
| *Thread* | Olive |
| *Tail* | Olive grizzle-cock |
| *Body* | Medium olive Antron (or similar fur) |
| *Rib* | Fine Swannundaze transparent olive |
| *Thorax* | As body |
| *Wing pad* | Two slips of recording tape |
| *Wing case* | Recording tape |
| *Legs* | Olive partridge |

The fly known as the dark olive (*Baetis atrebatinus*) is not very common in the UK but is quite widespread in Europe and also in Ireland. The following olive nymph was created by the Irish fly-tier, Thomas J. Hanna, author of *Fly Fishing in Ireland* (1933). A number of his patterns appear in Courtney Williams's *Dictionary of Trout Flies*. Even today some of his flies would be considered innovative.

### Dark Olive Nymph (*Baetis atrebatinus*) · Hanna · Ireland

| | |
|---|---|
| *Hook* | Mustad 9671, size 14 |
| *Thread* | Brown or olive |
| *Tail* | Dark olive cock, three fibres |
| *Body* | Dark olive seal fur |
| *Rib* | Gold wire |
| *Thorax* | As body |
| *Wing case* | Cock-pheasant tail fibres |
| *Legs* | Olive partridge |

Dark Olive Nymph (Irish)

The iron blue (*Baetis niger* or *B. muticus*) is common throughout Europe. The great North Country spider pattern, the Snipe & Purple, has been used, and is still being used for that matter, to imitate this dark ephemerid. Most nymphal patterns are basically the same; Skues's pattern given earlier (p. 26) is as good as any. The following pattern, like the Dark Olive, comes from Ireland. I give this dressing because it is sufficiently different from most of the usual ties.

### Iron-blue Nymph (*Baetis niger, B. muticus*) · Ireland

| | |
|---|---|
| *Hook* | Mustad 9671, sizes 14–16 |
| *Thread* | Black |
| *Tail* | Greenish-grey cock hackle, three fibres |
| *Body* | Cinnamon floss |
| *Rib* | Clipped, palmered, smokey-blue-grey hackle |
| *Thorax* | Fieldmouse fur |
| *Wing case* | Cock-pheasant tail fibres |
| *Legs* | Blue dun hen |

I sat in my small cockleshell of a boat amid a gaggle of other club members fishing our local club water. Fish were moving all around, but success was notable by its absence; very few, if any, rods curved into a fighting fish. I looked into my fly-box. I had tried all the usual large nymphs and peacock-herl-headed pupae; I had even run the gamut of exotic lures; but all to no avail. Finally, I selected a small, insignificant little nymph by John Goddard, the Olive PVC Nymph, and vowed that, if this did not work, then to hell with it, I was going home. Never was the last straw clutched with so very little hope and with only a thin veneer of conviction. I cast out this small, size 16 nymph and inched it back slowly. The very first cast caught me my best fish of the season – a rainbow that was not much short of 4 lb (1.8 kg) – which was duly netted. I sat back in the boat, smug, satisfied and certainly looking as though I knew what it was all about. 'A PVC nymph,' I informed all and sundry as they called to me across the water in the now half-light. 'They are taking pond olive nymphs,' I continued, knowing there was nobody else around with a fish to prove otherwise. Yes, there are times when, in the kingdom of the blind, the one-eyed man is truly king.

Goddard's PVC Nymph should really be classed as a broad-spectrum nymph, but it imitates the pond olive (*Cloëon dipterum*) so well that I feel justified in including it here. The pond olive nymph can be found on the water throughout the fishing season from May onwards. There have been many times when the trout on our local water have become preoccupied with this insect. I believe it prefers the smaller lakes and reservoirs to great expanses of stillwater.

### Olive PVC Nymph
#### (*Cloëon dipterum*) · Goddard · UK

| | |
|---|---|
| Hook | Mustad 3904A, sizes 14–16 (pre-weight with copper wire) |
| Thread | Yellow |
| Tail | Olive goose fibre |
| Body | As body |
| Rib | Narrow silver Lurex |
| Overbody | Wrapped PVC strip |
| Thorax | As for body not wrapped in PVC |
| Wing case | Dark cock-pheasant tail fibres |

The original pattern called for condor herl but, this being no longer available, goose or turkey quill makes a good substitute.

Olive PVC Nymph

Mention has already been made of C.F. Walker and his contribution to our knowledge of flies and fly-fishing; the next pattern is one of his.

### Pond Olive Nymph
#### (*Cloëon dipterum*) · C. F. Walker · UK

| | |
|---|---|
| Hook | Mustad 3904A, sizes 14–16 |
| Thread | Yellow |
| Tail | Brown partridge, few fibres |
| Body | Brown and ginger seal fur, thin |
| Rib | Silver wire (a silver wire tag is also given in the original dressing) |
| Thorax | Brown seal fur |
| Breathing appendages | Yellow-brown goose herl (original called for condor) |
| Legs | Short-fibred honey hen hackle |

Pond Olive Nymph

Walker also suggest another pattern using a more olive shade, to match nymphs that are of a lighter colour. Nymphs can vary in colour from water to water. He also imitates the lake olive with the same artificial dressing.

The slightly larger lake olive (*Cloëon simile*) is not quite so common as its smaller relation except in Ireland, where it is widespread and far more common. The insect is found on much larger expanses of water than the pond olive, which gives some justification for their names. If necessary, they can be distinguished by the shape of the gills, the second gill being the key (see illustration on p. 42). The first lake olive imitation to be described is one conceived by Joscelyn Lane in his book *Lake and Loch Fishing*.

*C. dipterum*     *C. simile*

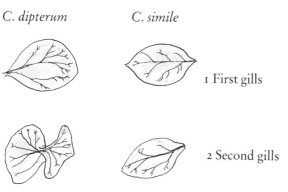

1 First gills

2 Second gills

Differences in gills of *Cloën* nymphs

## Lake Olive (*Cloëon simile*) · Lane · UK
*Hook*      Mustad 94840, sizes 12–14
*Thread*    Golden olive
*Tail*      Olive cock hackle fibres
*Body*      Olive silk
*Rib*       Fine gold wire
*Thorax*    Darker olive silk (not ball-shaped)
*Legs*      Olive cock hackle fibres below the hook

As stated earlier the lake olive is found in quite large numbers on many of the Irish loughs, so it is only fitting that, as a second example, I give an Irish pattern.

## Lake Olive Nymph (*Cloëon simile*) · Ireland
*Hook*      Mustad 9671, size 14
*Thread*    Olive
*Tail*      Brown-olive cock hackle fibres
*Body*      Medium olive floss silk
*Rib*       Gold wire
*Thorax*    Hare's ear
*Legs*      Dark olive cock, short and tied sparsely

Remaining with stillwater, we shall deal next with the nymph of the sepia dun (*Leptophlebia marginata*). The fly is found on the water from late April until late May. On my local water in Kent, southern England, there are sparse hatches at the same time as the larger *Ephemera danica* takes to the wing. This occurs during the last week in May. The nymph can be recognized by its dark brown colour and rather large side gills. Its tails are spread wide apart and are as long as the body. The first imitation is a pattern devised by the late Richard Walker.

## Sepia Nymph (*Leptophlebia marginata*) · R. Walker · UK
*Hook*      Mustad 94840, size 12
*Thread*    Black
*Tail*      Long sepia cock-pheasant tail fibres
*Body*      Black sheep's wool picked out at the sides to imitate the gills
*Rib*       Black floss silk
*Thorax*    Black sheep's wool, fairly flat
*Wing case* Cock-pheasant tail fibres
*Legs*      Cock-pheasant tail fibres swept back either side of the thorax

The next pattern was devised by my friend the late David Jacques, who taught me a lot about the angler's sedge, a subject on which he was an expert. He observed the natural sepia nymph in his home aquarium and mentioned that, due to the warm indoor temperatures, his insects hatched at the end of March.

## Sepia Nymph (*Leptophlebia marginata*) · Jacques · UK
*Hook*      Mustad 94840, size 12
*Thread*    Maroon or claret
*Tail*      Cock hackle fibres, widely spread
*Body*      Cock-pheasant tail fibres
*Rib*       Gold wire
*Thorax*    Black seal fur
*Wing case* As body
*Legs*      Honey or light red hackle with a dark list

The claret dun (*Leptophlebia vespertina*) hatches out a little later than the closely related sepia dun and can be found on the water at the end of June. C.F. Walker maintained, in his book *Lake Flies and Their Imitation*, that he could not see the slightest trace of the colour claret. Colour, like beauty, is found only in the eye of the beholder. No two people can see exactly the same subtleties of colour and shade, especially in something as small as a tiny insect, unless it is so bright and garish that no doubt could possibly arise. There is not a great deal of difference between this and the Sepia Nymph except the breathing filaments, which are more finely tapered in *L. vespertina*. The first pattern is the fly given by C.F. Walker to imitate both species.

## Claret Nymph
### (Leptophlebia vespertina, L. marginata)
C.F. Walker · UK

| | |
|---|---|
| *Hook* | Mustad 94840, sizes 14–12 |
| *Thread* | Black |
| *Tail* | Long, black hen hackle fibres, widely spread |
| *Body* | Dark brown and ginger seal fur, mixed |
| *Rib* | Silver wire |
| *Thorax* | Black seal fur |
| *Breathing appendages* | Fur picked out at the sides |
| *Legs* | Brown hen hackle, couple of turns |

The second fly is one of my own patterns.

## Claret Nymph
### (Leptophlebia vespertina) · Price · UK

| | |
|---|---|
| *Hook* | Mustad 94840, sizes 14–12 |
| *Thread* | Black |
| *Tail* | Three strands of brown mallard, widely spread |
| *Body* | Dark claret seal fur |
| *Rib* | Gold wire |
| *Thorax* | Black seal fur |
| *Breathing appendages* | Hair picked out at the sides |
| *Wing case* | Black goose quill |
| *Legs* | Brown partridge |

The March brown is still called in some books by its old name, *Rithrogen haarupi*, but in recent years it has been reclassified as *R. germanica*. Although found in the fly-boxes of fly-fishermen the length and breadth of the British Isles, it hatches out on very few rivers. The late March brown (*Ecdyonurus venosus*) is far more widespread in the British Isles and in Europe. The same nymphs can be used to imitate both species, as can the nymphs of the large green dun (*E. insignis*) and the large brook dun (*E. torrentis*). All are flat, broad-headed, stone-clinging nymphs, found in similar habitats and of similar habits. Even the nymph of the yellow May dun (*Heptagenia sulphurea*) can be reconciled to a good March brown nymph imitation.

## March Brown Nymph
### (Rithrogena germanica) · Wooley · UK

| | |
|---|---|
| *Hook* | Mustad 94840, sizes 10–14 |
| *Thread* | Orange |

March Brown Nymph

| | |
|---|---|
| *Tail* | Three short strands of brown mallard flank |
| *Body* | Any brown fur dubbing |
| *Rib* | Gold wire |
| *Thorax* | As body |
| *Wing case* | Woodcock quill fibre |
| *Legs* | Speckled grouse hackle, one turn |

The next pattern I devised was heavily influenced by some styles of nymphs I had encountered on a visit to Spain. The fly itself is not difficult to tie and yet has a degree of realism without sacrificing its fish-catching capabilities. I would describe the fly as semi-realistic.

## March Brown Nymph
### (Rithrogena germanica) · Price · UK

| | |
|---|---|
| *Hook* | Mustad 9672, sizes 12–14 (pre-weight with lead or copper wire if so desired) |
| *Thread* | Black or brown |
| *Tail* | Three fibres of cock-pheasant tail |
| *Body* | Hare fur and Antron mix |
| *Back* | Mottled turkey strip (first treated with a flexible cement) |
| *Rib* | Fine gold wire |
| *Thorax* | As body |
| *Legs* | Partridge hackle |
| *Wing case* | Mottled turkey |
| *Head* | As wing case |

To tie the fly, proceed as follows:

*Step 1* At the tail end of the hook tie in three cock-pheasant tail fibres for the tail so that they are spread well apart. At the same point, tie in a length of fine gold wire and a strip of mottled turkey feather. Dub the body fur onto the tying thread.
*Step 2* Take the fur-laden thread down the shank to the point indicated and then stretch the mottled turkey over the back. Finally, rib overall with the gold wire. Remove any surplus feather or wire. Now tie in a further strip of mottled turkey and a partridge hackle at this point. Dub a fresh amount of fur onto the tying thread.

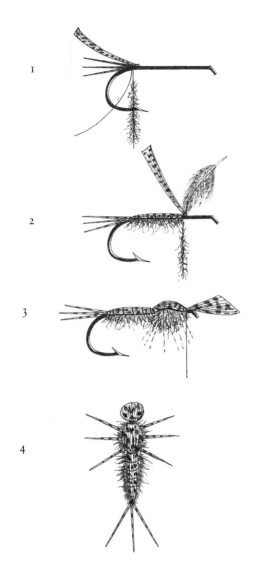

March Brown Nymph

**Step 3** Form the thorax, then wind on the partridge hackle across the whole thorax, palmer fashion. Now take the mottled turkey over the back to form the wing case, flattening it down with the thumb and finger.

**Step 4** Tie off and whip finish. Trim the surplus mottled turkey to a circular shape. Varnish the back, wing case and head. If desired, paint on two small, black eyes and, with a dab of varnish between thumb and finger, stroke the hackle fibres into six legs. With a dubbing needle pick out the fur at the sides of the nymph to simulate the gills of the natural nymph.

I collected my first large summer dun on a small reservoir at Powder Mills, Seddlescombe, near Hastings in Sussex. I was at the time corresponding with Richard Walker, and he also had found specimens on an adjacent reservoir: Darwell near Battle. We both concluded that the species was *Siphlonurus armatus*. This and the other two species, *S. lacustris* and *S. alternatus*, are found as far as the north of Scotland, but none could be described as very prolific. I have encountered them hatching at the end of May through June. They appear to be localized in distribution. I have since found a few specimens on Dartmoor in Devon. They can be found on both stillwaters and rivers all over Europe.

The largest concentration of this insect which I ever encountered was in Slovenia on the River Obrh, a small karst stream under the control of the Fisheries Research Institute of Ljubljana. It was pouring with rain when we first started to fish this stream and, sheltering under every conceivable leaf on the bankside trees, and under every nettle and bush, were millions of *Siphlonurus* spinners (probably *S. croaticus*), so many in fact that they clung all over us as we brushed past the foliage. The surface of the river was amass with these dark reddish-brown insects. Indeed, there were so many that I could well believe that the local farmers used them as fertilizer on their small garden patches.

The trout of the Obrh had had their fill of these dusky flies and, by the time we began to fish, their interest was focused on smaller olives; we were able to match these and subsequently enjoyed some good sport. I made a mental note that, if ever I were to fish the Obrh again before the big hatch (which is an annual occurence and not a now-and-again phenomenon), I would know exactly which nymph to put on to tempt the browns and rainbows. The imitation of the nymph given below is one of my own patterns, which I will certainly use.

### Large Summer Dun Nymph
**(*Siphlonurus* sp.)** · Price · UK

| | |
|---|---|
| *Hook* | Mustad 79580 longshank, sizes 12–14 |
| *Thread* | Brown |
| *Tail* | Brown-olive cock hackle fibres |
| *Body* | Brown-olive seal fur |
| *Rib* | Gold wire |

| | |
|---|---|
| *Thorax* | Olive and dirty yellow seal fur, mixed |
| *Breathing appendages* | Short-fibred olive hen hackle |
| *Wing case* | Brown feather fibres |
| *Hackle* | Short-fibred dark olive hen |

Pale watery is the name given to *Baetis fuscatus*, although it has also been used for other medium-to-small ephemerids in the past. *B. fuscatus* is well distributed throughout Europe, and the British Isles are no exception; it can be found on the water in May and at any time throughout the season until the autumn months. Nymphs devised to imitate the pale watery can also be used to imitate other species, such as the pale evening dun (*Procloëon bifidium*) and spurwings (*Centroptilum luteolum* and *C. pennulatum*).

The old West Country fly, the Tups Indispensable, was thought to be an imitation of the pale watery. The Skues pattern representing the nymphal stage of this insect emulates the Tups Fly in many ways, including the reddish colour of the thorax. Frank Sawyer gave a nymph for both the pale watery and the pale evening dun, in addition to his now-famous Pheasant Tail and Grey Goose Nymphs, I give both his patterns.

## Pale Watery Nymph
**(*Baetis fuscatus*)** · Sawyer · UK

| | |
|---|---|
| *Hook* | Mustad 3904A, size 14 |
| *Thread* | None (Sawyer used fine copper wire) |
| *Tail* | Ginger cock hackle fibres |
| *Body* | Fawn darning wool wound with the copper wire (extra weight can be achieved by a layer of copper wire as an underbody) |
| *Thorax* | Wood-pigeon primary feather |
| *Legs* | None |

## Pale Evening Dun Nymph
**(*Procloëon bifidium*)** · Sawyer · UK

| | |
|---|---|
| *Hook* | Mustad 3904A, size 14 |
| *Thread* | None |
| *Tail* | Tips of condor herl (or dyed goose) |
| *Body* | Browny-yellow condor herl (or dyed goose) wound with red copper wire |
| *Thorax* | Browny-yellow condor herl, wound with gold wire |
| *Legs* | None |

There are five fairly common species of *Caenis* in Europe: *C. macrura*, *C. robusta*, *C. moesta*, *C. rivulorum* and *C. horaria*. These are known collectively by fishermen as the angler's curse. All are small, broad-winged, white or light-coloured flies. They can hatch at any time during the season from May to September and, although they can hatch during the morning, in my experience most large hatches occur at dusk.

It had been hot all day; a white sun had burnt down, driving me off the water to seek some shade from a lonely tree that stood by the side of the lake where we had pitched our tent. The lake we were fishing lay not far from the mighty Columbia River in eastern Washington in the arid desert area. Lake Lennice, for that was its name, is a seep lake, i.e. a lake of clear water amid dry scrub and sandy dust. The water rises through the sand after travelling through volcanic conduits and channels from the water-bearing Columbia Basin.

After a few hours' rest, I gathered up my float tube and returned to the water. The sun had dipped down behind the hills, painting the sky pink; the clouds changed to mauve and purple as the heat went out of the day. I had not been fishing for more than 10 minutes, flippering my way at the edge of the weed patch and admiring a blood-red hunter's moon as it rose above the basalt escarpment, when I noticed that I was becoming covered in white insect confetti. I was in the middle of the largest hatch of *Caenis* I had ever witnessed. They poured over my clothing and across my float tube; they got into my eyes and up my nose; and their very numbers drove my friend Darrel Martin out of the water because they had so covered his glasses that he could not see. These benign little flies masked some less welcome winged visitors: sharp-tongued mosquitoes that, small as they were, endeavoured to devour me. Needless to say, there was no point in trying to match the hatch, so I used an ultra-large white fly to tempt the only trout of the evening.

*Caenis* is an important fly because trout like to feed on it, and there are a number of patterns devised to imitate the winged stage. There are, however, a number of fishermen who believe that there is little point in imitating the nymph and, to a degree, I agree with them. But others have devised and fished imitations succesfully, so who am I to say no. In the USA the equally small and frustrating *Tricorythodes* spp. occupy the wiles and guiles of the American fly-fisherman more so than species of *Caenis*, mainly because the activity related to the Trico generally occurs during daylight hours, so there is not quite the same frustration of tiny flies combined with selective fish, all compounded by the fading light.

The British Midlands fly-dresser, Bob Carnill, devised such a nymph for fishing just below the surface. Bob is probably one of the best fly-dressers working in England today and many of his patterns have received international acclaim.

### Caenis Nymph (*Caenis* sp.) · Carnill · UK

| | |
|---|---|
| *Hook* | Mustad 94840, sizes 14–16 |
| *Thread* | Black or brown |
| *Tail* | Three brown partridge hackle fibres |
| *Body* | Drab light brown swan or goose herl |
| *Rib* | Stripped peacock quill |
| *Thorax* | Hare's ear |
| *Wing case* | Biots from a heron primary feather, broad ends tied facing the rear, trimmed to shape |
| *Legs* | Partridge hackle fibres |

Caenis Nymph

\*    \*    \*

Over the last few years the world has grown a lot smaller. Fast, economical air-flights have made fishing in foreign places a practicality for most anglers. The increasing number of books published on flies and fly-fishing in various countries has opened up for all a knowledge of flies and fishing that is not limited to home waters. Political and geographical boundaries do not hinder the passage of good, killing fly patterns and the exchange of views and knowledge can now be described as truly international. I have sat and tied flies alongside local tiers at conclaves and fly-fairs in many countries and each time it has been a learning experience. I have fished with Slovenian flies in the UK, British flies in Spain, South African flies in New Zealand, American flies in most countries – every conceivable combination of fly and country – and I certainly hope to continue to do so.

The following nymphs, tied to represent particular mayfly species, come from a number of countries. Other patterns can be found in subsequent chapters. All are worth tying and certainly worth trying, whether in the fly's country of origin or in home waters.

### AMERICAN PATTERNS

### Western March Brown (*Rithrogena morrisoni*) · Arbona · USA

| | |
|---|---|
| *Hook* | Mustad 3906, size 12 |
| *Thread* | Brown |
| *Tail* | Brown partridge hackle fibres |
| *Body* | Dark reddish-brown dubbing |
| *Thorax* | As body |
| *Wing case* | Black goose quill |
| *Legs* | Brown partridge |

I have also seen the following pattern described as the Small Black Quill.

### Small Western Red Quill (*Rithrogena undulata*) · USA

| | |
|---|---|
| *Hook* | Mustad 3906, size 16 |
| *Thread* | Rusty brown |
| *Tail* | Brown partridge fibres |
| *Body* | Reddish-brown fur |
| *Rib* | Fine gold wire |
| *Thorax* | As body |
| *Wing case* | Black goose quill |

The next fly is found in the eastern and mid-western states of the USA. It is named after the doyen of American fly-fishing, Theodore Gordon, America's equivalent of our Halford and Skues rolled into one.

### Quill Gordon Nymph (*Epeorus pleuralis*) · USA

| | |
|---|---|
| *Hook* | Mustad 3904A, sizes 12–16 |
| *Thread* | Olive |
| *Tail* | Cock-pheasant tail fibres |
| *Body* | Light beaver fur |
| *Rib* | Brown thread |
| *Thorax* | As body |
| *Wing case* | White-tipped turkey tail quill |
| *Legs* | Brown partridge |

The next pattern was devised by Art Flick from an earlier pattern created by the pioneer fly-fisherman, Preston Jennings, author of *A Book Of Trout Flies*.

## American March Brown
### (Stenomena vicarium) · Flick · USA

| | |
|---|---|
| *Hook* | Mustad 3906, sizes 12–18 |
| *Thread* | Brown |
| *Tail* | Cock-pheasant tail fibres |
| *Body* | Red fox fur (two parts), amber goat hair (one part), mixed |
| *Rib* | Dark brown silk |
| *Thorax* | As body |
| *Wing case* | As tail |
| *Legs* | Brown partridge |

The following nymph is sometimes known as the Gray Fox as well as the Light Cahill.

## Light Cahill (Stenomena fuscum) · USA

| | |
|---|---|
| *Hook* | Mustad 3906b, sizes 10–18 |
| *Thread* | Cream |
| *Tail* | Lemon wood-duck fibres |
| *Body* | Creamy-tan fox fur |
| *Rib* | Brown thread |
| *Thorax* | As body |
| *Wing case* | Lemon wood-duck fibres, divided either side of thorax |

The burrowing nymphs are well represented in the USA, where there are many more species than in the UK. The following patterns are representative of some of the American species.

## Brown Drake Nymph
### (Ephemera simulans) · USA

| | |
|---|---|
| *Hook* | Mustad 9672 (3x), sizes 10–12 |
| *Thread* | Tan |
| *Tail* | Light tan partridge hackle fibres |
| *Body* | Tan rabbit mixed with cream fitch fur |
| *Rib* | Brown thread |
| *Thorax* | As body |
| *Wing pad* | Brown ostrich herl |
| *Legs* | As tail |

## Yellow Drake Nymph (Ephemera varia) · USA

| | |
|---|---|
| *Hook* | Mustad 9672 (3x), sizes 10–12 |
| *Thread* | Olive |
| *Tail* | Ginger hen hackle fibres |
| *Body* | Brown-olive fur dubbing |
| *Rib* | Yellow thread |
| *Thorax* | Brown-olive fur dubbing |
| *Wing case* | Mottled turkey |
| *Legs* | As tail |

The following fly has been known by anglers as the Coffin Fly, as well as the more accepted Green Drake.

## Green Drake Nymph
### (Ephemera guttulata) · USA

| | |
|---|---|
| *Hook* | Mustad 9672 (3x), sizes 10–8 |
| *Thread* | Olive |
| *Tail* | Olive partridge hackle fibres |
| *Body* | Cream fitch and light olive rabbit mixed |
| *Wing pad* | Dark brown ostrich clump |
| *Legs* | Light olive partidge |

## Dark Hendrikson Nymph
### (Ephemerella subvaria) · USA

| | |
|---|---|
| *Hook* | Mustad 3906b, sizes 10–14 |
| *Thread* | Olive |
| *Tail* | Lemon wood-duck fibres |
| *Body* | Grey-brown fox fur |
| *Rib* | Brown silk |
| *Thorax* | As body |
| *Wing case* | White-tipped turkey quill |
| *Legs* | Brown partridge |

## Light Hendrikson Nymph
### (Ephemerella rotunda) · USA

| | |
|---|---|
| *Hook* | Mustad 3906b, sizes 12–14 |
| *Thread* | Olive |
| *Tail* | Ginger hen hackle fibres |
| *Body* | Yellowish-brown dubbing |
| *Rib* | Brown silk |
| *Thorax* | As body |
| *Wing case* | Dark brown turkey quill |
| *Legs* | As tail |

## Pale Evening Dun Nymph
### (Ephemerella dorothea) · USA

| | |
|---|---|
| *Hook* | Mustad 94840, sizes 12–16 |
| *Thread* | Olive |
| *Tail* | Lemon wood-duck fibres (or substitute) |
| *Body* | Grey-brown fox fur |
| *Rib* | Gold wire |
| *Thorax* | As body |
| *Wing case* | Light grey goose or duck quill |
| *Legs* | Brown partridge hackle |

### Large Blue-winged Olive
### (Ephemerella cornuta) · USA

| | |
|---|---|
| *Hook* | Mustad 94840, sizes 12–16 |
| *Thread* | Olive |
| *Tail* | Hen-pheasant tail fibres |
| *Body* | Grey-olive dubbing |
| *Rib* | Gold wire |
| *Thorax* | As body |
| *Wing case* | Black turkey quill, flattening the thorax |
| *Legs* | Tan hen-pheasant fibres |

The next fly is referred to as the Small Blue-winged Olive or the Slate-winged Olive, a fly that appears in mid- to late summer.

### Slate or Small Blue-winged Olive
### (Ephemerella lata) · USA

| | |
|---|---|
| *Hook* | Mustad 94840, sizes 14–16 |
| *Thread* | Olive |
| *Tail* | Three goose quill fibres |
| *Body* | Grey-brown fox fur |
| *Rib* | Grey thread |
| *Thorax* | As body |
| *Wing case* | Grey goose quill fibres |
| *Legs* | Medium blue dun hen hackle |

### Tiny Western Olive
### (Pseudocloëon edmundsi) · USA

| | |
|---|---|
| *Hook* | Mustad 94859, size 20 |
| *Thread* | Olive |
| *Tail* | Pale ginger or honey cock hackle fibres |
| *Body* | Brown-olive dubbing |
| *Thorax* | As body |
| *Wing case* | Brown turkey quill |
| *Legs* | As tail |

### Iron-blue Quill Nymph
### (Baetis vagans, B. parvus) · USA

| | |
|---|---|
| *Hook* | Mustad 3906, size 16 |
| *Thread* | Olive |
| *Tail* | Wood-duck fibres |
| *Body* | Light olive-brown dubbing |
| *Thorax* | As body |
| *Wing case* | Black-dyed goose quill segment |
| *Legs* | Wood-duck fibres |

The next nymph is sometimes called the Black Drake Nymph and, by others, the Gray Drake Nymph. The scientific name is *Siphlonurus occidentalis*, and it is an important hatch on some waters of the western USA. The pattern given was created by the legendary western American fly-tier, 'Polly' Rosborough. I have had the privilege of tying flies with him at a number of conclaves in the USA and have also written a profile on him for one of the British magazines. His now-famous book, *Tying and Fishing the Fuzzy Nymphs*, is considered a classic.

### Black Drake Nymph
### (Siphlonurus occidentalis) · Rosborough · USA

| | |
|---|---|
| *Hook* | Mustad 38941 (3x), size 10 |
| *Thread* | Grey |
| *Tail* | Black-and-white guinea-fowl tied short |
| *Body* | Beaver fur from the belly with guard hairs |
| *Thorax* | As body |
| *Wing case* | Small tuft of black ostrich plume. |

Black Drake Nymph

### Great Western Lead-wing
### (Isonychia velma) · Brookes · USA

| | |
|---|---|
| *Hook* | Mustad 38941 (3x), size 10 |
| *Thread* | Olive |
| *Tail* | Green grizzle hackle fibres |
| *Body* | Mottled brown wool |
| *Rib* | One strand of purple wool and grey ostrich herl with an over-rib of gold wire |
| *Legs* | Green grizzle hackle, palmered over the thorax area |

### Emerging Calibaetis Nymph
### (Calibaetis sp.) · Janssen · USA

| | |
|---|---|
| *Hook* | Mustad 9671, sizes 12–16 |
| *Thread* | Grey |
| *Tail* | Grey Amherst-pheasant tail tippets |
| *Body* | Grey rabbit covered with clear PVC |
| *Thorax* | As body |
| *Wing case* | Grey duck or goose quill, lacquered |
| *Legs* | Wood-duck flank |

**Ostrich Calibaetis**
**(Calibaetis sp.)** · Arbona · USA

| | |
|---|---|
| *Hook* | Mustad 94845, sizes 12–16 |
| *Thread* | Grey |
| *Tail* | Grouse hackle fibres |
| *Body* | Grey ostrich herl |
| *Rib* | Grey thread |
| *Thorax* | As body |
| *Wing case* | Grey duck |

There are a number of patterns around to imitate the nymphs of *Hexagenia* spp. The following pattern, by Charles E. Brookes, is one such fly. It is extremely impressionistic.

**Genie May (Hexagenia sp.)** · Brookes · USA

| | |
|---|---|
| *Hook* | Mustad 9672, sizes 8–12 |
| *Thread* | Brown |
| *Tail* | Orange grizzle hackles |
| *Body* | Mottled brown fur dubbing |
| *Rib* | Purple yarn and grey ostrich wound together; cross-ribbed with gold wire (optional) |
| *Thorax* | As body |
| *Legs* | Orange grizzle cock, palmered through the thorax |

The small *Caenis* nymph is not often copied by the tiers in the USA, but the following pattern has been depicted in a number of books.

**Caenis Nymph** · USA

| | |
|---|---|
| *Hook* | Mustad 94859, sizes 16–26 |
| *Thread* | Black or brown |
| *Tail* | Three cock-pheasant tail fibres, widely spread |
| *Body* | Greyish-tan rabbit dubbing |
| *Rib* | Brown thread |
| *Wing case* | Short tuft of black rabbit |
| *Legs* | Fur picked out in the thorax region |

Like the *Caenis* nymph, there are very few patterns to imitate the tiny Trico nymph. These nymphs are small and not everyone's cup of tea; most people like to fish with something a bit more substantial. The following pattern was given by Rik Hafele and Dave Hughes in their book *Western Hatches*.

**Trico Nymph** · USA

| | |
|---|---|
| *Hook* | Mustad 94840, sizes 20–26 |
| *Thread* | Brown |
| *Tail* | Three fibres of cock-pheasant tail, tied short |
| *Body* | Tapered body of tan or light brown dubbing |
| *Legs* | Fur picked out in the thorax area |

NEW ZEALAND PATTERNS

When you think of New Zealand and the flies used there to catch the fabulous browns and rainbows, you could be forgiven for thinking only of the large Matuka-type flies and other bait-imitating lures which that country created. Nothing could be further from the truth. During a visit to both islands of that beautiful country, apart from dry imitations of cicadas and caddis, the only flies we used were small insect-imitating nymphs.

While I was there, I had the good fortune to be guided by knowledgeable fly-tiers Brian Hussey from Taupo, Frank Schlosser on the Ahuriri River, and the late Harry Rae on the blue ribbon river, the Mataura; all used small nymphs. I also received help and flies from Bryan and Nancy Tichborne and exchanged views with such writers as John Parsons and later, in the USA, with Tony Orman. The following few direct imitations are really the results of these people's help and knowledge.

Perhaps one of the best books to come out of New Zealand in the last decade was Norman Marsh's *Trout Stream Insects of New Zealand*; add to this Keith Draper's *Trout Flies in New Zealand* and Tony Orman's *Trout with the Nymph* and you are more than adequately equipped to fish with the nymph those crystal-blue waters in the Land of the Big White Cloud.

One of the largest of the New Zealand mayflies, *Ichthybotus hudsoni*, appears to be in decline. The species was named by the visiting English angler, J.C. Mottram, as 'The Mayfly', because of its size and slight resemblance to the British *Ephemera danica*. The natural nymph resembles in many respects the *E. danica* nymph but it is of a sandier colour and has more pronounced tusks. Mottram gave patterns for the dun and spinner stages, but not for the nymph. The nearest artificial to this insect is the pattern given by Keith Draper, who was not certain about the fly's origin but thought it might have been Bavarian.

## May Fly Nymph
### (Ichthybotus hudsoni) · Draper · NZ

| | |
|---|---|
| *Hook* | Mustad 79580, size 10 |
| *Thread* | Brown |
| *Tail* | Partridge tail feathers |
| *Body* | Off-white wool |
| *Rib* | Silver wire |
| *Thorax* | Yellow wool |
| *Wing case* | Brown partridge |
| *Legs* | Grey-partridge hackle fibres |

*Ichthybotus hudsoni*

## Striped Nymph
### (Zephlebia versicolor) · Marsh · NZ

| | |
|---|---|
| *Hook* | Mustad 9672, sizes 14–16 |
| *Thread* | Black |
| *Tail* | Cree or honey grizzle |
| *Body* | Stripped well-marked peacock quill |
| *Thorax* | Grey dubbing |
| *Wing case* | Dark grey mallard fibres |
| *Legs* | As tail |

Striped Nymph

## Grey Darter
### (Nesameletus ornatus) · Marsh · NZ

| | |
|---|---|
| *Hook* | Mustad 9672, sizes 12–16 |
| *Thread* | Brown |
| *Tail* | Brown partridge hackle fibres |
| *Body* | Sandy-grey hare fur |
| *Rib* | Copper wire |
| *Thorax* | As body |
| *Wing case* | Grey mallard quill segment |
| *Legs* | Brown partridge |

J.C. Mottram named the adult of the next fly the Pepper-winged Olive. He gave a pattern for this and the spinner but did not imitate the nymph.

## Orange Nymph (Zephlebia cruentata) · NZ

| | |
|---|---|
| *Hook* | Mustad 9672, sizes 12–14 |
| *Thread* | Orange |
| *Tail* | Brown partridge hackle fibres |
| *Body* | Orange wool |
| *Rib* | Fine silver wire |
| *Thorax* | Brown wool |
| *Wing case* | As tail |
| *Legs* | As tail |

## Orange Nymph
### (Zephlebia cruentata) · Marsh · NZ

| | |
|---|---|
| *Hook* | Mustad 9671 (2x), sizes 14–16 |
| *Thread* | Brown |
| *Tail* | Brown goose biots |
| *Body* | Ruddy-brown mohair |
| *Thorax* | Deep orange floss silk |
| *Wing case* | Light brown mallard flank |
| *Hackle* | Brown |

Unlike the European sepia nymph, the New Zealand nymph of the same name, *Zephlebia nodularis*, is easily recognized by its light-coloured legs. I have taken the liberty of amending an original Norman Marsh pattern to take this into account. The original nymph called for a black hackle but, because the legs on the natural are pale and not black, I have used ginger.

## Sepia Nymph
### (Zephlebia nodularis) · Marsh · NZ

| | |
|---|---|
| *Hook* | Mustad 9671 (2x), sizes 14–16 |
| *Thread* | Black |
| *Tail* | Light brown cock hackle fibres |
| *Body* | Mixed brown and black dubbing |
| *Rib* | Black thread |
| *Thorax* | As body |
| *Wing case* | Black feather fibre |
| *Legs* | Light brown or ginger hen |

Sepia Nymph

### New Zealand Mayfly Nymph
**(Oniscigaster sp.)** · Bragg · NZ

| | |
|---|---|
| *Hook* | Mustad 9672 (2x), sizes 10–14 |
| *Thread* | Olive |
| *Tail* | Olive cock hackle fibres |
| *Body* | Apple-green silk covered with PVC |
| *Thorax* | As body but pronounced |
| *Wing case* | Brown-speckled hen |
| *Legs* | As tail |

*Oniscigaster* sp.

The following pattern is yet another to imitate the grey darter. It was devised by a young tier, Peter Schasching, from Christchurch. It is tied to represent *Nesameletus ornatus* and an allied species, *N. flavitinctus*.

### Ornate Mayfly Nymph
**(Nesameletus ornatus)** · Schasching · NZ

| | |
|---|---|
| *Hook* | Tiemco 200, size 10 |
| *Thread* | Black |
| *Tail* | Three or four golden-pheasant tippet fibres or brown partridge |
| *Body* | Hare's ear dubbing |
| *Rib* | Gold wire |
| *Thorax* | Hare and rabbit fur, mixed |
| *Wing case* | Brown partridge, treated with varnish |
| *Legs* | Sparse brown partridge hackle |
| *Eyes* | Melted nylon monofilament |

Ornate Nymph

Other nymph examples from New Zealand will be found in subsequent chapters.

SOUTH AFRICAN PATTERNS

Today in South Africa more attention is being paid by the fly-fisherman to aquatic entomology. The likes of Neil Hodges, Tom Sutcliffe and Jack Blackman in Natal and Ed Herbst and Tony Biggs in Cape Province are educating the fly-fisherman into using natural representations of native insects and to the fact there is more to fly-fishing than Walker's Killer Fly. At the moment South African fly-fishermen are still, with a few exceptions, influenced by British and American nymph patterns.

One of the famous brown-trout rivers of South Africa is the Mooi River in Natal. This rises on an eastern spur of the main Drakensberg Range and, I believe, has one of the most constant flows of all the Natal streams. It has given its name to a fisherman's fly called the Mooi Moth. The natural is not, in fact, a moth but a mayfly (*Oligoneuriopsis lawrenci*), but it is certainly of significance on the Mooi River. The nymph, when full grown, is about ¾in (20mm) in length and is distinctly hump-backed. In the USA, there are a number of hump-backed nymphs of *Baetisca* sp. This South African nymph, although of a different species, may possibly look similar. The following imitation endeavours to imitate the nymph.

### Mooi Nymph
**(Oligoneuriopsis lawrenci)** · S. Africa

| | |
|---|---|
| *Hook* | Mustad 9672 (2x), sizes 8–10 (pre-weight the hook with lead wire to create the hump-back effect at the thorax) |
| *Thread* | Brown |
| *Tail* | Cock-pheasant tail fibres |
| *Body* | Grey, buff and olive dubbing, mixed |
| *Rib* | Black thread |
| *Thorax* | Brown dubbing |
| *Wing case* | Dark brown feather fibre |
| *Legs* | Brown partridge or francolin hackle fibres |

Mooi Nymph

## JAPANESE PATTERNS

In recent years fly-fishing has become extremely popular in Japan. I recall reading somewhere that there was evidence of fly-fishing there going back 500 years. In their waters, there are three indigenous game-fish; the yamame, a landlocked cherry salmon; the iwana, a species of char found in freestone rivers; and the amago. Brown, brook and rainbow trout have also been introduced. Close attention to detail and natural aptitude have combined to produce a number of fine skilled fly-dressers in the islands of Japan.

During a visit to the USA in 1990 I had the great pleasure of watching two such tiers display their talents. Nori Tashiro presented me with two of his books, alas, from my point of view, written in Japanese, containing excellent photographs. I have it on good authority that the titles are: *The Tashiro Nymphs and Naturals* and *The World of Tashiro Nymphs*. The other fly-tier was Masao Sakaguchi. Both live in Yokohama. Great emphasis is placed by them on the natural behaviour of the nymphs and the subsequent reaction of the trout to such behaviour. The swimming actions of various nymphs, both ephemerid and stoneflies, have been studied and photographed in detail by these two intrepid Japanese, and the style and type of artificial fly has been adopted to match as nearly as possible the appearance and action of the real thing. Most of the mayflies found in Japan, although similar to European and American ephemerids, are of different species.

### Ephemera Swimming Nymph
**(Ephemera japonica)** · Tashiro · Japan

| | |
|---|---|
| *Hook* | Tiemco 400T, bent shank, sizes 8–14 |
| *Thread* | Tan |
| *Tail* | Three strands of fine, natural ostrich herl tips |

Ephemera Swimming Nymph

| | |
|---|---|
| *Body* | Dirty yellow synthetic fur |
| *Rib* | Fine round gold tinsel |
| *Thorax* | As body |
| *Breathing appendages* | Natural fine ostrich herl |
| *Wing case* | Dark brown goose or turkey quill |
| *Legs* | Yellow partridge |

### Siphlonurus Swimming Nymph
**(Siphlonurus binotatus)** · Tashiro · Japan

| | |
|---|---|
| *Hook* | Tiemco 400T, bent shank, sizes 8–14 |
| *Thread* | Olive |
| *Tail* | Amherst-pheasant tippet fibres |
| *Body* | Pale green synthetic dubbing |
| *Back* | Barred wood-duck flank feather |
| *Rib* | Fine round gold tinsel |
| *Thorax* | As body |
| *Wing case* | Olive goose quill (crow quill during emerging period) |
| *Legs* | Grey-partridge hackle |

Both these pattens are tied with the dressing in the conventional hook-down position and also in the reverse with the hook up, both weighted in the thorax area. This is to simulate the action of the natural nymphs as they swim with their abdomen first up and then down. The flies can also be tied on conventional hooks. Nori Tashiro recommends that two such nymphs (one hook up and one hook down) be fished on a cast and that they be fished upstream and allowed to come back naturally in a dead drift.

### FISHING THE MAYFLY NYMPHS

There are many ways of fishing mayfly nymphs, depending on the type of nymph and the nature of the water to be fished. We have already learned that the nymphs themselves behave in different ways: some are crawlers, others swim, and some do not move very far from the bottom. The swimming nymphs travel through the water by means of a distinctive undulation of their abdomens; this up-and-down motion causes them to rise up in the water.

Trout will feed on nymphs in all depths of water: they will actively seek them close to the bottom or near weed-beds; they will take them in the main body of the water; and they will certainly feed upon them at the surface prior to hatching.

On fast-flowing rivers, nymphs are swept along in the main flow of the water for a considerable distance before they are able to reach the surface. Because of this, you will notice that hatches of fly usually occur in the slacker reaches after a stretch of fast water. Nymphs that have lived in the faster stretches among the rocks and pebbles cannot hatch out easily in such water. Trout know this and will lie in wait in the quieter water. It is their feeding zone or, if you like, their aquatic killing field. Lying just out of the main current, they will move to intercept and investigate any likely food item that enters their particular preserve.

Such holding areas are usually the haunts of bigger fish, the bullies that hold the best station, with lesser fish lined up behind. Take a good fish from such a spot and it will not be long before another takes its place. Where large boulders break up the current is another good place to find trout. They may be in front of, or even behind, such rocks and some will hold station to one side or the other, depending on the comfort of the lie and the break-up of the current created by the boulder.

A bend in the river can be a place where fish find both safety and a regular supply of food brought by the conflicting current that eddies and whirls in such places. On some rivers, fish will be found very close to the banks in riffle water about 3ft (90cm) deep and with a bottom made up of variously sized stones. On other rivers, trout may be found in similar water but away from the banks, perhaps even in the middle of the river. On the Madison River in Montana, USA, I found that all the good-sized fish were tucked well into the bank. The following year I fished the Hawea River in South Island, New Zealand, and here the fish were in the faster, deeper water in the middle of the river. So no hard and fast rule can apply. Each river is different and this is part of attraction of fly-fishing.

Fallen trees and other obstructions are places to find trout. Fish feel safe amid the tangle of roots and drowned branches; it is their safety zone, a place from which they can dart out and seize their food, before retreating to their bolt-hole. On weedy chalkstreams or spring creeks, where the

Swimming movement of mayflies

flow is even and the currents more benign, trout can be found anywhere in the river. Usually they retreat beneath the tresses of flowing weed; again this is their safety area from which they can move out into the channels to ambush nymphs and other prey.

Trout always prefer to have food brought to them and are extremely wary of expending their precious energy. Only small fish dart hither and thither, chasing nymphal shadows; big fish move from side to side to intercept their prey, sometimes dropping back or moving upstream a yard or two but always with deliberation and seldom at speed unless spooked. Watch such a fish discouraging another trout that moves into its domain. Such interlopers are given short shrift and are chased away without much ceremony, unless they are bigger; then, inevitably, the larger fish, will take over the station. If you happen to witness such a situation and see the intruder taking up its new position, get a nymph to it quickly; it will usually be so pleased to have found a good lie and so fired-up by the aggression used to seize the lie, that it will often take the first nymph that arrives.

On freestone or rain-fed rivers one of the most effective methods of fishing the nymph is in the dead drift. The nymph is cast up and across and, by mending the line, is drifted down to the anticipated positions of the lies at the same speed as the current. Takes can come at any time during the drift. The more weighted the nymph the closer to the bottom it will drift. You may need to add extra shot if you want to drift close to the bottom. Obviously, in deeper water, it is better to use sink-tip or, in some instances, full-sinking lines rather than floating ones.

A slight variation of the dead drift makes use of a take indictor – a little bead of coloured polystyrene slipped onto the leader – which enables you to see each take. If the water is about 3ft (90cm) deep, set the indicator 6ft (1.8m) from the fly. Pinch one lead shot, more if necessary, onto the leader about 6in (15cm) from the nymph. Cast upstream with this rig and watch the bead carefully. When the bead is above you and it hesitates or moves away from the normal line, strike. It could be the bottom but the chance of it being a fish is about 40 per cent. When the bead is directly in front of you and you get this divergence or hesitation in float direction, strike again; you have a 50 per cent chance of it being a trout. Finally, as the line flows downstream and you get a movement from the bead, strike once more; you have at least a 70 per cent chance of a fish because, this time, the fly has come off the bottom and has started to rise in the water, very much like a real insect.

Fishing across and down with weighted nymphs sometimes brings success. The takes often come as the nymph swings around in the current, just before the drag occurs. If there is no take, pull in the line in sharp jerks; this will often bring results. Feeding more line through the guides when fishing downstream extends the natural drift-time of the nymph.

On chalkstreams, you can, more often than not, see the fish feeding, so the use of aids, e.g. take indicators, is not necessary. (There are some who would say they are not necessary on freestone waters either, but that is another argument.) On such clear, even-flowing streams, the upstream drift with the induced-take is usually the most successful method. The fly is cast well ahead of the feeding fish and, when the nymph approaches the vicinity of the fish, the rod is lifted. This causes the nymph to rise within sight of the trout in a most natural manner, thus inducing the take. Rules on many of the English chalkstreams dictate that you can only fish upstream to the fish, so any method involving downstream techniques cannot apply. This upstream-only rule is often waived once the trout season has finished and grayling become the quarry; you may cast in any direction for these fish.

On smaller, clear stillwaters, where trout can be seen and targeted, weighted nymphs are the order of the day. Such fish, usually rainbows, patrol the water. Unlike brown trout on rivers, they do not hold station but actively swim around to seek their food. The weighted nymph is used to ambush such fish. By keeping a low profile and casting well ahead of the fish, you can drop the heavy nymph swiftly through the water to the bottom. At the fish's approach the fly is activated by raising the rod; this causes the nymph to rise in front of the marauding trout. One of the secrets of fishing such stillwaters for fish you can see is getting the depth right. This is not always as easy as it sounds. Retrieve nymphs in a figure-of-8 fashion, watching carefully the reaction of the fish to your fly; the take is quite often deceptive. A flash of white as the trout opens its mouth may be the only signal that the fish has taken; tighten immediately if you see this. A trout that is about to take a nymph seems to become excited: a shiver seems to run down the fish, the fins seems to extend, and there is an involuntary quiver of the tail.

# CHAPTER SIX

# STONEFLIES

## NATURALS

The Plecoptera (stoneflies) date back to the Carboniferous period and are perhaps not quite as primitive as the mayflies. The nymphs are easily distinguished from the mayfly nymphs because they possess only two tails (cerci) whereas most mayflies have three. They also have two claws at the end of their legs (the mayflies have only one) and three tarsal joints (mayflies have three, four or five, according to genus). Stoneflies generally prefer clean, highly oxygenated water and have a very low tolerance of pollution, so most species are found in fast-running water. Unlike the mayflies, they have no intermediate, sub-imago, winged stage; the nymphs hatch out directly into the mature, winged-insect form. Small species take a year to develop from egg to adult, medium-sized species take from 1 to 1½ years and the larger, impressive species can take up to 3 years. The smaller species in general are algae-feeders, while the larger species are highly carnivorous, feeding on a wide variety of aquatic larvae, etc.

The nymphs are bottom-crawlers, hiding beneath stones, hence their alternative name, 'creeper'. They rarely swim but, when they do, they propel themselves along by contortions of the body, with their legs acting as oars. This is why a number of artificials are tied on bent or curved hooks. Most species crawl out of the water to hatch, although some species will rise and hatch directly onto the surface, where they rest for a short while before flight. In the old days, larvae were collected and used as livebait for a wide variety of fish and were stored in special containers, often made from cow-horn. The larva in its final stages resembles, in many respects, the adult insect.

The distribution of the Plecoptera in the British Isles makes them a fly of the northern counties and of the Celtic fringes because it is in these areas that suitable habitat rivers are to be found. There are just one or two species found on the slower moving chalkstreams of the south. This distribution is reflected in the angling and fly-dressing literature of the UK. The angling writers of the south concentrated their efforts on the more glamorous mayfly, while the writings and patterns of the northern writers afforded an important niche for the more prosaic stonefly. Some of the earliest hatches to occur on British rivers are of various species of stonefly. Their very names indicate this: the February Red and Early Brown are two such examples.

In the USA, especially on the large freestone rivers in the Pacific West, the true importance of the various stoneflies is recognized and more than appreciated, with a plethora of patterns to imitate both the adult and nymphal forms. It is probably true to say that the hatches of stoneflies on such rivers mark them as being the prime insects as far as fishing is concerned. Many American anglers follow the large stonefly hatches from river to river.

In New Zealand the importance of the stonefly is now recognized by the number of imitations of some of the 20 or 30 native species. It is interesting to note that in Australia there is a species that is almost a direct link with the fossil stoneflies of the Carboniferous period. The stonefly has also achieved fishing status in Japan.

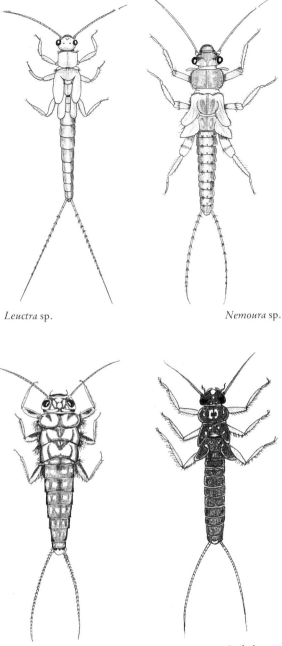

*Leuctra* sp.

*Nemoura* sp.

*Perla* sp.

*Perlodes* spp.

### Stoneflies of Angling Significance in the UK and Europe

| Scientific Name | Common Name | Length in mm |
|---|---|---|
| Chloroperla torrentium | Small Yellow Sally | 7–9 |
| Dinocras cephalotes | Large Stonefly | 16–33 |
| Diura bicaudata | Medium Stonefly | 9–17 |
| Isoperla grammatica | Yellow Sally | 11–16 |
| I. obscura* | Yellow Sally | 11–16 |
| Leuctra fusca | Needle Fly | 6–9 |
| L. geniculata | Willow Fly | 8–11 |
| L. hippopus | Needle Fly | 8–11 |
| Nemoura cinerea | Small Brown | 8–10 |
| N. picteti | Small Brown | 5–9 |
| N. sulcicollis* | Small Brown | 5–9 |
| Perla bipunctata | Large Stonefly | 16–33 |
| P. marginata*/** | Large Stonefly | 35–38 |
| Perlodes microcephala | Large Stonefly | 21–28 |
| Protonemura meyeri | Early Brown | 8–10 |
| Taeniopteryx nebulosa | February Red | 8–12 |

*Europe only

**This species was known until recently as *Perla maxima* and has been identified in Slovenia, France, Switzerland and possibly Spain.

Fly-tiers and fishermen all over Europe appreciate the various species of stonefly that hatch in fast-flowing rivers, from the Pyrenees to the Julian Alps, and have created a number of patterns to imitate them. Most species which have received the attention of fishermen in the British Isles are basically the same as those on the Continent, although because they have been isolated by the surrounding sea, a number have developed subtle changes, e.g. the underdeveloped, short wing on some males. This diminutive wing seems to occur more at high altitudes. There is also one species found only in the British Isles, *Brachyptera putata*, but this is not of fishing significance.

The number of stonefly species in the USA is far greater than in the UK, and they vary in size from the tiny black winter species to the huge salmon flies of the western waters that hatch out during June. I shall deal with only some of those patterns that our American fly-tiers and fisherman have deemed important from a nymph-fishing point of view. Had this book been devoted solely to stoneflies, both nymph and adult, I would have listed a greater number of smaller species because many are fished as dry flies and not just as nymphs. It also goes without saying that to list the many hundreds of different American species is beyond the scope of this book. Also listed are a few Japanese and New Zealand stonefly species that have received the attention of the fly dressers of those countries.

As far as the UK is concerned there are very few patterns tied to imitate specific stonefly nymphs.

There are some known simply as 'Stonefly Creepers' and that is about it. I have therefore created the patterns given in this chapter specifically for this book. There are a number of patterns now to be found on the Continent, many of which have been heavily influenced by some of the flies used in the USA. My earlier comments on spider-dressed flies also apply to the insects in this chapter, but, to my mind, with more effect. The larva of the stonefly resembles the adult in so many ways that flies tied as wet patterns by the early fly-dressers will still, I am sure, be of great value to the fishermen of the troubled streams. Those slim flies, such as the Dark Spanish Needle and the warm Partridge & Orange, will be taken by the fish as the larva of a stonefly; I, for one, continue to fish with such patterns in all corners of the world, wherever the water tumbles and riffles and the stonefly flutters above the troubled stream.

Today in the USA these soft-hackled flies have received fresh attention mainly because of the work of Sylvester Nemes and his books on the subject. There are few fly-shops in western America that do not have a selection of his patterns among the many hundreds of flies usually displayed.

### Non-European Stoneflies of Angling Significance

| Scientific Name | Common Name | Length in mm | Distribution |
| --- | --- | --- | --- |
| Acroneuria carolinensis | Great Brown Stone | 25–38 | USA |
| A. pacifica | Brown Willow Fly | 25–38 | USA |
| Allocapnia rickeri | Tiny Winter Black | 4–10 | USA |
| Auklandobius sp. | Blackstone Nymph | 20–25 | NZ |
| Austroperla cyrene | Brownstone Nymph | 11–15 | NZ |
| Calineuria californica | Golden Stone | 25–38 | USA |
| Desmonemoura pulchellum | Porcupine Quill | 7–13 | S. Africa |
| Isogenus mitsukonis | Yellow & Black | 12–15 | Japan |
| Isoperla & Isogenus spp. | Little Yellow Stone | 13–22 | USA |
| Isoperla mormona | Western Yellow Sally | 11–13 | USA |
| Moselia infuscata | Tiny Black Willow | 6–8 | USA |
| Nemoura banksi | Little Brown | 7–13 | USA |
| N. nigrita | Little Brown Stone | 7–13 | USA |
| Oyamia gibba | Yellow Stonefly | 20 | Japan |
| Phasganophora capitata | Eastern Golden Stone | 25–38 | USA |
| Pteronarcys badia | Dark Stone | 25–50 | USA |
| P. californica | Giant Salmon Fly | 25–50 | USA |
| P. dorsata | Giant Black Stonefly | 20–25 | USA |
| Stenoperla prasina | Green Stonefly | 20–25 | NZ |
| Taeniopteryx nivalis | Early Black | 12–24 | USA |
| Zelandoperla maculata | Perla Nymph | 20–25 | NZ |

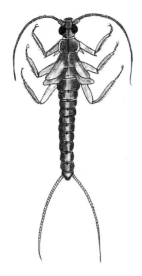

*Taeniopteryx* sp.

## ARTIFICIALS

### BRITISH AND EUROPEAN PATTERNS

Wherever you looked snow-capped peaks stabbed at the sky and the vista folded around you like a giant cloak. My eyes could hardly absorb it all; yet its magnificence was not too overpowering and you felt that you could get to the top of at least some of the mountains. The lower slopes were forested and green, sloping down to alpine meadows richly carpeted with wild flowers. We were in the midst of the Julian Alps in Slovenia, not far from the borders of Italy and Austria, in the valley of the beautiful Soča River. We were in a side-valley where a small river, the Lepena, gushed betwixt white limestone boulders and sang over shifting gravel; and a million caddis, dressed in the same gravel, crawled over the stones.

It was late May and myriad insects buzzed and hummed in the grass bordering the stream. The crystal water was cold but unaffected by snow-melt. The Soča, into which this small stream flows, is always affected by melting snow at this time of the year and changes from a clear cerulean to a pale, milky blue. I had been fishing upstream with a small, size 16 dry Adams and had taken one or two small brown trout in the fast riffling runs. I approached a place where a rickety footbridge crossed the river and here the water gushed between two large limestone rocks and into a deep pool. It was then that I noticed several large flies fluttering above the river; one landed on the water and was immediately engulfed by a trout, much larger than any of the fish I had so far been catching. I crept upstream and looked into the deep pool. It must have been 10ft (3m) deep, scoured from the soft limestone. In its clear depths several quite large trout finned in the churning, conflicting currents stirred up by the gushing stream.

I sat and watched yet another trout rise and take a large brown insect from the side of the pool; a hatch of large stoneflies had started. I caught one of these large insects and immediately recognized it as *Perla bipunctata* a species that was familiar to me from days spent on the River Exe in Devon. I looked down at my feet and there, crawling up my waders, was just such a nymph; it paused and, before my eyes, the nymphal skin split asunder and the dark adult emerged. Its yellow body flicked from side to side and the two spots showed clearly on its thoracic plate before it scurried off my foot to find sanctuary beneath the clutter of small stones.

## Large Perla Nymph
### (Perla bipunctata, P. microcephala, Dinocras cephalotes) · Price · UK & Europe

| | |
|---|---|
| *Hook* | Partridge K4 Piggy Back Hook, sizes 8–10, or Mustad 79580 longshank, sizes 6–10 (pre-weight with lead wire if desired) |
| *Thread* | Brown or black |
| *Tail* | Two brown goose biots |
| *Body* | Brown and orange fur dubbing, mixed |
| *Rib* | Transparent brown Swannundaze or similar |
| *Thorax* | As body |
| *Wing pads* | Brown goose treated with pliable varnish |
| *Legs* | Brown partridge wound as hackle over thorax |
| *Head* | As wing pads |
| *Antennae* | Two shorter brown goose biots |

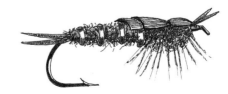

Large Perla Nymph

This fly is tied like any normal nymph, the only difference being the double wing case; this wing-case formation and an alternative method is depicted later (see p. 64). One of the largest European species, *Perla marginata*, can also be imitated by the above pattern. I have witnessed hatches of this large stonefly on the Lepena and, in early June, on the River Uneč in Yugoslavia; it is a magnificent creature relished by the trout and grayling of the fabled Uneč. It is also to be found on some Croatian streams.

The next pattern I devised using the convenient dubbing wicks.

### Large Stonefly Nymph
**(*Perla marginata*)** · Price · UK & Europe

| | |
|---|---|
| *Hook* | Mustad 79580, sizes 8–10 |
| *Thread* | Black |
| *Tail* | Two dark goose biots |
| *Body* | Orange dubbing wick |
| *Back* | Black dubbing wick |
| *Rib* | Gold wire |
| *Thorax* | As body |
| *Wing case* | As back |
| *Legs* | Brown partridge |
| *Eyes* | Burnt monofilament |
| *Antennae* | Hackle quills |

### Medium Stonefly Nymph
**(*Diura bicaudata*)** · Price · UK & Europe

| | |
|---|---|
| *Hook* | Mustad 9672, sizes 10–14 |
| *Thread* | Yellow or brown |
| *Tail* | Brown partridge hackle fibres |
| *Body* | Brown and orange hare fur, mixed |
| *Rib* | Gold wire |
| *Thorax* | As body |
| *Wing case* | Brown goose |
| *Legs* | Brown partridge |
| *Antennae* | Brown partridge hackle fibres (optional) |

Medium Stonefly Nymph

There are those who will tell you that trout do not take yellow flies. Do not believe them because trout most certainly do. I can recall one fine day in June, during a visit to the River Exe in Devon, when yellow flies were all that the trout were interested in. I had fished down a long riffle with the usual spider patterns to no avail and, where the river turned to meander through another meadow, I sat on the bank and watched the streams flow. Among my hobbies, if I had to list them, would be looking at water. I cannot resist looking over a bridge at the river below and imagining what fish are swimming in the dark currents beneath the stone arches. I have been known to stop the car after going over such a bridge, get out and walk back to look over the stone parapet, only to be confronted by railway lines! It is the risk you run when you indulge in such idiosyncratic behaviour. On this day, however, I was fishing and looking at the river from the waterside.

Where the stream turned to the right, it flowed beneath a tangle of willows, whose tresses kissed the water and played hither and thither in the conflicting current. A fence post stuck out of the water like a silent sentinel and fragments of a long-gone, barbed-wire fence dangled in the flow, catching weed and flotsam. Beneath this tangle of weed and willow, a good trout rose. It was not going to be an easy fish to take in such a difficult place but any angler worth his salt would at least make an attempt – and this angler was no exception.

It was then that I saw the small flies fluttering around the willow in a flicker of butter yellow. Could these bright yellow stoneflies be what the trout was taking? I could not see any reaction from the trout to the yellow sallies but, as far as I could see, there was nothing else on the water surface. I looked into my fly-box for something yellow, a colour which, generally speaking, I am not over-burdened with. The only flies I could find were some weighted Conrad Voss-Bark palmered nymphs (see p. 188), which should have been a golden olive but were a bit more yellow than they should have been. I tied one of these hairy nymphs onto my leader and cast in the direction of the grey fence post. Nine times out of ten I would have caught the post or one of the trailing branches of guardian willow but this time I dropped my fly between the two and it sank beneath the surface. I watched my leader uncurl and then stop; I tightened and was into the fish, a fine brown of about 1½lb (0.7kg), which, after a while, came to the net. Subsequent investigation of its stomach contents revealed a mass of yellow sallies.

Happiness is watching rivers.

### Yellow Sally Nymph
### (Isoperla grammatica) · Price · UK & Europe

| | |
|---|---|
| *Hook* | Mustad 9672, sizes 12–14 |
| *Thread* | Yellow |
| *Tail* | Brown partridge hackle (or yellow dyed grey partridge) |
| *Body* | Yellow hare fur and golden-stone Haretron |
| *Rib* | Gold wire |
| *Thorax* | Light brown hare fur and golden-brown Haretron |
| *Wing case* | Yellow goose |
| *Legs* | As tail |
| *Antennae* | Yellow goose fibres (optional) |

Yellow Sally Nymph

I could see from the surface of the water that the fish in the river were more than busy. Rise after rise appeared on the surface of the water; the splashy rise of small fish excited in their feeding and the more deliberate, less showy rises of what were better sized fish, worthy of the angler's attention. The river was the famed Uneč in Slovenia, a magical karst stream that gushed out of a giant cave near the village of Plannina southwest of Ljubljana. That morning we had elected to fish the upper part of this river, where it flows through the woods and has the definite feel of a rough stream. Further on, it glides between water meadows of wild flowers and is more reminiscent of a Hampshire chalkstream as it gracefully flows over fine gravel.

My companion had gone to the river sometime before me and I watched him wade carefully down the centre of the stream. 'What are they taking?' I enquired as I sat on a stump of a tree. 'Emergers,' Bozo Voljč replied. Dr Bozidar Voljč is possibly one of the best fishermen and fly-dressers in Slovenia and his articles are published in a number of European countries. He is perhaps best known for his series of Sedge and Stonefly patterns. 'Emerging what?' I asked. '*Chloroperla*, I think,' replied Bozo as he waded towards me. 'Look', he continued, as he showed me the nymphal skin of the small yellow sally he had taken from the water

surface. This is another example of another time and another place when trout and grayling were preoccupied with feeding on yellow flies, albeit of different species.

### Small Yellow Sally
### (Chloroperla torrentium) · Price · UK & Europe

| | |
|---|---|
| *Hook* | Mustad 80000BR, sizes 14–16 (may be weighted with copper wire) |
| *Thread* | Yellow |
| *Tail* | Brown partridge hackle fibre |
| *Body* | Dull yellow transparent PVC strip |
| *Thorax* | Yellow fur dubbing |
| *Wing case* | Dull yellow PVC |
| *Legs* | Brown partridge |

The nymphs of these bright stoneflies are a little more subdued in colour than the butter-yellow adults; this is why I favour using brown partridge for the legs and tail because it gives a more toned-down, realistic coloration.

The remaining species are all generally varying shades of brown and all are small and quite slim. I think no great purpose can be served in having an imitation for each species; the following pattern will serve to imitate all of them. If you wish, the colour of the dubbing may be varied from orange-brown to dark brown. The following nymph will serve to imitate the needle fly (*Leuctra fusca*), February Red (*Taeniopteryx nebulosa*), Early Brown (*Protonemura meyeri*), and any other similar-sized species.

### Small Stonefly Nymph · Price · UK & Europe

| | |
|---|---|
| *Hook* | Mustad 80000, sizes 12–16 |
| *Thread* | Black or brown |
| *Tail* | Two strands of cock-pheasant tail fibres |
| *Body* | Brown speckle flake (or fine Swan-nundaze, Body Glass or brown latex) |
| *Thorax* | Brown dubbing |
| *Wing case* | Two goose biots pointing over the body, with one tied over the thorax |
| *Legs* | Brown partridge |

Small Stonefly Nymph

Like the other nymphs this one also can be weighted with copper wire.

Marjan Fratnik of Milan, formerly from the village of Most na Soči in Slovenia, first introduced me to the joys and many delights of his beautiful native country. He showed me rivers and fish that, in the past, I could only dream of. Each year I make an annual pilgrimage to Slovenia, to fish its crystal waters. The following fly is one of his patterns. Like most of the flies in this book it can be pre-weighted e.g. with lead wire.

**Fratnik Stonefly Nymph** · Fratnik · Slovenia

| | |
|---|---|
| *Hook* | Mustad 79706, sizes 8–12 |
| *Thread* | Black or brown |
| *Tail* | Two olive goose biots |
| *Body* | Dark to medium olive natural fur (dyed dormouse is ideal) |
| *Rib* | Yellow thread |
| *Thorax* | As body |
| *Wing case* | Black Raffene varnished at least three times |
| *Legs* | Red squirrel hair |

The next two patterns were given to me by Juha Vainio of Konnevesi in Finland. The flies were actually tied by his friend, Veli Autti, a highly skilled fly-tier.

**Dark Stonefly Nymph** · Autti · Finland

| | |
|---|---|
| *Hook* | Mustad 79706, sizes 10–12 |
| *Thread* | Black or brown |
| *Tail* | Feather fibres |
| *Body* | Yellow-olive dubbing |
| *Back* | Dark brown feather fibre |
| *Rib* | Fine gold wire |
| *Wing case* | As back |
| *Legs* | As back |
| *Antennae* | Ptarmigan fibres |

**Light Stonefly Nymph** · Autti · Finland

| | |
|---|---|
| *Hook* | Mustad 79706, sizes 12–14 |
| *Thread* | Yellow or brown |
| *Tail* | Dirty yellow goose biots |
| *Body* | Olive-yellow dubbing |
| *Back* | Dirty yellow feather fibre |
| *Rib* | Fine lead wire |
| *Thorax* | As body |
| *Wing case* | As back |
| *Legs* | Yellow feather fibres |
| *Antennae* | Ptarmigan fibres |

Since the disintegration of the Iron Curtain, greater discourse has occurred between fly-dressers in the West and their brothers of the hackle in what was the Eastern Bloc. The following two stonefly nymphs come from the Czech Republic and were tied by Milos Zeman.

**Dark Stonefly Nymph** · Zeman · Czech Republic

| | |
|---|---|
| *Hook* | Mustad 7906, sizes 8–12 |
| *Thread* | Black |
| *Tail* | Two dark olive goose biots |
| *Body* | Black fur dubbing |
| *Rib* | Grey Swannundaze (or similar) |
| *Back* | Dark turkey, folded and layered in three folds |
| *Thorax* | Medium grey dubbing |
| *Wing case* | Light mottled turkey |
| *Legs* | Black hen hackle |

**Light Stonefly Nymph** · Zeman · Czech Republic

| | |
|---|---|
| *Hook* | Mustad 7906, sizes 8–12 |
| *Thread* | Black |
| *Tail* | Two light orange goose biots |
| *Body* | Light ginger dubbing |
| *Rib* | Light brown transparent Swannundaze |
| *Back* | Cinnamon turkey, folded and layered in three folds |
| *Thorax* | Orange Antron (or similar) |
| *Wing case* | Light mottled turkey |
| *Legs* | Two tufts of beige filoplume either side of thorax |

AMERICAN PATTERNS

Of all the aquatic creatures imitated by the fly-dressers in the USA, the stonefly nymph has received more than its fair share of attention, especially from those tiers who practise the art of ultra-realism in their craft. At a Federation of Fly Fishers Conclave I watched a number of these specialists apply their skills and was amazed at the resultant flies. Fly-tiers such as Bill Blackstone of Orange, California, produce flies of such ingenious detail that one would be hard put to differentiate between them and the natural creatures. Some tiers, such as Kent Bullfinch of Yreka, California, specialize in the nymphs of the indigenous stoneflies of the American west. These gentlemen are just two of many excellent American tiers who create stonefly patterns.

This preoccupation with the stonefly stems from the fact that, on the large freestone rivers of the west, the stonefly is the major aquatic insect, the equivalent of the mayfly on the Hampshire chalk-streams of the UK. Everyone looks forward to the annual appearance in June of these large, fluttering stoneflies, often following the hatch from river to river. Given the space, time and inclination, I could fill a book with all the available imitations found in the USA but, as with the list of naturals given earlier, I will confine myself to just a few.

Because of its very impressive size we shall look first at the largest of the stoneflies, *Pteronarcys californica*, known by anglers as the giant salmon fly. This is a nymph up to 2in (50mm) long – and that is big! In Europe there is *Perla marginata*, which is slightly smaller, measuring about 1½in (38mm). The first pattern was devised by the well-known fishing writer and fly creator, Randall Kaufmann. A visit to one of his fly-shops is an eye-opener and I purchased a number of patterns the last time I was in Seattle. Among the flies purchased was the Kaufmann Stone. This pattern of his would be descibed as impressionistic rather than naturalistic. It comes in a number of colours, black and brown being the most popular; there is also a golden shade that can imitate the nymphs of other large species of American stonefly nymphs, e.g. the eastern golden stone (*Phasganophora capitata*), and a brown version that could possibly imitate the brown willow fly (*Acroneuria pacifica*).

### Kaufmann Stone
**(*Pteronarcys californica*)** · Kaufmann · USA

| | |
|---|---|
| *Hook* | Mustad 9575, sizes 2–10, heavily leaded with up to 20 turns of flattened lead |
| *Thread* | Black, brown or yellow (depending on the species being imitated) |
| *Tail* | Two goose biots of appropriate colour |
| *Body* | Rabbit fur or angora goat (one part) and Haretron of matching colour (one part), mixed |
| *Rib* | Swannundaze of appropriate colour |
| *Thorax* | As body |
| *Wing case* | Three separate sections of turkey quill taking up half the hook length |
| *Antennae* | Goose biots |

Kaufmann Stone

As an alternative, the following pattern, created by Kent Bullfinch, is of a more realistic conception. It was given in *Patterns of the Masters*, which was produced by the Federation of Fly Fishers, and consists of a collection of the flies tied at the annual conclave.

### Salmon Fly Nymph
**(*Pteronarcys californica*)** · Bullfinch · USA

| | |
|---|---|
| *Hook* | Mustad 36890, sizes 8–4 |
| *Thread* | Pre-waxed orange |
| *Underbody* | Insulation wire |
| *Tail* | Black goose biots |
| *Body* | Size 32 latex rubber band marked with waterproof ink |
| *Thorax* | Orange furry foam marked with water-proof ink |
| *Wing cases* | Tyvac cut to shape |
| *Legs* | Black goose biots or micro-chenille |
| *Eyes* | Melted 80lb (36kg) BS nylon mono-filament |
| *Antennae* | Black boar bristle |

The fly is tied as follows:

*Step 1*  Cut two pieces of electric wire with the insulation still on.
*Step 2*  Strip both ends and tie either side of the hook shank (2a & b).
*Step 3*  Take a small piece of 80lb (36kg) BS monofilament and hold it in a pair of tweezers. Apply a flame to either side to form the eyes.
*Step 4*  Tie the eyes on top of the hook and take the thread down the shank. Then tie in a thin strip of orange furry foam and form a small butt of furry foam. Remove any surplus material.
*Step 5*  Tie a black goose biot either side of the butt of foam and then tie in the latex rubber band. Take the thread back up the shank.
*Step 6*  Form the abdomen by winding the rubber band up the shank to form a segmented body. Tie off and cut away any surplus.
*Step 7*  For the legs, tie in the six goose biots, or three lengths of micro-chenille, in the position indicated.
*Step 8*  Take the thread back to the legs nearest the abdomen and tie in a strip of orange furry foam. Wrap the foam up to the eye to form the thorax. Secure and remove any surplus.
*Step 9*  Prepare the wing cases, two of the first and one of the second. The originator uses a sheet of

Tyvac but any thin plastic strip, or even turkey quill feather fibre, will do.

*Step 10*   Tie in the wing cases.

*Step 11*   Complete the fly with a pair of antennae and finish with a whip finish and a dab of varnish. Kent also ties up this pattern as a wiggle nymph.

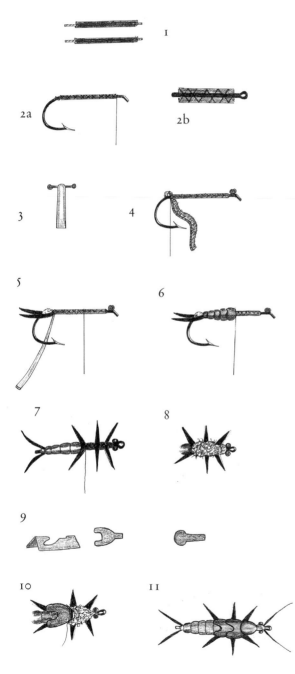

Salmon Fly Nymph

The next pattern is by Polly Rosborough and will suffice for both the golden stone (*Calineuria californica*) and the important large fly of the eastern seaboard, the eastern golden stone (*Phasganophora capitata*).

### Golden Stone Nymph
### (*Calineuria californica, Phasganophora capitata*) · Rosborough · USA

| | |
|---|---|
| *Hook* | Mustad 9672, sizes 6–4. |
| *Thread* | Tan |
| *Tail* | Teal flank fibres |
| *Back* | Rest of teal flank from tail |
| *Body* | Gold-coloured yarn |
| *Rib* | Tan and gold sewing thread |
| *Thorax* | As for body but tied fuller |
| *Wing pad* | Teal neck feather extending over the thorax |
| *Legs* | Fibres from teal neck feathers stroked either side and downwards |

Golden Stone Nymph

The American version of the European Yellow Sally, the Western Yellow Stonefly, is sometimes called the Mormon Girl. The species is *Isoperla mormona* and, in many respects, is very similar to our own young lady of a fly. I saw a number of these hatching one cool day on the South Fork of the Snake River in Idaho. Ernest Schwiebert gives a pattern for this nymph in his excellent book, *Nymphs*, which is now considered a classic.

### Western Yellow Stonefly
### (*Isoperla mormona*) · Schwiebert · USA

| | |
|---|---|
| *Hook* | Mustad 9671, sizes 10–12 |
| *Thread* | Yellow |
| *Tail* | Yellow hen hackle fibres |
| *Body* | Flat nylon monofilament over yellow thread body |

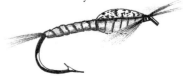

Western Yellow Stonefly

| | |
|---|---|
| *Thorax* | As body |
| *Wing case* | Pale yellow mottled feathers |
| *Legs* | Pale yellow hen hackle fibres |
| *Antennae* | As legs |

The Little Brown Stonefly Nymph and other similar species can be imitated by the next pattern, which I believe was devised by Eric Leiser, the author of *The Book of Fly Patterns*, in which it was called the Early Brown Stonefly Nymph. It is similar to the Early Brown sold by Orvis.

### Early Brown Stonefly Nymph
**(Nemoura sp.)** · Leiser · USA

| | |
|---|---|
| *Hook* | Mustad 9671, sizes 10–14 |
| *Thread* | Tan |
| *Tail* | Tan goose biots |
| *Body* | Medium brown fur dubbing |
| *Thorax* | As body |
| *Wing case* | Dark mottled turkey, folded and layered in three folds |
| *Legs* | Brown hen hackle fibres |

Early Brown Stonefly Nymph

The firm of Orvis sells a number of standard stonefly nymph patterns in their range of flies. The following are from their list.

### Early Black
**(Taeniopteryx nivalis)** · Orvis · USA

| | |
|---|---|
| *Hook* | Mustad 9671, sizes 10–14 |
| *Thread* | Black |
| *Tail* | Two Canada-goose fibres |
| *Body* | Dark almost black fur |
| *Thorax* | As body |
| *Wing case* | Black goose quill, folded |
| *Legs* | Dark blue dun |

### Little Yellow (Isoperla & Isogenus
**sp.)** · Orvis · USA

| | |
|---|---|
| *Hook* | Mustad 9671, sizes 12–16 |
| *Thread* | Yellow |
| *Tail* | Two amber goose biots |
| *Body* | Amber fur dubbing |

| | |
|---|---|
| *Thorax* | As body |
| *Wing case* | Cinnamon turkey quill, folded |
| *Legs* | Pale yellow hen |

I prefer to add a gold wire rib to the above three patterns.

Dave Whitlock's stonefly patterns have proved highly successful for many anglers. They are tied in both brown and black versions.

### Whitlock's Stonefly Nymph
**(Brown)** · Whitlock · USA

| | |
|---|---|
| *Hook* | Mustad 79580, sizes 4–8 |
| *Thread* | Brown |
| *Tail* | Brown goose biots or monofilament |
| *Body* | Reddish-brown synthetic dubbing |
| *Rib* | Gold wire |
| *Thorax* | Yellow Antron and fur, mixed |
| *Wing pads* | Folded Raffene |
| *Legs* | Grouse hackle |
| *Head* | As thorax |
| *Eyes* | Black bead eyes or burnt monofilament |
| *Antennae* | Boar's hair or monofilament |

The next two patterns use Swannundaze as the body material, which gives a very realistic, natural-insect look to the flies. The first pattern was sent to me over 12 years ago and was tied by the originator of Swannundaze, Frank Johnson of Lyndhurst, New Jersey.

### Swannundaze Stonefly Nymph · Johnson · USA

| | |
|---|---|
| *Hook* | Mustad 79580, sizes 2–8 (bent to shape) |
| *Thread* | Brown |
| *Tail* | Brown goose biots |
| *Body* | Brown transparent Swannundaze over dark yellow dubbing |
| *Thorax* | Dark yellow synthetic dubbing |
| *Wing pads* | Cock-pheasant 'church-window' feathers cut to shape |
| *Legs* | Brown goose biots, knotted for realism |
| *Head* | Built up with the tying thread and pheasant feather on the top |
| *Antennae* | Brown goose biots |

The Superior Fly Company of Edmonton, Alberta, sells a number of attractive and realistic fly patterns devised by Dan Cottrell, of which the following is one.

**Superfly Swannundaze Stonefly**
**Nymph** · Cottrell · USA

| | |
|---|---|
| *Hook* | Mustad 795580, sizes 2–10 |
| *Thread* | Brown |
| *Tail* | Brown goose biots |
| *Body* | Brown yarn over lead wire with transparent Swannundaze over yarn |
| *Thorax* | Brown rabbit fur |
| *Legs* | Tan cord, the thigh portion dubbed with brown rabbit |
| *Gills* | Tufts of orange yarn |
| *Wing case* | Brown yarn in three parts, varnished |
| *Antennae* | Tan cord |

NEW ZEALAND PATTERNS

I was viewing some slides taken by one of my South African fishing friends, Neil Hodges, who at the time was the editor of the South African Federation of Fly Fishers magazine. There were some excellent studies of damselfly and dragonfly nymphs when Neil said with great enthusiasm, 'Now have a look at this'. I picked up the viewer and there, staring back at me from the screen, was a nymph with two tails, a typical stonefly nymph with two distinct yellow spots on its pronotum (upper part of the front of the thorax). Neil's excitement stemmed from the fact that stoneflies are few and far between in South African rivers and imitations of the larval and adult forms do not, as a general rule, figure in the fly-wallets of South African anglers.

This cannot be said of New Zealand and, in recent years, New Zealand fly-fishers have been reproducing imitations of some of their native species. The rivers of both North and South Islands are perfect habitats for the stonefly; fast-flowing, crystal-clear and, in most cases pollution free. Their very appearance speaks to you of stoneflies. Some of the most important and prolific of these Antipodean stoneflies have been imitated by many of New Zealand's fly-tiers.

The first pattern comes from the Christchurch area and was an imitation of the long-tailed stonefly nymph, *Zelandoperla maculata*.

**Perla Nymph (*Zelandoperla maculata*)** · NZ

| | |
|---|---|
| *Hook* | Mustad 9671, sizes 10–12 |
| *Thread* | Black or brown |
| *Tail* | Two strands of cock-pheasant tail |
| *Body* | Stripped cock hackle quill overwound with a stripped peacock quill; body is flattened during the tying process |
| *Thorax* | Continuation of body but fatter |
| *Wing case* | Guinea-fowl feather |
| *Legs* | Guinea-fowl and cock-pheasant tail fibres |

Perla Nymph

There are a number of imitations of the next species, the green stonefly (*Stenoperla prasina*), a common fly on some rivers in South Island. The first pattern is one of Norman Marsh's creations; he describes the natural as having jade wing pads.

**Greenstone Nymph**
**(*Stenoperla prasina*)** · Marsh · NZ

| | |
|---|---|
| *Hook* | Mustad 9671, sizes 8–12 |
| *Thread* | Brown or green |
| *Tail* | Golden-pheasant flank fibres |
| *Body* | Olive seal fur and hare fur, mixed |
| *Rib* | Gold wire |
| *Thorax* | As body |
| *Wing case* | Green kea (or substitute dyed goose) |
| *Legs* | Ginger hen |

Tony Orman gives an alternative pattern, devised by his friend, Jim Ring, in *Trout with the Nymph*.

**Green Stonefly Nymph**
**(*Stenoperla prasina*)** · Ring · NZ

| | |
|---|---|
| *Hook* | Mustad 9671, sizes 8–12 |
| *Thread* | Green |
| *Tail* | Cock-pheasant breast-feather fibres |
| *Body* | Yellow mohair (12 parts), mid-olive silk (6 parts), hare's ear (1 part), yellow and green fluorescent silk (1 part); mixed |
| *Rib* | Gold wire |
| *Thorax* | Grey wool |
| *Wing case* | Grey-green feather from a mallard drake |
| *Legs* | Long-fibred Greenwell-cock hackle |

**Green Stonefly Nymph**
**(*Stenoperla prasina*)** · MacDonald · NZ

| | |
|---|---|
| *Hook* | Mustad 9671, sizes 8–12 |
| *Thread* | Olive |

| | |
|---|---|
| *Tail* | Olive-green goose biots |
| *Body* | Light green Swannundaze or Larva Lace, etc. |
| *Thorax* | Olive-green dubbing fur |
| *Wing case* | Brown-olive goose or similar feather fibre |
| *Legs* | None (fur of the thorax picked out) |

The black stonefly nymph (*Austroperla cyrene* ) is a smaller creature than the green stonefly nymph, but there are a number of patterns devised to imitate it. The first was depicted in the excellent New Zealand calendar for 1991, which was compiled by Nancy and Brian Tichborne, and is a pattern devised by Steven Willis of Christchurch.

### Gothic Stonefly Nymph
**(Austroperla cyrene)** · Willis · NZ

| | |
|---|---|
| *Hook* | Mustad 9671, sizes 10–12 |
| *Thread* | Black |
| *Tail* | Black goose biots |
| *Body* | Black seal fur (or substitute) |
| *Rib* | Copper or gold wire |
| *Back* | Peacock eye feather |
| *Thorax* | As body |
| *Wing case* | As back |
| *Legs* | Thorax fur picked out at the sides and divided into six legs |
| *Antennae* | Finer black goose biots |

Gothic Stonefly Nymph

The last of the New Zealand stonefly nymph patterns I am going to give is that tied to imitate the brown stonefly nymph (*Aucklandobius* sp.). Norman Marsh gives an effective pattern for this insect. The Blackstone Nymph depicted in the colour plate is tied in the same way as the Brownstone Nymph, but uses black Swannundaze.

### Brownstone Nymph
**(Aucklandobius sp.)** · Marsh · NZ

| | |
|---|---|
| *Hook* | Mustad 9671, sizes 10–14 |
| *Thread* | Brown |
| *Tail* | Brown goose biots |
| *Body* | Transparent brown Swannundaze or Larva Lace |

Brownstone Nymph

| | |
|---|---|
| *Thorax* | Brown mohair |
| *Wing case* | Brown feather fibre |
| *Legs* | Brown partridge |

These New Zealand patterns are worth trying on other waters. They can be just as effective in the UK and Europe as they are on the waters of their conception.

Japanese Patterns
These final patterns come from Japan where there are a number of native species of stonefly. The first, created by Masao Sakaguchi, is based on an earlier pattern by Nori Tashiro. It does not imitate a specific stonefly but can be used for a number of indigenous species, such as *Oyamia gibba*. Masao finds it a good pattern for the Japanese land-locked salmon, the yamame, and also for the iwana. Although by nature this fly is a broad-spectrum pattern, I include it because I am sure that it would work well in other waters far from Japan.

### Hare's Ear Stonefly Nymph
**(Oyamia gibba)** · Sakaguchi · Japan

| | |
|---|---|
| *Hook* | TMC 2302, curved shank, sizes 6–10 |
| *Thread* | Brown |
| *Tail* | Dark brown grouse hackle fibres |
| *Body* | Brown hare's ear |
| *Rib* | Fine round gold tinsel |
| *Thorax* | Yellow fur |
| *Wing case* | Striped brown partridge hackle |
| *Legs* | Brown partridge |

Hare's Ear Stonefly Nymph

The next pattern was devised by Nori Tashiro to imitate *Isogenus mitsukonis*, the Japanese version of the British yellow sally.

## Japanese Yellow Sally

**(Isogenus mitsukonis)** · Tashiro · Japan

| | |
|---|---|
| *Hook* | TMC 200R (3x), sizes 10–12 |
| *Thread* | Yellow |
| *Tail* | Yellow goose biots |
| *Body* | Yellow synthetic fur |
| *Rib* | Black silk |
| *Thorax* | As body |
| *Wing case* | Yellow feather fibre marked at the tips with black waterproof ink |
| *Legs* | Yellow grey-partridge |
| *Antennae* | Yellow goose fibres |

Japanese Yellow Sally

### FISHING THE STONEFLY NYMPH

Stonefly nymphs are not active swimmers but are found, as their name suggests, on the bottom amid the stones and gravel. Trout will seek them out down there but, more often than not, they will feed on nymphs that have been washed away by the current. The stonefly nymph swims in a laboured way by bending and unbending its body. This is why a number of artificials are tied on curved hooks, to simulate the action of the weakly swimming nymph. The artificial nymph is most successful when fished in the dead drift where it emulates the natural as it tumbles with the current. Trout will also take nymphs as they migrate to the shallows in order to hatch.

# CHAPTER SEVEN

# CADDIS NYMPHS

## NATURALS

Unlike the mayflies and the stoneflies, the caddis (or sedge) has an aquatic pupal stage as well as a larva. This means that the trout has two bites of the cherry, as it were, when it comes to feeding upon this creature beneath the surface of the water. The importance of the caddis has now become established in all parts of the fly-fishing world, although, for a long time, the mayflies received the most attention and the caddis was relegated to the second division of the list of angler's flies. The caddis belongs to the insect order Trichoptera (*trichos* meaning 'hairy' and *pteron* meaning 'wing'). This is self-descriptive; the wings of caddisflies are clothed in minute hairs, unlike those of the closely related moths and butterflies, which are covered in scales.

The caddis is to be found in a wide range of waters, from the minutest rill to the largest lake, from stagnant ditches to the purest of streams. Although many species hatch out during the hours of darkness, they are often seen on the wing throughout the day. Most species spend a year as a larva and pupation takes about 20 days. Some people believe that certain species may have more than one brood a year.

The adult caddisfly has been recognized as an angler's fly and worthy of imitation as far back as the 'Treatyse' in the *Boke of At Albans* and even Aelian's fly, in Macedonia, many centuries before, was probably a caddis. It is only comparatively recently, however, that the larva and pupa have been imitated, with the exception of the fly given by Robert Venables in the seventeenth-century. It was nevertheless appreciated that trout fed upon such creatures for here is what Walton had to say on the subject in his *Compleat Angler*:

I will tell you, scholar, several countries have several kinds of caddises, that differ as much as dogs do; that is to say, as much as a very cur and greyhound do. These be bred in very little rills, or ditches, that run into bigger rivers; and I think a more proper bait for those rivers than any other . . . I know not how, or of what, this caddis receives life, or what coloured fly it turns to; but doubtless they are the death of many trouts.

In this statement of Walton's we find a clue as to why imitations of the larva were so late in appearing in the lists of angler's flies: quite simply, early anglers used the live larvae as bait in the same way as they used the nymphs of stoneflies. It is likely that the old-time angler, as he turned over stones to collect stonefly creepers, took caddis larvae as well and impaled them on his hook. An imitation was not necessay because there were no restrictions placed upon fishermen in those days. Do not forget that, although many of the sporting gentlemen of old fished for sport, they also fished to eat. The practice of catch and release was certainly not in evidence. Apart from the name 'caddis' in its various old spellings, the larvae were also known as codbait, codworm and caddos worm, and there were probably other, local names.

Walton describes quite precisely at least three different species of caddis larvae, indicating at least some awareness of what was going on beneath the surface of the water. I feel, however, that he knew nothing about the true life-cycle of the caddis because, like many people who came after him, he believed that the caddis hatched out into the mayfly. He names one caddis 'The Piper' and describes it as being 1in (25mm) long with a case made from a reed stem. A second, which he calls 'The Cock-Spur', had a case of husks, small gravel and slime, and was sharp at one end. The third he describes as being not unlike a hedgehog.

Although it is not possible to identify positively a caddis by its case, those species that do make such portable shelters usually do so to a typical pattern. Some of the most important caddis species, important to the fisherman that is, do not make a larval case; some construct nets, webs or funnels and others are free-swimming, building a shelter for pupation only.

Worldwide there are a great number of caddis considered to be important from an angling point of view and I shall endeavour to give a fair representation of such species in the following lists. For simplicity I have grouped them into case-makers and non-case-makers, and I will indicate whenever possible the country where they are used as artificial flies. A more detailed account of the caddis can be found in the following: *Caddis and the Angler* (Solomon and Leiser, 1977), *Caddis Flies* (Gary LaFontaine, 1981) and my own book, *The Angler's Sedge*. The first two books deal with American species and their imitations, and the last mainly with British and European sedge.

| Scientific Name | Common Name | Length in mm |
|---|---|---|
| P. varia | Speckled Peter | 30+ |
| Potamophylax latipennis | Large Cinnamon Sedge | 23 |
| Sericostoma personatum | Welshman's Button | 15 |
| Silo nigricornis | Black Sedge | 8 |
| Trianodes bicolor | Bicolor Sedge | 35 |

*These species have no common name as such but, as they are closely allied to the cinnamon sedge (*Limnephilus lunatus*), I have given them the same name.

*Anabolia nervosa*

## Case-making Caddis (Eruciform Larvae)

### Case-making Caddis of the UK and Europe

| Scientific Name | Common Name | Length in mm |
|---|---|---|
| Anabolia nervosa | Brown Sedge | 26 |
| Athripsodes albifrons | Brown Silverhorn | 12 |
| At. aterrimus | Black Silverhorn | 18 |
| At. cinereus | Brown Silverhorn | 12 |
| At. nigronervosus | Black Sedge | 8 |
| Brachycentrus subnubilus | Grannom | 12 |
| Glyphotalius pellicidus | Mottled Sedge | 23 |
| Goera pilosa | Medium Sedge | 15 |
| Halesus digitatus | Caperer | 23–27 |
| H. radiatus | Caperer | 23–27 |
| Lepidostoma hirtum | Small Silver Sedge | 18 |
| Limnephilus flavicornis | Cinnamon Sedge* | 20–23 |
| Li. lunatus | Cinnamon Sedge | 20–23 |
| Li. marmoratus | Lane's Mottled Sedge | 20–23 |
| Li. politus | Cinnamon Sedge* | 20–23 |
| Li. rhombicus | Large Cinnamon Sedge | 20–23 |
| Mystacides azurea | Black Silverhorn | 15 |
| M. longicornis | Grouse-wing | 15 |
| M. nigra | Black Silverhorn | 15 |
| Odontocerum albicorne | Silver (or Grey) Sedge | 20 |
| Oecetis lacustris | Longhorn Sedge | 8 |
| Phryganea grandis | Great Red Sedge | 30–50 |
| P. obsoleta | Dark Peter | 30+ |
| P. striata | Great Red Sedge | 30–50 |

*Athripsodes atterimus*

*Anthripsodes cinereus*

*Brachycentrus subnubilus*

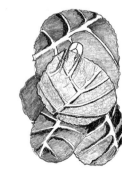

*Glyphotalius pellicidus*

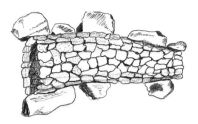

*Goera pilosa*

*Mystacides longicornis*

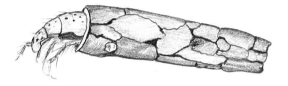

*Halesus digitatus*

*Mystacides nigra*

*Lepidostoma hirtum*

*Odontocerum albicorne*

*Limnephilus flavicornis*

*Phryganea grandis*

*Limnephilus lunatus*

*Phryganea striata*

*Mystacides azurea*

*Potamophylax latipennis*

*Sericostoma personatum*

*Trianodes bicolor*

There are other European species which are important to the fly-fisherman, especially in alpine and limestone areas, such as Switzerland, the Pyrenees and Slovenia; these karst limestone areas have an abundance of sedge species. In the northern hemisphere, the limnephilids are probably the most important of angling sedges because of the large number of species. There are very few limnephilids in the southern hemisphere although two or three species are recorded from Chile.

The list below is but a sample of the case-making species found in the fly-fishing countries listed. In the USA the number of caddis species, both case-makers and non-case-makers, runs into thousands. Those who wish to explore the American species further should refer to *Caddis Flies*, by Gary LaFontaine, or *Nymphs*, by Ernest Schwiebert.

### Non-European Case-making Caddis

| Scientific Name | Common Name | Length in mm | Distribution |
|---|---|---|---|
| Brachycentrus americanus | Grannom | 10–13 | USA & Japan |
| B. fuliginosus | American Grannom | 10–13 | USA |
| Dinarthodes japonica | Hairy-nosed Caddis* | 10–13 | Japan |
| Dicosmoecus sp. | Giant Orange Sedge | 35+ | USA |
| Helicopsyche albescens | Brown-horn Sedge | 10 | NZ |
| Hesperophylax designatus | Silver-striped Sedge | 25+ | USA |
| Heteroplectron americanum | Medium Brown | 15–20 | USA |
| Hydrosalpinx sericea | Elephant-tusk Caddis | 8–15 | S. Africa |
| Leptocerus schoenobates | — | 25 | S. Africa |
| Limnephilus coloradensis | Medium Cinnamon | 10+ | USA |
| Mystacides alafimbriata | Black Dancer | 15 | USA |
| Nectopsyche albida | White Miller | 12–16 | USA |
| Olinga feredayi | Horny-case Caddis | 10–15 | NZ |
| Petrothrincus circularis | Tortoise-case Caddis | 10–13 | S. Africa |
| Phryganea sayi | Rush Sedge | 30+ | USA |
| Platycentropus radiatus | Chocolate & Cream Sedge | 30+ | USA |
| Psiloptetra frontalis | Dark Blue Sedge | 11–12 | USA |
| Pycnocentrodes aurelea | Grey-horn Nymph | 8–15 | NZ |
| Py. aureola | Stone-case Caddis | 20+ | NZ |
| Pycnopsyche scabripennis | Large Red Sedge | 30+ | USA |
| Triplectides cephalotes | Stick Caddis | 20+ | NZ |
| T. obsoleta | Stick Caddis | 20+ | NZ |

*I do not whether this species has a common name in Japan but I have called it this because the adult has a long, hairy projection extending from the head.

## Non-case making Caddis
## (Campodeiform Larvae)

### British and European Non-case-making Caddis

| Scientific Name | Common Name | Length in mm |
|---|---|---|
| Diplonectrona felix | Yellow-spotted sedge | 17 |
| Hydropsyche augustipennis | Grey Flag | 17 |
| H. contubernalis | Marble Sedge | 17 |
| H. instabilis | Grey Flag | 17 |
| H. pellucidula | Grey Flag | 17 |
| Philopotamus montanus | Dark-spotted Sedge | 22 |
| Polycentropus flavomaculatus | Dark Sedge | 12–14 |
| Psychomyia pusilla | Small Yellow | 8 |
| Rhyacophila dorsalis | Sand Fly | 22–25 |
| Tinodes waeneri | Small Red Sedge | 15 |

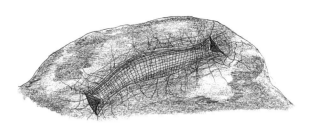

*Tinodes waeneri*

There are many other species of non-case-making caddis found in Europe which may be of importance on some rivers. There are, for example, over 20 species of *Rhyacophila* listed in the alpine and karst rivers of Slovenia and species such as *Hydropsyche saxonica* and *H. guttata* are abundant on many rivers in northern Spain. If it is difficult to list all the species that may be of importance to the European angler within the confines of a general book devoted to nymphs, then it is nigh on impossible to list all the American species. In North America the genus *Rhyacophila* has 100 known species and Gary LaFontaine gives over 20 as being of angling significance. The genus *Hydropsyche* has in excess of 70 species, with at least 15 mentioned by LaFontaine as being of angling importance. The same applies to the species from New Zealand and Japan. There are many more species other than those listed below.

There are, of course, caddis from other fly-fishing countries, such as Argentina, Chile and Australia, but to my knowledge no list of their native caddis equated with artificial flies has been compiled.

*Hydropsyche* sp.

*Rhyacophila* sp.

### Non-European Non-case-making Caddis

| Scientific Name | Common Name | Length in mm | Distribution |
|---|---|---|---|
| Aoteapsyche colonica | Grey Caddis | 10–15 | NZ |
| Chimarrha ambulans | — | 7–10 | S. Africa |
| C. atterrima | Little Black Sedge | 7–10 | USA |
| Hydrobiosis umbripennis | Green Caddis | 10–14 | NZ |
| Hydropsyche spp.* | Spotted Sedge | 8–25 | USA |
| H. tsudai | — | 25 | Japan |
| Hydropsychodes lateralis | — | 15 | S. Africa |
| Polycentropus cinereus | Summer Mottled Sedge | 7–12 | USA |
| Psychomyia flavida | Dinky Purple-breasted Sedge | 7–9 | USA |
| Rhyacophila spp. | Green Sedge | 6–25 | USA |
| Stenopsyche japonica | — | 25 | Japan |

*The sizes given are to cover a large range within this genus.

## ARTIFICIALS

Unlike the mayflies and stoneflies there have been only a few artificial patterns conceived with particular caddis species in mind. Flies tied to imitate caddis larvae have usually been broad-spectrum in their conception, i.e. they have been patterns that can imitate a number of different species. This also applies to the pupa or hatching adult; very few tiers have bothered to imitate specific pupa. Ernest Schwiebert did, however, make some attempt to tie patterns for a number of the American species. Gary LaFontaine devised a set of colour patterns to represent a wide range of pupa and larvae and, by selecting the colour and size of pattern, was able to imitate the naturals in this way. In the UK, apart from one or two artificials, size and colour patterns have been the usual way of imitating the larval and pupal stages of the caddis or sedge.

## LARVA PATTERNS OF CASED CADDIS

### BRITISH AND EUROPEAN PATTERNS

A number of caddis build their cases out of sand or fine gravel. The grouse wing (*Mystacides longicornis*), silverhorns (*Athripsodes albifrons*, *A. aterimmus*, *A. cinereus*, *M. azurea*, *M. nigra*), silver (or grey) sedge (*Odontocerum albicorne*) and Welshman's button (*Sericostoma personatum*) are examples of these, and the following pattern will serve to imitate all of them. The pattern can be tied on conventional 3x longshank hooks or on any of the larval-type hooks now available to the fly-tier. As the natural creature is found near the bottom, it is prudent to pre-weight the hook with copper or lead wire.

**Sand Caddis (species as above)** · UK

| | |
|---|---|
| *Hook* | Mustad 79580 or Partridge K14, sizes 8–14 |
| *Thread* | Black or brown |
| *Underbody* | Cream or green floss, coated in adhesive |
| *Overbody* | Fine sand |
| *Exposed body* | Fluorescent green floss |
| *Legs* | Brown partridge or soft hen hackle |

The next pattern will serve to imitate those species that utilize slightly larger pieces of gravel and small pebbles for their cases: the medium sedge (*Goera pilosa*) and a number of limnephilids. The first time

Sand Caddis

I tied this particular pattern, it caught a number of fine brown trout but the fly had one major drawback: it was too heavy to cast. Since then I have used a number of different materials; apart from small stones from my aquarium, light cat's litter or vermiculite serve the purpose well. I use superglue to stick on the case materials.

**Pebble Caddis (species as above)** · Price · UK

| | |
|---|---|
| *Hook* | Mustad 79580, sizes 8–12 |
| *Thread* | Black or brown |
| *Underbody* | Cream or light green floss |
| *Overbody* | Vermiculite stuck on with super-glue |
| *Exposed body* | Fluorescent green floss silk |
| *Legs* | Brown partridge or brown hen hackle |

Pebble Caddis

A number of caddis use leaf and other plant matter in the construction of their portable shelters and the next fly endeavours to simulate such species. The small silver sedge (*Lepidostoma hirtum*), grannom (*Blachycentus subnubilus*), red sedge (*Phryganea* spp.) and cinnamon sedge (*Limnephilus* spp.) are just a few that can be imitated with this pattern.

**Twig Caddis (species as above)** · UK

| | |
|---|---|
| *Hook* | Mustad 79580, sizes 8–14 |
| *Thread* | Black or brown |
| *Underbody* | Cream or light green floss |
| *Overbody* | Small pieces of natural and brown raffia stuck onto the underbody with the odd small twig for effect |
| *Exposed body* | As underbody |
| *Legs* | Light red hen or partridge (optional) |

Twig Caddis

The sedge *Trianodes bicolor* is a fairly widespread species, usually found in stillwater. All species of *Trianodes* swim quite actively around the weed-beds and in the main body of the water by means of their long, hairy middle legs. I have found this larva in many stomach contents of trout caught on reservoirs in southern England. In the sludge of the exposed insect food-mass, they could well have been mistaken for the tips of reeds.

### Green Stick *(Trianodes bicolor)* · UK

| | |
|---|---|
| *Hook* | Mustad 38941, sizes 12–14 |
| *Thread* | Green or black |
| *Underbody* | Green floss silk |
| *Overbody* | Green raffia |
| *Exposed body* | Green or yellow silk |
| *Hackle* | Ginger hen hackle |

One of the most effective patterns used on British reservoirs is a pattern called simply the Stick Fly. While this pattern can be used as a general, stillwater fly pattern (see p. 197), it can also be used as an imitation of a cased caddis. The following pattern works exceedingly well on all types of water. Like most cased caddis pattens it can be pre-weighted.

### Stick Fly (general cased caddis) · UK

| | |
|---|---|
| *Hook* | Mustad 79850, sizes 8–16 |
| *Thread* | Black |
| *Body (case)* | Bronze peacock herl |
| *Rib* | Fine gold or copper wire |
| *Exposed body* | Fluorescent green floss silk |
| *Legs* | Brown partridge |

Among the wealth of synthetic products available to today's fly-tier is a new plastic chenille which makes an ideal body medium to imitate the case of the caddis. I use black, brown or dark green.

### Cased Caddis (general cased caddis) · UK

| | |
|---|---|
| *Hook* | Mustad 79580 or Partridge, sizes 8–12 |
| *Thread* | Black or brown |
| *Body (case)* | Plastic chenille (brown, black or green) |
| *Exposed body* | Fluorescent green or white floss silk |
| *Legs* | Brown partridge |

The next fly was devised by Bob Carnill to imitate a broad-spectrum, cased caddis larva. It is pre-weighted with lead wire.

### Cased Caddis (general cased caddis) · Carnill · UK

| | |
|---|---|
| *Hook* | Mustad 38941 or Partridge K14, sizes 10–12 |
| *Thread* | Black |
| *Body* | Spun hare fur |
| *Rib* | Silver wire |
| *Exposed body* | White swan or goose herl |
| *Legs* | Black hen |

One of the most gifted of fly-tiers in the UK is the Yorkshire tier, Oliver Edwards. The following pattern is one of his which he calls the Peeping Caddis. I tie a similar fly using a real discarded caddis case, which I call the Ultimate Caddis.

### Peeping Caddis · Edwards · UK

| | |
|---|---|
| *Hook* | Mustad 79762, all sizes |
| *Thread* | Brown |
| *Body* | Hare fur, well picked out |
| *Rib* | Gold or silver wire |
| *Exposed body* | Light-coloured wool |
| *Legs* | Partridge hackle |
| *Head* | Tip of the wool body, burnt to form a little black blob |

A gold bead or lead shot can be added to this pattern to provide weight and also to keep the fly upright on the bottom. The bead is slipped onto the hook before any of the other materials. It is necessary to de-barb most hooks when applying beads.

Roman Moser from Austria is, without doubt, one of the most enlightened fly-tiers and expert fishermen in Europe today. His great skill is manufacturing unique dubbing mixtures from natural and man-made products, combining such items as chopped deer body hair with Antron or various carpet wools. He is best known for his sedge and caddis larval patterns and the methods of fishing them on his local River Traun. The following pattern uses chenille or the case of the caddis.

### Pebble-case Larva

**(*Limnephilus* spp.)** · Moser · Austria

| | |
|---|---|
| *Hook* | Mustad 79580, sizes 10–12 (copper wire for weight) |
| *Thread* | Brown |
| *Body* | Greyish-tan chenille |
| *Exposed body* | Deer hair and brown synthetic fibre, mixed |
| *Legs* | As exposed body |

### Plant-cased caddis

**(*Limnephilus* spp.)** · Moser · Austria

| | |
|---|---|
| *Hook* | Mustad 79850, sizes 10–12 |
| *Thread* | Brown. |
| *Body* | Dubbing of brown synthetic and clipped deer-hair fibres, mixed |
| *Exposed body* | Yellow hare's ear with brown latex over the back |
| *Legs* | Black cock hackle, sparse and clipped |

Luis Antunez divides his time between Madrid and his ranch in Chile where he has at least six rivers running through his land. I view his life-style with a certain degree of envy, what with the culture, wine and tapas of old Madrid and the hard-fighting fish which he has running up his rivers that flow from the Andes. He always provides me with some excellent fish-taking patterns.

### Deep Caddis Larva (general cased caddis)

Antunez · Spain

| | |
|---|---|
| *Hook* | Mustad 94840, sizes 8–10 (weighted with copper wire) |
| *Thread* | Black |
| *Body* | Hare fur |
| *Rib* | Black thread |
| *Exposed body* | Brown fur dubbing |
| *Legs* | Grey hackle fibres beneath the hook |

The next cased caddis comes from Finland, from the vice of Veli Autti, one of the best fishermen of that country.

### Cased Caddis · Autti · Finland

| | |
|---|---|
| *Hook* | Mustad 79706, sizes 10–12 |
| *Thread* | Black |
| *Body (case)* | Short chopped fibres of golden-pheasant tail dubbed onto the tying thread |

| | |
|---|---|
| *Exposed body* | Green silk |
| *Legs* | Golden-pheasant tail fibres |

The country of Croatia has had its fair share of troubles since it became independent and left the old republic of Yugoslavia. There are many fine rivers in the new republic, one being the Kupiča, a small river close to the borders of Slovenia. Mladen Merkas Goranin is a local artist and fly-tier from that area and fishes this river for trout and grayling with a wide number of excellent nymphs. Among the examples he sent me were two that serve to imitate the cased caddis of the brown sedge (*Anabolia nervosa*), the caddis that attaches long twigs to its case.

### M.M.G. Cased Caddis (dark) · Goranin · Croatia

| | |
|---|---|
| *Hook* | Mustad 79580, sizes 8–12 |
| *Thread* | Black |
| *Body (case)* | Dark brown hackle, grizzle hackle and dark brown seal fur twisted together, dubbed to the hook and clipped, leaving a few fibres at the head to simulate the legs |
| *Rib* | Gold wire |
| *Twigs* | Stripped hackle quills tied at the bend and at the head on top of the hook |

M.M.G. Cased Caddis (light) is tied in the same way but the case is made from a brown hackle, a badger hackle and ginger seal fur.

Mladen Merkas says that both these patterns are excellent for grayling, especially in cloudy or coloured water.

Holland can in no way be considered a game-fish country and yet there are many fine fly-tiers and excellent fly-fishermen in this flat land of tulips and dykes. One of the best trout fishermen from this country is Hans van Klinken, whose patterns are universally accepted throughout Europe. In his extensive repertoire, Hans has many caddis larvae and pupae patterns. The following cased pattern is just one of many which he sent to me.

### Cased Caddis · van Klinken · Holland

| | |
|---|---|
| *Hook* | Partridge H1A, sizes 10–12 |
| *Thread* | Black |
| *Body* | Gutterman glitter thread |
| *Thorax* | Light feather fibre (goose) |
| *Legs* | Starling hackle |

AMERICAN PATTERNS

The Clark Fork flows through the town of Missuola in Montana and is considered to be a good water for the caddis. On my first visit to this Big Sky State I drifted this river on a day so hot that no self-respeting sedge dared scorch its wings; only a few *Tricorythodes* mayflies dared brave the mid-day sun. The day before we had motored up to a smaller freestone stream called Rock Creek and walked through shady pines and bush to get to the river. On the way, we were scolded by chipmunks, who chittered and chattered at our approach. Multi-coloured grasshoppers flew in alarm from our feet with a whirring of fragile wings. Our guide, Dave Ruetz, suggested we try a little, dry Spruce Moth, which, although it did not capture a fish of memorable size, served its purpose well that morning.

After a while I stopped fishing and decided to spend some time turning over stones to see what creatures inhabited this river and was soon joined by Dave, who pointed out various species to me; he was a fully qualified aquatic biologist as well as a licensed guide. 'Look,' he said, pointing to a large cased caddis, 'That is the *Dicosmoecus*,' he continued, awaiting my reaction. 'Oh, the Giant Orange Sedge,' I replied with a degree of nonchalance. I think I went up in Dave's estimation with that reply; perhaps I was not as stupid as I looked after all. Little did he know that I had read about this species only a week or so before and it was about the only American species I could remember. This time, it was a case of a little knowledge doing no harm at all.

This large caddis is one of those species that, for reasons best known to itself, vacates the safety of its case and is swept away by the current to become very acceptable fare for the trout. I do not know what prompts this lemming-like activity. I suppose it can be described as insectivorous suicide.

The caddis described by Walton as looking like a small hedgehog could be any of a number of cased caddis. The species *Limnephilus rhombicus* is just one such caddis that builds itself a case of transverse twigs. An American pattern that has been in existence for some considerable time could well imitate a similar larva, in this instance, that of the species *Platycentropus radiatus*. Named by Gary LaFontaine as the Chocolate & Cream Sedge, it will also suffice to imitate a number of native American limnephilids. Because it uses

clipped deer hair as the main dressing ingredient, it is necessary to weight the fly with an underbody of lead wire in order to get it to sink. Ray Bergman in his book, *Trout*, credits the fly to Paul Young.

### Strawman Nymph (*Platycentropus radiatus*) · Young · USA

| | |
|---|---|
| Hook | Mustad 79580, sizes 8–12 |
| Thread | Black or brown |
| Tail | Sparse tail of grey-speckled duck fibres (now usually omitted) |
| Body | Roughly clipped deer hair |
| Rib | Yellow silk (optional) |
| Legs | None |

Try tying this pattern in reverse, as for the Oliver Edwards Peeping Caddis. It is really effective.

The next pattern is one ostensibly tied to represent the species *Hesperophylax*. One of the most beautiful-looking of the American sedge species is the silver-striped sedge (*H. designatus*). As its name suggests, this fly has wings that appear to be streaked with quicksilver, more like a moth than the usual drab sedge. This pattern would serve to imitate the larva of such a species. The pattern was created by Charles Brookes, author of *Nymph Fishing for Larger Trout*.

### Skunk-hair Caddis (*Hesperophylax designatus*) · Brookes · USA

| | |
|---|---|
| Hook | Mustad 38941, sizes 8–10 |
| Thread | Black |
| Body | Natural skunk tail, with a long black tip about 4in (10cm) long and a lighter root; the dark portion is wound on to imitate the case, the lighter portion the exposed body |
| Legs | Small black hen |

The fly is tied as follows:

*Step 1* Take the thread down the hook and there tie in a bunch of skunk hair by the black tips, about 1/8in (4mm) in thickness. Also tie in a length of copper wire

*Step 2* Return the thread back down the shank leaving room for the head and the hackle. Coat the thread on the hook with varnish.

*Step 3* Twist the skunk hair into a rope and twist in a clockwise motion around the shank. Tie off securely and cut off any surplus hair

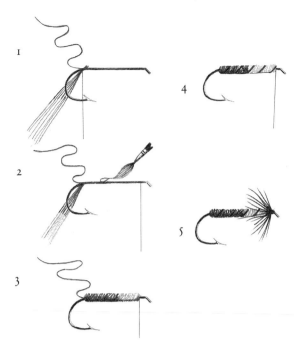

Skunk-hair Caddis

*Step 4* Wind on the copper wire rib anti-clockwise, tie off and cut off any surplus wire

*Step 5* Tie in and wind a small black hen hackle. Finish the fly with a neat head and whip finish. Varnish the head and the fly is now complete. Like all larval patterns this fly can be pre-weighted with lead or copper wire.

Ken Iwamasa is perhaps best known for his series of nymphs tied on curved hooks and dressed upside-down. These patterns were called 'Tarcher Nymphs'. He has also produced a very good pattern to imitate the larva of the American grannom, *Brachycentrus americanus*.

### American Grannom Larva (*Brachycentrus americanus*) · Iwamasa · USA

| | |
|---|---|
| *Hook* | Mustad 3906, sizes 12–16 |
| *Thread* | Black |
| *Body (case)* | Stripped peacock herls, forming a square shape, varnished |
| *Underbody* | Lead trimmed to shape either side of the shank |
| *Legs* | Dark brown cock hackle |

In his definitive book on the American caddis flies, Gary LaFontaine gives three patterns for the cased caddis: a Light Cased Caddis, a Medium Cased Caddis and a Dark Cased Caddis. These three patterns, tied in various sizes, should serve to imitate most species that construct a case of sorts.

### Light Cased Caddis (general cased caddis)
LaFontaine · USA

| | |
|---|---|
| *Hook* | Mustad 94840, sizes 6–12, front fifth bent upwards into a swimming-nymph style and remainder weighted with fine lead wire |
| *Thread* | Brown |
| *Body (case)* | Grey mallard and lemon wood-duck palmered and clipped |
| *Exposed body* | Pale yellow chenille |
| *Legs* | Brown and grey grouse hackle |

The Medium Caddis uses grouse and lemon wood-duck for the case and the Dark Caddis uses a dark brown hackle and a grouse hackle. All the other ingredients are the same as for the light version.

NEW ZEALAND PATTERNS

The caddisfly and its imitation is well appreciated in New Zealand where there are a number of killing patterns to imitate both cased and uncased caddis. The first is one given by Keith Draper in his book *Trout Flies in New Zealand*. It is a pattern tied to represent the species *Olinga feredayi* and was devised by R.K. Bragg of Christchurch, New Zealand. Like many of New Zealand's top fly-creators, Robert Bragg originated in England, arriving in New Zealand at the outbreak of World War Two. This pattern of Bragg's uses a detached body.

### Bragg's Caddis Larva
(*Olinga feredayi*) · Bragg · NZ

| | |
|---|---|
| *Hook* | Mustad 3904A, sizes 10–12 |
| *Thread* | Yellow |
| *Body* | Detached, from a piece of stout mono-filament covered with yellow floss |
| *Legs* | Small yellow grizzle hen |

Bragg's Caddis Larva

## Horn Cased Caddis
**(Olinga feredayi)** · Marsh · NZ

| | |
|---|---|
| *Hook* | Partridge Sedge Hook K2B or K4A, sizes 14–16 |
| *Thread* | Black or brown |
| *Underbody* | Yellow floss silk |
| *Overbody* | Stripped quill from a brown hen hackle |
| *Head* | Peacock herl |

Horn Caddis

## Smooth Cased Caddis
**(Olinga feredayi)** · Brown · NZ

| | |
|---|---|
| *Hook* | Partridge Sedge Hook K2B or KH4A, sizes 10–14 |
| *Thread* | Black or brown |
| *Underbody* | Copper wire |
| *Overbody* | Cassette recording tape coated with clear varnish |
| *Thorax* | Black fur dubbing |

The species *Pycnocentrodes aureola* makes its case out of sand or gravel. The Horn Caddis given by Keith Draper represents this species quite well.

## Horn Caddis
**(Pycnocentrodes aureola)** · Draper · NZ

| | |
|---|---|
| *Hook* | Mustad 3904, sizes 10–14 |
| *Thread* | Grey or black |
| *Body* | Grey wool varnished with clear lacquer |
| *Rib* | Silver wire |
| *Exposed body* | White wool |
| *Legs* | Few grizzle hackle fibres sticking out of the top |

In the Tichborne's New Zealand Trout Calendar there is another pattern which was tied by Bill McLay of Dunedin. It also serves as an imitation of *Pycnocentrodes* sp. and is very similar to the Draper pattern. It could also be used as an imitation of other stick caddisfly larvae, such as *Triplectides* sp.

## Sandy-cased Caddis · McLay · NZ

| | |
|---|---|
| *Hook* | Mustad 38941, sizes 8–12 |
| *Thread* | Black |
| *Body* | Grey wool |
| *Rib* | Copper wire |
| *Legs* | Brown partridge (or similar) tied beneath the hook |

### LARVA PATTERNS OF NON-CASED CADDIS

If the trout are prepared to take larvae encased in all manner of non-palatable materials then surely they would prefer to dine on larvae free of such inedible crusts. And so they do. The free-swimming species and those that build themselves nets and funnels and webs are an important item of a trout's diet. *Rhyacophila* and *Hydropsyche* spp. occur time and time again in the stomach contents of caught trout and today's angler is not slow in coming forward with a wealth of patterns to imitate such creatures.

As with the cased-caddis patterns, there are very few flies tied with individual species in mind. This is understandable because most species of free caddis, at first glance, look very similar to one another, and I am sure that trout also view the creatures in this way. Colour is the guiding factor; most larvae are usually shades of cream, green, grey or olive, although some tiers have also given patterns that are light brown and even washed-out pink. Most fly-tiers name their patterns under the generic terms *Hydropsyche* or *Rhyacophila* but some fall back on the term 'free-living caddis'.

### BRITISH AND EUROPEAN PATTERNS

I devised this first pattern some 12 years ago in two colour forms: green to imitate *Rhyacophila* spp. and cream to imitate *Hydropsyche* spp. I gave the dressing of this fly in *The Angler's Sedge*. It is worth relating here how one particular beginner, who did not know one fly from another, used the flies on a salmon expedition to Scotland; he hooked and landed two fish. To this day I am sure he did not know that he was using the wrong fly, but with two salmon to show for his ignorance, it would be a brave man who would tell him he was wrong.

## Latex Caddis-cream
**(Hydropsyche spp.)** · Price · UK

| | |
|---|---|
| *Hook* | Mustad 37160, sizes 12–20, or Partridge K2B, sizes 8–16 |
| *Thread* | Brown |

| | |
|---|---|
| *Body* | Light brown ostrich herl |
| *Rib* | Natural creamy-yellow latex |
| *Thorax* | Dark brown seal fur or substitute |
| *Legs* | Brown partridge |

This fly is tied as follows:

*Step 1*   Take the thread down the hook and tie in a strip of latex about ⅛in (4mm) wide and three or four strands of ostrich herl.

*Step 2*   Return the thread back along the shank to the point shown and then twist the ostrich herl into a rope and wind it up the shank. Tie off and cut away any surplus ostrich herl.

*Step 3*   Wind the latex up the shank, covering the ostrich herl but leaving gaps so that the herl protrudes in more or less equal segments. At this point dub onto the tying thread a pinch of brown fur.

*Step 4*   Form a thorax with the fur and tie in a partridge hackle by the point.

*Step 5*   Wind on the hackle; two or three turns will be sufficient. Finish with a neat small head, whip finish and varnish. The fly is complete.

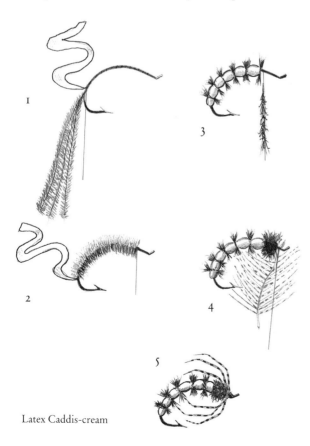

Latex Caddis-cream

Because ostrich herl is quite delicate and easily broken by the trout's teeth I have reversed the usual ribbing procedure. I first form the body out of ostrich herl and protect it by the latex thus eventually forming a body of latex with the ostrich now acting as a rib.

### Latex Caddis-green
**(*Rhyacophila* spp.)** · Price · UK
As above except:

| | |
|---|---|
| *Body* | Olive ostrich |
| *Rib* | Light green latex |

C.F. Walker in his book *Lake Flies and Their Imitation* gives a pattern for a free caddis larva, *Holocentropus dubius*. This larva forms silken nets beneath floating leaves on stillwater.

### Free Caddis Larva
**(*Holocentropus dubius*)** · C.F. Walker · UK

| | |
|---|---|
| *Hook* | Mustad Laser Point 79761, sizes 12–14 |
| *Thread* | Brown |
| *Body* | 3 parts yellow and 1 part green seal fur (or substitute) |
| *Rib* | Fine oval gold tinsel |
| *Legs* | Woodcock undercovert |
| *Head* | Cock-pheasant tail fibres |

In the British Isles the development of nymph-fishing over the last 30–40 years has, to a degree, coincided with the construction of a large number of reservoirs, which have then been opened up for trout-fishing. Flies and methods used have been biased towards this stillwater scene, so creatures such as the free-swimming caddis larva have not figured too much in the pattern lists of British anglers. In other parts of Europe this is not the case. Most Continentals favour the fishing of rivers and, to a certain extent, this also applies to the USA and New Zealand. As we will see later, there has been a far greater emphasis placed on pupal patterns suitable for stillwater fishing in the UK.

The next pattern given will imitate the larva of *Rhyacophila* spp. reasonably well. The pattern comes from Ireland.

### Sedge Nymph (general pattern) · Ireland

| | |
|---|---|
| *Hook* | Mustad 3123, sizes 10–12 |
| *Thread* | Brown |
| *Tail* | Short fibres of dark grouse |
| *Body* | Apple-green swan or goose herl |
| *Thorax* | Chestnut seal fur (or substitute) |

*Wing case*   Brown turkey
*Legs*           Dark grouse

The Idrija River flows into the beautiful River Soča in northwest Slovenia. It is a limestone river with abundant aquatic life; stoneflies and mayflies in a variety of species vie with sedges for the attention of the trout. The river is one of a number of crystal streams under the control of the Fishing Club of Tolmin, which issues day tickets to visiting anglers.

I first fished this stream about 8 years ago in the company of my now good friend Marjan Fratnik, who was born close to the banks of this river. I shall always be indebted to Marjan for introducing me to some of the finest fishing in the world. On our first visit another of our guides was Franko Gorjan, who comes from the small town of Tolmin. He is one of the local fly-tiers.

The sun was warm that first day, but the river ran cold, shaped and dappled by the linden trees that graced the banks. The coldness of the water was due in part to the residual ice-melt, the memory of the previous year's snow on the high mountains. I found it difficult to keep my feet in the river, what with the slippery rocks and the force of the water that pulled at my waders; so treacherous was it that my wife actually fell in and was carried 50yd (45m) or so downstream; after drying off she continued to fish.

I concentrated on fishing dry with small, grey flies and succeeded in taking a few trout. Above me, where the river spewed around some rocks in a welter of foam and riffled currents, Franko was taking much better fish than I was. I worked my way up the bank to him in an endeavour to see what fly he was using. 'A nymph', he said, or at least I thought that is what he said, for his English is only marginally better than my Slovenian (and I cannot speak Slovenian). He showed me the fly that he was using, a pattern that I was later to publish and christen on his behalf 'Franko's Nymph'. The simple nymphal pattern is an ideal impression of *Hydropsyche*, of which there are some half-a-dozen species and many other closely allied caddis in the Slovenian rivers.

### Franko's Nymph
**(*Hydropsyche* spp.)** · Gorjan · Slovenia
*Hook*      Mustad 79580, sizes 8–12
*Thread*   Black or brown
*Body*      Cream fur or wool
*Rib*         Gold wire

Franko's Nymph

*Thorax*   Brown fur or wool
*Legs*       Brown partridge

One of the best fishing videos that I have seen over the last few years was one featuring Roman Moser fishing the caddis on his beloved River Traun in Austria. This river is one of the finest in Europe and, over the years, some of the world's greatest anglers have fished its clear, clean water for trout and grayling. The following four patterns are some of the many flies he kindly sent me, flies that he uses on his river.

### Original Marbled Hydropsyche
**(*Hyropsyche* spp.)** · Moser · Austria
*Hook*      Mustad 79580, size 10
*Thread*   Black or brown
*Tail*        Short tuft of downy filoplume from a partridge hackle
*Body*      Light grey furry foam ('Body Gill')
*Back*      Brown latex marked with waterproof ink or pre-printed
*Legs*       Beard hackle of brown partridge
*Head*     Dubbed squirrel body fur

Original Marbled Hydropsyche

### Hydropsyche No. 2 · Moser · Austria
*Hook*      Mustad 79580, sizes 10–12
*Thread*   Brown
*Tail*        Short tuft of yellow filoplume
*Body*      Fine olive chenille
*Thorax*   Brown Antron (or similar)
*Legs*       None

### Hydropsyche No. 3 · Moser · Austria
*Hook*      Mustad 79580, sizes 10–12
*Thread*   Brown
*Tail*        Short tuft of grey filoplume

| | |
|---|---|
| *Body* | Olive hare and synthetic fur, mixed |
| *Thorax* | As body |
| *Wing case* | Brown latex |
| *Legs* | Sparse black hackle |

**Rhyacophila** · Moser · Austria

| | |
|---|---|
| *Hook* | Mustad 79580, size 10 |
| *Thread* | Brown |
| *Tail* | Short tuft white filoplume |
| *Body (main)* | Cream furry foam |
| *Back* | Green Raffene (Swiss Straw), varnished |
| *Belly* | Yellow Raffene, varnished |
| *Rib* | Brown thread |
| *Thorax* | Mixed synthetic fur and chopped deer body hair |
| *Wing case* | Brown Raffene |

The next pattern comes from Spain and was created by Luis Antunez; it is a simple *Rhyacophila* pattern, very similar to the Gill-ribbed Larva pattern created by Larry Solomon in the USA.

**Rhyacophila** · Antunez · Spain

| | |
|---|---|
| *Hook* | Mustad 94840, sizes 10–14 |
| *Thread* | Black |
| *Body* | Green latex |
| *Rib* | Bronze peacock herl |
| *Underbody* | Copper wire |
| *Head* | As rib |

I met Richardt Jensen, who hails from Esbjerg in Denmark, at a fly-fishing fair in Holland, where the very best of European and American fly-tiers were plying their art. Richardt's simple caddis-larva patterns use dubbing wicks (various furs pre-twisted onto copper wire).

**Yellow Thorax Caddis**

**Larva** · Jensen · Denmark

| | |
|---|---|
| *Hook* | Tiemco TMC 103BL, sizes 11–17 |
| *Thread* | Black |
| *Body* | Hare's ear or brown angora dubbing wick |
| *Thorax* | Yellow ostrich herl |
| *Legs* | Brown partridge hackle |

This last pattern could be used to imitate either a case- or a non-case-making caddis larva.

Hans van Klinken sent me a number of different free-swimming caddis larvae imitations and the following two are excellent fish-takers.

**Caseless Caddis No. 1** · van Klinken · Holland

| | |
|---|---|
| *Hook* | Partridge GRS 12 ST |
| *Thread* | Black |
| *Body* | Furry foam (green, cream, yellow or brown) |
| *Rib* | Grey monofilament nylon |
| *Back* | Clear flexible body (PVC sheet) |
| *Thorax* | Mink or fitch body fur well picked out to give the impression of legs |

The second represents a larva that has been swept from the bottom and is struggling in the rough and tumble of the stream.

**Lost Caddis** · van Klinken · Holland

| | |
|---|---|
| *Hook* | Partridge H1A, sizes 10–12 |
| *Thread* | Black |
| *Tag* | Fluorescent green flexible body (PVC sheet) |
| *Body* | Rabbit fur well picked out |
| *Legs* | Brown partridge |

Both *Rhyacophila* and *Hydropsyche* spp. have been imitated by Veli Autti of Finland, who combines modern and traditional materials.

**Caddis Larva** · Autti · Finland

| | |
|---|---|
| *Hook* | Mustad 79671, sizes 10–14 |
| *Thread* | Brown |
| *Body* | Yellow or olive seal fur |
| *Rib* | Gold wire |
| *Back* | Olive Swannundaze |
| *Thorax* | As back but marked with brown water-proof ink |
| *Legs* | Golden-pheasant tail fibres |

There is a traditional fly from France called the Plantreuse, which means 'Buxom Lass'. This fly is an artificial to represent *Hydropsyche* spp.

**Plantreuse (*Hydropsyche* spp.)** · France

| | |
|---|---|
| *Hook* | Mustad 79703, sizes 10–14 |
| *Thread* | Black |
| *Body* | Golden-yellow wool |
| *Underbody* | Lead wire |
| *Legs* | Brown partridge |

AMERICAN PATTERNS
As the reader would expect there are many patterns in the USA to imitate free-living caddis larvae because they are an important item of diet for the trout of the freestone rivers. This was

brought home to me on my first fishing trip to the famous Deschutes River in Oregon.

As I stepped into the cold water, on what was a very hot day, I held onto a streamside bush, partly to aid my progress into the fast water and also to avoid a cluster of poison-oak plants, which, if they had touched my bare legs, would have had me scratching for the rest of the week. The bush shook as I eased my naked limbs into the current and from it a cloud of sedges flew off in all directions. Some fell into the water where they were swept away; others returned to their green-leaf sanctuary. Every bush that lined the river was such a resting place for these insects; they must have numbered thousands.

I asked my companion, Rik Hafele, what species they were and was told that they were *Hydropsyche* but which of the many species found on the Deschutes he could not be sure without a more detailed examination. He went on to tell me that the *Hydropsyche* caddis was one of the most important insects on the river and, judging from their numbers, I was rather inclined to believe him. He suggested I use a Gold-ribbed Hare's Ear type of fly as that was a good representation of a small *Hydropsyche*.

I had one or two variations of this fly in my box, one with a rib of fluorescent green silk instead of the usual gold wire, and it was this pattern that I successfully used on my first day on this famous river, fishing it in a dead drift, so that it bounced along the bottom in the riffled water. This is how the natural larva behaves when swept away from the safety of its web.

In his excellent book, *Western Hatches*, co-written with Hughes, Rik gives a number of patterns to imitate the *Hydropsyche* larva, one of which, the Latex Caddis Larva, is a pattern from the vice of that very good innovative tier, Poul Jorgensen. This is an all-purpose pattern and, by ringing the changes of the colour of the body, most species can be imitated.

### Latex Caddis Larva
**(Hydropsyche spp.)** · Jorgensen · USA

| | |
|---|---|
| *Hook* | Mustad 3906, sizes 10–16 |
| *Thread* | Brown |
| *Underbody* | Lead wire |
| *Overbody* | Natural latex strip (coloured to imitate the various species) |
| *Thorax* | Dark brown rabbit fur with underside picked out to resemble legs |

Gary LaFontaine has five patterns with different body-colours to emulate the range of free-living caddis. All you have to do is match the pattern to the colour of the indigenous species. The variants are: Pale Green, Bright Green, Olive-brown, Yellow and Pink. I will only give one pattern here and leave the reader to change the body colour as required.

### Free-living caddis · LaFontaine · USA

| | |
|---|---|
| *Hook* | Mustad 37160 or Partridge K2B, all sizes |
| *Thread* | Brown |
| *Body* | Golden-yellow fur |
| *Rib* | Stripped brown cock hackle quill |
| *Thorax* | Brownish-yellow fur |
| *Legs* | Lemon wood-duck tied beneath the hook. |

The Polly Rosborough pattern, the Green Rock Worm, is an excellent pattern to imitate the larva of *Rhyacophila* spp. Like most of Polly's patterns, this is a no-nonsense fly that is simple to construct.

### Green Rock Worm
**(Rhyacophila spp.)** · Rosborough · USA

| | |
|---|---|
| *Hook* | Mustad 3906, sizes 8–14 |
| *Thread* | Black |
| *Body* | Green synthetic yarn |
| *Legs* | Green guinea fowl |
| *Head* | Black ostrich herl |

One American nymphal pattern has over the years become a classic fly, a standard that serves to imitate the free-living caddis, I refer to the Breadcrust, a pattern that is found in most American fly catalogues. It comes in two colour forms: green and orange.

### Breadcrust · USA

| | |
|---|---|
| *Hook* | Mustad 3906 or *37160*, all sizes |
| *Thread* | Green or orange |
| *Body* | Green floss or orange floss, depending on the pattern |
| *Rib* | Stripped brown cock hackle quill |
| *Legs* | Soft grizzle hen hackle |

Breadcrust

## NEW ZEALAND PATTERNS

My wife and I arrived in New Zealand after a long flight of nearly 24 hours. We were not going to fish until the following day, so our guide, Brian Hussey, drove us to visit some of the local sights. He showed us a nature reserve where steam hissed and swirled from an uneasy land. Mud bubbled and belched with sighs of gas and the earth was warm. Close to this park of steam and sulphur, New Zealand's longest river, the Waikato (*wai* means 'water' and *kato* means 'flow' in Maori), flows out of Lake Taupo and after a short distance, pours over Huka Falls. At one time this river was famous for its fly-fishing but the installation of control gates at Taupo, and as many as nine power stations along its length, have spoilt what was once a superb fishing river.

As we walked around the banks of the river, a medium sedge fluttered up from the water; at the time I only noted this in my mind without really appreciating its significance. In past years the Waikato was famous for its hatch of sedge. Although there was trout activity throughout the day it was at dusk that the river boiled with big fish, eager for the hairy-winged insects. A lodge was built above Huka Falls to cater for anglers who had travelled the length and breadth of the world to fish for the big rainbows of the Waikato. It was built by Alan Pye in the 1930s and he gave his name to a number of fly patterns, one of which is the Pye Nymph, a pupa pattern.

The two main species of caddis that brought fame to Huka Lodge and the Waikato were *Aoteapsyche colonica*, a free-swimming caddis, and a species of *Triplectides*. Brian Hammond, in his *New Zealand Encyclopedia of Fly Fishing*, states that it was probably the latter case-making species that caused the big nightly rise of trout.

Both islands of New Zealand have big trout that feed on caddis. The first pattern, which imitates a free-swimming caddis, is a fly devised by Frank Schlosser of Omarama, another excellent guide with whom I had the good fortune to fish in South Island, at the mouth of the Ahuriri River where it braids into Lake Benmore. Here you fish for brown trout as though they were bonefish, for they cruise the sandflats searching for all manner of titbits. Frank Schlosser originally came from Bavaria and has that love and appreciation for fish and fishing found in many sportsmen from that part of the world. Perhaps his only disappointment with his new country is that there are no grayling.

## Green Caddis Larva (general pattern)
Schlosser · NZ

| | |
|---|---|
| *Hook* | Mustad 79580, sizes 8–12 |
| *Thread* | Black |
| *Body* | Light green fur |
| *Rib* | Oval gold or silver tinsel |
| *Thorax* | Hare fur or similar |
| *Legs* | Fur picked out |

Norman Marsh also has a green caddis pattern to represent *Hydrobiosis* spp.

## Green Caddis (*Hydrobiosis* spp.) · Marsh · NZ

| | |
|---|---|
| *Hook* | Partridge K2B, sizes 14–16 |
| *Thread* | Black |
| *Tail* | Ginger hackle fibres, short tuft |
| *Body* | Green and yellow fur, mixed |

Another simple pattern to imitate the free-swimming *Hydrobiosis* caddis is a pattern tied by Mike Weddell. Mike was one of the finest tournament-casters in the world and I had the pleasure of working with him on a number of instruction courses at Grafham Water in the English Midlands before he left to start a new life in New Zealand.

## Green Caddis (*Hydrobiosis* spp.) · Weddell · NZ

| | |
|---|---|
| *Hook* | Mustad 3906, sizes 10–12 |
| *Thread* | Black |
| *Body* | Green synthetic fur |
| *Rib* | Gold wire |
| *Thorax* | Peacock herl |
| *Legs* | Two strands of peacock herl left unclipped and tied beneath the hook |

Like all these caddis imitations the fly can be weighted with lead or copper wire.

The Rangitaiki River flows between high banks and through the pine forest of Kaingoroa. It is a fine river, noted for its evening sedge rise. Brian Hussey and I visited this river late one evening, just to sample this rise. Alas we had spent perhaps just a little too long in the Taupo club because, when we arrived, it was almost dark, and I had just enough time to catch one fish on a sedge and, in the descending gloom of night, to fall over a large, tufted lump of tussock grass. We had missed the best of rise by an hour. Mind you, the beer was good! In The New Zealand and Trout Fly Calender 1990, beneath an excellent Nancy Tichborne water-colour of the Rangitaiki River, there is a fly pattern to imitate the sedge species *Hydrobiosis parumbripennis*, an insect common on this river. The pattern was devised by Garth Coghill and uses either Swannundaze or a similar product for the body.

### Free-swimming Caddis
**(Hydrobiosis parumbripennis)** · Coghill · NZ

| | |
|---|---|
| *Hook* | Partridge K2B, sizes 8–14 |
| *Thread* | Black or brown |
| *Body* | Green Swannundaze, Larva Lace (or similar) |
| *Thorax* | Brown fur |
| *Wing case* | Green quill |
| *Legs* | Light red hackle |

JAPANESE PATTERNS

Nori Tashiro from Japan has created many interesting nymph patterns, some of which I have given in earlier chapters. The following two patterns represent two species of free-living caddis, the first a rather large species, *Stenopsyche japonica*.

### Free-swimming Caddis *(Stenopsyche japonica)*
Tashiro · Japan

| | |
|---|---|
| *Hook* | Mustad 79580 or Tiemco equivalent, size 8 |
| *Thread* | Brown |
| *Tail* | Two short dark brown goose biots |
| *Body* | Dark brown ostrich herl (takes up half the shank) |
| *Rib* | Fine oval gold tinsel |
| *Thorax* | Brown synthetic dubbing same colour as ostrich herl |
| *Legs* | Six dark brown goose biots |

The second pattern imitates the species Hydropsyche tsudai.

### Caddis Larva *(Hydropsyche tsudai)*
Tashiro · Japan

| | |
|---|---|
| *Hook* | Partridge K2B or Tiemco equivalent, sizes 8–10 |
| *Thread* | Tan |
| *Tail* | Two short brown biots |
| *Body* | Pale green and tan synthetic fur, mixed |
| *Rib* | Gold wire |
| *Back* | Tan Raffene (or similar) |
| *Legs* | Brown biots |

CADDIS PUPA PATTERNS

The pupa or, to be more precise, the hatching adult (for the pupa of the caddis lies dormant within the larval case), is the most vulnerable stage in the life-cycle of the insect. As they rise to the surface, cocooned in a thin skin and buoyed up by gases, many fall victim to predatory fish. Some species drift for a considerable time before breaking through the surface film. So it is with little wonder that, world-wide, there is a plethora of patterns tied to represent this stage.

BRITISH AND EUROPEAN PATTERNS

Most patterns do not represent particular species but, just like some of the flies tied to represent the larva, colour series have been developed to cover most needs. About 12 years ago I worked with John Veniard and, at that time, we managed to have the sole franchise for the UK for Swannundaze. A phone call from Eric Leiser gave us the information on this then new product and he advised us to contact the manufacturer, Frank A. Johnson, in New Jersey. Among some of the patterns I devised at that time was a series of sedge-pupa patterns that proved their worth on a wide variety of waters. There were three colour variations, using clear amber, clear olive and clear brown Swanundaze, with different coloured underbodies to achieve an overall natural effect.

### Swannundaze Sedge Pupa · Price · UK

| | |
|---|---|
| *Hook* | Partridge K4A Grub Hook, sizes 8–12 |
| *Thread* | Brown |
| *Underbody* | Fluorescent red floss |
| *Overbody* | Transparent amber Swannundaze |
| *Rib* | Peacock herl slotted between the turns of the Swannundaze |
| *Thorax* | Brown natural or synthetic fur |
| *Wing case* | Cock-pheasant tail fibres |
| *Antennae* | Two strands of cock-pheasant swept backwards |
| *Legs* | Brown partridge |

The red fluorescent silk shines through the amber Swannundaze, looking like the blood and guts of a real insect. Use a yellow or green fluorescent for the clear olive pattern and red or yellow for the brown version.

The fly is tied as follows:

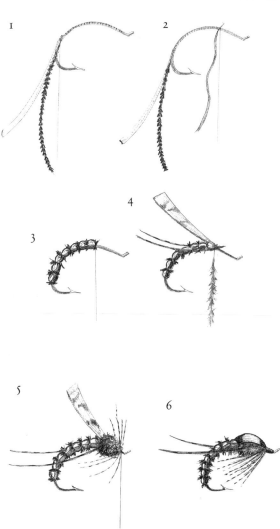

Swannundaze Sedge Pupa

the body. Cut off any surplus after tying off. Rib the Swannundaze with the peacock herl, allowing the herl to slip in between the turns of Swannundaze.

*Step 4*   Tie in a strip of cock-pheasant tail on top of the hook for the wing case. Tie in two strands of pheasant-tail fibres on either side of the hook. Dub onto the tying thread the brown fur dubbing.

*Step 5*   Wind on the dubbed thread and form the thorax, then wind on the partridge hackle about three turns.

*Step 6*   Take the cock-pheasant tail fibres over the back and tie off. Cut away the surplus feather. This wing case separates the hackle either side of the hook. Form a neat head and finish the fly in the usual way.

The well-known angling writer, John Goddard, created a series of pupa patterns for stillwater fishing which are still on the lists of most fly-suppliers in the UK.

**Goddard Pupa** · Goddard · UK

| | |
|---|---|
| *Hook* | Mustad 9672, sizes 10–12 |
| *Thread* | Brown |
| *Body* | Cream, brown, olive or orange fur, dubbed |
| *Rib* | Fine silver tinsel |
| *Thorax* | Brown condor herl substitute |
| *Wing case* | As thorax |
| *Legs* | Sparse honey hackle |

Goddard Pupa

*Step 1*   Wind the thread down the hook and tie in the strand of peacock herl for the rib. Before tying in the Swannundaze, cut the material into a point and nibble the end slightly; this adds a few serrations, which help to secure the material when you tie it. Now tie in the Swannundaze, taking care to keep the curved side of the material uppermost; this provides the finished fly with a good segmented abdomen. The other side of the Swannundaze strip is flat.

*Step 2*   Take the tying thread back along the shank to the point shown, and tie in the length of red fluorescent floss.

*Step 3*   Take the floss down the shank and back again. Follow this with the Swannundaze to form

I find light-coloured cock-pheasant tail perfectly acceptable for this pattern.

The following patterns were devised by the late Richard Walker, whose contribution to the world of angling in the UK is unsurpassed. The first fly is one that represents the pupa of such species as *Mystacides*. He called it the Shorthorn.

**Shorthorn** · R. Walker · UK

| | |
|---|---|
| *Hook* | Mustad 3904A, sizes 10–14 |
| *Thread* | Brown |
| *Body* | Dark brown feather herl |
| *Rib* | Yellow thread |
| *Thorax* | Green or yellow fluorescent wool |

| | |
|---|---|
| *Wing case* | Strip of black Lurex |
| *Legs* | Brown partridge tied as two bunches flanking in the body |

Walker devised the next pattern to imitate the pupa of species such as *Ocetis lacustris* or *O. ochracea*, known as the Longhorns. These stillwater sedges are common on many English day-ticket reservoirs.

**Longhorn Sedge Pupa** · R. Walker · UK

| | |
|---|---|
| *Hook* | Mustad 3904A, sizes 8–12 |
| *Thread* | Light yellow |
| *Body* | Amber wool, two-thirds of the shank |
| *Rib* | Fine oval gold tinsel |
| *Thorax* | Chestnut wool |
| *Legs* | Brown partridge hackle, two turns |
| *Antennae* | Two cock-pheasant strands sloping backwards |

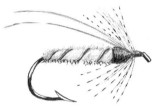

Longhorn Sedge Pupa

Another body colour used in this pattern is sea green. The rest of the fly follows the pattern above.

Roger Fogg, the author of that excellent book *The Art of the Wet Fly* has a couple of good fish-taking pupa patterns. Like the Swannundaze Sedge Pupa given on p. 185, these two flies rely on the underbody shiny through the latex overbody.

**Latex Pupa** · Fogg · UK

| | |
|---|---|
| *Hook* | Partridge K2B Sedge Hook, sizes 12–20 |
| *Thread* | Brown |
| *Underbody* | Fluorescent lime-green floss |
| *Overbody* | Tapered cream latex |
| *Thorax* | Chestnut-brown ostrich herl |
| *Legs* | Chestnut-brown hen |

The other version uses fluorescent orange silk or wool as an underbody with orange-coloured latex over.

One of the most interesting and beautiful books I have read over the last few years has come from Spain. It is the lifetime's work of the author Rafael del Poso Obeso. Entitled *Moscas para La Pesca*,

this large book is crammed with excellent colour photographs of the aquatic insects found in the Province of Léon in northern Spain. This is where the famous Spanish work on fly-tying was born, namely the *Manuscrito de Astorga* by Juan de Bergera, a work published about 24 years before Isaak Walton's *Compleat Angler*. This book will, I am sure, be of equal importance to future generations. The author depicts an interesting series of sedge pupa patterns sufficiently different from the British flies to be included here.

**Spanish Sedge Pupa** · del Poso Obeso · Spain

| | |
|---|---|
| *Hook* | Partridge K4A Grub Hook, sizes 8–12 |
| *Thread* | Black |
| *Body* | Olive, grey or brown dubbing |
| *Rib* | Brown or green Swannundaze |
| *Wings* | Cut turkey or goose quill |
| *Legs* | Cock-hackle fibres* sloping backwards |
| *Antennae* | Horse-hair, cock-pheasant tail fibres or other long fibres |

*The hackle used on these pupae are fibres from the famous *coq de léon* feathers.

The interesting feature of this style of fly lies in the fact that the antennae are tied in first at the bend of the hook and, when all the other ingredients have been tied in, taken over the back and tied in at the head.

**Grannom Pupa** · Antunez · Spain

| | |
|---|---|
| *Hook* | Mustad 3904A, size 12 |
| *Thread* | Brown |
| *Body* | Light brown polypropylene dubbing (or other synthetic fibre) |
| *Rib* | Dark brown thread |
| *Thorax* | Reddish-brown polypropylene dubbing |
| *Wings* | Grey mallard slips |

**Ucero (hatching pupa)** · Antunez · Spain

| | |
|---|---|
| *Hook* | Mustad 3904A, sizes 10–12 |
| *Thread* | Red |
| *Tail* | Short tuft of cinnamon Antron (or similar synthetic) |
| *Body* | Cinnamon Antron (or similar synthetic) |
| *Rib* | Dark brown thread |
| *Hackle/Legs* | Same as body, tied as a collar and teased out so that it flares over the body |
| *Head* | Red |

In the town of Nova Gorica, close to the Italian/ Slovenian border, Branko Gasparin, with his brother, runs one of the finest seafood restaurants I have ever eaten in. Every time I have stopped there I have had a gastronomic banquet of great delight. Branko, as well as being a restaurateur, is an excellent fly-fisherman and fly-tier. I first gave his pattern in *The Angler's Sedge* and called it the Gasparin Pupa.

### Gasparin Pupa · Gasparin · Slovenia

| | |
|---|---|
| *Hook* | Mustad 9672, sizes 8–12 |
| *Thread* | Pre-waxed black |
| *Body* | Cream-coloured foam plastic |
| *Thorax* | Peacock herl |
| *Legs* | Few fibres of light ginger or honey hackle |

The first recorded account of fly-fishing took place in Macedonia; it appeared in the work of the Roman writer Aelian. Today, working in the town of Skopje, in modern Macedonia, is a fly-tier of great excellence: Andrij Urban, a retired Major in the Yugoslav air force. He is carrying on a tradition that goes back nearly 2,000 years. In Chapter 7, I shall be giving a number of his emerger patterns but, for now, the following sedge pupa is one of his. Andrij specializes in subtle fur mixes, using hare, rabbit, dormouse, seal and modern man-made synthetics to create bodies that scintillate in the light, with guard hairs projecting from the body to give life to the flies.

One of the most effective caddis pupa patterns for the River Unec in Slovenia and for other rivers in the area is the following latex pattern. I was given the fly on the banks of the River Unec on a day when the water was high and the prospect of sport with the dry fly was non-existent. Using this pattern, I caught both trout and grayling – many of a decent size – on a day I had written off.

### Latex Pupa · Slovenia

| | |
|---|---|
| *Hook* | Mustad 94840, sizes 10–14 |
| *Thread* | Brown or black |
| *Body* | Natural latex over yellow silk with small dots painted on either side |
| *Thorax* | Brown cock pheasant tail |
| *Wing case* | As thorax |
| *Antennae* | Two cock-pheasant tail fibres, swept backwards |

There is also a green version, which uses green latex for the body.

### Sedge Pupa · Urban · Macedonia

| | |
|---|---|
| *Hook* | Mustad 94840, sizes 8–12 |
| *Thread* | Black |
| *Body* | Mixed fur dubbing to achieve an overall orange colour (other variations, including, ginger, are also tied) |
| *Wings* | Grey mallard slips |
| *Legs* | Sparse brown partridge hackle |
| *Head* | Grey fur mix (hare fur) |

The area in France around Limousin is famous, just like Léon in Spain, for its cockerels, which are bred purely for show and for their excellent hackles. The feathers shine like glass and are used by many of the French fly-dressers of that area for a wide range of dry and wet flies. The firm of Guy Plas operates in this area at Marcillac-La-Croisille, near Limoges. Not only is the firm famous for its quality fishing tackle but it also sells a wide range of specialist flies. The following pattern has been used with great success on many rivers in Europe from Spain to Yugoslavia.

### Phryga-Nymph · Guy Plas · France

| | |
|---|---|
| *Hook* | Mustad 3906B or VMC 8527, sizes 8–10 |
| *Thread* | Yellow |
| *Body* | Yellow and brown dubbing fur, mixed (or olive, brown, green and orange) |
| *Rib* | Brown silk |
| *Wings* | Brown-mottled hackle fibres flanking the body |
| *Hackle* | Ash grey on top of the hook |

I remember discussing flies with George Lenzi, a well-known French angling journalist. We had been fishing the Unec River at Plannina in Slovenia and, after a good day with the hard-fighting grayling, were relaxing in our pension after a hearty meal and one or two glasses of slivovitz. He informed me of a fly that he said was known as the Gypsy's Fly and was famous right throughout France.

I was later to receive such a fly from Raymond Rocher, an untidy raggle-taggle of a fly, called 'Peute', which I believe is feminine and translated means 'ugly'; compared with most other flies, ugly she certainly is. The secret of the fly was allegedly given to Henri Bresson, the famous French fly-tier, by a gypsy on the banks of a river; it was all to do with the semi-magical powers of the feathers from the breast of a female mallard at certain times of the year, or so the story goes. Magic or not, this fly is still used with great success by many French anglers. It is similar in many respects to the American pattern, Carey's Special, and, to my mind, both imitate a hatching sedge. The fly is sometimes called the Bresson Sedge.

**Peute (Bresson Sedge)** · Bresson · France
| | |
|---|---|
| *Hook* | VMC 8527, sizes 10–18 |
| *Thread* | Yellow |
| *Body* | Yellow thread |
| *Legs* | Female mallard breast feather, tied swept back |

There are many other French patterns tied with the pupa of the caddis in mind. The famous firm of Devaux of Champagnole produces a number of such flies in its range of artificials. Its Att series of nymphs depicts a number of them, and its Ato series of small grub-like flies also show patterns that resemble the sedge pupa very closely.

The Scandinavians have long appreciated the sedge in all three stages of its life-cycle. The following series of pupae, tied by Karsten Fredrikson, were sent to me by Sigverdt Steffensen of Tranbjerg in Denmark. There are four colour variations: dark brown, light brown, green and orange.

**Karsten Pupa** · Fredrikson · Denmark
| | |
|---|---|
| *Hook* | Partridge K4A Grub Hook, sizes 8–12 |
| *Thread* | Black or brown |
| *Body* | Latex coloured the required shade (the gold tinsel shines through) |
| *Underbody* | Copper wire covered with flat gold tinsel |
| *Thorax* | Sandy-coloured hare fur (or similar) complete with guard hairs |
| *Wings* | Grey duck wing slips |
| *Legs* | Thorax fur picked out |
| *Antennae* | Golden-pheasant tail fibres |

The use of gold, silver and other types of beads on the heads of flies is a common practice in many European countries. The following patterns are, to my mind, small pupa patterns that serve to imitate the newly emerged caddis. The bead shines in such away that it attracts the fish; perhaps they see it as a bubble of air, and the weight of the bead helps to keep it near the bottom. Although these flies will take trout, they are extensively used for the grayling. They are generally fished on the dead drift.

Fishing is never that easy on the Soča River. Its very clarity after the snow-melt has gone makes the fish all-seeing; at least most of the time they seem to see me. We arrived at the river close to where it flows into the dammed-up area at Most Na Soči (Bridge on the Soča); the blue water was fast-moving and a lot deeper than it looked. You wade this stream with great care.

I stepped into the current and tentatively waded out as far as my chest-waders would allow; I felt the coldness of the water even through my neoprenes and the current clutched and pulled at my legs. The gravel beneath my feet started to shift and it was sometime before I could say I was stable and not likely to be swept away. With my heels dug in firmly, I began by casting my gold-headed fly across the stream towards the far bank where one or two fish rose beneath the shade of inaccessible cliffs. My line drifted with the fast current and was swept downstream. Three casts later, at the end of the drift, my line shot out across the flow and I was into a fish. It fought hard in the current and leapt three times before I could net it. I easily slipped the barbless hook out of its top lip, the gold bead shining as though it was an item of jewellery worn only by regal fish. I roughly measured my Prince of Fish against the marks painted on my rod. It was just over 18in (46cm) long. Its large dorsal fin gleamed purple and red; its sides were suffused with pink as though it was blushing at being caught; I slipped it gently back into the blue water to fight another day. There is an old East European saying, 'Grayling live on the bottom of rivers and feed solely on nuggets of gold'. Well, it was my little nugget of gold on the head of my fly that tempted the fish to take that evening in the chill waters of the Soča.

**Goldkopfnymphe** · Austria
| | |
|---|---|
| *Hook*\* | Partridge Moser CS20 or similar, sizes 8–12 |
| *Thread* | Brown |
| *Head* | Gold metallic bead (slipped on before other materials) |
| *Body* | Cream, olive or brown synthetic dubbing |
| *Rib* | Gold wire |
| *Thorax* | Brown synthetic dubbing |
| *Antennae* | Few hackle fibres pointing backwards from the thorax (optional) |

\*Any hook will serve providing you can slip the

bead over the bend of the hook. Partridge K4 Grub Hooks with the barb flattened are ideal.

### Hare's Ear Goldkopfnymphe · Austria

| | |
|---|---|
| *Hook* | Partridge Moser CS20 or similar, sizes 8–14 |
| *Thread* | Brown |
| *Head* | Gold metallic bead |
| *Body* | Hare's ear |
| *Rib* | Gold wire |
| *Thorax* | Hare's ear |

Roman Moser gave me two such bead-headed flies, which he uses on the Traun River. The first he uses in clear water and the second in dark or cloudy water. Roman is continually changing his patterns and developing new materials and dubbing mixtures; fly-tying for him is an on-going experience. He told me on one occasion that his flies pass through so many variations that he eventually arrives back at square one, with the first fly he was endeavouring to develop.

### Clear-water Pupa · Moser · Austria

| | |
|---|---|
| *Hook* | Partridge Sedge Hook, sizes 8–10, barb flattened |
| *Thread* | Brown |
| *Bead* | Gold metallic |
| *Body* | Fluffy brown-grey wool |

Clear-water Pupa

### Dark-water Pupa · Moser · Austria

| | |
|---|---|
| *Hook* | Partridge Sedge Hook, sizes 8–10, barb flattened |
| *Thread* | Brown |
| *Bead* | Gold |
| *Body* | Cream furry foam |
| *Back* | Spectraflash sheet |

Dark-water Pupa

| | |
|---|---|
| *Rib* | Copper wire |
| *Legs* | Soft grey hackle |

The next Austrian pattern does not have a bead head and is quite conventional.

### Sedge Pupa · Austria

| | |
|---|---|
| *Hook* | Mustad 3904A or similar, sizes 10–16 |
| *Thread* | Brown or yellow |
| *Body* | Tan, brown or cream synthetic dubbing |
| *Thorax* | Lighter buff synthetic dubbing |
| *Wings* | Printed synthetic wing material |

Francesco Palu of Udine in Italy is a larger-than-life character. I have watched him fish with his unusual carbon fly-rod, a telescopic affair that allows the angler to select different lengths of rod according to the water that he is fishing: at one minute a brook rod, it can become a long rod suitable for stillwater the next. He also used a long tapered leader that was, in fact, a double length of nylon. He is perhaps best known for his flies, and sells a complete range of sedge, stonefly and mayfly patterns, some of which he kindly gave me. Among his nymph patterns there are a number of bead-headed flies similar to the Goldkopfnymphe.

### Golden Perla · Palu · Italy

| | |
|---|---|
| *Hook* | Mustad 38930 or Partridge K4, sizes 12–16, barb flattened |
| *Thread* | Black or brown |
| *Head* | Gold metallic bead |
| *Body* | Peacock herl |
| *Back* | Strip of gold tinsel |
| *Legs* | Soft light red hen hackle |

### Lucifero · Palu · Italy

| | |
|---|---|
| *Hook* | Mustad 38930, sizes 14–16 |
| *Thread* | Black |
| *Head* | Pearl bead |
| *Tail* | Short tuft of red cock hackle fibres |
| *Body* | Bronze peacock herl |
| *Legs* | Dark ginger cock or hen |

### Diabolica Perla · Palu · Italy

| | |
|---|---|
| *Hook* | Partridge K4, sizes 12–16 |
| *Thread* | Black |
| *Head* | Pearl bead |
| *Tail* | Few fibres of dark blue-dun cock hackle |
| *Body* | Orange fur or wool |
| *Rib* | Fine oval gold tinsel or wire |
| *Legs* | Dark blue dun cock |

The following fly was sent to me from Switzerland where it is used to take the shy grayling of the rivers in the Jura region; they are generally fished on small hooks.

### Swiss Bead-head Pupa · Switzerland

| | |
|---|---|
| *Hook* | Mustad 3904A, size 14–20, barb flattened |
| *Thread* | Black |
| *Head* | Silver metallic |
| *Body* | White plastic strip |
| *Thorax* | Black feather fibre |
| *Legs* | Sparse black hen |

Swiss Bead-head Pupa

Hans van Klinken from Holland is well known to British anglers; his work has appeared in a number of British fly-fishing periodicals, the Fly Dresser's Guild Magazine and the papers of the Grayling Society. He is an innovative fly-tier with a number of excellent fish-taking patterns to his credit. Most of his patterns will take trout and grayling with great ease. In one such nymph, instead of a shiny bead, a lead split shot is used; this is crimped onto a small piece of nylon monofilament and tied in at the head of the fly instead of the more usual gold bead. It is there to provide weight and weight alone. What this nymph of his represents I am sure I do not know but, to my mind, it resembles a sedge pupa more than any thing else, so I felt it worthy of inclusion.

### Leadhead Nymph · van Klinken · Holland

| | |
|---|---|
| *Hook* | Partridge H1A, sizes 8–16 |
| *Thread* | Brown |
| *Head* | Small lead split shot crimped to nylon monofilament and tied in firmly at the top of the head |
| *Tail* | Wound brown partridge hackle (I interpret this so-called tail as the trailing legs of the insect) |
| *Tip* | Fluorescent lime-green wool or silk |
| *Body* | Well-picked-out brown fur; hare is ideal |

The next van Klinken pattern is the Summer Pupa, a fly that catches bream and orfe, and has also accounted for a 32in (82cm) carp on one occasion. It is an unweighted pattern and is fished slowly in the shallows of the lakes.

### Summer Pupa · van Klinken · Holland

| | |
|---|---|
| *Hook* | Partridge GRS 12ST, sizes 12–18 |
| *Thread* | Black |
| *Body* | Pale olive Haretron |
| *Rib* | Brown thread |
| *Thorax* | Grey Haretron |
| *Legs* | Starling |

Another Hans van Klinken fly is used for both bream and rudd but will also take trout.

### Amber Pupa · van Klinken · Holland

| | |
|---|---|
| *Hook* | Partridge GRS 12ST, size 14 |
| *Thread* | Grey |
| *Body* | Two layers of fine amber Nymph Rib (or similar) |
| *Thorax* | Dark dun Haretron |
| *Legs* | Partridge hackle |

Veli Autti from Finland, whose excellent larval patterns were given earlier, also produces some excellent caddis pupae.

### Caddis Pupa No. I · Autti · Finland

| | |
|---|---|
| *Hook* | Partridge Grub Hook, sizes 10–14 |
| *Thread* | Brown |
| *Body* | Orange mohair |
| *Thorax* | Olive Antron |
| *Head* | Hare's ear |

### Caddis Pupa No. 2 · Autti · Finland

| | |
|---|---|
| *Hook* | Mustad 79706, sizes 10–14 |
| *Thread* | Black |
| *Body* | Light brown Antron |
| *Back* | Brown Swannundaze |
| *Rib* | Brown monofilament |
| *Thorax* | Hare fur and black marabou |
| *Legs* | As thorax |

### Caddis Pupa No. 3 · Autti · Finland

| | |
|---|---|
| *Hook* | Mustad 79706, sizes 10–14 |
| *Thread* | Brown |
| *Body* | Light green Antron, ribbed with green ostrich |
| *Back* | Olive Swannundaze |
| *Rib* | Gold wire |
| *Head* | Hare fur and black marabou |
| *Legs* | As thorax |

### AMERICAN PATTERNS

In the fly selections of the USA there are innumerable patterns tied to represent the pupal stage of the caddis. Many are broad-spectrum patterns created in a variety of sizes and colour variations so that most species are covered. The following simple patterns are sold by a number of fly-dressing houses.

### Small Black Pupa · USA

| | |
|---|---|
| *Hook* | Mustad 37160, sizes 16–20 |
| *Thread* | Black |
| *Body* | Black synthetic or dark iron-blue dun |
| *Legs* | Beard hackle of black cock hackle fibres |
| *Head* | As body |

### Little Sand Pupa · USA

| | |
|---|---|
| *Hook* | Mustad 37160, sizes 14–20 |
| *Thread* | Brown |
| *Body* | Light yellow synthetic fur |
| *Wings* | Grey mallard quill segments |
| *Legs* | Beard hackle of brown partridge |
| *Head* | Medium brown synthetic fur |

### Small Green Pupa · USA

| | |
|---|---|
| *Hook* | Mustad 37160, sizes 16–20 |
| *Thread* | Olive |
| *Body* | Olive-green synthetic fur |
| *Legs* | Beard hackle of brown partridge |
| *Head* | As body |

### Speckled Sedge Pupa · USA

| | |
|---|---|
| *Hook* | Mustad 3906, sizes 12–16 |
| *Thread* | Brown |
| *Body* | Light brown fur (original called for mink) |
| *Rib* | Australian opossum fur thinly spun onto the tying thread |
| *Wing* | Grey mallard tied short |
| *Legs* | Brown partridge tied beneath and either side of the hook in two bunches |
| *Head* | Brown beaver fur |

After the emerging caddis has bitten through its pupal chamber, it is completely enclosed in a natal skin; gases are trapped within this skin to help the emerging insect to rise through the water. Gary LaFontaine evolved a set of patterns using sparkle yarn (Antron) to simulate the shine of the trapped gases. He created two types of pattern, a deep-water pupa and an emerging pupa, both using this material. In his selection he gives 15 different deep pupae and 15 emergers. I will give an example of each here.

### Dark Grey Deep Pupa · LaFontaine · USA

| | |
|---|---|
| *Hook* | Mustad 94840, various sizes |
| *Thread* | Grey |
| *Underbody* | Medium grey fur (half) and dark brown fur (half), mixed and dubbed; sparkle yarn (Antron) |
| *Overbody* | Grey sparkle yarn |
| *Legs* | Lemon wood-duck or dark grey hen hackle fibres beneath and at the sides of the body |
| *Head* | Dark grey marabou fibres or grey fur |

The emergent equivalent has a rudimentary wing of coastal deer hair.

### Dark Grey Emergent Pupa · LaFontaine · USA

| | |
|---|---|
| *Hook* | Mustad 94840, various sizes |
| *Thread* | Grey |
| *Underbody* | Medium grey fur (half) and dark brown fur (half), mixed and dubbed |
| *Overbody* | Grey sparkle yarn |
| *Wing* | Dark grey deer hair |
| *Head* | Grey marabou or grey fur |

Other colours in the LaFontaine series are: Brown & Yellow, Brown & Bright Green, Ginger, Brown, Black, Grey & Yellow, Grey & Brown, Grey & Green, Brown & Orange, Brown & Dark Blue, Black & Yellow, White, White & Bright Green, Tan & Pale Green. All patterns are tied in more or less the same way, as follows.

*Step 1* For the Deep Pupa pre-weight the hook with lead or copper wire, then take the thread down the shank. I always coat the lead and the thread with a little varnish at this stage as an anti-slip device; this prevents the lead and the subsequent dressing from turning around the hook.

*Step 2* At the tail end tie in a bunch of sparkle yarn already teased out. Onto the tying thread dub on the fur/sparkle yarn mixture.

*Step 3* Take the fur-laden thread up the shank and form the body.

*Step 4* Divide and separate the sparkle yarn and take half over the back, so that it covers the back and halfway down the sides.

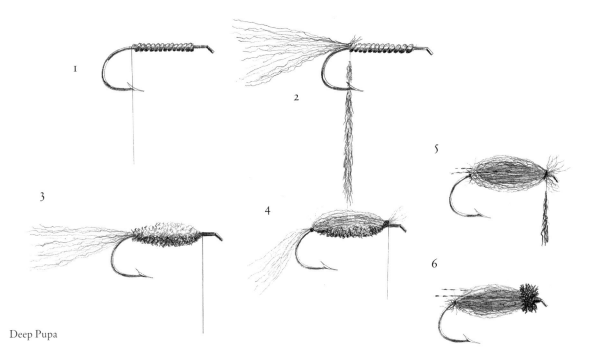

Deep Pupa

*Step 5* Repeat with the remaining sparkle yarn underneath the hook and up the sides, so that the body is more or less covered by the yarn. At each side tie in a few fibres of lemon wood-duck, and dub some fur or brown marabou onto the tying thread.

*Step 6* Wind on the head and finish the fly as usual.

For the Emergent Pupa the tying is the same as for Step 5 then, instead of the lemon-duck fibres, a sparse bunch of deer hair is tied in on the top of the hook to form a wing.

The Grannom, in this instance the American species, is one of the few caddis to have an imitation tied to represent the pupal stage. In Chapter 4 I gave patterns devised by Halford and Skues to represent the larvae of the British species. This following pattern is tied possibly to represent the American species, *Brachycentrus americanus*.

### Grannom Pupa
#### (*Brachycentrus americanus*) · USA

| | |
|---|---|
| *Hook* | Mustad 3906, sizes 12–16 |
| *Thread* | Brown |
| *Body* | Australian opossum or similar reddish-brown fur |
| *Rib* | Fine gold wire |

| | |
|---|---|
| *Wings* | Grey mallard wing quill slips tied short either side of body |
| *Legs* | Brown partridge tied beneath the hook |
| *Head* | Dark brown fur (beaver) |

The following pattern, created by Polly Rosborough, imitates the large orange sedge (*Discosmoecus*), which hatches out on a number of Oregon rivers in late summer.

### Dark Emergent Caddis
#### (*Discosmoecus* spp.) · Rosborough · USA

| | |
|---|---|
| *Hook* | Mustad 3906B, size 10 |
| *Thread* | Black |
| *Body* | Burnt-orange yarn |
| *Rib* | Burnt-orange thread |
| *Legs* | Dark furnace cock hackle extending the length of the body with the fibres removed from the top and bottom |

JAPANESE PATTERNS

I have read that the caddis species *Brachycentrus americanus* is also found on some of the rivers in Japan, including the Akan. The following pattern is one by Masao Sakaguchi; he uses a special hook available only in Japan. The nearest available here is the Partridge Piggy Back Hook Z14.

**Brachycentrus Caddis Pupa** · Sakaguchi · Japan

| | |
|---|---|
| *Hook* | Partridge Z14, sizes 10–14 |
| *Thread* | Black |
| *Body* | Bright green synthetic fur |
| *Rib* | Pearl Flashabou |
| *Thorax* | Dark brown blended synthetic fur |
| *Head* | As thorax |
| *Eyes* | Burnt monofilament |
| *Wing* | Slips of dark brown goose |
| *Antennae* | Brown mallard fibres |

**Dinathrodes Pupa** · Tashiro · Japan

| | |
|---|---|
| *Hook* | Mustad 94840 or similar, sizes 12–14 |
| *Thread* | Brown |
| *Body* | Light brown synthetic fur mix |
| *Rib* | Gold wire (optional) |
| *Thorax* | Dark brown synthetic fur mix |
| *Eyes* | Burnt monofilament nylon |
| *Wing* | Dark grey duck or goose wing quill |
| *Legs* | Light red hackle fibres tied beneath the hook |
| *Antennae* | Brown mallard fibres |

## NEW ZEALAND PATTERNS

Alan Pye, who built the Huka Lodge alongside Waikato River in New Zealand, created a number of patterns. The following is a pupa pattern.

**Pye's Nymph** · Pye · NZ

| | |
|---|---|
| *Hook* | Mustad 3906, sizes 10–12 |
| *Thread* | Brown |
| *Body* | Ginger fur tied full and plump |
| *Legs* | Ginger hackle tied sparsely and sloping backwards |

**Emerging Caddis** · Marsh · NZ

| | |
|---|---|
| *Hook* | Mustad 37160,* or Partridge Sedge Hook, sizes 18–20 |
| *Thread* | Brown |
| *Body* | Hare fur, including grey underbody, and black seal fur, mixed |
| *Thorax* | As body |
| *Wing case* | Mottled turkey |
| *Legs* | Hare fur guard hairs |

*The Mustad 37160 is a much larger hook than its rating suggests. If the Partridge Hook is used, then I would suggest using sizes 12–14.

Fly-tiers throughout New Zealand are producing a number of new pupa and other nymph patterns, most of which have not yet been published. I think that, before long, another book on modern New Zealand patterns will be required.

## FLOATING PUPAE

Occasionally, for various reasons, some pupae become trapped in the surface film. A number of patterns have been evolved to imitate the floating pupae. The following three flies are representative of such imitations.

### Moser's Floating Pupa · Moser · Austria

| | |
|---|---|
| *Hook* | Mustad 3904A or Partridge G3A, sizes 10–14 |
| *Thread* | Brown |
| *Tail* | Deer hair |
| *Body* | Natural or brown deer hair, tied along the hook and not spun |
| *Head* | Thin polyurethane foam |

### Floating Micro-pupa · Antunez · Spain

| | |
|---|---|
| *Hook* | Mustad 9578A, sizes 18–20 |
| *Thread* | Olive or brown |
| *Body* | Green seal fur (or substitute) |
| *Rib* | Brown silk |
| *Thorax* | Brown seal fur (or substitute) |

### Floating Pupa · USA

| | |
|---|---|
| *Hook* | Mustad 9672, sizes 12–18 (can be bent to shape) |
| *Thread* | Black |
| *Body* | Sparse clipped deer hair |
| *Thorax* | Fluorescent lime ostrich |
| *Legs* | Grey partridge |

## FISHING THE CADDIS

Trout will actively seek larvae from the bottom of the lake or river. They have been known to 'browse' on such creatures as they crawl along the bottom, so it would seem reasonable to assume that an imitation inched along the bottom should prompt the correct response from the trout. It is more certain that trout will take larvae whose fragile hold on the rocks and stones has been broken by a strong current; these larvae drift helplessly in the main body of the water. Likewise dead drifting artificials will bring positive results. The same thing applies to the pupae; in their rise from the bottom to the surface, it is obvious that they are going to be carried some considerable way by the current before emerging, so fish the pupae on rivers in a dead drift. The video by Roman Moser, *Fishing the Caddis*, illustrates this method well.

On stillwater, caddis pupae are best fished in the sink-and-draw method, i.e. by casting the pupa out on a fairly long leader, allowing it to sink, then retrieving the line in long, steady pulls with pauses in between. This imitates the rise of the natural insect through the main body of the water.

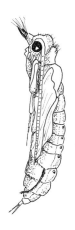

Caddis pupa

# CHAPTER EIGHT

# DAMSELS AND DRAGONS

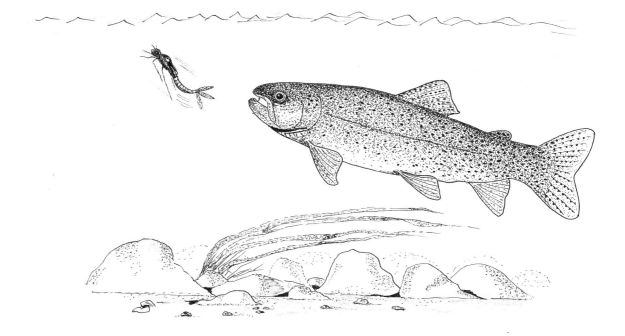

Millions of years before Man walked the face of the earth, dragonflies flew amid the giant feathery ferns. They have been around almost unchanged since then. Fossil evidence shows that at one time at least one species had a wing span of over 3ft (90cm). They must have looked quite formidable as they flew over the steaming swamps and marshes, presumably seeking insect prey that may have been proportionally as large. This was the Jurassic period when their only company was the dinosaurs. If an adult was that large, the nymphs must have been at least 2ft (60cm) long. Perhaps it is a good thing that such species have gone the same way as the dinosaur because it would certainly add an element of danger to wading! I feel sure their formidable jaws would fit neatly around my skinny ankles.

Both groups of insects belong to the insect order Odonata, the slim-bodied damselflies belonging to

the sub-order Zygoptera and the larger, more robust dragonflies to the sub-order Anisoptera. There is one other primitive sub-order, Aniso-zygoptera, represented by a single species in Japan. Of the two main sub-orders, the damselflies are the more important as far as fly-fishing is concerned because, on most waters, they are found in far greater numbers than their larger cousins. For this reason, there are more imitations of the damsel nymph than of the dragonfly nymph. Nevertheless, the larger nymphs of the dragonfly can be an effective pattern on most stillwaters.

It is not usual for the fly-tier to imitate a particular species, although Ernest Schwiebert attempts to do this in his book, *Nymphs*. Most fly-tiers create broad-spectrum patterns in a wide variety of colours selected to match the naturals found in the water; they are not generally interested in individual species. The usual colours are shades

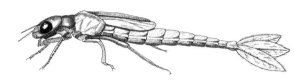

Damselfly nymph

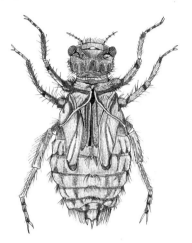

Dragonfly nymph

of brown, green, tan, olive, watery olive and, in some cases, almost black.

Distinguishing between the damsel and dragonfly nymphs is very simple. The damsel nymphs are long and slim with three flat tails (lamellae), which are, in effect, breathing appendages. The dragonfly nymphs on the other hand are bulky and fat, with no obvious tails, and the end of the abdomen bears short spikes. The dragonfly nymph breathes through a special chamber in the anus. The measure of a successful fly is the number of fish that it fools. Damsel and dragonfly nymphs are among the easiest to construct. Damsel nymphs must be tied slim with an active tail to simulate the lamellae. Dragonfly nymphs, on the other hand, must be tied bulky because they are fat, substantial creatures, a good mouthful for the ever-hungry trout. The two creatures are predators and, like all predators, they spend much of their time slowly stalking their prey. This tells us that the artificial must be fished comparatively slowly. When a damsel nymph is disturbed, e.g. by a trout, it puts on a fair turn of speed and moves with great undulations of the body in what best can be described as a sinuous wiggle. Dragonflies cannot do this; they escape by blowing water out of the breathing chamber in the anus – a primitive form of jet propulsion.

The common species described are those that I consider to be the species of most significance for the fly-fisherman in the UK. Compared with the rest of the world, the UK is not served very well by the order Odonata; there are just 42 species, some of which are on the decline due to habitat loss and the indiscriminate use of various pesticides and insecticides in agriculture. By noting the species of the adults flying in an area, the angler can determine which nymphs are likely to be found within a stream or lake. Common sense will tell you that, if there are large numbers of adults, the water will hold equally large numbers of nymphs.

## DAMSELFLIES

### NATURALS

**BANDED AGRION (Agrion splendens)**
This species prefers fast-flowing rivers with muddy bottoms. The adult is easily recognized by its metallic colour, blue in the male and green in the female. The male has a blue band across its wings, and the females have greenish-tinged wings. The *Agrion* nymphs have well-pronounced, forward-facing antennae.

Size of mature nymphs: 1¼–1¾in (30–45mm). Emergence: mid-May to August.

*Agrion* damselfly nymph

## BEAUTIFUL DEMOISELLE (Agrion virgo)

A creature of fast-flowing rivers with stony or pebble bottoms, this species is very similar to the previous damsel but the wing of the male is an overall brown. The female also has brownish wings. The nymph is very similar in appearance to that of *A. splendens*.

Size of nymph: 1¼–1¾in (30–45mm). Emergence: mid-May to September.

## LARGE RED DAMSEL FLY (Pyrrhosoma nymphula)

This red-bodied damsel, with black markings on the tip of the abdomen, is one of the earliest to hatch out. It occurs in a wide variety of waters, from slow-moving rivers to almost stagnant ponds. In past years, however, I have seen large numbers on the River Torridge in Devon and, at those times, this was anything but slow-flowing.

Size of nymph: (¾–⅞in), 20–22mm. Emergence: May to mid-August.

## COMMON BLUE DAMSEL (Enallagma cyathigerum)

One of the most widely distributed species in the UK and Europe, this damsel prefers large lakes with plenty of marginal vegetation. The adult male has a bright blue abdomen with black banding. The female is usually a sombre, dark-straw colour, although there are also variant blue female forms. The nymph has a tinge of olive-green.

Size of nymph: ¾–1in (20–25mm). Emergence: mid-May to mid-September.

## BLUE-TAILED DAMSEL (Ischnura elegans)

Also known as the common ischnura, this damselfly, as its name suggests, is one of the most common in the UK. It is recognized by its dark body with a bright blue band on the eighth abdominal segment. It favours slow rivers, ponds, small lakes and boggy areas. Size of nymph: ⅝–¾in (15–20mm). Emergence: end of May to end of September.

## COMMON COENAGRION (Coenagrion puella)

Also known as the azure damselfly, this species favours weedy ponds, canals and slow-moving rivers. Like the common blue damsel, the males are blue with black markings. The female is darker, with yellow markings on the abdomen near the thorax. The nymphs are mostly brown, rarely green.

Size of nymph: ¾–1in (20–25mm). Emergence: mid-May to mid-August.

## GREEN LESTES (Lestes sponsa)

In some areas this species is known as the emerald damselfly and is fairly well distributed. As its name indicates, the adult insects, both male and female, are of an emerald-green colour. This damselfly rests with its wings half-open. Its favoured habitats are rush-fringed lakes and large ponds.

Size of nymphs: 1–1½in (25–35mm). Emergence: mid-June to end of September.

\* \* \*

There have been a number of occasions during my fishing life when I have been astounded and enthralled by the great numbers of hatching damselflies. One occasion occurred on the River Torridge in Devon when large numbers of red damsels carpeted the river as they mated and oviposited. Surprisingly, this frantic activity did not seem to interest the trout one little bit. The other occasions happened many miles away from this West Country river, and all of them will remain in that part of my memory that I reserve for all the goods times I have spent on the water.

Lake Lenore lies in the scab lands of eastern Washington State, in the American northwest, a hot, semi-arid land carved by a giant, cataclysmic flood and fashioned by volcanoes many ages ago. It is an alkaline lake, set like a jewel amid this hot desert and fringed by basalt cliffs, making a suitable backdrop for a Western film. The lake was stocked a number of years back with Lahotan cut-throat trout, a strain of cut-throat trout that originally came from Nevada. This fish is one of the largest game-fish in North America and, although we did not catch ultra-large fish during our visit, we were happy with fish up to 6lb (2.7kg). As we paddled across the lake in our float tubes, thousands upon thousands of damsels hatched, the nymphs crawling all over our tubes and our clothing in what can only be described as a mega-hatch or, as our American cousins would probably now say, 'A mother of all hatches'. The damsel nymph on Lenore must surely be a prime food source for the trout.

Thousands of miles away across the Pacific we find the anglers' Eldorado – New Zealand – another country fashioned by volcanoes. Lake Otamangakua is a man-made lake near Taupo in North Island, a water famous for its trophy-sized

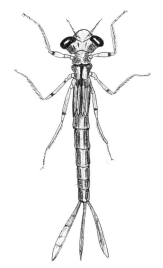

Damselfly nymph

**Damselflies of Angling Significance in the USA**

| Scientific Name | Common Name |
| --- | --- |
| Agria violacea | Purple Damsel or Civil Bluet |
| Enallagma civile | Bright Olive |
| Hataerina americana | Great Olive Damsel |
| Ischnura barberi | Barber's Forktail |
| I. verticalis | Medium Olive Fork-tail |
| Lestes disjunctus | Speckled Olive |
| L. inaequalis | Dark Olive Damsel |

Australia, South Africa, Argentina and Chile all have large numbers of damsels, as well as dragonflies, and perhaps one day will be produced in a fly-fishing book devoted to their native flies.

## ARTIFICIALS

Both C.F. Walker, in *Lake Flies and Their Imitation*, and Joscelyn Lanc, in *Lake and Loch Fishing*, give examples of artificial damsel nymphs. Bill Blades, in *Fishing Flies and Fly Tying*, gives examples of realistic patterns to imitate both the damsel and the dragonfly nymph. These books are among the first to give an importance to the damselfly nymph and, although these flies will still catch their fair share of trout, other more recent patterns have superseded them.

Unless the fly is devised to float or to be fished close to the surface, all the patterns given can be weighted with lead or copper wire if so desired. The reader will note that most of the patterns given are various shades of olive, although I would think that there are as many, if not more, brown natural nymphs than olive ones. By changing the colour of the material from olive to brown, darker variations can be achieved. I have had success with damsel nymphs that were black in colour.

### BRITISH AND EUROPEAN PATTERNS

The first of the patterns is a very basic fly indeed but, over the years, it has accounted for many fish for me. It can best be described as a simple Stick Fly.

brown and rainbow trout. On this water the air was alive with the whirring wings of red damselflies. At any one time, at least half-a-dozen pairs could be mating on our fishing hats, such was their number. They formed a thin red line the length of our resting fly-rods. It is little wonder that, on this water, the damsel nymph fly is considered to be one of the most killing of patterns.

A couple of years ago, during a hot August, not the best time for fishing anywhere, I was in the mountains of central Spain, fishing the upper reaches of the Tajo, one of the main rivers of the Iberian peninsula. On this particular river the dazzling blue *Agrion* damsels were on the wing, fluttering in weak flight along the entire stretch of water, their dark wings rustling like the sound of dead leaves in a breeze. The bankside vegetation changed to dark blue with these insects as they coupled. Without a doubt a damsel nymph would have been the right fly to use on this river a few weeks earlier.

The two most important species found in New Zealand are the red damsel *Xanthocnemis zealandica* and the blue damsel *Austrolestes colensonis*. There are, of course, other species found in the Antipodes but these two in particular have had flies tied to represent the nymphal stage.

When it comes to the USA, we have the problem of almost too many species to consider. There are approximately 450 different species of Odonata compared to the meagre 42 in the UK. The following shortlist of nymphs are but half a dozen of those that have interested the American angler.

Damselfly Stick

**Green-tail Damsel** · Price · UK

*Hook*      Mustad 79850, sizes 8–14
*Thread*    Olive
*Tail*      Fluorescent green silk or wool
*Body*      Olive and brown fur, mixed with a small amount of fluorescent orange fur (I once used natural seal fur but these days tend to use SLF or similar dubbing)
*Rib*       Fluorescent green silk or gold wire
*Hackle*    Olive partridge

The next pattern and its variations are a little more realistic but again fairly simple to tie. The hook I use in the dressing is called the Swimming-nymph hook, a pattern now produced by most of the world's hook-makers, including Partridge of Redditch (the K6ST) and, more recently, O. Mustad & Son of Norway (the 80150BR). The flies are tied upside-down in the hope of imparting a little more action and realism to the fly when retrieved.

**Swimming Olive Damsel** · Price · UK

*Hook*      Swimming-nymph Hook, sizes 8–14, weighted on the underside with a strip of lead
*Thread*    Olive
*Tail*      Short tuft of olive marabou, lighter than the body (the best, if you can get it, is the small slipper marabou)
*Body*      Medium olive and light brown dubbing mixed with a small amount of orange or dyed goose or turkey feather fibre to give a slimmer body
*Rib*       Oval gold tinsel
*Thorax*    As body
*Wing case* Olive Raffene
*Hackle*    Olive partridge
*Eyes*      Black bead or burnt nylon

Swimming Olive Damsel

**Brown Damsel** · Price · UK

As for the above, except:
*Tail*      Brown marabou
*Body*      Dark brown dubbing with a small amount of orange added (or brown turkey or goose feather)
*Hackle*    Brown partridge

**Purple Damsel** · Price · UK

As for the Olive Damsel except:
*Tail*      Purple marabou
*Body*      Purple feather fibre
*Thorax*    Black dubbing
*Legs*      Black hen hackle

I know this variation is somewhat unrealistic but I tied it because I had seen some South African dragonfly nymph patterns in this colour and, frankly, could not resist tying some damsels in the same overall shade. I have a thing about the colour purple. The first time I tried it out I took three rainbows in very quick succesion. Whether I would have taken them on more natural colours I do not know; perhaps the fish also had this thing about the colour purple! Over a 3-week period, the same nymph took in excess of 30 trout and one errant pike. Because purple is at the blue end of the spectrum, the fish may see it a little better. There are many modern steelhead patterns in use today tied in this most royal of colours.

Peter Lapsley is one of Britain's gifted angling writers and, at one time, ran a successful stillwater fishery in Hampshire. He is a believer in simplicity of fly design and his pattern to imitate the damsel nymph reflects this. This pattern is consistent fish-taker and I believe that the gold tinsel underbody is part of the reason for the fly's success because it shines through the fur dubbing, imparting and almost living glow.

**Golden Damsel Nymph** · Lapsley · UK

*Hook*        Mustad 79850, sizes 8–12
*Thread*      Bright yellow
*Tail*        Short tuft of cock-pheasant tail fibres
*Underbody*   Flat gold tinsel
*Abdomen*     Golden-olive, almost yellow, seal fur (or substitute)
*Rib*         Fine oval gold tinsel
*Thorax*      As abdomen
*Legs*        Grey partridge
*Head*        Bright yellow

Readers of *Trout Fisherman* will be familiar with the work of Bob Carnill, one of England's finest fly-tiers. For more years than I care to remember, the pages of this monthly magazine have been graced with Bob's innovative flies, creations that are the epitome of meticulous fly-tying. The following damsel nymph is one of his.

**Olive Damsel** · Carnill · UK

| | |
|---|---|
| *Hook* | Mustad 9671 or similar, sizes 12–14 |
| *Thread* | Green |
| *Tail* | Three olive cock hackle points |
| *Body* | Olive swan or goose herl |
| *Rib* | Fine oval gold tinsel |
| *Thorax* | Olive fur dubbing |
| *Wing case* | Olive feather fibre |
| *Legs* | Olive partridge hackle |
| *Eyes* | Olive-coloured beads with black pupils |

Olive Damsel

One of the most consistent captors of large fish from all types of water must be Pete Cockwill. Time and time again when I have been fishing with him he has caught not only more but inevitably larger fish than I have. I have come to the sad conclusion that Pete is a better fisherman that I am – but everybody knows that. The following pattern is one that he uses on some of the clearwater fisheries in Hampshire, during the time of the damselfly. This fly is similar to the American Wooly Bugger, both in design and in its action in the water.

**Long-tailed Damsel** · Cockwill · UK

| | |
|---|---|
| *Hook* | Mustad 79580, size 8, weighted with about 2in (5cm) of lead wire |
| *Thread* | Olive |
| *Tail* | Olive marabou, 1in (2.5cm) long |
| *Body* | Medium olive seal fur (two-thirds) and dark olive seal fur (one-third) |
| *Rib* | Yellow thread or oval gold tinsel |
| *Wing case* | Olive feather fibre |
| *Legs* | Long-fibred olive hen hackle |

The late Richard Walker has many flies to his credit and the Lamb's Wool Damsel Nymph is one. In his introduction to this fly in *Modern Fly Dressings*, he did not consider the damselfly to be an important element in the trout's diet. Today I feel sure he would have changed his mind for, without doubt, the damselfly larva is an integral part of the trout's larder, especially on most of the smaller stillwater fisheries.

**Lamb's Wool Damsel Nymph** · R. Walker · UK

| | |
|---|---|
| *Hook* | Mustad 79580, size 8 |
| *Thread* | Pale brown |
| *Tail* | Bunch of short olive-green cock-pheasant tail |
| *Body* | Equal parts of orange and cobalt-blue lamb's wool, tapered |
| *Rib* | Brown thread |
| *Legs* | Grass-green dyed grey partridge |

The damselfly nymph comes into its own for stillwater fly-fishing, whether on natural lakes, man-made ponds or fisheries. The European fly-fisherman is generally a river man and prefers to fish the tumbling stream and rippling brook; this is why there are so few damselfly nymph imitations to be found on the Continent.

Finland is a land of many lakes so it is not surprising that Finnish fishermen have come to appreciate the importance of the damselfly nymph during the summer months. The following pattern comes from the vice of Veli Autti.

**Damsel Nymph** · Autti · Finland

| | |
|---|---|
| *Hook* | Mustad 9671, sizes 10–12 |
| *Thread* | Olive |
| *Tail* | Three olive ostrich barbules |
| *Body* | Olive rabbit |
| *Thorax* | As body |
| *Legs* | Olive goose biots |
| *Eyes* | Silver bead chain |

Damsel Nymph (Finland)

Among the fishing fraternity the German tackle firm of Traun River Products is well known throughout Europe and the owner, Rudi Heger, is equally famous. The firm pioneered the sale of man-made products for fly-dressing. Wing materials, pre-printed for sedges and mayflies, and sheets of latex mottled to create realistic nymphs are just some of the products of this company. In their recent book, *Modernes und Einfaches Fliegenbinden*, Rudi Heger and Thomas Wolfle included patterns for both damsel and dragonfly nymphs using modern materials. I give two versions of their damsel here.

**Fluffy Damsel** · Wolfle · Germany

| | |
|---|---|
| *Hook* | Partridge H1A, sizes 6–10 |
| *Thread* | Brown |
| *Tail* | Short tuft of olive grizzle marabou |
| *Body* | Olive fluffy lead (a lead-wire wool twist) |
| *Legs* | Collar of olive grizzle marabou |
| *Head* | Olive Antron |
| *Eyes* | ⅛in (3mm) heavy glass eyes |

**Spectra Damsel** · Wolfle · Germany

| | |
|---|---|
| *Hook* | Partridge H1A, sizes 6–10 |
| *Thread* | Olive-brown |
| *Tail* | Spectraflash hair (similar to Crystal Hair) |
| *Body* | Olive fluffy lead with Spectraflash hair over the back |
| *Legs* | Collar of olive grizzle marabou |
| *Head* | Medium olive Antron |
| *Eyes* | ⅛in (3mm) glass eyes |

SOUTH AFRICAN PATTERNS

Trout were first successfully introduced into South Africa in 1890 and since that time have become the quarry of an ever-growing band of fly-fishermen. Before the establishment of proper hatcheries, a shipment of ova from the UK was kept alive in tanks at the local brewery in Cape Town. In South Africa, as far as the rivers are concerned, it is either feast or famine. Sometimes they rage in brown, swollen floods, carrying all before them – earth, trees, beast and man. At other times they diminish to mere trickles. It is a miracle that trout have survived at all in such a harsh and demanding environment. This contrast of drought and flood may account for the scarcity of mayflies and stoneflies in South African waters.

Most of the rivers that flow from the Drakensbergs contain either brown or rainbow trout, as do the streams in the eastern Cape. Even some of the thin waters of the western Cape still provide testing fly-fishing. The numerous dams or reservoirs to be found throughout the country, many on private farmlands, all contain fish, in most instances trout, but others are stocked with black bass, another successful introduction. In recent years a number of attractive man-made fisheries have also been established. With so much stillwater available it is little wonder that there are a number of patterns tied to represent the native species of damsels and dragonflies for, unlike the mayflies, these insects are to be found in profusion.

The first of the South African damsel-nymph patterns was created by Hugh Huntley. I had the great pleasure of travelling with him from Pietermaritzburg to the Drakensburgs to fish the famous Umzumkulu River. (*Umzumkulu* means 'big river'.) We sped up the road in a continual cloud of cigarette smoke as we chain-smoked the miles away. Here was a man that was not only, in all probability a much better fisherman than I, but he also smoked more than I did. I am told by some of Hugh's friends that, when he fishes this particular nymph, he first casts out, then lights a cigarette and only when he has finally smoked it down to the tip does he start the retrieve.

**Huntley's Damsel** · Huntley · S. Africa

| | |
|---|---|
| *Hook* | Mustad 79580, sizes 6–12 |
| *Thread* | Olive |
| *Tail* | Olive cock hackle tips |
| *Body* | Dark olive wool or seal fur |
| *Rib* | Oval gold tinsel |
| *Legs* | Soft-olive hen hackle |
| *Head* | Peacock herl |

Another pattern by Huntley uses red chenille for the eyes and mobile marabou for the tail. I am told that this pattern can be very deadly.

**Red-eyed Damsel Nymph** · Huntley · S. Africa

| | |
|---|---|
| *Hook* | Mustad 79580, sizes 8–12 |
| *Thread* | Brown |
| *Tail* | Brown marabou and two strands of Crystal Hair |
| *Body* | Brown marabou with Crystal Hair down the sides |
| *Thorax* | Brown marabou |
| *Head* | As thorax |
| *Eyes* | Red chenille |

The late John Beams was one of South Africa's best-known anglers with many flies to his credit. This simple damsel is one of his patterns.

**Beams' Damsel** · Beams · S. Africa

| | |
|---|---|
| *Hook* | Mustad 79580, sizes 8–10 |
| *Thread* | Black |
| *Tail* | Brown feather fibres |
| *Body* | Brown silk or wool, tapered |
| *Thorax* | Peacock herl |
| *Legs* | Natural red cock palmered through the thorax |

AMERICAN PATTERNS

In recent years the number of patterns evolved in the USA to imitate the various species of damselflies has been legion. The following patterns are but a small sample.

The grand old man of American fly-tying, Polly Rosborough, is renowned throughout the USA for his 'Fuzzy' flies. These look-alive patterns rely on the mobility of the materials used in their construction to impart a natural life to the fly. He is not of the school of direct imitation; his patterns are best classed as impressionistic. The following pattern is one of his.

**Green Damsel** · Rosborough · USA

| | |
|---|---|
| *Hook* | Mustad 79580, sizes 8–12 |
| *Thread* | Green-olive |
| *Tail* | Golden-olive marabou lighter than the body |
| *Body* | Medium olive Antron (or similar synthetic) |
| *Rib* | Length of the tying thread |
| *Wing tuft* | Olive marabou, darker than the body |
| *Legs* | Olive teal or mallard tied beneath the hook |

To my mind, Randall Kaufmann can best be described as a fly-tier's fly-tier. His many patterns are designed with one thing in mind and that is the catching of fish. All his flies are tied with plenty of mobility, the important factor in all good flies. His patterns imitating damsels and dragonfly nymphs are such flies, flies you can fish with confidence.

**Marabou Damsel** · Kaufmann · USA

| | |
|---|---|
| *Hook* | Mustad 9671, sizes 8–10 |
| *Thread* | Olive |
| *Tail* | Medium olive marabou |
| *Body* | As tail |
| *Rib* | Copper wire |
| *Wing tuft* | As tail |
| *Legs* | None |

In his book *Designing Trout Flies* Gary Borger gives many new and innovative patterns. Most of Gary's flies are what I would describe as no-nonsense flies. They are simple in concept and design and, as I have said many times, it is usually the simple fly that takes the trout. The next pattern is an imitation of the damselfly nymph.

**Marabou Damsel** · Borger · USA

| | |
|---|---|
| *Hook* | Mustad 3906, sizes 10–14 |
| *Thread* | Olive or brown |
| *Tail* | Tuft of marabou |
| *Body* | Dubbed marabou, one-third of the shank |
| *Thorax* | Dubbed marabou or fur |
| *Wing case* | Peacock herl |
| *Legs* | Guard hairs of the fur or marabou fibres picked out |

Borger also ties this pattern with mixed-colour marabou: brown and pale yellow, olive and brown and purple.

There are many examples of Dave Whitlock's flies in this book. His work is known throughout the fly-fishing world and his fly patterns are second to none. His Damsel Wiggle Nymph is considered by many to be one of the best.

**Damsel Wiggle Nymph** · Whitlock · USA

| | |
|---|---|
| *Rear hook* | Straight-eyed longshank, cut off at the bend |
| *Thread* | Olive or brown |
| *Tail* | Ostrich or marabou tips |
| *Abdomen* | Sparkle yarn (Antron or similar); Raffene (Swiss Straw) for back |
| *Rib* | Fine gold wire |
| *Front hook* | Mustad 94842, sizes 8–10, weighted with lead wire |
| *Thorax* | Sparkle yarn as for abdomen |
| *Wing case* | Raffene (Swiss Straw) |
| *Head* | Sparkle yarn with Raffene over the top |
| *Eyes* | Burnt nylon monofilament |
| *Linkage* | Fine piano wire (or similar) |

John Newbury of Chewelah, Washington State, also ties a similar pattern of wiggle nymph, but he cuts off the front hook, not the rear.

**Damsel Wiggle Nymph** · Newbury · USA

| | |
|---|---|
| *Rear hook* | Mustad 79671 or similar, sizes 12–14 |
| *Thread* | Light olive |
| *Tail* | Short tuft of light olive marabou |
| *Body* | Thinly dubbed olive synthetic fibre with light olive Raffene (Swiss Straw) over the back |
| *Breathing appendages* | Short tuft of olive marabou |
| *Front hook* | Short-shank, ring-eyed hook, about size 12 |
| *Thorax* | Olive synthetic dubbing well picked out to imitate the legs |
| *Wing case* | Light olive Raffene, which also goes over the head |
| *Head* | As thorax |
| *Eyes* | Black beads |

### FISHING THE DAMSEL NYMPHS

Damselfly nymphs can be fished at any depth. Sometimes it is best to fish the artificial close to the bottom in the vicinity of weed-beds. The artificial should be fished slowly, emulating the slow-stalking natural. Occasionally quicken the retrieve because, when disturbed by a large predator such as a fish, the damsel swims in a fast wriggling motion that usually prompts the trout to take. Some patterns are best fished just under the surface, imitating the behaviour of the real nymph as it makes its way up prior to hatching. On such occasions the fly should be retrieved fairly fast, with plenty of movement to the rod tip in order to activate the mobile tails of the fly.

# DRAGONFLIES _____

### NATURALS

The larger, more robust dragonflies are seldom, if ever, found in very great numbers; most species are territorial, driving off competitors from their particular stretch of water. Some species, however, are more numerous than others. The broad-bodied libellula, with bright blue-bodied males and yellow-bodied females, can often be seen in fair numbers, and the red common sympetrum is to be found in comparative abundance, usually towards the end of summer. But the largest of the common dragon-flies in the UK, such as the brown, southern and

Dragonfly nymph

common aeshnas, are solitary fliers, flitting and hovering close to the water, even flying at anglers to inspect them and investigate their intrusion into their domain. Because there are only one or two of these large darter, or hawker, dragonflies on the wing does not mean that there are only a few nymphs beneath the surface. There could be a considerable number because a single female can lay hundreds, if not thousands, of eggs.

The following British species are the most common and widely distributed and therefore probably of importance to the nymph-fisherman.

### BROWN AESHNA (Aeshna grandis)
Common from the Midlands southwards, this species breeds in lakes, ponds and slow-moving canals.

Size of nymph: 1¾–2¼in (45–56mm). Emergence: July to October.

### GOLD-RINGED DRAGONFLY (Corduligaster boltonii)
This species is found mainly in the southwest of England. I remember many years ago capturing a fine specimen at Fernworthy Reservoir in Devon; after photographing it I released it to grace somebody else's day. The nymph is a shy creature, covering itself in dead leaves and detritus. It ambushes its prey rather than actively stalking it as the other species do. Its preferred habitat is swift-moving, sandy-bottomed streams.

Size of nymph: 1½–1¾in (35–45mm). Emergence: end of May to August.

### COMMON SYMPETRUM (Sympetrum striolatum)
This reddish, medium-sized dragonfly is most abundant in southern England. It is found in ponds, lakes and slow-moving canals.

Size of nymph: about ⅝in (17–18mm). Emergence: mid-June to end of October.

### BROAD-BODIED LIBELLULA (Libellula depressa)
Still fairly common in the southeast of England, this species is found in ponds, lakes and slow-

moving canals. The nymph is short, stubby and hairier than many other dragonfly nymphs.

Size of nymph: about 1in (23–25mm). Emergence: mid-May to beginning of August.

\*     \*     \*

Patterns to imitate dragonfly nymphs figure highly in the fly-boxes of the American angler, especially since the growth of interest in stillwater fishing in recent years. A number of the many American species has been imitated by flydressers and the following four species are just a sample.

### Dragonflies of Angling Significance in the USA

| Scientific Name | Common Name |
|---|---|
| Aeshna constricta | Giant Dragonfly |
| Anax junius | Green Darner |
| Libellula pulchella | Ten-spot Skimmer |
| Sympetrum ribicundulum | Common Red Skimmer |

On most American waters which I have had the privilege to fish, damsels and dragonflies were found in profusion and I seemed to spend as much time photographing them as I did trying to pit my wits against the trout.

## ARTIFICIALS

The nymph of the dragonfly is one of the most ferocious predators found beneath the surface of the water. It will feed on a wide variety of creatures, including small fish. Some species will grow to at least 3in (70mm) or more and trout will feed avidly upon them if given the chance. In the UK there are very few patterns tied to imitate the large dragonfly nymph but, in other parts of the world, patterns abound.

### British and European Patterns

Many years ago I devised a simple dragonfly nymph pattern for use on the smaller stillwaters. It became one of the flies sold by the mail-order company run by Dermot Wilson at Nether Wallop Mill in Hampshire. When the Orvis Company took over the business, many of the flies on the original list continued to be sold under the Orvis banner. It is somewhat gratifying to see that this pattern of mine still remains on the Orvis list. I tied the original fly with a wool body. I bought the wool, a subtle mixture of dark brown and olive, at

a local shop and, after almost 20 years, I still have some left.

### Dragonfly Nymph · Price · UK

| | |
|---|---|
| Hook | Mustad 79580, sizes 6–10, weighted with lead wire |
| Thread | Brown |
| Tail | Two short points of brown or olive goose biots |
| Body | Olive-brown wool tied fat |
| Rib | Green or yellow thread |
| Legs | Brown partridge hackle |
| Head | Peacock herl |

A pattern similar to the above was created by Glyn Hopper, an excellent fly-tier from Kent, who runs a tackle business in the village of Lamberhurst near the famous fly-fishing reservoir, Bewl Water.

### Dragonfly Nymph · Hopper · UK

| | |
|---|---|
| Hook | Kamasan B830 medium shank, or similar |
| Thread | Black |
| Tail | Olive goose biots |
| Body | Green-olive seal fur |
| Rib | Fine oval silver tinsel |
| Thorax | Peacock herl |
| Legs | Olive partridge |
| Head | As thorax |

Hopper's Dragonfly Nymph

I tied up the next pattern using the versatile dubbing wicks. These fur-laden copper wire strands speed up the tying of flies and the resultant patterns look very good.

### Dubbing-wick Dragonfly Nymph · UK

| | |
|---|---|
| Hook | Mustad 79580, sizes 6–10 |
| Thread | Black |
| Tail | Very short goose biot spikes |
| Body | Two or three dubbing wicks of different natural colours (olive, brown-green, black, etc.) twisted together; the body is fatter at the rear and tapers towards the head |

Dubbing-wick Dragonfly Nymph

| | |
|---|---|
| *Legs* | Cock-pheasant tail fibres |
| *Eyes* | Dumb-bell eyes painted to match or contrast with body |
| *Head* | As body or dark brown dubbing wick |

The following pattern was created by the innovative fly-tier Davy Wotton.

**Wotton's Green Dragon** · Wotton · UK

| | |
|---|---|
| *Hook* | Partridge Straight-eyed Streamer, size 6 |
| *Thread* | Dark olive |
| *Tail* | Two goose biot tips |
| *Body* | Woven from dubbed olive SLF thread |
| *Rib* | Clear monofilament |
| *Thorax* | Dark olive SLF |
| *Wing case* | Olive Raffene |
| *Legs* | Knotted micro-chenille |
| *Head* | Olive SLF |
| *Eyes* | Red chenille |

Wotton's Green Dragon

The commercial fly-tying company of Fulling Mill Flies, based in Reigate, Surrey, has a wide and multi-national list of well-tied flies. Among its selections is an excellent dragonfly nymph pattern.

**Dark Brown Dragonfly Nymph** · Fulling Mill Flies · UK

| | |
|---|---|
| *Hook* | Mustad 79580 or similar, sizes 6–10 |
| *Thread* | Brown |
| *Tail* | Chestnut-brown marabou |
| *Body* | Chestnut-brown dubbing |
| *Thorax* | As body |
| *Wing case* | Dark turkey |
| *Legs* | Cock-pheasant tail fibres tied beneath |
| *Head* | As body |
| *Eyes* | Black beads |

I have already given a damsel nymph created by Veli Autti of Finland. The following fly is his dragonfly nymph. It is simple, realistic and highly effective.

**Dragon Nymph** · Autti · Finland

| | |
|---|---|
| *Hook* | Mustad 79580, sizes 8–14 |
| *Thread* | Black or brown |
| *Body* | Brown and grey marabou, mixed and dubbed |
| *Thorax* | As body |
| *Wing pads* | Cock-pheasant tail fibres |
| *Legs* | As wing pads |
| *Head* | As body |
| *Eyes* | Burnt monofilament nylon |

Dragon Nymph

Visits to a local wool, craft or hobby shop can often reward a tier with many useful materials. Roman Moser found a flat chenille material on one such visit and with it created the following dragonfly nymph.

**Moser Dragon** · Moser · Austria

| | |
|---|---|
| *Hook* | Partridge SH3, size 8 |
| *Thread* | Olive |
| *Tail* | Short tuft of olive grizzle marabou |
| *Body* | Olive-brown multi-coloured chenille |
| *Wing case* | Raffene |
| *Legs* | Sparse cock hackle fibres |
| *Head* | Brown or olive polypropylene dubbing |
| *Eyes* | Green or brown beads |

## NEW ZEALAND PATTERNS

The next pattern was given by Keith Draper in *Trout Flies in New Zealand*. It is one of his own tyings.

**Brown Dragonfly Nymph** · Draper · NZ

| | |
|---|---|
| *Hook* | Mustad 79580, sizes 8–12 |
| *Thread* | Brown |
| *Tail* | Short tuft of black squirrel |
| *Body* | Brown chenille |
| *Legs* | Brown partridge |

This next fly is slightly more complicated to tie because it has a woven body. This is also a New Zealand fly, created by the well-known fly-tier John Morton, of Christchurch. He calls the fly Annie's Nymph, Annie being a diminutive of Anisoptera.

**Annie's Nymph** · Morton · NZ

| | |
|---|---|
| *Hook* | Mustad 79580, sizes 8–12 |
| *Thread* | Black |
| *Underbody* | Green rabbit fur over lead |
| *Overbody* | Woven with olive and brown Swann-undaze, brown on top, olive below |
| *Legs* | Olive-green partridge |
| *Wing case* | Brown-mottled turkey |

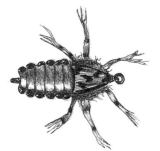

Annie's Nymph

Another Christchurch angler, R.K. Bragg, is responsible for the next two patterns. His work appears in Keith Draper's book. The first is almost like the traditional Woolly Worm.

**Bragg's Dragonfly Nymph** · Bragg · NZ

| | |
|---|---|
| *Hook* | Mustad 79580, sizes 8–10 |
| *Tail* | Barred squirrel tail tied short |
| *Body* | Fluorescent lime chenille |
| *Legs* | Soft mustard grizzle hackle palmered along the body |

**Dragonfly Kea Nymph** · Bragg · NZ

| | |
|---|---|
| *Hook* | Mustad 79580, sizes 8–12 |
| *Thread* | Broad |
| *Tail* | Green kea feather fibres (a natural greeny-grey feather) |
| *Body* | Brown seal fur (or substitute) tied fat |
| *Rib* | Copper wire |
| *Wing case* | Green kea feather, tips tied down to imitate the legs |
| *Legs* | See wing case |

Among a whole set of patterns sent to me from New Zealand was a dragonfly nymph tied by Martin Langlands of Christchurch. From what I can see, there are a lot of good fly-tiers in Christchurch and the following realistic dragonfly nymph bears witness to this

**Furry-foam Dragon** · Langlands · NZ

| | |
|---|---|
| *Hook* | Mustad 90240, sizes 8–10 |
| *Thread* | Olive |
| *Body* | Creamy-yellow dubbing, tied fat |
| *Back* | Light brown furry foam, the edges and the tip of the body marked with darker brown waterproof ink |
| *Rib* | Brown Swannundaze |
| *Thorax* | Dirty yellow dubbing |
| *Wing case* | Cock-pheasant tail fibres |
| *Legs* | Dirty yellow goose biots marked with waterproof ink |

Furry-foam Dragon

## SOUTH AFRICAN PATTERNS

Much of the fly-fishing in South Africa takes place on large and small reservoirs, known as 'dams'. The dragonfly nymph figures highly in the fly-wallets of most South African fly-fishermen. The following two patterns were sent to me by Andy Krajewski, now living in Stellenbosch in the western Cape. Andy is best known for his excellent saltwater patterns. The first uses spun and clipped klipspringer antelope hair and the second uses duiker hair. Both patterns can be weighted with lead wire.

## Klipspringer Dragonfly Nymph
Krajewski · S. Africa

| | |
|---|---|
| *Hook* | Mustad 79580, sizes 6–10 |
| *Thread* | Black |
| *Tail* | None |
| *Body* | Klipspringer (or deer) body hair, spun and clipped to shape |
| *Thorax* | Hare fur or similar |
| *Head* | As thorax |
| *Wing case* | Cock-pheasant tail fibres |
| *Eyes* | Black chenille |

## Duiker Dragonfly Nymph · Krajewski · S. Africa

| | |
|---|---|
| *Hook* | Mustad 79580, sizes 6–10 |
| *Thread* | Black |
| *Tail* | Fat bunch of duiker hair (or grey squirrel tail) |
| *Body* | As tail |
| *Thorax* | Dubbed duiker hair (or hare) |
| *Wing case* | Cock-pheasant tail fibres |
| *Head* | As thorax |
| *Eyes* | Black chenille |

AUSTRALIAN PATTERNS

Dragonfly nymphs in Australia and Tasmania are often called mud-eyes and there are a number of different patterns tied to represent them, many of which are just called Mud-eyes. The following pattern was tied up by Fulling Mill Flies for the Australian market.

## Mud-eye · Fulling Mill Flies · Australia

| | |
|---|---|
| *Hook* | Mustad 79580, sizes 8–10 |
| *Thread* | Brown |
| *Tail* | None |
| *Body* | Brown chenille |
| *Wing* | Hen-pheasant tail fibres |
| *Legs* | Brown partridge |
| *Head* | Light brown chenille |
| *Eye* | Green-glass eye |

I have seen other less complicated Mud-eye dressings with fat, tapered bodies of dubbed fur and lead dumb-bell eyes.

The next pattern was depicted by Charles Jardine in his excellent best-seller, *Sotheby's Guide To Fly Fishing*. The fly is a deer-hair creation used on the large lakes of Australia and waters such as Lake Pedlar in Tasmania, home of large, cruising brown trout.

## Cordallid · Australia

| | |
|---|---|
| *Hook* | Mustad 79580, sizes 4–10 |
| *Thread* | Black |
| *Body* | Deer hair spun and clipped |
| *Waist* | Black tying thread |
| *Wing* | Deer hair, unclipped |
| *Head* | As body |

This pattern can be weighted with lead wire before applying the deer hair.

The following pattern is named after Lake Jindabyne in New South Wales and is purported to represent a dragonfly nymph. I have to admit you have to stretch your imagination to accept this.

## Jindabyne Special · Australia

| | |
|---|---|
| *Hook* | Mustad 7958, sizes 2–12 |
| *Thread* | Black |
| *Tail* | Black or red wool tuft |
| *Body* | Black wool |
| *Thorax* | Black wool |
| *Wing* | One black and one royal-blue mallard tied flat on the top of the hook |
| *Hackle* | Orange, tied swept back alongside the body. |

I believe that many of the patterns from New Zealand that are similar to the Jindabyne special are taken by the trout as dragonfly larva. Flies such as the Mrs Simpson and, in South Africa, the standby of all South African anglers, the Walker's Killer, probably also work well as a dragonfly nymph.

AMERICAN PATTERNS

In the USA patterns to imitate the dragonfly larva are legion. They come in all shapes and sizes, and all types of materials are used in their construction. Some are extremely realistic; others are impressionistic. One of the first American tiers to experiment within the school of realism was, without doubt, Bill Blades. Examples of his ultra-real flies are depicted in his book, *Fishing Flies and Fly Tying*. His work is the forerunner of many more recent innovations. Among his patterns there are a number of damsel and dragonfly nymphs which are so realistic that they seem to be about to crawl off the page. Are these realistic patterns effective? In my opinion, a good impressionistic fly with plenty of movement will outfish them every time. The next pattern, conceived by Gary Borger, is such a fly.

**Fur Chenille Dragon** · Borger · USA

| | |
|---|---|
| *Hook* | Mustad 79580 or similar, sizes 2–8, weighted |
| *Thread* | Brown |
| *Body* | Dark brown fur spun on a loop of brown yarn |
| *Legs* | Rusty-brown pheasant rump |

Other colours are: natural rabbit on green yarn, or olive synthetic fur on olive yarn.

This type of fly is similar in concept to the Assam Dragon, a fly given by Charles E. Brookes in his classic book, *Nymph Fishing for Larger Trout*.

**Assam Dragon** · Brookes · USA

| | |
|---|---|
| *Hook* | Mustad 79580, sizes 4–10 |
| *Thread* | Brown |
| *Body* | Strip of rabbit or any other fur tied in and wrapped around the shank. |
| *Legs* | Large-fibred brown grizzle or pheasant body feather |

Yet another pattern in the same vein, with plenty of pulsating movement but different materials, is the Filoplume Dragon, a fly created by Gene Armstrong of Seattle. These soft, ultra-mobile feathers are being used more and more where once they were discarded.

**Filoplume Dragon** · Armstrong · USA

| | |
|---|---|
| *Hook* | Mustad 79580, sizes 4–10 |
| *Thread* | Brown or olive, depending on the colour being tied |
| *Tail* | Few mallard flank-feather fibres and cock-pheasant rump-feather fibres |
| *Body* | Brown or olive filoplume tied densely |
| *Rib* | Copper wire |
| *Thorax* | Dubbing rope of olive or brown angora with Antron well picked out underneath |
| *Wing case* | Blue-green cock-pheasant back feather |
| *Legs* | Tips of wing-case feather |

The last time I was in the USA I went into one of Randall Kaufmann's super fly shops. Although I tie most of my own flies I cannot resist buying other people's patterns and I suspect I am not alone in this. Two of the flies I bought were dragonfly nymph patterns, one floating and one sinking.

**Lake Dragon** · Kaufmann · USA

| | |
|---|---|
| *Hook* | Mustad 79580, sizes 4–8 |
| *Thread* | Olive or brown to match the pattern being tied |
| *Tail* | Olive or brown marabou tuft |
| *Body* | Olive or brown Haretron blended with a mixture of blue, purple, green, amber-brown and rust goat hair to provide highlights for the dubbing |
| *Rib* | Copper wire |
| *Thorax* | As body but not as wide |
| *Head* | As thorax |
| *Wing case* | Brown or olive turkey cut into a V-shape and lacquered |
| *Eyes* | ⅛in (3mm) glass beads or burnt nylon monofilament |

**Floating Dragon** · Kaufmann · USA

| | |
|---|---|
| *Hook* | Mustad 79580, sizes 4–8 |
| *Thread* | Olive |
| *Tail* | Olive grizzle marabou |
| *Body* | Spun and clipped olive deer hair, clipped flat underneath and the back marked with brown-olive waterproof ink |
| *Wing case* | Olive turkey feather cut into a V-shape and lacquered; the wing case should half cover the legs at the sides of the body |
| *Head* | Dark olive Antron |
| *Eyes* | Burnt nylon monofilament |

Floating Dragon

This pattern is ideal with a sunk line and short leader because the buoyancy of the deer hair keeps it off the bottom. On the retrieve the fly dives; when the retrieve is stopped the fly slowly rises.

I could not end this selection of American dragonfly-nymph patterns without including the dragonfly nymph of my friend Darrel Martin of Tacoma. Darrel is a wizard when it comes to weaving bodies and this pattern of his highlights this skill.

**Martin's Dragon** · Martin · USA

| | |
|---|---|
| *Hook* | Mustad 79580, sizes 6–8, with the shank slightly bent |
| *Thread* | Brown |
| *Tail* | None |
| *Body* | Woven with two chenilles of light and dark olive |
| *Legs* | Two bunches of knotted cock-pheasant tail fibres |
| *Head* | Dubbed olive marabou fibres |
| *Eyes* | Black bead chain or burnt nylon monofilament |

Martin's Dragon

CANADIAN PATTERNS

The next pattern was tied by Gerry Beck of Manitoba, Canada. He simply called it Gompus.

**Gompus** · Beck · Manitoba

| | |
|---|---|
| *Hook* | Mustad 79580, size 8 |
| *Thread* | Olive |
| *Body* | Green-olive wool or dubbing, weighted with lead and tied fat |
| *Thorax* | Medium olive dubbing |
| *Head* | As thorax |
| *Legs* | French-partridge hackle |
| *Eyes* | Burnt black monofilament or bead eyes |

The Superfly Company of Edmonton, Alberta, are purveyors of fine flies and on their extensive list is a chenille Dragon of excellent realism. It comes in brown, olive and black.

**Dragonfly Nymph** · Superfly Company · Alberta

| | |
|---|---|
| *Hook* | Mustad 79580, sizes 6–10 |
| *Thread* | Brown or black |
| *Body* | Chenille over polypropylene |
| *Thorax* | As body |
| *Wing case* | Brown yarn (optional) |
| *Legs* | Brown braided fishing line with dark grey or brown dubbing on the thigh portions |
| *Head* | As body |
| *Eyes* | Bead chain |

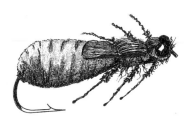

Dragonfly Nymph (Superfly)

*FISHING THE DRAGONFLY NYMPH*

I have found that all dragonfly nymphs are best fished a slow figure of 8 retrieve, with just the occasional spurt when the retrieve is almost complete.

# CHAPTER NINE

# MIDGES AND MOSQUITOES

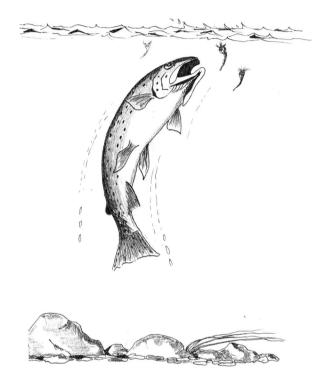

Larvae and pupae of the aquatic Diptera are important creatures in the food cycle of both rivers and stillwater and, of all the aquatic Diptera, the Chironomidae are probably the most significant. In some waters these non-biting midges hatch out in veritable clouds and it has been noted that densities of larvae on the bottom of some waters can number between 10,000 and 100,000 per square yard. Now that is a lot of midge by anybody's stretch of the imagination and it is little wonder that they are a prime food source for fish, including trout.

The phantom midges (Chaoboridae) also play a part in the diet of fish. These small, almost transparent larvae and pupae can also be found in large numbers in stillwater. The mosquitoes (Culicidae) that whine and dine, usually on me, are also taken by fish. The small *Dixa* midges (of the family Dixidae) are sometimes found in sufficient numbers to interest trout and other fish but are of lesser importance. Aquatic crane flies (Tipulidae) and their larvae have been imitated by fly-tiers on both sides of the Atlantic. Some horse flies (Tabanidae) and hover flies (Syrphidae) have aquatic larvae, many of which are large and plump, forming an occasional juicy morsel for fish.

The blackflies (Simuliidae) of fast-flowing streams are also preyed on by fish but few patterns exist because they are so small. Nevertheless they make their presence felt. I remember one occasion in northern Quebec when I covered myself in insect repellent but forgot the exposed area at my sleeve cuffs. The result was something like 20 bites on each forearm and excruciating itching all night.

## CHIRONOMID MIDGES

### NATURALS

The larvae of this family are slender and rounded, generally with 12 body segments behind the head. They have two false legs at the front and two at the rear. The mature larva can vary in size from $1/16$in to over $3/4$in (2mm to over 20mm), depending on the species. Those species that live in deeper water are generally red in colour because of the haemoglobin within their system; they are commonly known as bloodworms. Those that live in shallower water are often colourless, yellowish or, sometimes, green. Most species build web-lined tunnels in which they mature to the pupal stage. Other species trundle along the bottom in a detritus-covered shelter. Larvae of the species *Chironomus* and *Tanypus* have been found in the deepest part of Lake Geneva, Switzerland, and chironomids have also been dredged up from 330ft (100m) in Lake Taupo, New Zealand.

From time to time, the larva will leave the sanctuary of its tunnel to visit the better-oxygenated

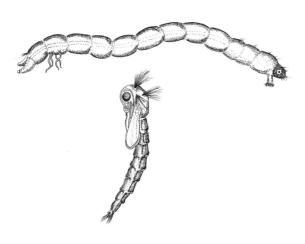

Chironomid larvae and pupa

levels of the water and replenish its oxygen supply. It absorbs the gas through its skin. Once satisfied with another shot of oxygen it wriggles back down to the bottom where it quickly constructs a new tunnel. This migration to oxygenated water levels is the danger time for the bloodworm, the time when it is likely to be preyed on by a number of different species of fish, including trout. On lakes and reservoirs, after a period of windy weather, the mud of the shoreline is often churned up by the action of wind and wave, and creatures such as chironomids, that live in the mud are washed out of their chambers and hiding-holes. Trout often patrol these muddy margins in search of such 'wash-out' food.

The chironomid starts to pupate in its tunnel or just outside. Unlike the larva the pupa has breathing filaments situated on top of the thorax. When it is time to emerge the pupa rises in the water, into the vulnerable area just below the surface. If the conditions and surface tension are right, it adopts a horizontal posture and the adult fly breaks out of the pupal skin. Some people believe that the pupa rises to the surface to test the tension and, if it is not right, descends again, rising and falling until the conditions are amenable to hatching. In the past chironomid midges have always been thought of as creatures of stillwaters and imitations of the insect have been used on lakes and reservoirs, but in recent years the use of such midges on rivers has increased. John Goddard has often written on this subject, for he has caught many good-sized fish on rivers such as the Test in Hampshire by observing the trout feeding on the midge.

There are 400–500 identified species of chironomid in the UK. In the USA the figure would be somewhere about 2,000. New species are being identified around the world each year. The species most frequently mentioned in angling books is *C. plumosus*, but the descriptions show such a divergence in size and colour that I tend to agree with John Goddard when he says that they may well be subspecies and may eventual be reclassified. Another common species that thrives in water with some sewage pollution is *C. riparius*.

The following list includes species mentioned in various angling books. As further scientific studies are carried out on this much neglected insect, this list will no doubt become longer. In the UK, chironomids are generally known as 'buzzers'. In Germany the term 'buzzer' (*brummer* in German) is reserved for the blowflies (Calliphoridae).

## Chironomid Midges of the UK

| Scientific Name | Common Name |
| --- | --- |
| Camptochironomus tentans | Yellow-striped Midge* |
| Chironomus anthracinus | Blue & Black Midge (Black Midge) |
| Ch. plumosus | Golden Dun Midge |
| Ch. plumosus | Grey Boy (Orange & Silver Midge) |
| Ch. plumosus | Large Green Midge |
| Ch. plumosus | Large Red Midge |
| Ch. plumosus | Olive Midge |
| Ch. riparius | Brown Midge* |
| Endochironomus albipennis | Blagdon Green Midge |
| Glyptotendipes pallipes | Small Brown Midge |
| Microtendipes pedellus | Small Red Midge |
| Polypedilum nebuculosus | Small Black Midge |

*Author's term.

The following list is of midges found in American waters which have been mentioned in various publications. There are of course many hundreds, if not thousands, more.

## Chironomid Midges of the USA

| Scientific Name | Scientific Name |
| --- | --- |
| Chironomus plumosus | C. stigmaterus |
| C. lobifera | C. utahensis |
| C. modestus | Tanypus arcticus |
| C. nigritus | T. carneus |

In New Zealand, *Chironomus zealandicus* is a common species.

In John Robert's book *A New Illustrated Dictionary of Trout Flies*, a reference and patterns are given for a *Dixa* Midge. The source of this information was the late Alec Pearlman, who published an article in *Trout & Salmon* way back in 1978. The article describes a certain midge that hatched from his local water. He eventually came to the conclusion, after seeking advice, that it was a species of *Dixa*, namely *D. aestivalis*. From his description, and from the appearance of this fly in the small black-and-white photograph, I doubted this identification; also his fly was twice as big as any known *Dixa*. I corresponded with him on this matter and, after a while, he was able to furnish me with some specimens. On seeing these flies, I was still convinced that I was looking at a species of chironomid and sent some to the Natural History Museum in London for identification. They told me it was *Camptochironomus tentans*.

By coincidence, 12 months later, another article appeared in *Trout & Salmon*, describing at length the midges of the author's water and mentioning and describing *C. tentans*. Alec Pearman, on reading this article, and armed with the information that I had passed on to him, wrote a letter to the magazine stating that his original fly may have been misidentified. For the record, *C. tentans* is a medium-sized midge with a jet-black abdomen and distinct yellow stripes on the thorax.

## ARTIFICIALS

Trout-fishing in the British Isles since World War Two has centred very much on stillwaters. Large public reservoirs, stocked with brown and rainbow trout and close to urban areas, have made fly-fishing available to many more people than in the past. The creation of many smaller put-and-take trout fisheries has also added to the area of water available. Flies and methods developed on such waters have made the British angler second to none when it comes to stillwater fishing. This is reflected in the number of patterns created to imitate the larval and pupal forms of the midges. There are more patterns in the UK than in the rest of the world put together. In Europe the number of fly-fishermen is small when compared with the UK and certainly with the fly-fishermen of the USA. Both the Americans and the Continentals have centred their fishing on rivers, largely neglecting the stillwater scene. This is now changing in the USA and the number of books and articles in the angling press on fishing lakes is certainly increasing.

In South Africa most fishermen are accomplished in stillwater fishing because good trout rivers are few and far between, and fishing is more easily available on the many dams and reservoirs. Until recently, the flies used in South African waters were British and American in origin but that is now changing as a new breed of angler-tier begins to imitate the indigenous insects.

New Zealand is a land of many lakes, and even more rivers, and the choice of the true New Zealand angler is, I am sure, to fish the fast-flowing streams, stalking large trout. When it comes to lake-fishing, the New Zealand angler has, in the past, contented himself with large lure-type flies and, even today, the most common method of catching fish on lakes such as Taupo is to trail one's flies behind a moving boat. I was lucky in my choice of guides when I was in that lovely country. Brian Hussey in North Island fished almost exclusively with nymphs and dry flies and Frank Schlosser in South Island did the same thing. Whether we fished Lake Otamangakua for rainbows with Damsel Nymphs or Lake Benmore in South Island with Pheasant Tails it was excellent small-fly-fishing.

### LARVA IMITATIONS

#### BRITISH PATTERNS

This first pattern, which I developed about 20 years ago, has stood the test of time. The fly is still included in the Orvis range of flies for the UK. It may be weighted.

**Marabou Bloodworm** · Price · UK

| | |
|---|---|
| *Hook* | Mustad 79671, sizes 12–14 |
| *Thread* | Red |
| *Tail* | Red marabou |
| *Body* | Red silk tied with undulations |
| *Rib* | Fluorescent red silk |
| *Head* | Peacock herl |

I tend to use this next pattern of mine more than any other.

**Swannundaze Bloodworm** · Price · UK

| | |
|---|---|
| *Hook* | Swimming-nymph Hook, sizes 10–14 |
| *Thread* | Red |
| *Tail* | Short tuft of fluorescent red floss |

| | |
|---|---|
| *Underbody* | Fluorescent red floss |
| *Overbody* | Clear or brown Swannundaze |
| *Head* | Red silk or red copper wire |

Swannundaze Bloodworm

Another effective colour combination is transparent yellow Swannundaze over red fluorescent silk. Fish often take these flies on the drop as they slowly and erratically fall through the water.

I gave a Peter Lapsley damsel fly pattern in the last chapter. This fly of his also uses marabou to give the pattern integral life.

### Wobble-worm · Lapsley · UK

| | |
|---|---|
| *Hook* | Partridge K2B, sizes 12–14 |
| *Thread* | Red |
| *Tail* | Red marabou |
| *Underbody* | Silver Lurex |
| *Overbody* | Red seal fur (or substitute) |
| *Head* | Lead split shot painted red |

Lapsley also gives both a green and a buff version, using a gold underbody and appropriately coloured seal fur and head.

John Roberts, in his *New Illustrated Dictionary of Trout Flies*, gives this pattern by Chris Kendall, which was Optima power gum, an elastic material normally used as a shock-absorber between the leader and the fly-line.

### Bloodworm · Kendall · UK

| | |
|---|---|
| *Hook* | Partridge K2B, sizes 8–18 |
| *Thread* | Red |
| *Tail* | Red marabou |
| *Body* | Red Optima power gum (red silk on the small sizes) |
| *Thorax* | Weighted with lead wire covered with an equal mixture of red and olive seal fur |

An ultra-simple pattern, the Chammy Bloodworm, relies on the natural mobility of chamois leather. The free ends of the leather move enticingly in the water and, on retrieve, look very much like a natural bloodworm in their movement. I was first shown this fly by Brian Clarke, but I am not certain of the originator.

### Chammy Bloodworm · UK

| | |
|---|---|
| *Hook* | Mustad 79672, sizes 10–14 |
| *Thread* | Red |
| *Body* | Thin strip of red chamois leather, tied in the middle of the hook with both ends free |

One of the finest anglers ever to fish the banks of the large Midlands reservoirs was without doubt Arthur Cove. A number of flies have been credited to him and the Red Diddy is a very simple one, which he created to imitate the bloodworm.

### Red Diddy · Cove · UK

| | |
|---|---|
| *Hook* | Partridge CS7, size 8 |
| *Thread* | Red |
| *Tail* | Piece of red elastic bank cut to taper at the end |
| *Body* | Red silk |
| *Rib* | Gold wire |

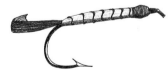

Red Diddy

One of the earliest larva patterns, this next one was created by John Goddard. He tied it up in both red and green and used dyed feather slips as the tail.

### Red Larva · Goddard · UK

| | |
|---|---|
| *Hook* | Mustad 79580, sizes 8–12 |
| *Thread* | Brown |
| *Tail* | Slip of red goose or swan with a natural curve |
| *Body* | Red condor substitute with red fluorescent floss over |
| *Rib* | Narrow flat, silver tinsel |
| *Thorax* | Buff condor-herl substitute |

Red Larva

Just substitute green materials for the red to imitate the green larva.

## AMERICAN PATTERNS

There are many British patterns to imitate the bloodworm, which is more than I can say for the rest of the fly-fishing world. One of the few American writers to give any importance to this larval stage is Ernest Schwiebert. In his definitive book, *Nymphs*, he gives two larval imitations, one for *Chironomus* and the other for *Tanypus*, a closely related species. In both cases he imitates the smaller species of midge.

**Chironomus Larva** · Schwiebert · USA
| | |
|---|---|
| *Hook* | Orvis Premium (1x), sizes 14–24 |
| *Thread* | To match body colour |
| *Body* | Red, brown, purple, olive, grey, amber, cream – a whole range of natural colours |
| *Gills* | In essence, the tail a short bunch of fibres as body colour |
| *Hackle* | Short tuft of hackle fibres to match the body and to imitate the false legs (prolegs) |

**Tanypus Larva** · Schwiebert · USA
| | |
|---|---|
| *Hook* | Mustad 9523, sizes 14–20 |
| *Thread* | Brown |
| *Tail* | Dark blue-dun hackle fibres tied around the bend |
| *Body* | Brown, olive, green or tan floss |
| *Thorax* | As body |
| *Rib* | Gold wire |
| *Antennae* | Short tuft of blue-dun hackle fibres |

Many things in life occur more by accident than design and so it is with fly-tying. A fly tied to represent one creature can become an excellent imitation of another. The San Juan Worm, a simple fly tied to represent an aquatic annelid worm, makes a very good bloodworm imitation.

**San Juan Worm** · Borger · USA
| | |
|---|---|
| *Hook* | Mustad 37160, sizes 2–10 |
| *Thread* | To match body colour |
| *Body* | Fluorescent orange, red or pink yarn |
| *Rib* | Silver wire for the pink and the orange, copper wire for the red |

San Juan Worm (Borger)

Gary Borger maintains that it is the shape of the hook which imparts a natural wiggle to the fly as it descends through the water.

**San Juan Worm** · USA
| | |
|---|---|
| *Hook* | Mustad 3904A, sizes 8–12 |
| *Thread* | Red |
| *Body* | Suede chenille, the ends tapered in a flame and tied in the middle of the hook with both ends free |

San Juan Worm

Charles E. Brookes gives a pattern to imitate the lighter colour of the midge larvae using chamois leather as a tail.

**Cream Wriggler** · Brookes · USA
| | |
|---|---|
| *Hook* | Mustad 94843, size 14 |
| *Thread* | Brown |
| *Tail* | Cream chamois |
| *Body* | As tail |
| *Legs* | Grey partridge |

Cream Wriggler

The final pattern in this larval section is one of Randall Kaufmann's, which he says was designed to imitate *Tendipes* sp.

**Bloodworm Larva** · Kaufmann · USA
| | |
|---|---|
| *Hook* | Mustad 79580, sizes 12–22 |
| *Thread* | Red |
| *Tail* | Red marabou |
| *Body* | As tail |
| *Breathing filaments* | Pale grey marabou or clear Antron |

Bloodworm Larva

## PUPA IMITATIONS

### BRITISH AND EUROPEAN PATTERNS

The creation of large reservoirs may well have triggered the British angler's awareness of the importance of the midge in the trout's diet and of the effectiveness of flies tied to imitate these midges on these large expanses of water. The traditional Duck Flies of Ireland, used for many years on the great Irish loughs, were the fore-runners of today's buzzer patterns, but the anglers that fished the natural lakes were steeped in tradition and seldom delved into the entomological intricacies of the waters which they fished. They contented themselves with traditional, albeit well-tried, wet-fly patterns and did not expand their aquatic horizon.

In Chapter 4, mention was made of Dr Bell, of Blagdon fame, and of his patterns created from observing the stomach contents of caught fish. The man-made water of Blagdon was one of the first reservoirs open to fishing in the early years of this century and must be considered as the first water to prompt thinking anglers into the wiles and guiles of what went on under the surface of stillwater. They created patterns that deviated from the normal wet fly and tied flies that more closely resembled the real insect. Today, if you drive down the lanes and roads of the Blagdon area, where the larger Chew Valley Reservoir has since been built, the hedgerows smoke with dancing midges, telling you that, although the water is home to splendid trout, it is also the habitat of the chironomid.

I devised the following fly many years ago in what I can describe as my marabou-tail period. I put this mobile feather, fragile as it was, on many of my nymphal patterns and the pupa of the midge was never ignored. I have always felt that an artificial fly must have a degree of in-built life and this can be achieved, at least, in this case, by the mobility of the delicate marabou feather.

**Marabou Buzzer** · Price · UK

| | |
|---|---|
| *Hook* | Mustad 3906, sizes 10–14 |
| *Thread* | Black (or other colours to match body) |
| *Tail* | Black marabou (or other colours to match body) |
| *Body* | Black floss (or red, brown, green, grey, orange or olive) |
| *Rib* | Fine, oval silver tinsel |
| *Thorax* | Peacock herl |
| *Breathing filaments* | White marabou tuft |

Marabou Buzzer

Geoffrey Bucknall is well known to the British angler for his many books, his articles in the angling press and his many fly patterns. The following fly was an early pupa pattern which he called the Footballer, because of the black-and-white stripes of the body; I suppose it was reminiscent of the colours of such teams as Newcastle United.

**Footballer** · Bucknall · UK

| | |
|---|---|
| *Hook* | Mustad 9143, sizes 10–14 |
| *Thread* | Black |
| *Body* | Black-and-white horsehair tied in alternate bands up the body (black-and-white hackle stalks can also be used) |
| *Thorax* | Peacock herl |
| *Breathing filaments* | Fluorescent white floss |

Richard Walker tied many different midge-pupa flies and the following still catches fish for me. The pattern is tied in a range of colours but I have found black to be the most effective.

**Red-tip Buzzer** · R. Walker · UK

| | |
|---|---|
| *Hook* | Mustad 79672, sizes 8–16 |
| *Thread* | Black |
| *Body* | Black floss with a tip of fluorescent red floss; the body is taken around the bend of the hook |
| *Rib* | Fine silver wire |
| *Thorax* | Peacock herl or black turkey |
| *Breathing filaments* | Fluorescent white wool |

Some of the best imitations of chironomid pupa have been devised by Bob Carnill. His various Poly-rib Pupae are, in my opinion, the most realistic available. These are tied in the following colours: black, brown, olive, claret, orange and green. I give the black version here.

**Poly-rib Pupa** · Carnill · UK

| | |
|---|---|
| *Hook* | Partridge K2B or similar Sedge Hook, sizes 10–14 |
| *Thread* | Black |
| *Tail* | Short tuft of fluorescent floss |
| *Body* | Black goose or similar feather |
| *Rib* | Fine polythene or PVC allowing the dyed goose to show through |
| *Thorax* | Black mole |
| *Thorax cover* | Body feather fibre |
| *Wing* | Two tips of goose biot, orange or white |
| *Breathing filaments* | Fluorescent white wool in two tufts |

John Goddard is known, and has fished, all over the world and he is Britain's leading angling entomologist. His famous sedge pattern, the Goddard Caddis, developed with Cliff Henry many years ago, is used in every fly-fishing country. The following pupa pattern is one of his flies.

**Hatching Midge Pupa** · Goddard · UK

| | |
|---|---|
| *Hook* | Mustad 79672, sizes 10–14 |
| *Thread* | To match body colour |
| *Tail* | White, fluorescent wool, tied around the bend |
| *Underbody* | Appropriately coloured fluorescent silk or wool |
| *Overbody* | Strip of PVC sheet |
| *Rib* | Flat silver tinsel |
| *Thorax* | Brown turkey or peacock herl |
| *Breathing filaments* | Fluorescent white wool |

Among the many flies sent to me for this book was a set of midge pupae tied by Tony Deacon, from Wadhurst, in East Sussex. Tony spent his formative years in South Africa and has just retired from the editorship of the Fly Dresser's Guild Magazine. I give three of his pupae here.

**Red-banded Pupa** · Deacon · UK

| | |
|---|---|
| *Hook* | Mustad 79672, sizes 10–16 |
| *Thread* | Black |
| *Body* | Black silk with two turns of red tinsel near the thorax |
| *Overbody* | Clear nylon monofilament, slightly flattened |
| *Thorax* | Black fur dubbing |
| *Breathing filaments* | Fluorescent white wool |

Deacon's Red-banded Pupa

**Small Olive Pupa** · Deacon · UK

| | |
|---|---|
| *Hook* | Partridge K4A Grub Hook, sizes 14–18 |
| *Thread* | Olive |
| *Body* | Olive silk |
| *Overbody* | Nylon monofilament |
| *Thorax* | Olive dubbing |
| *Breathing filaments* | Fluorescent white wool |

**Black Pupa** · Deacon · UK

| | |
|---|---|
| *Hook* | Partridge K4A, sizes 12–16 |
| *Thread* | Black |
| *Body* | Black silk |
| *Overbody* | Nylon monofilament |
| *Thorax* | Black dubbing |
| *Breathing filaments* | Fluorescent white wool |

Joscelyn Lane in his book, *Lake and Loch Fishing*, gives a very simple pattern to imitate the midge pupa. All he uses is brown silk. Lane recommends a silver hook if one is available.

**Midge Pupa** · Lane · UK
*Hook*      Mustad 9479, sizes 14–16
*Thread*    Brown
*Tail*      Brown silk (salmon-fly thickness)
*Body*      As tail
*Rib*       Fine gold wire
*Thorax*    As body but three thicknesses of silk

The following dressings are designed to imitate the pupa in the surface film, just prior to emergence. This is when pupae are at their most vulnerable. I use the first pattern on my local water in Kent and have had a fair degree of success with it. The fly relies on the flotability of the now famous *cul de canard* (CDC) feather.

**Emerging Midge** · Price · UK
*Hook*      Mustad 9479, sizes 10–14
*Thread*    Black or grey
*Body*      Grey dubbing, using CDC fibres
*Rib*       Silver wire
*Thorax*    Dubbed CDC veiled by two CDC feathers; tips can be left unclipped

One of the most popular and effective Buzzer patterns of recent years must be the Shipman Buzzer, a simple fly created by David Shipman. This pattern is fished in the surface film and moved very slowly indeed; on occasions it is just left with no retrieve at all. The usual pattern given is fiery brown or orange but other colours can be just as effective.

**Shipman's Buzzer** · Shipman · UK
*Hook*      Mustad 79642, sizes 10–14
*Thread*    To match body colour
*Tail*      Fluorescent white silk or, better still, Antron
*Body*      Fiery brown seal fur
*Rib*       Pearly tinsel
*Breathing  As tail
filaments*

The Suspender Midge is most popular on reservoirs and, in recent years, on rivers. John Goddard developed the suspender concept from Charles E. Brookes and took it a stage further by using more buoyant plastics rather than enmeshed poly-propylene dubbing.

**Suspender Midge** · Goddard · UK
*Hook*      Mustad 79642, sizes 10–16
*Thread*    Black (or other colours to match the body)
*Tail*      White fluorescent wool tied around the bend
*Body*      Black seal fur (or red, orange, olive, brown or green)
*Rib*       Fine silver wire
*Thorax*    Peacock herl with a small polystyrene or ethafoam ball enmeshed in nylon tied in

The next pattern uses deer hair as the buoyancy aid and was created by the late Dave Collyer, whose untimely death in a road accident was a great loss to the fishing world.

**Hatching Buzzer Pupa** · Collyer · UK
*Hook*      Mustad 79642, sizes 8–12
*Thread*    Black (or other colours to match body)
*Body*      Black silk (or red, orange, olive or claret)
*Rib*       Flat silver gold or copper tinsel
*Thorax*    Deer hair spun and clipped into a ball shape

Bob Church has many patterns credited to him and the following fly is one of his. It represents the large red chironomid just as it is hatching.

**Brown Emerging Midge** · Church · UK
*Hook*      Mustad 79642, sizes 10–16
*Thread*    Brown
*Butt*      Fluorescent yellow floss silk
*Body*      Hare fur
*Legs*      Palmered dark furnace

The next pattern I obtained from Andrij Urban, from Skopje, Macedonia. This is another pattern using *cul de canard* feather.

**Urban Emerging Pupa** · Urban · Macedonia
*Hook*      Mustad 79642, sizes 10–14
*Thread*    Black
*Tail*      Short tuft of CDC
*Body*      Black fur dubbing
*Rib*       Fine blue tinsel
*Thorax*    Black dubbing with CDC looped over the back

The last pattern of the five emergers comes from Germany and utilizes some of the many man-made products sold by the Traun River Company of Rudi Heger.

**Spectra Bubble Midge Pupa** · Wolfle · Germany
*Hook*      Partridge L3A, sizes 12–22
*Thread*    Black
*Body*      Spectraflash hair
*Thorax*    Olive Antron with a polystyrene or ethafoam ball retained in nylon stocking material

I have already given a number of patterns in this book from the vice of Roman Moser and this next pattern of his is used mainly on quiet or still portions of a river. I suspect that it would also work well when fished in a dead drift.

**Hatching Chironomid Pupa** · Moser · Austria
*Hook*      Roman Moser Arrowpoint, sizes 12–18
*Thread*    Black
*Body*      Black Raffene
*Rib*       White Raffene
*Thorax*    Brown and grey deer body hair, not spun but dubbed and mixed
*Wing*      White Raffene marked, if so desired, with waterproof ink

Roman Moser treats his Raffene (Swiss Straw) with material to make it more durable. I use Dave's Flexament or Floo Gloo for this purpose.

AMERICAN PATTERNS
One of the few books from the USA to deal in any depth with patterns to represent the midge pupa is Gary Borger's *Designing Trout Flies*. The following patterns are his.

**Sparkle Midge Pupa** · Borger · USA
*Hook*      Mustad 79703, sizes 14–28
*Thread*    To match body colour
*Body*      Dubbed sparkle yarn (black, grey, golden-olive and green)
*Thorax*    To match body colour, weighted with lead or copper wire

**Jumbo Lake Pupa** · Borger · USA
*Hook*      Mustad 79706, sizes 8–14
*Thread*    To match body colour
*Tail filament*   White sparkle yarn
*Body*      Sparkle yarn (black, olive-green, orange-brown)

*Rib*       Silver or pearly for the black and olive, copper for the orange-brown
*Thorax*    Weighted with lead or copper wire, peacock herl over
*Breathing filaments*   White sparkle yarn

Jumbo Lake Pupa

Gary adds a piece of white, closed-cell foam to an unweighted pattern to create a suspender pupa.

A midge-pupa pattern from the 1950s devised by Richard B. Thompson and called simply the T.D.C. (Thompson's Delectable Chironomid), is used for lake-fishing in the American northwest.

**T.D.C.** · Thompson · USA
*Hook*      Mustad 3906B, sizes 6–16
*Thread*    Black
*Body*      Black wool
*Rib*       Fine silver thread
*Collar*    White ostrich

Sidney A. Neff of Pennsylvania has had experience of fishing in Ireland and other parts of Europe and is well aware of the importance of the midge in fishing the large Irish lakes. The following pattern was given in the book *Masters of the Nymph*, edited by Michael Migel and Leonard M. Wright Jr.

**Chironomid Pupa** · Neff · USA
*Hook*      Mustad 3906B, sizes 18–26
*Thread*    To match body colour
*Body*      Dirty yellow, amber, brown, grey or olive swan herl
*Rib*       To match tying thread
*Thorax*    Ostrich herl to match body colour

One of the most popular of pupa patterns used in the USA is a fly originating on the San Juan River – the Brassie. A simple concoction of copper wire and a fur ball, the pattern originated in Colorado.

There are some who consider this fly to be a caddis pupa and no doubt it will work well as such a creature.

**Brassie** · USA

| | |
|---|---|
| *Hook* | Mustad 3906B or any Midge Hook, sizes 8–26 |
| *Thread* | Red or brown |
| *Body* | Copper wire |
| *Thorax* | Button of any fur, synthetic or natural |

The next pattern was tied by the American tier, Tim Coleman, and imitates a pupa complete with a string of fine bubbles. To achieve this effect he uses a strand of silver Crystal Hair.

**Crystal Chironomid** · Coleman · USA

| | |
|---|---|
| *Hook* | Mustad 80050BR, sizes 16–22 |
| *Thread* | Black |
| *Tail* | Single strand of silver Crystal Hair |
| *Body* | Black tying thread, lacquered |
| *Rib* | Silver wire |
| *Thorax* | Black tying thread, lacquered |
| *Wing case* | Cock-pheasant tail fibres |
| *Breathing filaments* | Tuft of white marabou |
| *Legs* | Grouse hackle fibres (optional) |

CANADIAN PATTERNS

Of the following patterns, one comes from Quebec, three from British Columbia, one from Manitoba and one from Ontario.

**Midge Pupa** · Vincent · Quebec

| | |
|---|---|
| *Hook* | Mustad 3906B, sizes 10–28 |
| *Thread* | Black |
| *Tail* | Black hackle fibres (optional) |
| *Body* | Stripped peacock quill |
| *Thorax* | Black fur dubbing |
| *Legs* | Black hackle fibres |

**YDC** · Yoshida · British Columbia

| | |
|---|---|
| *Hook* | Mustad 9671, sizes 6–16 |
| *Thread* | Black |
| *Body* | Thinly dubbed black polypropylene |
| *Rib* | White thread |
| *Thorax* | White ostrich |
| *Thorax back* | Cock-pheasant rump or oak turkey |

**Irv's Carrot Chironomid** · Ross
British Columbia

| | |
|---|---|
| *Hook* | Mustad 3906B, size 10 |
| *Thread* | Black |
| *Body* | Carrot-coloured floss |
| *Rib* | Gold or silver wire |
| *Collar* | White ostrich herl |

On a recent visit to Manitoba I had the good fortune to meet Gerry Beck, one of the area's leading fly-fisherman and tiers. He gave me two pupa patterns: one of his own for fishing Steep Rock Lake in the Porcupine Mountains, and the other from a tier in British Columbia, Jim Kilburn.

**Steep Rock Pupa** · Beck · Manitoba

| | |
|---|---|
| *Hook* | Mustad 94840, sizes 10–12 |
| *Thread* | Brown |
| *Body* | Hare fur |
| *Rib* | Yellow thread |
| *Thorax* | As body |
| *Hackle* | Brown partridge |

**Kilburn Pupa** · Kilburn · British Columbia

| | |
|---|---|
| *Hook* | Mustad 90240, Salmon Hook, sizes 10–12 |
| *Thread* | Black |
| *Tip* | Oval silver tinsel, few turns |
| *Body* | Hare fur (or similar) |
| *Thorax* | As body |
| *Breathing filaments* | Two tufts of white yarn either side of the thorax |

The next pattern was tied by Ian James of Guelph, Ontario, and was depicted in *Flies for Trout* by Dick Stewart and Farrow Allen whose series of fly-pattern books are some of the best on the subject available today.

**Copper Buzzer** · Allen · Ontario

| | |
|---|---|
| *Hook* | Mustad 94840, sizes 12–18 |
| *Thread* | Black |
| *Body* | Copper wire |
| *Thorax* | Orange or black seal fur (or substitute) |
| *Breathing filaments* | White floss silk, clipped |

NEW ZEALAND PATTERNS

Norman Marsh, in his book *Trout Stream Insects of New Zealand*, gives a pattern to imitate an Antipodean midge, which is probably *Chironomus zealandicus*.

**Midge Pupa** · Marsh · NZ

| | |
|---|---|
| *Hook* | Mustad 79642, sizes 16–18 |
| *Thread* | Olive |
| *Tail* | White rabbit cheek fur |
| *Body* | Green seal fur (or substitute) |
| *Thorax* | Dark grey rabbit underfur |
| *Breathing filaments* | White rabbit cheek fur |

Midge Pupa

There are many more patterns to imitate the pupa of the midge, some of which are to be found in later chapters.

### FISHING THE MIDGE PUPA

A trout will take midge pupae close to the bottom prior to their rising. It will feed avidly on the rising pupae in the main body of the water and will also take them just under the surface and in the surface film when they are on the point of hatching. On stillwater these are the areas where you fish the fly. Use a leader as long as the prevailing conditions will allow. Fishing with a leader of about 20ft (6m) in strong winds does pose a lot of problems, at least it does for me. Arthur Cove fished with leaders of anything up to 30ft (9m).

It is quite usual to fish with a team of three flies usually of different colours and sometimes of different weights; the heaviest fly should be at the point and the lightest on the top dropper. If you are fishing close to the top, grease the leader up to the fly so that it hangs just below the surface. The retrieve must be ultra-slow or non-existent; allow the leader and fly-line to be taken by the natural flow of the water. It is essential to watch the line at all times because the slightest hesitancy in the normal speed and direction of the line could mean a take. I have friends who believe in fishing only weighted pupae. These are cast out and allowed to sink and the line is then retrieved in the sink-and-draw method. This emulates the natural rise of the pupa. In clear water, you can see the fish following behind the fly and this does wonders for the adrenalin flow. Quite often pupa-feeding fish can be seen swimming in almost a straight line, taking the flies as they move in a feeding lane. I find the best method is to cast the fly well ahead into the path of the fish and then leave it stationary. The fish just sip it in along with all the naturals.

In times of strong wind a team of pupae fished quickly through the surface film is often successful because the insects that are hatching are caught on the surface and moved by the water quite quickly. The trout expect to see their prey moving at speed and that is how you should fish the artificial. The natural midge can be trapped in the scum lines that often form on reservoirs; trout are often found in the vicinity of these because they know that insect life becomes trapped there. On rivers the midge pupae and larvae are best fished in a dead drift in the riffle water. On the quieter sections and larger pools I have always found it prudent to fish as though I was on stillwater and I use some of the methods that prove successful there.

## PHANTOM MIDGES

### NATURALS

The phantom midges (Chaoboridae) are similar in many respects to mosquitoes and, to some extent, chironomids. Like chironomids, but unlike mosquitoes, the adults do not bite! A distinguishing feature of the adult male is the heavily plumed antennae which gave the insect its alternative name of 'plumed gnat'.

The larvae, which are about ⅝in (15–16mm) long when fully mature, are transparent predators which feed in the main body of the water on a wide range of small creatures, e.g. rotifers, mosquito larvae and other larval dipterans. The phantom larva hardly moves at all but remains transparent and motionless in the water, seizing its prey when the opportunity arises.

The pupae are free-living in the water and look very similar to those of mosquitoes. They have a touch more colour than the larvae; I have seen specimens with a distinct watery-green colour to the abdomen and a brownish thorax. On top of the thorax, there are two donkey-like 'ears', which are thought to be stabilizers, enabling the creature to

Phantom midge larvae and pupa

rise, fall and hold station in the water. I am told that, if these 'ears' are removed, the creatures remain on the bottom and are unable to rise. I usually tell my audience, when I give talks on entomolgy, that when the 'ears' are removed the pupa also become very deaf!

Phantom midges are creatures of lakes, reservoirs and ponds. They can occur in very large numbers and, at such times, trout will certainly feed upon them. From time to time in the summer I have found them in the stomach contents of caught trout. A number of fly patterns have been devised to imitate the larval and pupal forms of this innocuous little fly.

It is hard to believe that creatures as small as this could also be food for Man but this is the case. David Livingstone, the great missionary explorer, discovered people living on the banks of Lake Nyasa eating 'kunga cake', a food made entirely from the larvae and pupae of the local phantom midge, sifted from the lake.

The commonest British species are thought to be *Chaoborus flavicans* and *C. crystallinus*.

## ARTIFICIALS

Peter Gathercole is one of Britain's leading angling photographers and many of his excellent pictures are published in the angling press each month. He is also the foremost macro-photographer working on fishing subjects in the British Isles today. The following pattern is one from his vice.

**Phantom Larva** · Gathercole · UK

| | |
|---|---|
| *Hook* | Mustad 79706, sizes 14–16 (or equivalent silver hook) |
| *Thread* | Brown |
| *Underbody* | If a silver hook is not used, wrap the shank in silver Lurex with a few turns of tying thread at the front and rear |
| *Overbody* | Clear polythene |
| *Legs* | Short white cock hackle |

The next pattern of mine was published in 1993 in *Practical Gamefishing* and for this fly I used transparent Larva Lace.

**Phantom Larva** · Price · UK

| | |
|---|---|
| *Hook* | Longshank silver hook, size 14, bent slightly to impart a little action to the fly |
| *Thread* | White |
| *Tail* | Very short tuft of white marabou |
| *Body* | Two dots painted on the hook shank |
| *Overbody* | Transparent Larva Lace tied down at both ends |
| *Hackle* | None |

Phantom Larva

**Phantom Larva** · Lapsley · UK

| | |
|---|---|
| *Hook* | Ring-eyed, sizes 14–16 |
| *Thread* | Brown |
| *Body* | Pale yellow floss |
| *Rib* | Flat, silver tinsel |
| *Thorax* | Small button of cock-pheasant tail behind the eye |

I tend to agree with John Roberts when he thought that this pattern resembled the pupa more than the larva.

**Phantom Pupa** · Goddard · UK

| | |
|---|---|
| *Hook* | Mustad 79672, size 16 |
| *Thread* | Brown |
| *Body* | White silk |
| *Overbody* | Both body and thorax covered with clear PVC strip |

| *Rib* | Fine flat silver tinsel |
| *Thorax* | Orange silk |

**Phantom Pupa** · Gathercole · UK

| *Hook* | Mustad 79672, sizes 14–16 |
| *Thread* | Brown |
| *Tail* | White feather fibres, cut square |
| *Body* | White silk with clear polythene over |
| *Rib* | Fine silver wire |
| *Thorax* | Amber seal fur |
| *Wing case* | Light brown feather fibres |
| *Head* | Tuft of white feather fibres as for tail |

**Phantom Pupa** · Collyer · UK

| *Hook* | Mustad 94845, sizes 10–16 |
| *Thread* | White |
| *Body* | Flat silver tinsel |
| *Rib* | Fine oval silver tinsel |
| *Overbody* | Polythene strip (optional) |
| *Thorax* | Small button of peacock herl |
| *Hackle* | Short, white hen |

Fly-tiers are ever optimistic, as you can see from the last few patterns. Although the phantom pupa has a small amount of colour, the larva is completely transparent, except for a couple of dark patches. No matter how clever we think we are in trying to achieve transparency in our flies, we still cannot hide the fact that, running through our imitations there is a hook and this, alas, can never be disguised. I am glad to say we still keep trying.

### FISHING THE PHANTOM MIDGE

How do you fish a creature that remains motionless for most of the time? The short answer is to cast out and hope for the best and, if you are going to retrieve, do so very, very slowly. You will take fish on the patterns without a doubt but, if the trout view our patterns as phantom midge larvae, then I for one am surprised. I think they take them because they look edible.

## MOSQUITOES _____

### NATURALS

Each of us, at sometime or another, has been bitten by a mosquito but most of us, thank goodness, will not have been bitten by any disease-carrying species. In temperate climates, if not in the tropics, such diseases have been more or less eradicated. Also the malaria-carrying mosquito belongs to the genus *Anopheles* (subfamily Anophelinae) and is less commonly encountered than the comparitively harmless *Culex* spp. (subfamily Culicinae). Incidentally, it is only the female mosquito that bites.

In some areas, however, the mosquito can prove a real pest, as those fishermen who fish in places such as the wilderness of northern Canada can vouch. In such areas each angler may well be accompanied by a personal swarm of mosquitoes, whining all day above and around his head and seeking every opportunity to feast on his blood.

The larva and pupa of the mosquito are found close to the surface, for they are aeropneustic, i.e they do not absorb oxygen from the water but obtain it directly from the air. They do this by penetrating the surface film, with a siphon in the larva and with respiratory horns in the pupa. Look at any rain barrel or small pond of stagnant water and you will see the larvae and pupae clustering near the surface. *Anopheles* larvae lie horizontally at the surface while *Culex* larvae hang vertically.

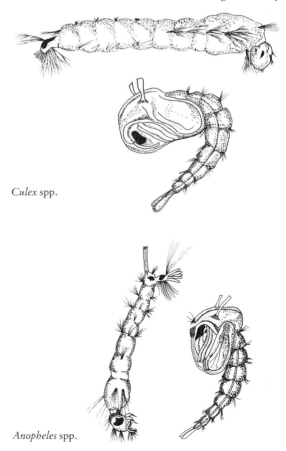

*Culex* spp.

*Anopheles* spp.

When disturbed they wriggle down to deeper water for safety. Mosquitoes are found in all types of water: ponds, lakes, even small, semi-permanent puddles and in the quiet portions of rivers.

How important are they from a fishing point of view? Well, on the scale of 1–10 (10 being the most important), I would put them at about 1. Having said that, there will be times when a trout will actively feed on the larvae and pupae if they are available.

## ARTIFICIALS

There are a number of patterns tied to imitate both forms. I am of the opinion that, although the flies are tied with the mosquito in mind, it is possible that some trout take such imitations as chironomids. In fact I will go even further and say that some early patterns tied to represent the pupae of mosquitoes were, in all probability, imitations of chironomid pupae because fisherman and tier did not really know the difference.

### BRITISH PATTERNS
I gave these patterns for a mosquito larva and pupa in volume 1 of my book *Stillwater Flies*.

**Mosquito Larva** · UK

| | |
|---|---|
| *Hook* | Mustad 9671, sizes 12–14 |
| *Thread* | Grey |
| *Body* | Grey silk |
| *Rib* | Black thread |
| *Hackle* | White cock hackle clipped short |

**Mosquito Pupa** · UK

| | |
|---|---|
| *Hook* | Mustad 9479, sizes 12–14 |
| *Thread* | Grey |
| *Body* | Grey silk taken around the bend of the book |
| *Rib* | Black thread |
| *Thorax* | Largish ball of dubbed mole fur |

Dave Collyer gave a similar pupal pattern using stripped peacock quill and a mole-fur thorax.

### AMERICAN PATTERNS
Polly Rosborough in his book, *Tying and Fishing the Fuzzy Nymphs*, gives a simple, basic pattern for a mosquito larva that worked for him on the upper Williamson River.

**Mosquito Larva** · Rosborough · USA

| | |
|---|---|
| *Hook* | Mustad 38941, sizes 14–16 |
| *Thread* | Grey |
| *Tail* | Finely barred guinea-fowl feather about ⅜in (9mm) long |
| *Body* | Smoky-grey yarn tied thinly |
| *Rib* | As tying thread |
| *Legs* | Small bunch of guinea-fowl hackle fibres |
| *Head* | Built up a bit thicker than the body (Polly adds a black dot for an eye) |

Another of the Polly Rosborough collection is the Tan Midge Pupa. In his description, he refers to the adult as a biting fly and further suggests that it belongs to the *Anopheles* genus of mosquito. The fly is tied in reverse, with the head and hackle at the bend, and it is fished in the surface film.

**Tan Midge Pupa** · Rosborough · USA

| | |
|---|---|
| *Hook* | Mustad 38930, size 10 |
| *Thread* | Pale tan |
| *Body* | Pale tan fuzzy yarn |
| *Thorax* | Turn of black ostrich |
| *Hackle* | Short grizzle hackle |

**Mosquito Larva** · Rosborough · USA

| | |
|---|---|
| *Hook* | Mustad 9671, sizes 14–20 |
| *Thread* | Black |
| *Tail* | Short tuft of grizzle hen hackle fibres |
| *Body* | Stripped peacock quill |
| *Thorax* | Peacock herl |
| *Breathing filaments* | As tail |

The next pupal pattern is one from Randall Kaufmann.

**Mosquito Pupa** · Kaufmann · USA

| | |
|---|---|
| *Hook* | Mustad 9671, sizes 14–20 |
| *Thread* | Olive |
| *Tail* | Short tuft of grizzle marabou |
| *Body* | Stripped peacock quill |
| *Rib* | Copper wire |
| *Thorax* | Peacock herl |
| *Wings* | Grizzle hen hackle tips |

## FISHING THE MOSQUITO

There is not much I can say regarding fishing the larvae and pupae except that both naturals are extremely active when disturbed, wriggling in the water at quite a fast rate. Bearing this in mind, a retrieve with plenty of action imparted to the rod tip may well tempt a fish to take. Otherwise fish as one would for chironomids.

## SIMULIUM MIDGES

### NATURALS

These small biting midges are sometimes called blackflies, reed smuts or buffalo gnats and, in Scotland, birch flies. They are usually found in fast water. I can remember an occasion when I was fishing from a canoe on the Delay River, in the Ungava peninsula of northern Quebec. We were approaching some whitewater rapids when I noticed the air above the troubled water was black with swarming midges. They hung above the river like a net of black muslin. As we passed through the swarm we became covered with these small, biting flies, much to our general discomfort. Shooting the rapids was one thing. Being bitten to death at the same time was something else.

It has been known for cattle to be killed by mass attacks of *Simulium*; they get so distressed that their hearts just give up. In New Zealand I once suffered bitten hands but, on that occasion, it was the even smaller sandflies that did the damage. I have come to the conclusion that I have been bitten in nearly every country in the world and, each time, I suffer from acute swelling and itching. This can be relieved only by liberal quantities of Scotch Whiskey rubbed into the offending parts and poured down the throat in generous amounts. It is almost worth getting bitten to partake of the cure.

The larvae, which are about ¼in (8mm) in length, are found attached to rocks, stones, logs and aquatic vegetation. They anchor themselves with fine silk line, up to a yard long, to prevent themselves being swept away. Using these silk lines they can descend downstream. Trout could possibly take them when they are detached and in the main body of the water.

The pupae, on the other hand, form little, open-ended cocoons in which they remain until it is time to hatch. If trout are going to take the aquatic forms of *Simulium*, it is the larva and not the pupa that we should be interested in. In the UK we have about 41 different species. Goodness knows how many there are in the USA. Professor L.C. Miall in his book *Aquatic Insects* mentions the following common species.

**Common Simulium Midges**

| *Scientific Name* | *Distribution* |
| --- | --- |
| Simulium latipes | UK |
| Simulium ornatum | UK |
| Simulium pictipes | USA |
| Simulium reptans | UK |

Of the UK species, *S. ornatum* appears to have the widest distribution and *S. latipes* and *S. reptans* occur in stony streams and in fast-flowing, weedy streams respectively. Patrick McCafferty, in *Aquatic Entomology*, quotes *S. vittatum* as being common in the USA, although *S. pictipes* is recorded as being abundant on the Ausable River. One species, *S. equinum*, attacks horses.

*Simulium* midge larva

### ARTIFICIALS

Imitations of *Simulium* midges are not very common. As far as the adult is concerned I have always done well with a small size 18 Kill Devil Spider fished in the film. It is possible that the trout take it as the adult or the larva; I do not know for certain.

As far as a nymph pattern is concerned, the following fly may well work. I tie the pattern in reverse so that the leader can, with a stretch of the imagination, represent the fine anchor thread which the larva makes.

## LARVA PATTERN
### Simulium Larva · UK

*Hook*   Midge Hook, sizes 16–22
*Thread*  Black
*Body*   Built-up fat at the eye, tapered to the bend and pre-weighted with copper wire
*Legs*   Few wisps of black cock hackle fibres tied in what is normally the tail position.

Simulium Larva

## EMERGER PATTERNS

One of the more common of the 60 odd species in South Africa is *S. chutteri*. Many fish feed on these tiny flies, including catfish. Two other species have larvae about ⅝in (13mm) in length: *S. debegene* and *S. dentulosum*. Ed Herbst of Cape Town sent me a pattern to imitate the emerging midge.

### Simulium Emerger

*Hook*    Mustad 80100BR, size 18
*Thread*  Ultra-fine thread (Spiderweb)
*Body*    Formed from twisting silver wire and copper together and dubbing with grey Antron (this dubbing is a mere fuzz)
*Hackle*  Black cock hackle stripped down one side

# CHAPTER TEN

# OTHER TRUE FLIES

## CRANE FLIES

### NATURALS

The crane flies, daddy-long-legs or harry-long-legs belong to the family Tipulidae or to the closely allied family Limnobiidae. Another group, the phantom crane flies, belong to the family Ptychopterida.

From a fly-fishing point of view, the most important crane fly species as far as the UK and Europe are concerned are wholly terrestrial. Crane flies such as the very common *Tipula paludosa*, whose larvae are known by farmers, gardeners and green-keepers alike as leatherjackets, provide the angler with great sport in early autumn, when they are blown onto the water in considerable numbers.

There are, however, a number of species with aquatic larval forms and these are often taken by trout. Many are truly large creatures. The largest British species, *T. maxima*, is just such a specimen with a totally aquatic larva that exceeds 1in (25mm) in length. As an adult it has the distinction of having the largest wingspan (2¾in/65mm) of any British fly, as well as a body length of about 3⁵⁄₁₆in (32mm). Most crane fly larvae are vegetarian, but there is a species, *Dicranota*, that feeds exclusively on *Tubifex* worms. Many crane fly larvae live in tunnels in the mud, feeding on vegetable matter.

The larva has a small, retractable head at one end and a breathing spiracle, which can hold a bubble of air, at the other. The body has 11 segments. Most larvae are a dirty off-white or grey but some are a palish olive. Pupation takes place out of water. Whereas there are about 300 species of aquatic and terrestrial crane fly in the UK, in the USA, as one would expect, the number increases to about 3000, with about 30 aquatic species. Ernest Schwiebert gives imitations for ten different species, the largest being the giant crane fly, *T. abdominalis*. This species has a larva up to 1¾in (45mm) long.

The following species could well be of interest to the fisherman. For a more complete coverage of the American species refer to Ernest Schwiebert's book, *Nymphs*.

### Crane Flies of Angling Significance in the UK and USA

| Scientific Name | Common Name | Distribution |
|---|---|---|
| Dicranota bimaculata | — | UK |
| Epiphragma bella | Riffle Crane Fly | USA |
| Helius americanus | Little Olive | USA |
| Pedicia rivosa | — | UK |
| Ptychoptera albimana | — | UK |
| P. contaminata | — | UK |
| Tipula abdominalis | Giant Crane Fly | USA |
| T. augustipennis | Summer Crane Fly | USA |
| T. bicornis | Orange Crane Fly | USA |
| T. furca | Whirling Crane Fly | USA |
| T. maxima | Giant Crane Fly | UK |

### ARTIFICIALS

The first pattern imitates *Tipula maxima* and was first given in my book *Stillwater Flies*. It uses latex for the body.

**Crane Fly Larva** · Price · UK

| | |
|---|---|
| *Hook* | Mustad 79580, sizes 6-10 |
| *Thread* | Grey or black |
| *Body* | Natural latex, coloured with grey waterproof ink |

Crane fly larva

| | |
|---|---|
| *Underbody* | Lead wire |
| *Rib* | Oval, gold wire |
| *Spiracles* | Grey or white hackle clipped right down |

Crane Fly Larva

In the USA there are far more patterns to imitate this plump and juicy larva, which, I suppose, is to be expected with so many more species to consider. The next pattern was given by Craig Matthews and John Juracek in their small book, *Fly Patterns of the Yellowstone*. They discovered large numbers of crane fly larvae in the Madison River. Subsequently they have used this pattern successfully for rainbows on that river and on the equally famous Henry's Fork.

**Giant Crane Fly Larva** · Matthews & Juracek · USA

| | |
|---|---|
| *Hook* | Mustad 79580, sizes 6-10 |
| *Thread* | Olive |
| *Tail* | Short tufts, ¼in (5mm), of cock-pheasant tail fibres |
| *Body* | Olive-yellow rabbit dubbed roughly over 25 turns of lead wire and olive wool |
| *Rib* | Gold wire |
| *Thorax* | Brown Australian opossum or rabbit |

This next pattern of theirs imitates a slightly smaller species.

**Summer Crane Fly Larva** · Matthews & Juracek USA

| | |
|---|---|
| *Hook* | Mustad 79580, sizes 10-14 |
| *Thread* | Brown |
| *Tail* | Short tuft of grey cock-pheasant back feather |
| *Body* | Light grey muskrat |

Summer Crane Fly Larva

| | |
|---|---|
| *Rib* | Fine gold wire |
| *Thorax* | Medium grey dubbing |

Ernest Schwiebert lists ten patterns for the eastern and western rivers in his book, *Nymphs*. For the record I give one here and advise the reader to refer to the others in Schwiebert's masterly book.

**Little Olive Crane Fly Larva** · Schwiebert · USA

| | |
|---|---|
| *Hook* | Mustad 79580, sizes 12-14 |
| *Thread* | Dark grey |
| *Tail* | None |
| *Body* | Blue-grey muskrat dubbing |
| *Rib* | Fine oval tinsel |
| *Antennae* | Dark blue-grey hackle fibres |

The famous Muskrat Nymph of Polly Rosborough is yet another imitation of the crane fly larva.

**Muskrat Nymph** · Rosborough · USA

| | |
|---|---|
| *Hook* | Mustad 9671, sizes 8-16 |
| *Thread* | Black |
| *Body* | Muskrat, beaver belly and rabbit underfur, blended |
| *Legs* | Guinea-fowl fibres (omit for a more realistic imitation – the natural has no legs as such) |
| *Head* | Black ostrich herl |

The final pattern was devised by Gary Borger and comes in four different colours.

**Fur Crane Fly Larva** · Borger · USA

| | |
|---|---|
| *Hook* | Mustad 37160, sizes 6-10 |
| *Thread* | To match body (according to species being imitated) |
| *Tail* | Cock-pheasant tail barbs tied short |
| *Body* | Dirty orange mohair or sparkle yarn (no. 1), dirty tan sparkle yarn (no. 2), olive sparkle yarn (no. 3), grey sparkle yarn (no. 4), all weighted with copper or lead wire |
| *Rib* | Copper (Nos 1 & 2), silver (nos 3 & 4) |
| *Head* | Peacock herl |

Fur Crane Fly Larva

**Swimming Mayfly Nymph** UK

**Walker's Mayfly Nymph** UK

**March Brown Nymph** UK

**Large Dark Olive Nymph** UK

**March Brown** USA

**Dark Hendrikson** USA

**Dark Olive Nymph** Ireland

**Iron-blue Nymph** Ireland

**Olive PVC Nymph** UK

**Sepia Nymph** UK

**Olive Dun Nymph** UK

**Pale Evening Dun Nymph** USA

**March Brown Nymph** UK

**Brown Drake Nymph** USA

**Light Hendrikson** USA

**Green Drake** USA

**Large Blue-Winged Olive Nymph** USA

**Iron-Blue Quill Nymph** USA

**Quill Gordon Nymph** USA

**Caenis Nymph** USA

**Trico Nymph** USA

**Light Cahill** USA

**Small Western Black Quill** USA

**Ephemera Swimming Nymph** Japan

**Siphlonurus Swimming Nymph** Japan

**Ostrich Calibaetis** USA

**Japanese Nymph 1**

**Mooi Nymph** South Africa

**Kakahi Nymph** New Zealand

**Grey Darter** New Zealand

**Ornate Nymph** New Zealand

**Orange Nymph** New Zealand

**Sepia Nymph** New Zealand

**EMERGERS**

**Mayfly Emerger** UK

**Dark Olive** UK

**Medium Olive** UK

**Light Olive** UK

**Grey Emerger** UK

**Claret Emerger** UK

**March Brown Emerger** UK

**Tups Emerger** UK

**Hare's Ear Emerger** UK

**Pale Emerger** UK

**Sedge Pupa** Macedonia

**Orange Emerger** UK

# STONEFLY NYMPHS

**Superfly Swannundaze Stonefly Nymph**
USA/Canada

**Kaufmann Stone**
USA

**Dark Stonefly**
Czech Republic

**Whitlock's Stonefly Nymph**
USA

**Light Stonefly Nymph**
Czech Republic

**Tumbling Stone**
Germany

**Salmon Fly Nymph**
USA

**Stonefly Nymph**
Austria

**Large Perla Nymph**
UK

**Swannundaze Stonefly Nymph**
USA

**Golden Stone Nymph**
USA

**Stonefly Nymph**
Spain

**Crocheted Stonefly Nymph**
Norway

**Blackstone Nymph**
New Zealand

**Brownstone Nymph**
New Zealand

**Fratnik Stonefly Nymph**
Slovenia

**Dark Stonefly Nymph**
Finland

**Light Stonefly Nymph**
Finland

**Perlodes Bicolor**
Germany

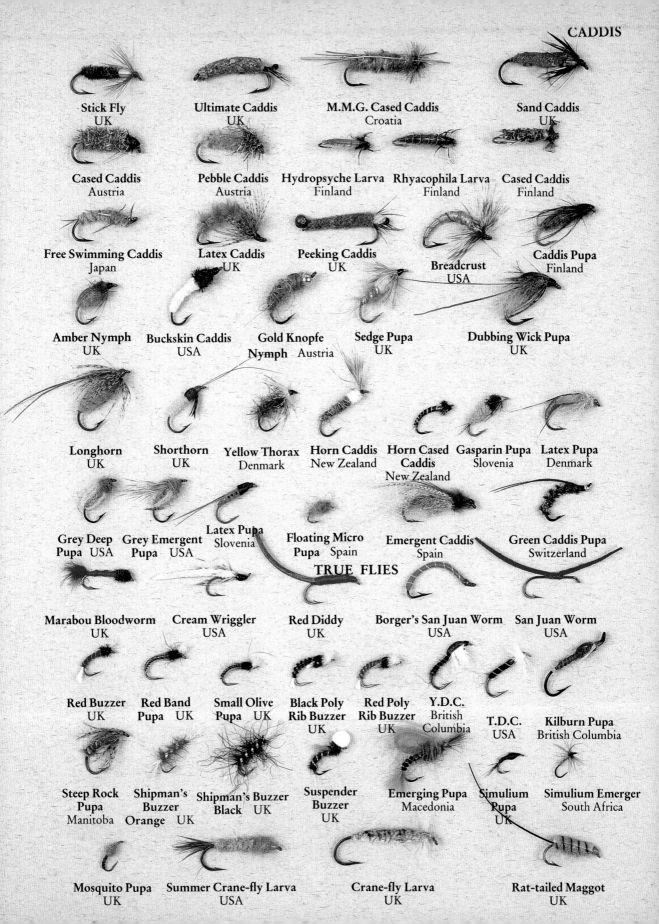

**Stick Fly**
UK

**Ultimate Caddis**
UK

**M.M.G. Cased Caddis**
Croatia

**Sand Caddis**
UK

**Cased Caddis**
Austria

**Pebble Caddis**
Austria

**Hydropsyche Larva**
Finland

**Rhyacophila Larva**
Finland

**Cased Caddis**
Finland

**Free Swimming Caddis**
Japan

**Latex Caddis**
UK

**Peeking Caddis**
UK

**Breadcrust**
USA

**Caddis Pupa**
Finland

**Amber Nymph**
UK

**Buckskin Caddis**
USA

**Gold Knopfe Nymph** Austria

**Sedge Pupa**
UK

**Dubbing Wick Pupa**
UK

**Longhorn**
UK

**Shorthorn**
UK

**Yellow Thorax**
Denmark

**Horn Caddis**
New Zealand

**Horn Cased Caddis**
New Zealand

**Gasparin Pupa**
Slovenia

**Latex Pupa**
Denmark

**Grey Deep Pupa** USA

**Grey Emergent Pupa** USA

**Latex Pupa**
Slovenia

**Floating Micro Pupa** Spain

**Emergent Caddis**
Spain

**Green Caddis Pupa**
Switzerland

**TRUE FLIES**

**Marabou Bloodworm**
UK

**Cream Wriggler**
USA

**Red Diddy**
UK

**Borger's San Juan Worm**
USA

**San Juan Worm**
USA

**Red Buzzer**
UK

**Red Band Pupa** UK

**Small Olive Pupa** UK

**Black Poly Rib Buzzer**
UK

**Red Poly Rib Buzzer**
UK

**Y.D.C.**
British Columbia

**T.D.C.**
USA

**Kilburn Pupa**
British Columbia

**Steep Rock Pupa**
Manitoba

**Shipman's Buzzer Orange** UK

**Shipman's Buzzer Black** UK

**Suspender Buzzer**
UK

**Emerging Pupa**
Macedonia

**Simulium Pupa**
UK

**Simulium Emerger**
South Africa

**Mosquito Pupa**
UK

**Summer Crane-fly Larva**
USA

**Crane-fly Larva**
UK

**Rat-tailed Maggot**
UK

# DAMSELS AND DRAGONFLIES

**Green-tail Damsel**
UK

**Golden Damsel**
UK

**Brown Swimming Damsel**
UK

**Purple Swimming Damsel**
UK

**Olive Damsel**
UK

**Damsel Nymph**
Finland

**Crocheted Damsel Nymph**
Norway

**Marabou Damsel**
USA

**Wiggle Damsel**
USA

**Dragon Nymph**
Finland

**Red-eyed Damsel Nymph**
South Africa

**Brown Dragonfly Nymph**
UK

**Mud-eye**
Australia

**Dragonfly Nymph**
Austria

**Crocheted Dragonfly Nymph**
Norway

**Dragonfly Nymph**
UK

**Gompus**
Canada

**Green Dragon**
UK

**Martin's Dragon**
USA

**Klipspringer Dragon**
South Africa

**Dubbing-wick Dragonfly Nymph**
UK

**Dragonfly Larva**
Canada

**Furry-foam Dragon**
New Zealand

**Annie's Nymph**
New Zealand

**Floating Dragon**
USA

**Assam Dragon**
USA

**Lake Dragon**
USA

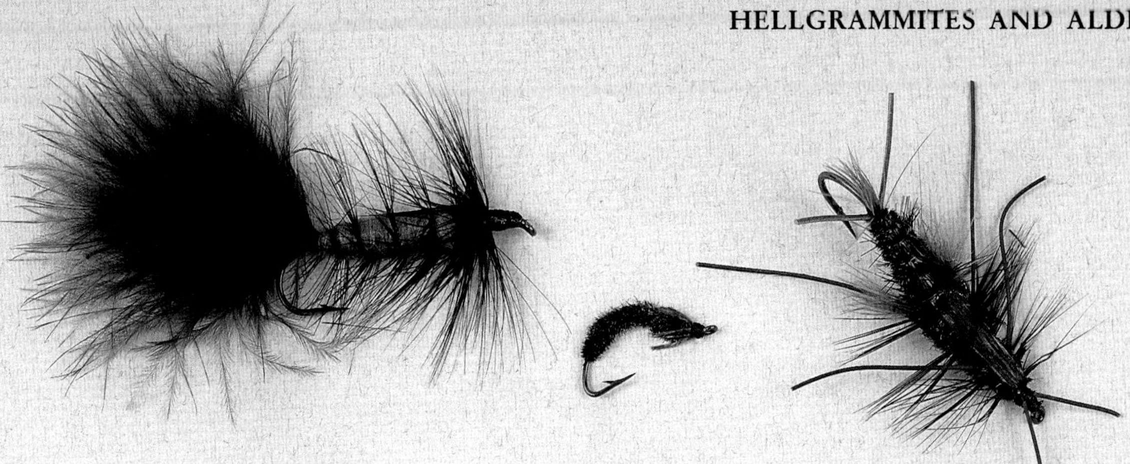

**Woolly Bugger**
USA

**Dobson-fly Larva**
New Zealand

**Bossbobs Hellgrammite**
USA

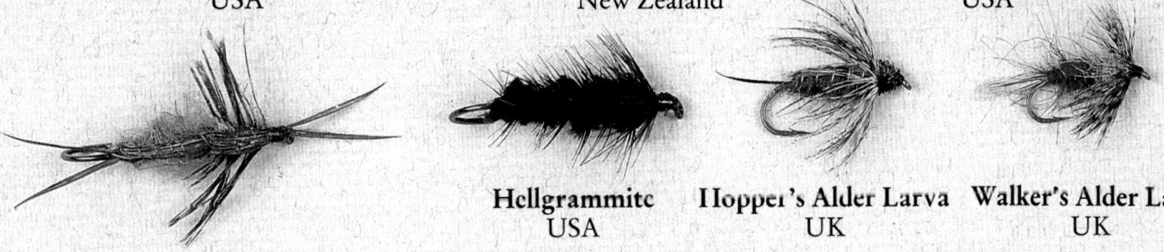

**Hellgrammite**
USA

**Hopper's Alder Larva**
UK

**Walker's Alder Larva**
UK

**Kaufmann's Hellgrammite**
USA

## BUGS AND BEETLES

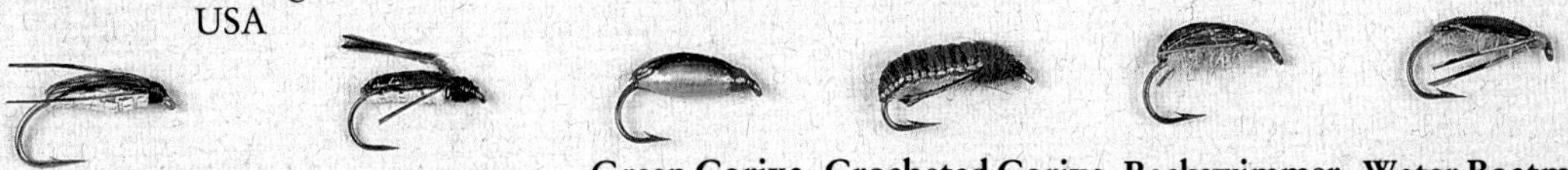

**Silver Corixa**
UK

**Large Brown Corixa** UK

**Green Corixa**
UK

**Crocheted Corixa**
Norway

**Backswimmer**
USA

**Water Boatman**
New Zealand

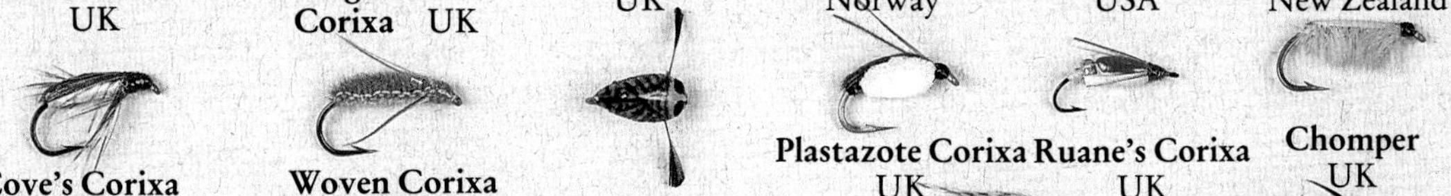

**Cove's Corixa**
UK

**Woven Corixa**
UK

**Carnill's Corixa**
UK

**Plastazote Corixa**
UK

**Ruane's Corixa**
UK

**Chomper**
UK

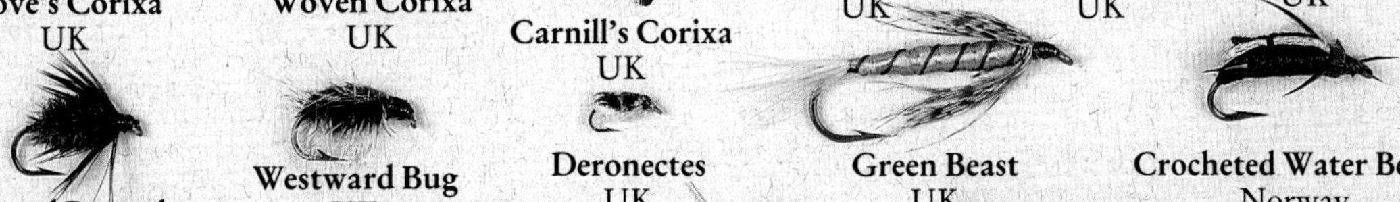

**Black and Peacock Spider** UK

**Westward Bug**
UK

**Deronectes**
UK

**Green Beast**
UK

**Crocheted Water Beetle**
Norway

## HARE'S EARS AND PHEASANT TAILS

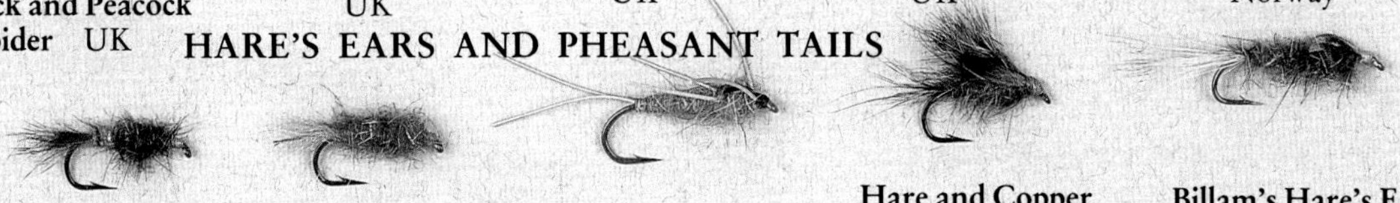

**Gold-Ribbed Hare's Ear** UK

**Orange Hare's Ear**
UK

**Rubberlegs Hare's Ear** USA

**Hare and Copper**
New Zealand

**Billam's Hare's Ear**
UK

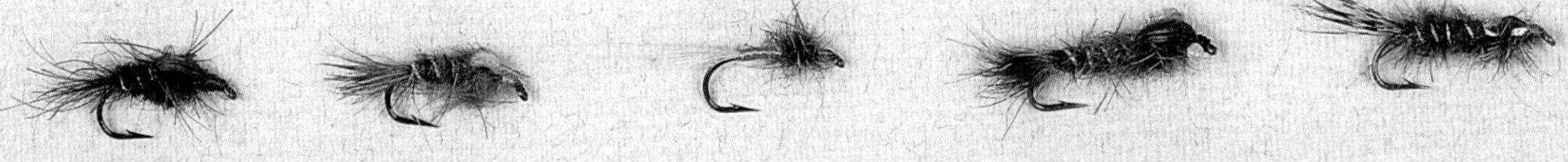

**Brown Hare's Ear**
USA

**Olive Hare's Ear**
UK

**Poil de Lièvre Nymphe**
France

**Mono-eyed Hare's Ear** USA

**Flashback Hare's Ear**
USA

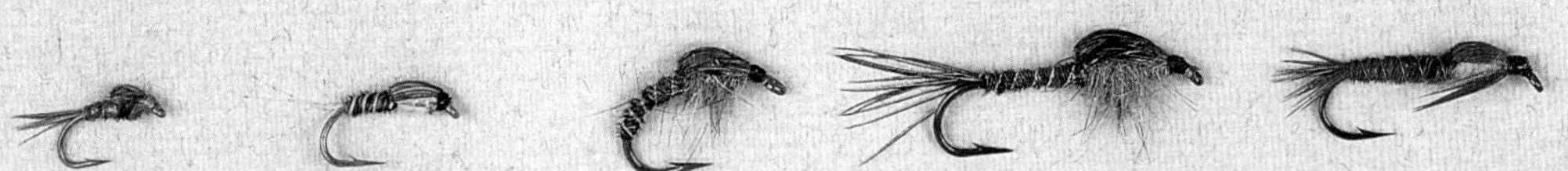

**Sawyer's Pheasant Tail** UK

**Pearly Pheasant Tail** UK

**Cove's Pheasant Tail** UK

**Long-shanked Pheasant Tail** UK

**Church's Pheasant Tail** UK

# CRUSTACEA

**Soft Shell Crayfish**
USA

**Clouser's Crayfish**
USA

**Fulling Mill Crayfish**
UK

**G.P.W. Crayfish**
Germany

**Mysis Relicta**
Scandinavia

**Bead-back Shrimp**
UK

**Mysis Shrimp**
USA

**Shrimper**
UK

**Red-spot Shrimp**
UK

**Blazevicev Rakusac**
Croatia

**M.M.G. Racusac**
Croatia

**Catfish Shrimp**
Austria

**Edwards' Freshwater Shrimp**
UK

**Dead Scud**
USA

**Bighorn Scud**
USA

**Hare's Ear Shrimp**
UK

**Eelskin Shrimp**
Slovenia

**Gamma**
France

**Eildon Shrimp**
Australia

# LEECHES

**'Lectric Leech**
USA

**Chamois Leech**
USA

**Black Leech**
UK

**Black & Brown Leech**
UK

**Egg-sucking Leech**
USA

**Stick Fly**

**Lead Bug**

**Copper Nymph**

**Clipped Coachman**

**Chew Nymph**

**Eyebrook Nymph**

**Conrad Voss Bark Nymph**

**Bewl Green Nymph**

**Green Rabbits**

**Carrot Nymph**

**Wonder Nymph**

**Bewl Beacon**

**Colnels Creeper**

**Fraser Nymph**

**B.W. Nymph**

**Collyer's Green Nymph**

**Collyer's Black Nymph**

**Twinkle Nymph**

**Hare's Ear Goldhead**

**Gold Nugget Orange Tag**

**Gold Nugget Stickfly**

**Dove Bug**

**Diawl Bach**

**Green DF Partridge**

**Hopper's Copper**

**Green Squirrel**

**Gerroff**

**Montana Stone**
USA

**Green Montana**
UK

**Montana Wasp**
UK

**Mayfly Nymph**
Italy

**Alletson's Brown Nymph**
South Africa

**T.V.N. Nymph**
South Africa

**Malcolm's Joseph**
South Africa

**Pallaretta**
Spain

**Pallaretta Variant**
Spain

**Quiver Nymph**
Austria

**Plecionka**
Poland

**Pika Nymph**
Slovenia

**Dormouse Nymph**
Slovenia

**Polifeitus**
Slovenia

**G.P.W. Nymph**
Germany

**Red-back Nymph**
Italy

**B.G. Emergent Pupa**
Germany

**Dendif Nymph**
Germany

**Pheasant and Orange**
France

**M.M.G. Grey Nymph**
Croatia

**Exotic Nymph**
Croatia

**Pfandl Nymph**
Germany

# AMERICAN NYMPHS

All-purpose Light    All-purpose Medium    All-purpose Dark    Rabbit Strip Nymph

Genie May    Natant Nylon Nymph    Ida May    Red Squirrel Nymph

Casual Dress    Big Hole Demon    Riffle Devil    Grey Squirrel Nymph

Picket Pin    Bitch Creek Nymph    Doc Sprately

Fledermaus    Black Rubber Legs    Simulator    Riffle Devil

Zug Bug    Prince Nymph    Atherton Medium    Atherton Dark    Atherton Light

Beaver Nymph    Martinez Nymph    Tellico    Carrot Nymph    Ted's Stonefly

Burlap Caddis    Near Enough    Burke's Nymph    Full Back    Dette's Isonychia

## FISHING THE CRANE FLY LARVAE

For most of the time crane fly larvae must be occasional food for trout. They are not active creatures, swimming around in large numbers or hatching from the surface like midges or ephemerids. I think that trout find, by accident, individuals that have been swept out of their safe havens down in the weeds, mud and detritus. On rivers I would tend to fish them on the dead drift; a large, juicy creature is not likely to be turned down by the fish.

Some years ago on Weirwood Reservoir in Sussex, during a long hot spell and in low-water conditions, a local angler who fished the water regularly was catching far more fish than anyone else, and these were generally much larger – trout up to 4lb (1.8kg). He fished an area where the shallows extended well out into the reservoir and he used to wade out into these shallows, causing as much disturbance as he could with his feet over quite a wide area so that the muddy water drifted ahead of him. When he thought he had created enough disturbance, and the muddy water was drifting outwards, he proceeded to cast a weigthed, plump larva pattern along the edges of this coloured water. The muddy water brought trout from the deeper water to mop up any 'wash-out' food caused by the disturbance.

I have seen this method – shuffling's one feet and allowing the mud and fine gravel drift downstream – work on rivers for grayling. They can be seen following the cloudy water almost up to the source of the disturbance. I have already mentioned, when discussing fishing bloodworms, the times after windy weather when midge larvae are washed out of their burrows. The same situation can occur with crane fly larvae.

## AQUATIC HOVER FLIES

### NATURALS

These flies belong to the family Syrphidae and the individuals that we are interested in, the drone flies, belong to the subfamily Eristalinae.

Hover flies are familiar to most people; the adults generally mimic the appearance of wasps, although the aquatic drones tend to mimic bees, hence the name 'drone'. The larvae of drone flies live in water, of a sort: drains, the mud and ooze of streams and ponds, even wet, smelly, farmyard manure; in fact in all the places where no self-respecting trout is likely to be found. The only reason for their inclusion here is that, from time to time, they are washed out of the disgusting areas they call home and end up in the main body of the water. It is then that trout are likely to feed upon them.

The larvae are known as rat-tailed maggots because of the long, telescopic breathing tube which they possess. This tube acts as a type of snorkel; the creature, safe underwater, can thrust this tube through the surface to replenish its air supply.

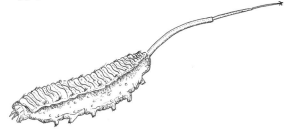

Rat-tailed maggot

Drone flies are highly successful insects; they spread from Asia to the USA, colonizing the western states by 1870 and spreading to the rest of the country by 1884. According to Gilbert, in his booklet *Hover Flies*, the fly reached New Zealand in 1888. Another interesting fact about this resilient fly is that the larva of at least one species is capable of giving birth to further larvae without ever having become an adult. Like the crane flies, the larvae come onto dry land in order to pupate.

The following are some of the species that have aquatic or semi-aquatic larval forms.

**Drone Flies of Angling Significance in the UK**

| Scientific Name | Scientific Name |
| --- | --- |
| Eristalis arbustorum | E. pertinax |
| E. intricarius | E. tenax |

The same species, I believe also occur in the USA.

### ARTIFICIALS

If I had been the only one to have created artificials to imitate the drone fly larva then perhaps I would not have included these insects in this book. But I am somewhat pleased to note that others have endeavoured to copy that rat-tailed maggot, so I include this insect with a small degree of justification.

**Rat-tailed Maggot** · Price · UK

| | |
|---|---|
| *Hook* | Mustad, 94841, sizes 8-12 |
| *Thread* | Grey or black |
| *Tail* | Stripped hackle stalk |
| *Body* | Grey fur mixed with a little fluorescent white fur or wool |
| *Back* | Natural latex |
| *Rib* | Black silk or oval silver tinsel |

**Rat-tailed Maggot** · R. Walker · UK

| | |
|---|---|
| *Hook* | Mustad 94841, size 12 |
| *Thread* | Grey |
| *Tail* | Bleached cock-pheasant tail fibre |
| *Body* | Hare's ear and fluorescent white wool, mixed |

**Rat-tailed Maggot** · Thomas · UK

| | |
|---|---|
| *Hook* | Mustad 94841, size 12 |
| *Thread* | Grey |
| *Tail* | Undyed swan fibres |
| *Body* | Fluorescent white wool |
| *Head* | Brown ostrich herl, two turns |

Rat-tailed maggot

\*    \*    \*

Other dipterans have aquatic larvae but they are of little significance from a fly-fishing point of view. A few dressings to imitate the larvae of snipe and soldier flies are given by Ernest Schwiebert in *Nymphs* and there are some South African patterns for the snipe fly, *Atherix androgyna*, which swarms on some rivers in mid-summer to lay its eggs.

# CHAPTER ELEVEN

# WATER BUGS

## NATURALS

The order Hemiptera, the true bugs, includes both terrestrial and aquatic insects. It is a very wide and diverse group which includes the various plant bugs, shield bugs, stink bugs, assassin bugs and even bed bugs. Most are either sap- or blood-suckers and at least one terrestrial species is a carrier of Chagas's disease. As far as this book is concerned, however, we are interested only in the aquatic members of this order. Some of these aquatic bugs feed on other creatures by stabbing them with their sharp rostral beaks and injecting them with a corrosive liquid which dissolves their vitals so that they can be easily sucked up. The two families of water bug which are of particular interest to the fly-fisherman are the Notonectidae and the Corixidae. Other aquatic true bugs, such as the water scorpion and water stick insect, are not really of our concern.

### NOTONECTIDAE

Better known as water boatmen, wherrymen, boat flies and backswimmers, these insects lie upside-down in the surface film awaiting their prey, which includes other insects and larvae, tadpoles or even small fish. (As a matter of interest, if these insects are placed in a tank lit from below, they lie the other way up.) They are sensitive to any sub-surface disturbance and will descend to attack their pray with their sharp rostral beak and inject their toxic saliva. A word of warning here. Handle these creatures with care because a stab from them is as painful as that from a wasp or bee.

They are good fliers and will often leave their home water to find other more suitable habitats. After the eggs hatch out, the infants undergo five instar stages in the 5 months or so before they reach adulthood. When the backswimmer dives beneath the surface, air becomes trapped on its abdomen by a series of longitudinal bristles and is held there as a bubble by hydrofugous (unwettable) hairs. The underside of the insect thus appears very silvery. These insects are found all over the world but, in the UK, there are four species, five if the smaller, allied species, the lesser water boatman, is included. Most British species are approximately ⅝–¾in (14–15mm) long while the lesser water boatman is about 1⁄16–⅛in (2–3mm).

### Water Boatmen of the UK and Europe

| Scientific Name | Common Name |
|---|---|
| Notonecta glauca | Common Water Boatman |
| N. maculata | — |
| N. marmorea | — |
| N. obliqua | — |
| Plea atomaria | Lesser Water Boatman |

The most abundant and widely distributed species is *N. glauca*. *N. obliqua* prefers more acid conditions and *N. marmorea* favours brackish waters. Concrete reservoirs and stony pools are the home of *N. maculata*, and *Plea atomaria* can sometimes be found in very large numbers feeding on daphnia.

In the USA there are many more species and subspecies, of which a few are included in the list below.

### Non-European Water Boatmen

| Scientific Name | Common Name | Distribution |
|---|---|---|
| Anisops assimilis | Common Backswimmer | NZ |
| Buenoa margaritacea | Pale Moon-wing Blackswimmer | USA |
| Notonecta irrorata | Gray-winged Backswimmer | USA |
| N. undulata | Grouse-winged Backswimmer | USA |
| Plea striola | Pygmy Bug | USA |

## CORIXIDAE

A little confusion creeps in because these insects are also known as lesser water boatmen; other common names include water singer and common corixid. In the UK there are just over 30 species and subspecies of corixid. In the USA in excess of 100 species have so far been identified. Corixids are found from the far north of Iceland as far south as the Antipodes. They occur in ice-cold pools and even in water emanating from hot springs. Although very similar in appearance to backswimmers, they do not swim upside-down; neither do they spend most of their time at the surface and, as far as diet is concerned, they feed on algal matter on the bottom. They ascend to the surface from time to time to replenish their oxygen supplies and, like the backswimmers, the corixids retain a bubble of air on their abdomen by means of hydrofugous hairs. They are extremely able and fast swimmers and to witness their ascent and descent through the water is like looking at beads of quicksilver. Most species have particular water requirements and tolerances and, if the water quality, falls short of these, the insects just fly away; their place is then taken by another species which finds the habitat more to its liking. Like the notonectids, the corixids undergo five moults, or instars, before reaching maturity. This takes about 3 months and the adults are usually encountered in the month of July. The adults vary in length from ⅜–¾in (9–15mm), depending on the species.

### Corixids of the UK and Europe

| Scientific Name | Common Name |
| --- | --- |
| Corixa affinis | — |
| C. dentipes | — |
| C. panzeri | — |
| C. punctata | Common Corixid |

The common corixid, *C. punctata*, prefers the weedy, alkaline waters found in ponds and the backwaters of slow-flowing rivers. *C. dentipes* has been identified as a British species only since 1928 but is common throughout Europe, while *C. affinis*, from north Africa, is at its northern limit in Europe. Chironomid larvae, as well as algae, feature in the diet of *C. panzeri*, which sports a chequered pattern on its elytra.

There are, of course, other species that could well figure in the diet of the trout, including the much smaller subspecies *Hespercorixa*, of which

*Corixa* sp.

there are about five species in the UK. These vary in size from ¼in to ⅜in (6mm to 9mm). Although there are many more species in the USA and the rest of the world, and although there are a great number of artificial patterns tied to imitate the corixa, very little has been written in the fishing books about the species being imitated. Even Schwiebert in his book, *Nymphs*, gives only one species, *Arctocorixa alternata* (Corixa Bug), suggesting that it is prototypical of all the species which are difficult to identify. Norman Marsh also gives only one pattern in his book on New Zealand species which he refers to as *Sigara arguta* (Water Boatman).

## ARTIFICIALS

It was a hot day in midsummer, one of those days when the fish were either ready to be caught or, because of the temperature, were sulking somewhere in the depths, fighting shy of any offering. I was fishing a small stillwater in Tenterden, in Kent, and am pleased to report that the trout did not skulk and I had one or two nice fish to show for all my sweat. But my companion on that occasion, Davy Wotton, seemed to be always fighing a fish and he must have caught and released about 20 fine trout to my one or two. He had placed himself close to a reed-bed where the water shallowed off.

When this sort of situation occurs I pretend it is not happening and go about my own business, trying to ignore the fact that someone is doing better than I am. Pride, I suppose, prevents me even asking what fly was doing the damage. But a 10:1 ratio was too much to bear. Curiosity tinged with a degree of envy prompted me to go over and see what he was using; whatever it was seemed to be more palatable to the fish than anything I was giving them. He was using a small, size 14 Corixa. He had noticed the trout coming into the shallows to take these small, silvery insects and had benefited from the observation. It always pays to stop, look and appraise the situation before fishing but it was something that he did and something I did not.

Mind you, I had the biggest catch of the day: a fine, fat, Kentish sheep, caught on my back cast! It trotted off on its woolly legs at a rate of knots, with my reel screaming and me running behind until my hook finally released itself from the thick fleece. There are jokes about Welshman and sheep, and I suppose this has to be one of them.

BRITISH PATTERNS
I tied up my first imitation some 25 years ago, when I was a lot younger – and even had hair. I wanted a simple pattern to imitate the small corixids found on my local lake. I had observed these little creatures in my aquarium, swimming up to the surface for air and diving down with the air, like a silver bubble, attached to their abdomen. The fly still appears in the Orvis Fly catalogue in the UK.

**Silver Corixa** · Price · UK
*Hook*      Mustad 3904A, sizes 12–15
*Body*      Flat silver Lurex
*Rib*       Oval silver tinsel
*Back*      Cock-pheasant tail fibres, lacquered for durability
*Paddles*   Two cock-pheasant tail fibres

Silver Corixa

The late Richard Walker had a number of patterns to imitate the Corixa. This first pattern imitates very well the final instar of a number of species.

**Yellow Corixa** · R. Walker · UK
*Hook*      Mustad 3905A, size 14
*Thread*    Brown
*Body*      Primrose silk

*Back*      Olive-green goose, varnished
*Paddles*   Two olive-green goose fibres (optional)

**Large Brown Corixa** · R. Walker · UK
*Hook*      Mustad 3904, size 10
*Thread*    Black
*Body*      White floss silk
*Rib*       Flat silver tinsel
*Back*      Brown-speckled turkey
*Paddles*   Two speckled turkey fibres

Arthur Cove in his book *My Way with Trout* gives three variations of the Corixa.

**Corixa** · Cove · UK
*Hook*      Mustad 3904, sizes 8–14
*Thread*    Brown
*Body*      White Terylene
*Rib*       Silver wire
*Back*      Cock-pheasant tail fibres
*Legs*      Small brown or white hen

**Green Corixa** · Cove · UK
*Hook*      Mustad 3904A, sizes 12–14
*Thread*    Olive
*Body*      White Terylene
*Rib*       Silver wire
*Back*      Green cock-pheasant tail fibres
*Legs*      Small green hackle

Green Corixa (Walker)

**Silver Corixa** · Cove · UK
*Hook*      Mustad 3904A, sizes 10–14
*Thread*    Black
*Body*      Flat silver tinsel
*Rib*       Silver wire
*Back*      Cock-pheasant tail
*Legs*      Small brown hen hackle

The late Dave Collyer created an interesting pattern using Plastazote as the body medium. This fly should be fished on a short leader with a sunk or sink-tip line. When you retrieve, the fly dives in a most realistic manner.

**Plastazote Corixa** · Collyer · UK
*Hook*      Mustad 94840, sizes 10–14
*Thread*    Black
*Body*      White Plastazote shaped and glued to the hook
*Back*      Cock-pheasant tail fibres
*Paddles*   Two cock-pheasant tail fibres

The next two patterns are a little more complex to tie than those already given. The first was created by Bob Carnill and is extremely realistic. The second was tied by Terry Ruane, a master in the use of synthetic materials.

**Carnill Corixa** · Carnill · UK
*Hook*      Drennan Midge Hook, short shank (or similar), sizes 10–12
*Thread*    Unwaxed white
*Underbody* White wool over lead or copper wire if weighted
*Belly*     Silver liquid glitter
*Back*      Piece of white plastic taken from a small food container, cut to a finger-nail shape, and coloured and marked with waterproof ink
*Paddles*   Two hackle stalks with fibres left at the tips

Carnill Corixa

To tie this fly, proceed as follows:

*Step 1*   Tie in the paddles, followed by the white wool underbody.
*Step 2*   Superglue the back to the body.
*Step 3*   Reverse the hook and fill the body cavity with liquid glitter. Allow to dry for 24 hours.
*Step 4*   Mark the back with waterproof marker pens to achieve a realistic effect.

This fly of Terry Ruane's incorporates a small bead to imitate the bubble of air and another pearl oval to imitate he body of the insect.

**Ruane's Corixa** · Ruane · UK
*Hook*       Partridge K12ST, size 16
*Thread*     White
*Air bubble* Clear bead
*Body*       Oval pearl bead
*Back*       Light brown lacquer
*Paddles*    Two grey duck fibres

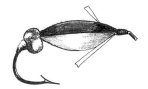

Ruane's Corixa

The air-bubble bead is slipped on over the hook barb and the oval pearl bead must have a centre hole wide enough to go over the eye of the hook. The beads are held in place by the tying thread, which is well varnished.

AMERICAN PATTERNS

The first of the American patterns was created by the Montana tier, A1 Troth, and is called simply the Backswimmer. This, of course, imitates one of the notonectids.

**Backswimmer** · Troth · USA
*Hook*      Mustad 7957BX , sizes 10–14
*Thread*    Olive
*Body*      Olive tinsel chenille
*Back*      Mottled turkey
*Paddles*   Olive goose biots

**Backswimmer** · Hughes · USA
*Hook*      Mustad 3904A, sizes 12–16
*Thread*    Brown
*Body*      Sandy-orange seal fur or substitute
*Back*      Cock-pheasant tail or mottled turkey with clear PVC over
*Paddles*   Cock-pheasant tail barbs

Dave Hughes also devised this next pattern. Dave is one of the most prolific writers in the USA today, with many excellent books to his credit, including one on the Deschutes River, a river which I had the pleasure fishing with him in 1991.

**Water Boatman** · Hughes · USA
*Hook*      Mustad 3904A, sizes 12–20
*Thread*    Light olive

| | |
|---|---|
| *Body* | Golden-olive seal fur or substitute over lead wire |
| *Back* | Natural or olive turkey quill |
| *Paddles* | Cock-pheasant tail fibres |

Water Boatman

One of the simplest of patterns to come out of the USA is depicted in *Flies (The Best One Thousand)* by Randall Scott Stetzer and was created by Bill Beardsley.

**Corixid** · Beardsley · USA
| | |
|---|---|
| *Hook* | Mustad 3906B, sizes 16–20 |
| *Thread* | Dark olive |
| *Body* | Dark olive rabbit tied on loosely |

I first saw the next pattern or a very similar one in an American fly-fishing publication. Like the Ruane pattern given earlier, this too used a bead to simulate the air bubble.

**E.T.'s Corixa** · Tainton · USA
| | |
|---|---|
| *Hook* | Mustad 9671, size 8–12 |
| *Thread* | Black |
| *Air bubble* | Silver bead glued into place |
| *Body* | Peacock herl over foam strip (lead underbody is optional) |
| *Back* | Black latex |
| *Paddles* | Two strands of black rubber hackle |

E.T.'s Corixa

NEW ZEALAND PATTERNS

**Water Boatman** · Orman · NZ
| | |
|---|---|
| *Hook* | Mustad 3904A, sizes 12–14 |
| *Thread* | Brown |
| *Tag* | Flat silver tinsel, two turns |
| *Body* | Cream wool or seal fur |
| *Rib* | Flat silver tinsel |
| *Back* | Cock-pheasant tail fibres |
| *Legs* | Ginger hen hackle clipped off at the top |

**Water Boatman** · Marsh · NZ
| | |
|---|---|
| *Hook* | Mustad 3904A, size 16 |
| *Thread* | Black |
| *Body* | Green and yellow synthetic dubbing |
| *Back* | Kea father (substitute with turkey) |
| *Paddles* | Pheasant tail fibres |

SOUTH AFRICAN PATTERN
The final pattern comes from South Africa but owes a lot to the English patterns. It was given in the book *Flies and Fly Fishing in South Africa*, written by my good friend Jack Blackman.

**Corixa** · Blackman · S. Africa
| | |
|---|---|
| *Hook* | Mustad 3904, sizes 12–14 |
| *Thread* | Black |
| *Body* | White or cream floss silk |
| *Rib* | Brown silk |
| *Back* | Woodcock feather |
| *Legs* | Cream hen hackle |

*FISHING THE WATER BUG NYMPH*

The corixids and, to a degree, the backwimmer are creatures of the water margins. They are not generally found in the main body of the water but prefer fairly shallow habitats of between 1 and 3ft (30 and 90cm). It is in these shallow waters that you should fish the artificials. Look for these insects near weed- and reed-beds, and in areas on reservoirs where old paths, roadways, ditches and hedgerows enter the water.

Corixa patterns make ideal ambush flies for cruising trout. Watch for such fish as they swim slowly, seeking out titbits here and there. Cast a Corixa pattern well ahead of the fish and allow it to sink. As the fish approaches, slowly lift the rod to activate the fly and retrieve in a long, slow pull; this movement imitates the natural as it rises in the water to replenish its air supply. Fish any buoyant fly in the same way but use a sinking or sink-tip line. If the water is 2 or 3ft (30 or 90cm) deep, use a leader of this length. The fly will be on the surface but, on retrieval, it will dive down, imitating the insect as it returns with its bubble of air. I have sometimes used a Corixa pattern on a dropper when fishing a lure. Because the natural insects swim fairly quickly, it is an ideal pattern in shallow lakes when using a lure on the point; fish will take both.

# CHAPTER TWELVE

# WATER BEETLES

Beetles belong to the insect order Coleoptera, which contains more species than all the other insect groups put together. Beetles are to be found throughout the world, from hot, sandy deserts to the icy wastes. There are about 370,000 identified species but entomologists believe that any number up to 5 million has yet to be classified. In the UK, there are about 4,000 species and, in the USA, somewhere in the region of 30,000; these figures are quite staggering.

## NATURALS

A large number of beetles are entirely aquatic in their habitat: some are active swimmers, some are found at the surface, and some creep and crawl along the bottom. Do trout feed upon them? The short answer is yes. Trout certainly feed avidly on terrestrial beetles that fall accidentally onto the water, judging from the number of patterns that have been created to imitate them: the Coch y Bonddu, Marlow Buzz, Eric's Beetle and Fern Web in the UK; the Tri Tree Beetle in Australia; and very effective Green Manuka and Brown Beetles in New Zealand. In the USA the terrestrial beetle imitations include a pattern to imitate the equivalent of our Coch y Bonddu, the Japanese Beetle.

If trout are going to expend energy by rising to the surface to take such fare it seems reasonable to assume that they will dine equally happily on similar creatures that shared their watery habitat. Very little study has been done into the relationships between the fish and aquatic beetles and their larvae, and this is evident in the very few patterns available to the angler. I may well be wrong but the sparsity of imitations is probably because anglers have not yet come to appreciate the relationship between trout and aquatic beetles. With so many other insect foods available to the trout it has not seemed important. Ernest Schwiebert, in his book *Nymphs*, gives 20 different species of aquatic beetle

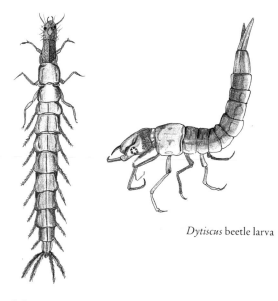

*Dytiscus* beetle larva

Beetle larva

larvae and his imitations of them. (There are, in the USA, some 1,000 different species of aquatic beetle.) He is the only author, and his the only book, that has devoted so much space to aquatic beetle larvae as the prey of trout.

A few years ago, on Bewl Water in Kent, down the arm called Hook Straight, I caught a number of trout close to the weedy shore line. At least two of the fish had the larvae of the beetle *Dytiscus marginalis* in their stomach contents.

I have kept both larval and adult *Dytiscus* in an aquarium in my living room and was quite appalled at their vicious predatory behaviour. Nothing was safe: tadpoles, caddis larva, minnows and sticklebacks all fell victim to these creatures. They seized their prey in their sickle-like jaws and just sucked it dry. Witnessing this, I felt loathe to put my hand in the water; they made dragonfly nymphs look like cissies. Not long afterwards, the adults decided that they had had enough of their enforced home and took flight for ponds anew.

One was found in the kitchen sink; the others, I believe, ended up in the toilet, and there a final dive took them right around the bend. I was not sorry to see them go.

## ARTIFICIALS

Adult as well as larval patterns are included in this chapter.

### BRITISH PATTERNS

The first pattern is a well-tried favourite of the British stillwanger angler, a fly popularized by the late Tom Ivens, one of the pioneers of reservoir fly-fishing. The Black & Peacock Spider is thought by many to represent a snail but I am of the opinion that the creature is taken by the trout as an aquatic beetle.

**Black & Peacock Spider** · Ivens · UK
| | |
|---|---|
| Hook | Mustad 94840, sizes 8–20 |
| Thread | Black |
| Body | Bronze peacock herl |
| Hackle | Soft black hen |

Black & Peacock Spider

Richard Walker created a series of flies called the Chompers, small, broad-spectrum patterns tied to represent a number of small aquatic bugs and creatures. The white-bodied version was ideal as a standby for the *Corixa*. The olive, brown and black versions make simple aquatic beetle representations.

**Chompers** · R. Walker · UK
| | |
|---|---|
| Hook | Mustad 3904A, sizes 8–16 |
| Thread | To match pattern colour |
| Body | Ostrich herl (black, olive, green, brown, white, etc.) |
| Back | Raffene (Swiss Straw) sometimes matching body, sometimes contrasting; varnish after tying in |

The next pattern was one of my own, tied to represent the larva of *Dytiscus marginalis*, which I found in the stomach contents of the trout from Bewl Water.

**Dytiscus Larva** · Price · UK
| | |
|---|---|
| Hook | Mustad 79580, size 6 |
| Thread | Brown |
| Tail | Brown hackle fibres |
| Underbody | Brown wool |
| Overbody | Latex, coloured with brown waterproof ink along the back |
| Thorax | Brown seal fur or synthetic dubbing |
| Wing case | Latex to match overbody colour |
| Legs | brown partridge |

Since publishing the above pattern, more modern materials have come onto the fly-tying market and the following version makes use of some of these.

**Dytiscus Larva No. 2** · Price · UK
| | |
|---|---|
| Hook | Mustad Swimming Nymph 80150BR, size 6 |
| Thread | Black or brown |
| Tail | Short tuft of brown hackle fibres |
| Body | Dirty yellow dubbing wick |
| Back | Brown PVC (Body Flex) |
| Rib | Transparent nylon tying thread |
| Thorax | As body |
| Legs | Brown partridge or grouse hackle, tied flat between the thorax and wing case |
| Wing case | As back |
| Head | Brown marabou or synthetic brown dubbing |
| Eyes | Black bead chain |

*Dytiscus* Larva No. 2

I have caught a number of fish on our local water and, on examining the stomach contents, have found a number of small, yellowish aquatic beetles of the species *Deronectes*. I tied up the following pattern to represent them.

**Deronectes Beetle** · Price · UK
*Hook*     Mustad 94840, sizes 16–18
*Thread*   Yellow
*Body*     Yellow seal fur (or substitute)
*Back*     Yellow Raffene marked with black water-
           proof ink
*Legs*     Body fur picked out

The next pattern, imitating a large beetle larva, was tied by Alan Pearson, no stranger to big stillwater trout.

**Green Beast** · Pearson · UK
*Hook*     Mustad 79580, sizes 6–10
*Thread*   Green
*Tail*     Green cock hackle fibres
*Body*     Grass-green silk over lead wire
*Rib*      Fine silver wire
*Legs*     Long-fibred brown partridge

Green Beast

Alan also tied a general-purpose pattern that imitates an aquatic beetle.

**Grizzle Beetle** · Pearson · UK
*Hook*     Mustad 94840, sizes 8–10
*Thread*   Black
*Body*     Black ostrich over lead wire
*Hackle*   Palmered grizzle cock
*Back*     Cock-pheasant, tail fibres; this back
           forces the hackle fibres to splay outwards

Dave Collyer christened his version of the *Dytiscus* larva the Water Tiger Nymph. Another name for this predacious creature is the Water Tiger.

**Water Tiger** · Collyer · UK
*Hook*     Mustad 79580, sizes 8–10
*Thread*   Light brown
*Tail*     Pale sepia tips of condor herl substitute

*Body*      Pale sepia condor herl substitute
*Rib*       Copper wire and peacock herl
*Thorax*    Olive-yellow dubbing
*Wing case* As body
*Legs*      Brown partridge either side of the
            thorax

The next pattern was given by John Roberts in his *A New Illustrated Dictionary of Trout Flies*.

**Buff Bug** · UK
*Hook*     Mustad 3906B, size 12
*Thread*   Brown
*Body*     Light brown wool
*Back*     Mottled turkey feather
*Legs*     Two strands of turkey either side of the
           body

AMERICAN PATTERNS
The famous American fly, the Wooly Worm, is no doubt sometimes taken by the fish as a beetle larva. It is a good, searching nymph pattern for riffle water. The following three patterns fall into this palmered-body type of fly. The first was created by Charles E. Brookes, whose book, *Nymph Fishing for Larger Trout*, is considered to be a classic, I also consider his book on Henry's Fork to be one of the best books I have read about a river and its environs. He found a strange larva in a riffle on the Firehole River and it took some time to identify; it eventually turned out to be a *Dytiscus* larva.

**Riffle Devil** · Brookes · USA
*Hook*     Mustad 79580, sizes 4–8
*Thread*   Olive
*Body*     Olive chenille
*Legs*     Palmered ginger cock hackle

Randall Kaufmann produced a multi-purpose dry fly called the Stimulator, a pattern that could imitate a caddis-, a stonefly or even a grasshopper. The nymph equivalent of this fly is called the Simulator, a broad-spectrum pattern that can imitate a number of aquatic creatures, among them the larva of an aquatic beetle.

**Simulator** · Kaufmann · USA
*Hook*     Mustad 79580, sizes 4–10
*Thread*   Claret
*Tail*     Two red-brown goose biots or a
           short tuft of red-brown marabou

| | |
|---|---|
| *Body* | Bronze peacock herl over lead wire (other versions use brown or black dubbed fur bodies) |
| *Body hackle* | Dark furnace palmered along the body then clipped |
| *Legs*<br>*(front hackle)* | Dark furnace palmered over the thorax area |

**Raggle Bomb** · USA

| | |
|---|---|
| *Hook* | Mustad 9671, sizes 8–14 |
| *Thread* | Black |
| *Underbody* | Tapered olive wool |
| *Overbody* | Peacock herl |
| *Hackle* | Palmered ginger cock with two turns at the head |

Raggle Bomb

Eric Leiser, in his *Book of Fly Patterns*, gives an example of an aquatic adult beetle called, simply, the Diving Beetle.

**Diving Beetle** · USA

| | |
|---|---|
| *Hook* | Mustad 3906, size 12 |
| *Thread* | Black |
| *Body* | Rust-coloured dubbing over lead wire |
| *Back* | Black Raffene (Swiss Straw) |
| *Legs* | Grouse hackle tied in before the back is wrapped over the body |
| *Head* | Black Raffene, the end of the back material folded over and tied down |

### FISHING THE BEETLE

On stillwaters, fish all such beetle larvae or adult beetle patterns close to the bottom, although the Black & Peacock Spider can prove quite effective near the surface. Fish close to weedbeds; this is where the natural lives and where trout expect to find them. Good-sized browns often cruise up from the deeper areas of the water to seek their sustenance in the shallow waters around the weedbeds. On rivers, many of the larval patterns are good searching flies when fished in the dead drift, in the fish-holding riffles.

# CHAPTER THIRTEEN

# ALDERS AND HELLGRAMMITES

## ALDERFLIES

### NATURALS

The alderflies, or orl flies as they are sometimes called, are well known to all anglers. These sedge-like insects, darkish brown in colour, belong to the order Neuroptera, family Sialidae, and are seen on the wing from May through to June. I have no doubt that trout take these flies when they are blown onto the water. Some angler's extol the virtues of this insect and recommend its use as an artificial. Charles Kingsley, author of the children's classic *The Water Babies*, was an avid fly-fisherman and wrote about the value of this fly. I, however, am one of those fishermen who has never caught a fish on the dry Alder and I suspect I am not alone. Imitations of the larvae, however, have caught fish for me and they are an important fly during the month of April on some rivers and smaller stillwaters.

When the prevailing weather and water conditions are right, the larva of the alderfly will decide it is time to pupate; this can be as early as March. As a larva, it lives down in the mud and detritus, leading the life of an efficient predator. When it is time to pupate, it leaves the water and digs a small hole in the soil close to the water's edge; there, for a week or so, it is quiescent and eventually changes into the adult fly.

I have found hundreds of pupating alders at my local lake; they seem to be gregarious. I found them by accident when I slipped off a 2ft (60cm) concrete promontory wall and, on standing up in the water, noticed what appeared to be alder larvae floating on the surface. On closer examination I could see that they were pupae. I scraped away the thin topsoil on the concrete promontory and, sure enough, there were dozens of small, curled-up pupa lying beneath the soil.

Examination of the stomach contents of caught fish on my local lake during the month of April at

Alder larva

times reveals alder larvae, occasionally as many as 10 or 12. Without doubt the alder larva is an important fly for early months of the season. The mature larva is approximately ¾–1in (20–25mm) long and its abdomen bears seven pairs of breathing filaments and what appears to be a single tail. This tail is also a breathing appendage.

The following species are a few that should interest the angler; all are very similar in general appearance.

**Alderflies of Angling Significance**

| Scientific Name | Distribution |
| --- | --- |
| *Sialis lutaria* | UK & Europe |
| *S. californica* | USA |
| *S. cornuta* | USA |
| *S. fuliginosa* | UK & Europe |
| *S. hamata* | USA |
| *S. infumata* | USA |
| *S. mohri* | USA |
| *S. nigripes* | S. UK & Ireland |
| *S. rotunda* | USA |

## ARTIFICIALS

The first pattern is a fly devised by C.F. Walker and is probably the first Alder larva fly to be tied.

**Alder Larva** · C. F. Walker · UK

| | |
|---|---|
| *Hook* | Mustad 3906, sizes 10–12 |
| *Thread* | Brown |
| *Tail* | Honey or ginger hackle point |
| *Body* | Brown and ginger seal fur, tapered |
| *Rib* | Oval gold tinsel and palmered sandy hen hackle |
| *Thorax* | Hare's ear |
| *Legs* | Brown partridge |
| *Head* | As thorax |

Stuart Canham is one of Britain's leading fly-tiers of the realistic school. Many of his flies have been illustrated in a number of British magazines. He is equally good at tying the ornate, fully dressed salmon flies.

**Alder Larva** · Canham · UK

| | |
|---|---|
| *Hook* | Partridge CS2, sizes 8–10 |
| *Thread* | Olive or brown |
| *Tail* | White marabou |
| *Body* | Ginger seals fur |
| *Rib* | Gold wire |
| *Back* | Brown Raffene |
| *Thorax* | Medium olive or brown seal fur |
| *Gills* | As tail |
| *Wing case* | As back |
| *Legs* | Brown partridge |

The next pattern is Bob Carnill's version, which, in many respects, is very similar to the Canham fly.

**Alder Larva** · Carnhill · UK

| | |
|---|---|
| *Hook* | Mustad 79580, size 10 |
| *Thread* | Brown |
| *Tail* | Medium brown goose biot |
| *Body* | Brown and chestnut mole, mixed |
| *Back* | Plain or mottled feather fibre |
| *Thorax* | As body |
| *Wing case* | As back |
| *Legs* | Brown partridge |
| *Gills* | Pale ginger hen palmered down the body |

The final pattern is another of Glyn Hopper's, tied in the same style as his Dragonfly Larva given earlier.

**Alder Larva** · Hopper · UK

| | |
|---|---|
| *Hook* | Kamasan B/830, mediumshank, sizes 10–14 |
| *Thread* | Brown |
| *Tail* | Single brown goose biot |
| *Body* | Brown seal fur (two parts), ginger seal fur (one part) and fluorescent orange seal fur (one part), mixed |
| *Rib* | Copper wire |
| *Back* | Golden-pheasant tail fibres |
| *Legs* | Brown or grey partridge hackle |

Alder Larva

## FISHING THE ALDER

The time for fishing the alder larva is in early April when they migrate from the camouflage of the silt and detritus to the dry land to pupate. It is at this time that the trout take notice of these creatures and feed avidly on them. I tend to fish these nymphs on a sunk or sink-tip line and retrieve in a slow figure of 8.

## HELLGRAMMITES

### NATURALS

The Dobson flies and fishflies, of the order Megaloptera, are close relatives of the alder but neither occur in the UK or Europe. In other parts of the world, however, the larvae of these creatures can be important fishing flies. Both belong to the family Corydalidae: the Dobson flies to the subfamily Corydalinae and the fishflies to the subfamily Chauliodinae.

The larvae of the Dobson flies are known as hellgrammites, crawlers or, sometimes, toe-biters. They are large nymphs, measuring anything up to 3½in (90mm) long when fully mature. They are creatures of well-oxygenated, fast-moving water. The larvae of the fishflies tend to favour the quieter portions of a river where there is plenty of detritus and leaf litter to hide in. Both larvae have eight pairs of breathing filaments along their abdomen

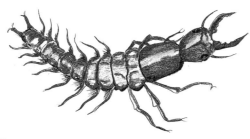

Hellgrammite

and the end of the bodies have two prolegs, each with a tiny hook. From a fly-tying point of view, both are very similar in appearance. They are big nymphs and their imitations are usually equally large. Most species are very dark, almost black, in colour. Like the alder larvae, they come out of the water to pupate.

**Dobson Flies of Angling Significance**

| Scientific Name | Distribution |
| --- | --- |
| Archichauliodes diversus | NZ |
| Chauliodes pectinicornis | USA |
| Chloroniella perngueyi | S. Africa |
| Corydalis cornuta | USA |

Other insects closely allied to these formidable creatures are the *Spongilla* flies and some species of lacewings, a number of which have aquatic or semi-aquatic larvae. These larvae are not usually of interest to the angler.

## ARTIFICIALS

From a fishing point of view, these nymphs are probably the largest of the aquatic insects we are likely to come into contact with, although some water beetle larvae run them a close second. They are the kind of nymphs I like: there is nothing delicate or small about the natural larvae or their imitations; they are man-sized nymphs, nymphs I have no trouble threading onto my leader; they do not stress my tired eyes. The hellgrammites are aggressive creatures that think nothing of trying to bite you with their formidable mandibles. Because they do not occur in European waters the anglers of the UK and Europe are unlikely to fish patterns to imitate them. However, they look so edible that I feel sure British reservoir trout would not be averse to taking them. Flies such as the Montana Stonefly Nymph have proved to be highly effective

on British stillwaters, even though the large stoneflies which the fly is supposed to imitate do not exist there; yet the trout take the Montana avidly, so why not the hellgrammite?

As if to prove a point, the first of the imitations is such a fly. Where would I be without the Woolly Bugger? It has taken fish for me all over the world. In the UK, this fly would be classed as a lure for use on reservoirs, but a glance at fly-catalogues from the USA will show you this highly mobile marabou fly is always placed firmly amid the ranks of the nymph and is fished more often than not on rivers.

We were in the town of Missoula in Montana and were due to take a float with a local guide, Dave Ruetz, on the famed Clark Fork. It was to be an early morning start, not the best thing after a night at the Duelling Daltons, trying to get on the wrong side of a bottle of Jack Daniels. Nevertheless we were ready and by the side of the river at 6 a.m., bleary-eyed and almost rarin' to go. The faint mist that clung to the river as we started out began to evaporate as the sun rose higher in the sky. We soon left the town behind and slowly drifted with the lazy current of the Clark. A large beaver swam ahead of us, not sure of our intentions, but keeping about 20yd (18m) from the raft, until, slightly piqued that his morning swim was being disturbed, he slapped the water with his broad, flat, frying-pan tail and swam to the left-hand bank.

For some unexplained reason the fish were decidedly uncooperative that morning: hoppers and sedges prompted no response at all. Royal and Grey Wulffs were tried and put back into the box as they too failed miserably. All I had to show for the drift after the first hour was one, rather lonesome squawfish. 'Put this on', said Dave, passing me a large, heavily weighted, marabou-befeathered Woolly Bugger. A nod is as good as a wink to a blind man, so, with no more ado, the fly was on and sent on its way to the far bank.

This was no mean feat, believe me, for there was so much lead in the fly that there was a real danger of taking off Dave's head as he plied the oars just behind me. As quickly as it takes for a lump of head to sink I was into a fish, a fine Clark-Fork rainbow that could not resist the allure of the Woolly Bugger. It was the first of many and I went home extremely satisfied. The only thing that marred the day was my forgetting to put sun-block on my legs. It is very rare for me to wear shorts and, after the drift, my thighs were red and

swollen. As I lay on the bed in the motel, with cold wet flannels on my legs and a glass of Jack Daniels to take away the pain, I swore eternal friendship to the Woolly Bugger. It is now a pattern I am seldom without, no matter where I fish.

The Woolly Bugger started life on the eastern seaboard of the USA and was created by Russell Blessing of Pennsylvania as an imitation of the hellgrammite. Nowadays it is common to see Woolly Buggers tied up in a wide variety of single colours but the original pattern is as follows.

**Woolly Bugger** · Blessing · USA

| | |
|---|---|
| *Hook* | Mustad 79580, sizes 2–10 |
| *Thread* | Black |
| *Tail* | Black marabou plume (nowadays silver Crystal Hair is usually added) |
| *Body* | Dark olive wool or chenille |
| *Hackle* | Palmered black cock hackle |

Woolly Buggers are generally pre-weighted with lead wire but, for best effect, the fly should be tied unweighted with a lead shot or two crimped onto the leader, 6–8in (15–20cm) from the fly. This shotting of the leader helps to activate the tail fly when it is retrieved with a figure-of-8 retrieve.

The next fly was given to me by my friend, Darrel Martin, who is the fly-tying editor of the American publication *Fly Rod and Reel*. The fly was sent to him by a correspondent, Bob Long Jr of Chicago, and cock hackle and rubber legs are used to create a high degree of mobility.

**Bossbobs Hellgrammite** · Long · USA

| | |
|---|---|
| *Hook* | Mustad 79580, sizes 4–6, shank bent upwards |
| *Thread* | Black |
| *Tail* | Few fibres of soft, brown filoplume and two strands of black rubber |
| *Body* | Peacock herl, palmered with a black hackle then clipped over a prepared 'Nymphform' body |
| *Rib* | Gold wire |
| *Back* | Brown feather fibre or Raffene (Swiss Straw), lacquered |
| *Breathing filaments* | Short tuft of filoplume either side |
| *Thorax* | Peacock herl, palmered with a black cock hackle unclipped |
| *Legs* | Black rubber |
| *Wing case* | Brown feather fibre, lacquered |
| *Antennae* | Two strands of black rubber |

Randall Kaufmann's pattern is slightly less complex to tie but nevertheless just as effective. It is tied commercially by Umpqua Feather of Oregon.

**Kaufmann's Hellgrammite** · Kaufmann · USA

| | |
|---|---|
| *Hook* | Mustad 79580, sizes 2–8 |
| *Thread* | Brown |
| *Tail* | Brown goose biots or single goose fibres |
| *Body* | Brown Antron, picked out at the sides to imitate breathing appendages |
| *Rib* | Copper wire |

| | |
|---|---|
| *Back* | Cock-pheasant tail fibres |
| *Thorax* | As body |
| *Legs* | Speckled hen saddle hackle tied over the thorax |
| *Wingcase* | As back |
| *Antennae* | As tail |

In recent years Dave Whitlock has tied many of his flies upside-down, presumably to avoid catching them up on the bottom when fishing. His version of the hellgrammite is no exception and is very similar to the Kaufmann fly.

### Whitlock's Hellgrammite · Whitlock · USA

| | |
|---|---|
| *Hook* | Mustad 79580, sizes 2–8 |
| *Thread* | Brown |
| *Tail* | Two brown goose biots |
| *Body* | Dark grey fur |
| *Rib* | Copper wire |
| *Back* | Dark grey Raffene (Swiss Straw) |
| *Thorax* | As body |
| *Legs* | Mottled brown hen feather |
| *Wing case* | Dark grey Raffene (Swiss Straw) |
| *Antennae* | Brown goose biots |

Whitlock's Hellgrammite

In his book *Popular Fly Patterns*, Terry Hellekson gives a very simple basic pattern for the hellgrammite which should not prove difficult for even the most inept beginner to fly-tying.

### Hellgrammite · Hellekson · USA

| | |
|---|---|
| *Hook* | Mustad 79580, sixes 4–8 |
| *Thread* | Black |
| *Body* | Black chenille |
| *Legs* | Black and brown saddle, palmered up the body; hackles are clipped top and bottom and trimmed down the sides, tapering from ¾in (2cm) at the head to almost nothing |

The Norman Marsh imitation of the larva of New Zealand's indigenous Dobson fly is a much simpler creation than the American patterns. In my opinion it looks more like a pupa than larva.

### Dobson Fly Larva · Marsh · NZ

| | |
|---|---|
| *Hook* | Mustad 37160, sizes 12–14 |
| *Thread* | Black |
| *Body* | Bronze peacock herl |
| *Thorax* | As body |

The final New Zealand pattern was created by Jim Ring and was given in Tony Orman's book, *Trout with the Nymph*.

### Hellgrammite · Ring · NZ

| | |
|---|---|
| *Hook* | Mustad 79580, size 4 |
| *Thread* | Black |
| *Tail* | Black cock hackle fibres |
| *Body* | Bronze peacock herl over lead wire |
| *Legs* | Black cock hackles tied in bunches, not palmered up the body, clipped |

### FISHING THE HELLGRAMMITE

The hellgrammite patterns are usually weighted so that they can be fished close to the bottom. They are also very effective flies when fished in the dead drift. They are excellent flies to try when no obvious insects are on the water.

# CHAPTER FOURTEEN

# CRUSTACEA

## FRESHWATER SHRIMPS _____

### NATURALS

The freshwater shrimps belong to the family Gammaridae (order Amphipoda) and are well distributed worldwide. The commonest European species is *Gammarus pulex*, a creature found in lakes, streams and rivers. The other species which is fairly common is *G. lacustris*. Both shrimps vary in size from approximately $\frac{5}{16}$in to 1in (12mm to 25mm). The males are larger than the females. (There is freshwater mysid shrimp, a relict of the last Ice Age, which is 4in (10cm) long. Imagine what a source of food it would be for trout if it lived in British rivers and lakes!)

The freshwater shrimp is an important item of food for all fish, including trout. I have even seen small pike regurgitate a veritable jam of shrimp when I have brought them to the net. As far as the trout is concerned, I believe the shrimp to be more important during the months when acquatic insect activity is at its lowest; the shortage of hatching ephemerids and caddis make the trout hunt and scavenge for whatever is available, and the shrimps are always available. A properly presented shrimp will take fish on any river at any time.

In the USA there are approximately 90 different species of freshwater shrimp, or 'scuds' as they are called, many of which are of interest to the fly-fisherman. New Zealand has a number of species, and there are at least seven in Australia.

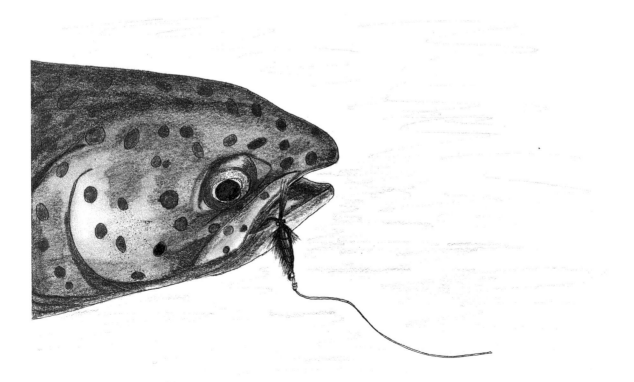

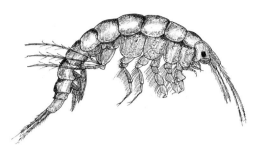

*Gammarus* sp.

Most species of shrimp swim on their sides although there are one or two that swim in a vertical position. There is no specific mating period; reproduction can take place throughout the year. The number of eggs laid can vary from as few as 20 to as many as a 1,000, depending on food availability, the age of the shrimp and prevailing water conditions. The female carries the eggs in a brood pouch beneath her thoracic plates. The colour of the shrimp can vary from nondescript grey or pale yellow to pale or even dark olive. They feed on dead animal and vegetable matter. Dead shrimps turn a pretty shade of yellow or orange.

The following are some of the commoner species which are of interest to the fisherman.

**Freshwater Shrimps of Angling Significance in the UK and Europe**

| Scientific Name | Distribution |
| --- | --- |
| *Carinogammarus roeselli* | Europe |
| *Crangonyx pseudogracilis*\* | UK |
| *Gammarus duebeni* | Ireland |
| *G. fosarum* | Europe |
| *G. lacustris* | N. UK & Europe |
| *G. pulex* | UK & Europe |
| *G. tigrinus*\*\* | UK & Europe |

\*Introduced to the UK from North America. Blue-green in colour, it swims in an upright position.
\*\*Usually found in brackish water but some fisheries in the UK are brackish.

Other British species are found in places such as caves, deep wells and underground rivers and therefore are of no interest to the fishermen.

The following are a few of the American *Gammarus* and *Hyalella* species that have interested the fly-fisherman, plus a couple of species from the southern hemisphere.

**Non-European Freshwater Shrimps of Angling Significance**

| Scientific Name | Common Name | Distribution |
| --- | --- | --- |
| *Crangonyx gracilus* | Tan Scud | USA |
| *Gammarus fasciatus* | Grey Scud | USA |
| *G. lacustris* | Olive Scud | USA |
| *G. limnaeus* | Olive Scud | USA |
| *G. minus* | Yellow Scud | USA |
| *G. nigroculus* | Freshwater Shrimp | S. Africa |
| *Hyalella americana* | Tiny Yellow Scud | USA |
| *H. azteca* | Tiny Olive Scud | USA |
| *H. knickerbockeri* | Tiny Grey Scud | USA |
| *Paratya curvirostris* | Freshwater Shrimp | NZ |

A few seasons ago, I was fishing Lake Lenore, in the barren scablands of eastern Washington with my wife Madeleine and my good friend Darrel Martin. We float-tubed this lake and sought hard-fighting Lahotan cut-throat trout from this alkaline water. We all took fish and I spent one night fishing among the weed-beds. As the moon came up and the odd coyote called, singing to the pale moon, I left the water and we deflated our tubes. The following day, at the nearest gas station, we once more inflated our float tubes to continue our search for the large Lahotan. On close examination, my tube was covered with literally thousands of small olive-green scuds – possibly *Hyalella azteca* – and, without a doubt, they must figure highly in the diet of the fish in Lake Lenore.

## ARTIFICIALS

Depending on species, freshwater shrimps, or scuds, can vary in size from ¼in (6mm) to almost 1¼in (30mm). Observation of your waters will tell you what size of fly to use. Most patterns are usually tied on curved hooks (Partridge K4A or Mustad 80200BR), thus more or less imitating the natural shape of the shrimp. A swimming shrimp, however, is elongated in profile rather than curved. I shall give the hooks as described by the originators but bear in mind that the same patterns could be tied up realistically on hooks such as the Mustad 80050BR or Partridge K12ST, both of which are ideal for imitating the profile of a swimming shrimp.

BRITISH AND EUROPEAN PATTERNS

The first shrimp pattern is a fly of John Goddard's that seems to have stood the test of time. He was one of the first tiers to use clear plastic for emulating the back of the shrimp.

**Shrimper** · Goddard · UK

| | |
|---|---|
| *Hook* | Mustad 3123, sizes 10–14 |
| *Thread* | Orange |
| *Body* | Olive-brown seal fur over copper wire, tied in a hump at the hook's centre |
| *Back* | Clear PVC or polythene |
| *Legs* | Palmered honey cock hackle |

John sometimes adds a touch of orange to the body dubbing.

Richard Walker's pattern is still popular with many anglers.

**Shrimp** · R. Walker · UK

| | |
|---|---|
| *Hook* | Mustad 79672, sizes 10–14 |
| *Thread* | Reddish-brown |
| *Body* | Olive wool |
| *Underbody* | Flat strips of lead wire on top of the hook to build up a hump |
| *Back* | Three or four coats of clear varnish |
| *Legs* | Ginger cock hackle palmered down the body then clipped top and sides |

Neil Patterson has many effective patterns to his credit, including the unusual Funnel Dun series of dry flies. He is an observant and thinking angler and I admire his work immensely. Included in his fly selections is this shrimp pattern, which is becoming a standard fly with many fishermen, both on stillwater and on rivers. Neil believes that the red spot seen on some naturals could be the early stages of egg formation. I think it is more likely to be an infestation caused by a small worm known as the proboscis roundworm (*Echino-rhynchus* sp.), a common parasite of *Gammarus* shrimps and usually a shade of red.

**Red-spot Shrimp** · Patterson · UK

| | |
|---|---|
| *Hook* | Partridge K2B Sedge Hook, sizes 8–15 |
| *Thread* | Olive |
| *Body* | Lead wire then dubbed olive seal fur and mohair with a centre of fluorescent red wool |
| *Rib* | Gold wire |
| *Back* | Two layers of clear plastic over body and rib |
| *Legs* | Body fur picked out |

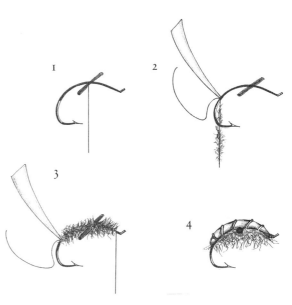

Red-spot Shrimp

This pattern is far easier to tie than it looks.

*Step 1* Tie a length of fluorescent red wool or red floss roughly in a middle of the hook.
*Step 2* Tie in the back material and the rib in at the bend and dub the fur onto the tying thread.
*Step 3* Form the body by taking the fur-laden thread back down the shank. Follow this with the back and then the rib.
*Step 4* Trim the flourescent wool either side and pick out the body fur for legs.

The next pattern, one of mine, is a fly that works well in cloudy water. The fish seem to see this colour well in such conditions. It is also successful on small, clear-water fisheries where it has the advantage of being seen not only by the trout but also by the angler.

**Golden Shrimp** · Price · UK

| | |
|---|---|
| *Hook* | Mustad 80200BR, sizes 8–14 |
| *Thread* | Yellow |
| *Back* | Clear PVC or natural latex |
| *Rib* | Yellow Terylene thread over back and body |
| *Underbody* | Lead wire |
| *Legs* | Palmered golden-olive cock hackle clipped at the sides and back |
| *Antennae (tail)* | Golden-olive hackle fibres (the fly is tied in reverse and the head of the shrimp is at the bend) |

The next fly comes from Slovenia, where it is used for both trout and grayling. The materials are unusual: dormouse tail for the body and eel skin for the back (the skin is taken from the side of the eel just before the colour changes to white). The fly was devised by Ljubo Pintar from the village of Most na Soči on the River Soča. I consider this river to be the most beautiful river in Europe and I am not alone in this belief. It is the home of the marbled trout (*Salmo marmoratus*). In very small sizes of 18 and below, this fly was used extensively on the River Gačka in Croatia.

**Eel-skin Shrimp** · Pintar · Slovenia

| | |
|---|---|
| *Hook* | Mustad 80200BR, sizes 8–18 |
| *Thread* | Black |
| *Tail* | Short tuft of grey or olive hackle fibres (optional) |
| *Body* | Grey natural dormouse tail or olive dormouse tail |
| *Back* | Eel skin |
| *Rib* | Clear monofilament nylon |

Eel-skin Shrimp

The next pattern imitates *Gammarus fosarum*. Tied by Ivo Blazevicev, it is used on the Kupa River for trout and grayling. The river now forms the border between Croatia and Slovenia (where it is called the Kulpa). *Rakusac* means 'shrimp' in Croatian.

**Blazevicev Rakusac** · Blazevicev · Croatia

| | |
|---|---|
| *Hook* | Mustad 80200BR, sizes 10–18 |
| *Thread* | Cream or light brown |
| *Tail* | Cream cock hackle fibres |
| *Body* | Golden-cream fur over lead wire |
| *Rib* | Black thread |
| *Back* | Honey-coloured plastic or latex |
| *Legs* | Fur picked out |

Mladen Merkas Goranin, from Skrad in Croatia, created the next pattern, which imitates a dead shrimp, hence the colour orange. Like the preceding fly, it is used on the Kupa and other streams, such as the Kupiča, a small, crystal-clear river which I had the pleasure of fishing in May 1993. It is usually fished in the summer months for grayling.

**M.M.G. Rakusac** · Goranin · Croatia

| | |
|---|---|
| *Hook* | Mustad 80200BR, sizes 8-18 |
| *Thread* | Orange |
| *Body* | Cream seal fur (three parts), yellow seal fur (one part) and orange seal fur (one part) over lead wire |
| *Back* | Yellow plastic similar to Spectraflash* or clear polythene |
| *Rib* | Gold wire |

*I have found the ideal material on a dress of my granddaughter's Barbie doll. I am trying to persuade her to change the elegant ball-gown to a mini-skirt, so far without much success!

T. Preskawiec is best known in France, and in the rest of Europe for that matter, for his sedge pattern, the Preska Sedge. This shrimp pattern uses pike scales for the back. How effective is this fly? I do not know, but I have tied up a few just in case.

**Gamma** · Preskawiec · France

| | |
|---|---|
| *Hook* | Mustad 94841, sizes 10–12 |
| *Thread* | Grey |
| *Body* | Two palmered grey hackles over lead wire |
| *Back* | Two pike scales, dyed or coloured beige with waterproof ink |

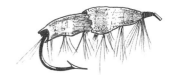

Gamma

The German for shrimp is *Bachflohkrebs* and the following pattern by Thomas Wolfle makes use of materials supplied by Traun River Products.

**Bachflohkrebs** · Wolfle · Germany

| | |
|---|---|
| *Hook* | Partridge L3A, sizes 12–18 |
| *Thread* | Dark grey |
| *Body* | Light grey Antron |
| *Back* | Grey marbled latex |
| *Rib* | Gold wire over body and back |
| *Legs* | Antron dubbing picked out |
| *Antennae* | Cree hackle fibres |

Bachflohkrebs

Roman Moser of Austria ties a similar pattern to this last fly using an iridescent Spectraflash back. He used it on the famous River Traun in Austria. A number of British tiers have subsequently copied this type of fly, using the same materials, and fished it on a number of the major reservoirs in the UK.

I created the next fly for want of something to tie at the Federation of Fly Fishers' Conclave in Eugene, Oregon, a few years ago. If nothing else, the pattern was a little different and had the bonus of actually catching fish.

**Bead-back Shrimp** · Price · UK

| | |
|---|---|
| *Hook* | Mustad 80050Br, sizes 8–10 |
| *Thread* | Grey |
| *Body* | Hare's ear and Antron, mixed |
| *Back* | Silver, gold or clear bead chain |
| *Antennae* | Grey hackle fibres |
| *Eyes* | Burnt monofilament |

To tie this fly, proceed as follows:

*Step 1* Load the tying thread with dubbing and take it down the shank.
*Step 2* Tie the bead chain across the back with the dubbing taken between the separate beads. If metal bead chain is used then no extra weight is required but if plastic bead chain is used the hook can be pre-weighted with lead or copper wire.

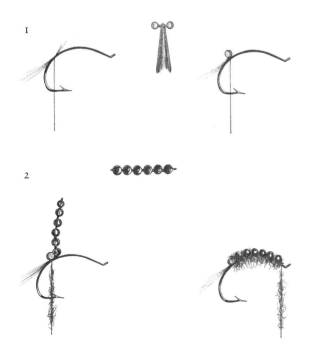

3

Bead-back shrimp

*Step 3* The finished fly. Eyes are formed by melting a small length of monofilament nylon held in a pair of tweezers.

AMERICAN PATTERNS
The outdoor-writer Ted Trueblood produced a shrimp pattern in the early 1950s that is still in use today. The fly is a broad-spectrum pattern that can represent other aquatic creatures, but it was originally conceived as a freshwater shrimp. It is sometimes known as Trueblood's Shrimp Nymph.

**Trueblood's Otter Nymph** Trueblood · USA

| | |
|---|---|
| *Hook* | Mustad 3906, sizes 8–16 |
| *Thread* | Brown |
| *Tail* | Brown partridge hackle (actually antennae) |
| *Body* | Otter and seal fur, blended |
| *Legs* | Brown partridge hackle fibres |

Trueblood's Otter Nymph

Many American shrimp patterns make use of deer or elk hair for the back of shrimp patterns and this is no exception.

**Olive Shrimp** · USA

| | |
|---|---|
| *Hook* | Mustad 3906, sizes 8–10 |
| *Thread* | Olive |
| *Body* | Insect-green synthetic dubbing |
| *Back* | Olive elk hair |
| *Legs* | Palmered olive cock hackle |

The fly-tying skills of Al Troth of Montana are known all over the fly-tying world. All of Troth's patterns catch fish not anglers.

**Scud** · Troth · USA

| | |
|---|---|
| *Hook* | Mustad 7957B, sizes 6–12 |
| *Thread* | Olive |
| *Tail* | Olive hackle fibres tied well down the bend of the hook |
| *Body* | Synthetic fur: olive (two parts), grey, (two parts), red (one part) and orange (one part) |
| *Rib* | Clear monofilament |
| *Back* | Clear PVC film |

The Nyerges Shrimp is a very simple fly, devised by Gil Nyerges of Washington State, that imitates, among other things, a freshwater scud. I have always maintained that the simpler the fly, the more effective it usually is. This fly is sometimes called Nyerges Nymph.

**Nyerges Shrimp** · Nyerges · USA

| | |
|---|---|
| *Hook* | Mustad 9672, sizes 8–12 |
| *Thread* | Olive |
| *Body* | Dark olive chenille |
| *Legs* | Palmered brown cock hackle trimmed back and sides |

Nyerges Shrimp

I was given the next fly by its creator, Len Holt. Len fishes the Colorado River below Glen Canyon Dam. The weedy areas become exposed when the water is held back, killing the resident shrimps which are washed out of the weeds when the dam is next opened. The trout downstream of the dam have become accustomed to this free, pre-prepared food coming down to them. Very recently, greater control over the release of water from the dam has meant a more constant flow of the river, which will be to the eventual benefit of the fishery.

**Dead Scud** · Holt · USA

| | |
|---|---|
| *Hook* | Mustad 3906, sizes 8–12 |
| *Thread* | Orange |
| *Body* | Orange chenille (there is also a yellow version) |
| *Back* | Light deer or elk hair, the fine end is left as a tail and a small tuft is left at the head |
| *Legs* | Palmered grizzle cock |

Dave Whitlock has created many scud patterns, as a glance through the pages of various books and publications will show. I believe this pattern to be one of his best impressions of a swimming shrimp.

**Whitlock's Scud** · Whitlock · USA

| | |
|---|---|
| *Hook* | Mustad 80050BR or 94842, sizes 8–12 |
| *Thread* | Olive |
| *Feelers* | Wood-duck or mallard fibres |
| *Body* | Dubbed muskrat and beaver with some synthetic fibres to yield a grey body with olive undertones |
| *Back* | Grey Raffene (Swiss Straw) or polythene |
| *Rib* | Oval silver tinsel |
| *Legs* | Partridge hackle fibres |

Many of the Blue Ribbon rivers of Montana have individual scud patterns named after them. The following two are examples.

**Bighorn Scud** · USA

| | |
|---|---|
| *Hook* | Mustad 3906B, sizes 8–16 |
| *Thread* | Pink |
| *Tail* | Pink hackle fibres |
| *Body* | Pink Antron |
| *Back* | Clear PVC or similar plastic |
| *Rib* | Clear or pink nylon monofilament |
| *Feelers* | Pink hackle fibres |
| *Legs* | Body fur picked out |

There are also peach and orange versions of this last pattern.

**Yellowstone Scud** · USA

| | |
|---|---|
| *Hook* | Mustad 80200BR, sizes 10–16 |
| *Thread* | Orange |
| *Body* | Pinkish-orange Antron |
| *Rib* | Gold or copper wire |
| *Back* | Clear plastic |
| *Legs* | Fur picked out |

*FISHING THE SHRIMP*

Shrimps can be fished slowly close to the bottom and the retrieve speeded up from time to time, in order to imitate the fast swimming action of the shrimp when disturbed by a predator. On rivers, fishing the fly in a dead drift is probably as good a way as any. On chalkstreams a weighted shrimp, cast upstream into the clear areas between the weed-beds and allowed to sink slowly and move with the stream's flow, is most effective. Heavily weighted shrimps cast upstream into the hurly-burly of small weirs and mill races often produce better than normal fish.

✻　　✻　　✻

Before we leave the freshwater shrimps I must mention one small, shrimp species that is not a member of the Gammaridae. This true shrimp is *Mysis relicta*, a relict of the last Ice Age that lives in a number of lakes in Sweden, Denmark and the former USSR. It has also been recorded in the waters of the Lake District in the UK. In North America, it is found in waters such as Lake Superior and, in Ireland, in Loughs Neagh, Derg, Erne and Corrib. It appears to be one of the most important items in the diet of the pollan, the indigenous whitefish of Lough Neagh. It is possible that this creature may be of importance on some waters. The American firm, Umpqua Feather, gives a pattern for this particular creature.

**Mysis Shrimp** · Umpqua Feather Merchants · USA
| | |
|---|---|
| *Hook* | Tiemco Nymph Hook, sizes 16–20 |
| *Thread* | White |
| *Tail* | White hackle fibres cut short with a slightly longer strand of pearl Flashabou on the top |
| *Body* | Dubbed thin white fur |
| *Rib* | Pearl Flashabou |
| *Legs* | White ostrich palmered over the body |
| *Eyes* | Burnt black nylon monofilament |

Mysis Shrimp

Charles Jardine, in his book *Sotheby's Guide to Fly Fishing*, gives a similar pattern from Scandinavia to imitate this tiny creature.

**Mysis relicta** · Scandinavia
| | |
|---|---|
| *Hook* | Mustad 80150BR, sizes 12–14 |
| *Thread* | White |
| *Tail* | White marabou tuft |
| *Body* | White marabou dubbed |
| *Rib* | Pearl Flashabou or Mylar |
| *Eye* | Burnt black nylon monofilament |

Just for the record, there is a freshwater prawn, found in certain lakes in Sweden and Finland, which goes under the name of *Gammaracanthus loricatus*. Ernest Schwiebert gives a pattern for another species of shrimp, the small, iridescent fairy shrimp. In the UK, this shrimp, *Chirocephalus diaphanus*, inhabits small, temporary rainpools and should not really come into contact with our quarry, the trout. In some of the deeper lakes of Canada there are so-called opossum shrimps (order Mysidacea), which can be up to 1¼in to (30mm) long and are a food source for the lake trout. As far as I know, these have not yet been imitated.

## WATER LICE

### NATURALS

The water louse, hog louse or slater to give its several names, belongs to the family Asellidae of the order Isopoda. In the USA it is known as the sow bug or cress bug. These small crustaceans resemble their close relative, the familiar terrestrial woodlouse. Water lice are tolerant of all waters except very fast-flowing streams. Like freshwater shrimps, they are scavengers, existing on all manner of dead animal and vegetable matter. They are ¼–¾in (10–20mm) long, with seven pairs of legs. The females carry their eggs near the base of the first four pairs of legs and, when they hatch, continue to carry the infant lice. Also like freshwater shrimps, they can be food for trout. When I have had both creatures in an aquarium the water lice were always eaten first by the fish, mainly because they could not move as fast as the more mobile shrimps.

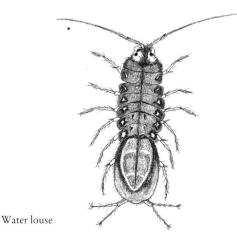

Water louse

Various species of *Asellus* are found all over the world. Not much has been written about them in Australia, but this may be because they have yet not been imitated there. Norman Marsh gives them a mention in his book *Trout Stream Insects of New Zealand*.

**Common Water Lice of Angling Significance**

| Scientific Name | Distribution |
| --- | --- |
| Asellus aquaticus | UK & Europe |
| A. communis | USA |
| A. meridianus | UK & Europe |
| A. occidentalis | USA |

### ARTIFICIALS

There are not as many imitations of the water louse compared with the number of patterns tied to emulate the shrimp but, like the shrimp, I believe these creatures are an important winter food for fish. It is possible that shrimp patterns could be taken by trout as water lice and *vice versa*.

BRITISH PATTERNS

The first fly is an early pattern created by C.F. Walker and given in his book *Lake Flies and Their Imitation*.

**Freshwater Louse** · C.F. Walker · UK
| | |
| --- | --- |
| Hook | Mustad 79672, sizes 12–14 |
| Thread | Black |
| Body | Grey and brown hare's ear flattened horizontally |
| Rib | Silver oval tinsel |
| Legs | Brown partridge, palmered rear half of body only |

The next fly was tied by Ann Douglas, who for many years tied flies with me. She is an excellent tier and has given many classes at evening institutes on the gentle art of fly-tying. In her pattern, she represents the egg-bearing female.

**Egg-bearing Louse** · Douglas · UK
| | |
| --- | --- |
| Hook | Mustad 79672, sizes 10–14 |
| Thread | Black |
| Body | Mole and hare fur (first third), green Raffene twised and knotted to form nodules (second third), hare and mole fur (last third) |

| | |
| --- | --- |
| Back | Brown mallard flank |
| Legs | Brown partridge |
| Antennae | Brown partridge fibres |

Geoffrey Bucknall's pattern is similar to that of C.F. Walker but different enough to be included here.

**Water Louse** · Bucknall · UK
| | |
| --- | --- |
| Hook | Mustad 79672, size 14 |
| Thread | Olive |
| Body | Pale olive seal fur or wool |
| Rib | Fine oval tinsel |
| Legs | Two bunches of grey partridge extended from the rear of the hook |

Water Louse

**Water Louse** · Gathercole · UK
| | |
| --- | --- |
| Hook | Mustad 79672, sizes 10–12 |
| Thread | Brown |
| Tail | Brown partridge fibres |
| Body | Grey rabbit |
| Rib | Silver wire |
| Back | Grey-brown feather fibre |
| Legs | Brown partridge laid across the back |
| Antennae | As tail |

Another pattern created by Peter Lapsley is also very similar to the C.F. Walker fly.

**Freshwater Louse** · Lapsley · UK
| | |
| --- | --- |
| Hook | Mustad 79672, sizes 12–14 |
| Thread | Light brown |
| Underbody | Lead wire, flattened horizontally |
| Body | Brown and grey hare fur trimmed flat on top |
| Rib | Fine silver tinsel |
| Legs | Guard hairs picked out |

AMERICAN PATTERNS

The book *Fishing the Midge* by Ed Koch was published in 1970 and among his 'midge' patterns was one which he referred to as a maverick; this was his tying of the freshwater louse or, as it is known in the USA, cress bug.

**Cress Bug** · Koch · USA
| | |
|---|---|
| *Hook* | Mustad 80100BR, sizes 16–22 |
| *Thread* | Grey |
| *Body* | Grey foam |
| *Back &* | Black ostrich herl |
| *collar* | |

Cress Bug

I presume this pattern would be weighted to get it down in the water.

It would indeed be strange if Dave Whitlock, who has imitated practically everything that moves in or on the water, had not imitated the louse. The following pattern is his interpretation of this small crustacean.

**Sow Bug** · Whitlock · USA
| | |
|---|---|
| *Hook* | Mustad 3906, sizes 20–26 |
| *Thread* | Grey |
| *Tail* | Two grey duck biots, half the body length |
| *Body* | Muskrat and synthetic fibre in equal parts, dubbed |
| *Rib* | Gold wire |
| *Back* | Clear PVC or polythene |

Randall Kaufmann gives an imitation similar to the Whitlock pattern using a feather-fibre back. The brilliant fly-tier, Poul Jorgensen, ties an all-fur pattern as follows.

**Cress Bug** · Jorgensen · USA
| | |
|---|---|
| *Hook* | Mustad 3906, size 16 |
| *Thread* | Olive |
| *Body* | Olive muskrat over medium-brown mink fur, clipped top and bottom |

## FISHING THE WATER LOUSE

The freshwater louse is best fished as close to the bottom as possible because it is not an active swimmer like the shrimp. Fish also in the vicinity of weed-beds because trout often make forays into the weed in order to dislodge such creatures from their green haven. Fish the artificial in a dead drift in the channels between such weed-beds.

## WATER FLEAS (DAPHNIA)

### NATURALS

There are many hundreds of species of water fleas, or daphnia, which belong to the crustacean family Calyptomera of the order Cladocera. The largest species, *Daphnia magna*, at ³⁄₁₆in (5mm) long, is just about possible to imitate but to copy size for size would be a little foolish because the imitation would be just one in possibly millions of naturals. There is no doubt that trout feed on daphnia, for most of us have, at some time, caught fish spewing out a pinkish jam of them.

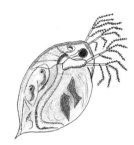

*Daphnia* sp.

I remember one frustrating evening on a local lake when the fish were obviously feeding on something but I knew not what. I had thrown virtually the entire contents of my fly-box at these stubborn fish to no avail when, in a mood of desperation, I put on a small Partridge & Orange wet fly. I was rewarded almost immediately with a plump 2lb (1kg) rainbow which had daphnia dripping from its jaws. I imparted this information to another angler who was having the same difficulties. He put on a Grenadier Nymph, another orange fly, and soon he was also enjoying good sport. We continued to do so for an hour or two until the feeding binge was over.

### ARTIFICIALS

Trout, when they are feeding on daphnia, appear to have no size hang-up; they will take a fly considerably larger than the minute naturals they are gulping.

With this in mind, I tied the following nymph to use when trout are preoccupied with this small crustacean, but in a size that will make them sit up and take notice.

**Orange Nymph** · Price · UK

| | |
|---|---|
| *Hook* | Mustad 80200BR, sizes 12–14 |
| *Thread* | Orange |
| *Body* | Orange synthetic fibre |
| *Rib* | Oval gold tinsel |
| *Back & antennae* | Orange goose with two tufts sticking beyond the eye; the back can be varnished for durability. |

Orange Nymph

This pattern can also be tied in pale green to imitate the daphnia species of this colour.

### FISHING DAPHNIA

Fish this pattern on a floating line and long leader and cast into the feeding area. Bring back with a slow figure-of-8 retrieve and, if this does not work, strip the larger sizes of the nymph through the shoal. Daphnia are usually found in the higher levels of the water on dull days or at night; sunshine drives the creatures down into the depths.

## CRAYFISH

I suppose we are stretching both imagination and plausibility in describing as a nymph creature as large as a crayfish, but, if we include the freshwater shrimp, it would seem reasonable to include this creature. It is not a dry fly and is certainly not a fish-imitating streamer or bucktail. Neither is it a garish and gaudy attractor. Furthermore, you would fish such a creature in much the same way as you would many of nymphs already described. So I feel reasonably justified in including it in a book on nymphs.

### NATURALS

Crayfish belong to the family Astacidae of the order Decapoda and are found throughout the world. They thrive best in clean, alkaline waters and have long been a source of food for Man as well as fish. In the USA they are also known as crawdads or crawfish. The creatures resemble in many ways their saltwater cousin, the lobster; almost a replica of this gourmet's delight, they are only about 4in (10cm) long when fully grown.

Crayfish like waters with plenty of holes in the bank and submerged logs, even discarded tins are places where they can hide. They are true scavengers, feeding on dead fish and other animals; they also take worms, snails and other aquatic creatures. Armour-plated and generally of a dark olive-brown colour, like the lobster, they possess two strong claws which they use to tear their prey and for defence. For most of the time they are nocturnal, emerging from their holes to scuttle along the bottom on their many legs. When attacked, they retreat backwards with a powerful jerking of their tails.

In many parts of Europe the crayfish has been in decline, mainly because of disease and river pollution. The single native species in the UK is the white-clawed crayfish. In the USA there are over 280 species and subspecies, which is why American imitations of this creature are legion.

It is true to say that many American imitations were devised to take the large- and small-mouthed bass but a number are used to tempt trout. In New Zealand it is appreciated that the native big trout will feed on koura and grow fat. In the UK, with the decline of the crayfish, imitations are few and far between and I know of no one who actually goes out to take fish on crayfish imitations. Roger Daltrey has recently stocked his Lakedown fishery in Sussex with crayfish and they are thriving.

\*       \*       \*

It was hot, hotter than hell and twice as sweaty. It was August and I was in a small hotel in the mountains of central Spain, just outside the tiny

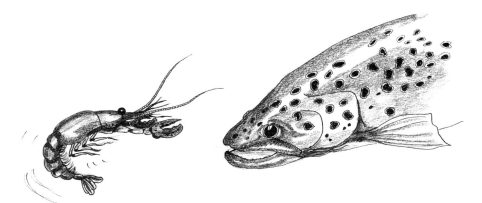

village of Peralejos de Las Truchas, beside the upper reaches of the Tajo River, in the Province of Guadalajara. The Tajo is one of the main rivers of Spain, winding like a blue vein from east to west through the centre of the country. It crosses the frontier with Portugal, where it becomes the mighty Tagus before pouring its Iberian soul into the Atlantic at Lisbon.

When we ventured out to fish it was in the cool of the evening and the fish we caught were the wild, dark brown trout of Spain. I suppose the largest fish we tempted with our flies was about 1½lb (0.7kg) but I believe that some of 2lb (0.9kg) come out quite regularly. For most of the day I sat in the cool of the bar, drinking ice-cold *cerveza*;

with temperatures approaching 100°F (38°C) outside this seemed the most sensible thing to do. 'Lucky', the barman, told me that, a few years ago, it was quite common to catch fish of 4½–6¾lb (2–3kg) with great regularity but things had now changed. 'Poaching?' I asked. 'No. Crayfish,' he replied. 'All the crayfish in the river were wiped out by a disease brought in by an imported American species. Our crayfish were susceptible and died,' he continued sadly. 'Yes, this river was famous for its crayfish and the trout grew fat on them.' I sympathized as I poured another beer, saddened at the demise of the Tajo crayfish, and also of those in our own waters, and reflecting on what might have been had they still lived in the river.

**Common Species of Crayfish**

| Scientific Name | Common Name | Distribution |
|---|---|---|
| *Astacus fluviatilis** | Red-clawed Crayfish | Europe |
| *Astacus leptodactylis* | Asian Crayfish | Asia & Europe |
| *Astacus pallipes* | White-clawed Crayfish | UK |
| *Cambarus bartoni**** | Eastern Crayfish | USA |
| *Oronectes sanborni* | – | USA |
| *O. rusticus* | – | USA |
| *O. luteus* | – | USA |
| *O. punctimanus* | – | USA |
| *O. propinquas* | – | USA |
| *Paranephrops* spp.** | Koura | NZ |
| *Portamobius trowbridgei**** | Columbia River Crayfish | USA |

*Arriving in the UK as an escapee, specimens were found on several rivers and streams in southern England. Bred in France for human consumption, take it from me, they are delicious.

** There are three species recorded in New Zealand, where they are called *koura*, a Maori word.

*** In *Freshwater Biology*, Ward and Whipple describe these two species as being abundant in the USA. Bear in mind that the names may have changed during the 70 years or so since this book was published.

## ARTIFICIALS

The first pattern was given to me by Fulling Mill Flies and although it is sold in the UK, it was probably devised for the American market. The fly is tied in reverse.

**Crayfish** · Fulling Mill Flies · UK

| | |
|---|---|
| *Hook* | Mustad 79580, sizes 4–8 |
| *Thread* | Red |
| *Tail, body, back & antennae* | Natural deer hair tied down with red thread leaving a short tuft for the tail; the rest taken over the thorax, tied down and left projecting over the bend as antennae |
| *Thorax* | Olive-green chenille |
| *Legs* | Brown partridge |
| *Claws* | Cut hen-pheasant feathers |
| *Eyes* | Burnt monofilament nylon |

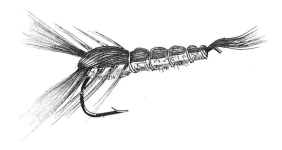

Crayfish

One of the most popular patterns coming out of the USA in recent years is another from Dave Whitlock. It is featured in many recent fly-tying books. Not only is this fly tied in reverse, it is also tied upside-down.

**Soft-shell Crayfish** · Whitlock · USA

| | |
|---|---|
| *Hook* | Mustad 79580, sizes 2–8 |
| *Thread* | To match overall colour |
| *Tail* | Raffene (Swiss Straw) to match body colour |
| *Back* | As tail |
| *Body* | Antron in orange, olive or sand |
| *Rib* | Monofilament nylon |
| *Legs* | Grizzle hen dyed to match body colours |
| *Mouthparts* | Short tuft of deer hair dyed to match body colours |
| *Eyes* | Black beads |
| *Antennae* | Moose mane, or peccary, dyed to match body colours |
| *Claws* | Hen-pheasant or hen back feathers to match body colours, lacquered for durability |

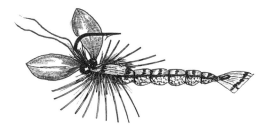

Soft-shell Crayfish

Bob Clouser is renowned for his Clouser Deep Minnows and among the many patterns he ties is a crayfish imitation which makes use of the modern furry foam.

**Clouser's Crayfish** · Clouser · USA

| | |
|---|---|
| *Hook* | Mustad 79580, sizes 4–8 |
| *Thread* | Tan |
| *Underbody* | Lead wire either side of the hook |
| *Antennae* | Cock-pheasant tail fibres |
| *Nose* | Hen mallard flank tip |
| *Body* | Pale green sparkle yarn |
| *Legs* | Bleached grizzle hackle |
| *Back* | Furry foam (brown, tan or olive) |
| *Head* | As back |
| *Claws* | Hen mallard flank cut to shape |

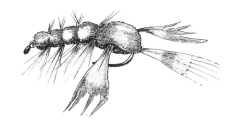

Clouser's Crayfish

Two years ago I had the pleasure of drifting down the Deschuttes River with Rik Hafele, an excellent fisherman, freshwater biologist and inventive fly-tier. The next pattern is one of his.

**Crawdad Creeper** · Hafele · USA

| | |
|---|---|
| *Hook* | Mustad 79850, sizes 6–8 |
| *Thread* | Olive |
| *Body* | Olive yarn or dubbing |
| *Legs* | Hen-pheasant body feather |
| *Back* | Red squirrel tail |
| *Tail* | As back |
| *Claws* | As back |

One of the simplest patterns was devised by Ed Howey, using wool and chenille.

**Crawdad Shredder** · Howey · USA

| | |
|---|---|
| *Hook* | Mustad 79671, sizes 2–12 |
| *Thread* | Brown |
| *Tail* | Cock-pheasant neck feather |
| *Underbody* | Lead wire or, for the unweighted pattern, olive wool |
| *Body* | Olive chenille, fatter in the thorax region |
| *Claws* | Deer body hair |

The New Zealand species, the kuora, was imitated by the famous New Zealand lure, the Fuzzy Wuzzy. This was the creation of Fred Fletcher of Waitahanui Lodge and it is still used on Lake Taupo.

## FISHING THE CRAYFISH

Crayfish are found near the bottom of the river, which is where foraging trout expect to find them. It goes without saying that this is where we fish our artificials. A pattern pre-weighted with lead will go down well enough with a sufficiently long leader. Try fishing some of the buoyant deer-hair patterns on a very short leader with a fast-sinking line. Crayfish are generally nocturnal scavengers but some can be found during daylight hours.

In South Africa, Chile and Argentina there may well be some species of crayfish but it is another crustacean, the crab, on which the trout feed and wax fat. In some waters freshwater crabs are prolific enough to be one of the main items of diet for the larger trout. Many trout in South Africa feed almost exclusively on *Potomon perlatus*, a species that I have seen on a number of rivers in South Africa. On the Umzumkulu these crabs are also the food of the clawless otter (*Aonyx capensis*); there were piles of broken crab shells at various places along the bank where these delightful creatures had been feasting. I am sure that some South African fishermen already have imitations of the freshwater crab.

# CHAPTER FIFTEEN

# LEECHES

## NATURALS

Although not exactly creatures from the Black Lagoon, leeches, in the eyes of most people, are creatures from beyond the pale. Who can forget Humphrey Bogart's reaction in the classic film, *African Queen*, when he came out of the water covered in these bloodsuckers? I think most of us would behave in the same way given the same situation. The true fact is, however, that very few leeches are capable of sucking mammalian blood. Most feed on insects, molluscs, amphibians, fish and fish eggs, as well as on other leeches.

In the old days, doctors were known as 'leeches' because all doctors at that time used to bleed their patients, either by opening veins or by applying medicinal leeches (*Hirudo medicinalis*). So common was this practice that the medicinal leech became virtually extinct in the wild in the UK and millions of these creatures were imported from the Continent in order to keep the blood flowing. In recent years there has been a resurgence in the use of leeches for some medical problems and they are now bred in sterile laboratory conditions. The European medicinal leech has been introduced into the USA. Such blood-sucking leeches can exist for about 12 months on one feed of blood.

That trout feed on leeches is indisputable but how often is perhaps another question. Are leeches important in the diet of the trout? The answer to this would, I think, be no. With so many other creatures available I suspect that the leech is way down on the menu of our quarry. But, having said that, there are times, certainly in some waters where there are large populations of leeches, when they must be important because of their sheer weight of numbers.

*Piscicola* sp.

Contracted Leech

Some species of leech are active swimmers, moving by an up-and-down undulation of the body. Most are able to expand and contract their bodies, one moment looking like a black blob and the next like an elongated worm. Other leeches move by creeping about the bottom in the detritus, in much the same way as a looper caterpillar, propelling themselves along by suckers at either end of their bodies.

The species most commonly seen by anglers is *Piscicola geometra*, a small leech about 1–2in (2.5–5cm) long. This thin olive-green leech, with distinct lighter bands, is usually found attached to trout that have been swimming close to the bottom. I have noticed the greatest incidence to be early in the season. One of the commoner large British and European species is the horse leech (*Haemopsis sanguisuga*). At one time this leech was believed to attach itself to the mouthparts and nostrils of drinking horses, but the truth is that the creature's mouthparts are not strong enough to bite through a horse's skin. Its usual diet consists of other aquatic creatures, such as caddis, other leeches and worms and, very occasionally amphibians.

One common American species, *Placobdella parasitica*, is often found in large numbers on the legs of snapping turtles, upon whose blood they

feed. Another common American species, *Proto-clepsis occidentalis*, which is very transparent compared with other species, is considered to be one of the fastest of all leeches, whether creeping or swimming. It often pursues and attacks frogs and fish. There is at least one species of leech that actually leaves the water at night to hunt earthworms.

When fully extended, the horse leech attains a length of over 4in (100mm); the medicinal leech can achieve a length of 6in (150mm) when fully mature. There is another species in British waters that is distinctly reddish-brown in colour, *Erpodella octoculata*. This species, which is about 2in (50mm) long, is completely insectivorous and swallows its prey whole. In the UK there are about 14 different species compared with over 60 in the USA. Most leeches are hermaphrodite and are capable of self-fertilization. In some species, the adults care for the young, which can be seen attached to them. Some fishing books state that leeches are blind but they do, in fact, have small eyes situated on the head; there are ten in the medicinal leech. Most leeches prefer shallow water, about 2–3ft (60–90cm) deep, and can be found in all types of habitat, from small stagnant ponds to swiftly flowing, crystal rivers.

*Erpodella* sp.

## ARTIFICIALS

It has been assumed by some that many of the traditional Black Lures could well be taken by fish for leeches and I suppose that this could be true. Flies such as Cliff Henry's Black Bear Lure could be one such pattern because it is very similar in construction and appearance to a number of the American leech imitations.

Most of the following patterns would not be termed as nymphs by fishery managers who run waters by nymph and dry-fly rules. I for one would not like to test the rules by fishing these patterns on such waters but, where no such rules apply, then I would have no qualms. The other thing I like about these patterns is that they are big, brash and bold, and I have always been a lot happier tying flies with plenty of meat! Not for me the size 28 dry flies, tiny little things that I cannot see. I leave those sorts of fly to the likes of my friends Darrel Martin and Oliver Edwards. They tie them far better than I ever could.

All imitations of the leech have one thing in common: mobility. All the flies use materials that are highly active in the water: marabou, rabbit strips and even chamois leather. All are used in an endeavour to imitate the natural movement of the real creature.

BRITISH PATTERNS

The first pattern is an amendment of a much earlier fly which I tied solely in black. Nowadays I combine both brown and black to give a dual-colour effect to the fly.

**Brown & Black Leech** · Price · UK
| | |
|---|---|
| *Hook* | Mustad 79580, sizes 6–10 |
| *Thread* | Black |
| *Tail* | Black marabou with brown marabou over |
| *Body* | Black wool or tinsel chenille over lead wire |
| *Wing* | Alternate tufts of brown and black marabou filling up the hook |

The next pattern is a simple fly which happens to be a favourite of my wife, Madeleine, who fishes it very, very slowly close to the bottom.

**Black Leech** · Price · UK
| | |
|---|---|
| *Hook* | Mustad 80150BR, size 8 |
| *Thread* | Black |
| *Tail* | Black marabou or dyed rabbit fur |
| *Body* | Dubbed black seal fur over lead wire |

Bob Church gives a leech pattern in his book *Guide to Trout Flies*. This is a basic, nymph-shaped fly, dressed in 'bible black'.

**Black Leech** · Church · UK
| | |
|---|---|
| *Hook* | Mustad 79850, 8–10 |
| *Thread* | Black |
| *Tail* | Long black cock hackle fibres or black marabou |
| *Body* | Black suede chenille over lead wire |
| *Back* | Black feather fibre |
| *Hackle* | Black hen |

NORTH AMERICAN PATTERNS

There are more patterns found in the American fly-pattern lists than in the rest of the world put together. Many are used to take large-and small-mouthed bass; others are used to great effect in Alaskan waters to take the many species of fish found in the wilderness rivers and lakes. The leech is a far more important fly for the American fly-fisher than it is for the British and European fisherman.

The first leech fly from the USA is a highly mobile filoplume pattern, tied in three versions: natural grey, black and olive.

**Filoplume Leech** · USA
| | |
|---|---|
| *Hook* | Mustad 79580, sizes 6–10 |
| *Thread* | Black or brown |
| *Tail* | Filoplume (grey, black or olive) and a few strands of Crystal Hair |
| *Body* | Filoplume (grey, black or olive) wound up the hook |
| *Rib* | Silver wire |

The next pattern is very similar but uses grizzle marabou. At one time these feathers, the soft, fluffy feathers found at the base of grizzle saddle capes, could not be given away. Today most fly-shops sell them dyed in a wide range of natural colours.

**Davis Leech** · USA
| | |
|---|---|
| *Hook* | Mustad 79580, sizes 6–10 |
| *Thread* | Olive |
| *Tail* | Soft olive grizzle marabou |
| *Body* | Olive wool or yarn |
| *Wing* | Rest of tail feather tied down with a silver ribbing, Matuka-style |

Most leech patterns bear a strong resemblance to the Woolly Bugger. In fact, in some instances, you will be unable to differentiate between them and I am sure the trout cannot either. The next pattern, by Dave Whitlock, is such a fly. A Woolly Bugger in everything but name, he calls it the Lectric Leech.

**'Lectric Leech** · Whitlock · USA
| | |
|---|---|
| *Hook* | Mustad 36890 (Salmon Hook), sizes 2–10 |
| *Thread* | Black |
| *Tail* | Black marabou with bronze peacock herl over and blue Flashabou either side |

*Body*    Black wool or dubbing with bronze peacock herl and blue Flashabou either side

*Hackle*    Black, palmered over the wool, herl and Flashabou

*Head*    Black incorporating blue Flashabou

Egg-sucking Leech

'Lectric Leech

In recent years leech-type patterns have become very popular in Alaska where they are used to take some of the large Alaskan rainbows that feed on the eggs from the various salmon. The first pattern is a simple marabou fly used mainly for stillwater fishing. There is also a purple version of this fly called simply Lake Leech.

### Black Marabou Leech · USA

*Hook*    Mustad 79580, sizes 6–10
*Thread*    Black
*Tail*    Black marabou
*Body*    Rest of the marabou plume twisted into a rope and wound up the hook shank

One of the most popular patterns from Alaska in recent years, and used for steelhead, is without doubt the Egg-sucking Leech. The fly looks like a Wooly Bugger with the addition of a colourful head.

### Egg-sucking Leech · USA

*Hook*    Mustad 79580, sizes 4–10
*Thread*    Black
*Tail*    Black marabou
*Body*    Black chenille
*Hackle*    Softish black saddle hackle palmered up the body
*Head (Egg)*    Ball of fluorescent chenille in either pink, red, orange or sometimes green; some craft shops sell pompons, little balls of chenille ideal for this fly

The Egg-sucking Leech can also be tied up with the addition of a dumb-bell weight to make it fast-sinking.

The bass fisherman uses a number of leech patterns in pursuit of his quarry, many of which, I must admit, are somewhat garish, exaggerated and often quite unrealistic. The following two, however, arc excellent fish-catching flies, despite their appearance.

### Whitlock's Chamois Leech · Whitlock · USA

*Hook*    Mustad 36890, sizes 2–6
*Thread*    Brown
*Tail*    Brown chamois-leather strip, marked with waterproof ink (optional); a ball of red polypropylene yarn tied under the tail to give it support
*Body*    Brown polypropylene dubbing over lead wire
*Back*    Chamois leather as for tail
*Rib*    Clear monofilament
*Hackle*    Mottled hen hackle

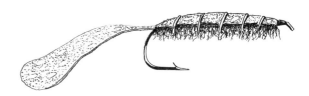

Whitlock's Chamois Leech

The Chamois Leech can be tied up in black, tan or dark olive.

Larry Dahlberg, the creator of that fine deer-hair pattern, the Dahlberg Diver, created the next fly but, instead of using chamois, he used latex cut to give more movement to the fly.

**Larry's Leech** · Dahlberg · USA

| | |
|---|---|
| *Hook* | Mustad 3366, sizes 2–8 |
| *Thread* | Brown |
| *Tail* | Brown latex cut in a spiral |
| *Body* | Brown rabbit strip would up the shank |
| *Eyes (weight)* | Chrome dumb-bell |

The following two patterns imitate the reddish-brown leeches.

**Mini Leech** · Kaufmann · USA

| | |
|---|---|
| *Hook* | Mustad 80050BR, size 10 |
| *Thread* | Red |
| *Tail* | Red marabou with strands of pearl and red Crystal Flash |
| *Body* | Red and pearl Crystal Flash twisted together with red goat hair well picked out |

The next pattern comes from Canada and was tied by Kelvin McKay.

**Canadian Blood Leech** · McKay

British Columbia

| | |
|---|---|
| *Hook* | Mustad 79580, sizes 6–10 |
| *Thread* | Black |
| *Body* | Maroon and black mohair picked well out so that it flares around the body and trails behind the fly as a tail |

The final leech pattern is one by Gary Borger. All of Gary's flies have that touch of magic, integral life. In the water, Gary's flies behave exactly like the real thing and his leech imitations are no exception. He ties them up in black, brown and olive.

**Strip Leech** · Borger · USA

| | |
|---|---|
| *Hook* | Mustad 79580, sizes 2–8 |
| *Thread* | To match the body colour |
| *Tail* | Bunch of chartreuse marabou fibres as long as the shank |
| *Body* | Mohair (or similar) well brushed out |
| *Rib* | Silver or copper wire (copper with the brown version) |
| *Wing* | Rabbit strip extending beyond the hook to about the same distance as the marabou tail secured by the rib |
| *Hackle* | Cock-pheasant rump |

## FISHING THE LEECH

How do you fish these leech patterns? Well the short answer is, fish them where the fish expect to find them. In stillwater they should be fished near the bottom; floating lines and a fairly long leader are adequate for shallow areas. Sink-tip and full-sinking lines are better for deeper water. With all highly mobile flies give plenty of action to the fly by retrieving with a varied figure-of-8 retrieve and activate the rod from time to time; this causes the fly to undulate in a most enticing manner in the water. On rivers with fairly deep, fast water, free-drift the flies close to the bottom. In long, deep pools treat the water as though it were a small lake and fish the flies with plenty of rod action. On riffle water 2–3ft (60–90cm) deep lift the rod as the fly approaches the fish-holding areas; this causes the leech pattern to rise in front of the fish and generally prompts a positive take. Leech patterns, like hellgramites, are good searching flies to be used where big fish can be expected and where there is no other obvious insect activity.

# PART III

# ADDITIONAL ARTIFICIALS

# CHAPTER SIXTEEN

# HARE'S EARS AND PHEASANT TAILS

If the fly-tier had only the fur of the hare and feathers from the ring-necked pheasant, he would still be able to tie a wealth of patterns just using these traditional materials. They are probably the most important natural materials in the palette of the fly-tier.

## HARE'S EAR

The fur of the hare is one of the most versatile of materials, with its broad range of colours and textures, from soft, grey underfur to the sharp, brown and black, bristle-like hair from the ears. Worldwide this fur has been used to create a large number of nymph patterns, starting with the famous, traditional Gold-ribbed Hare's Ear, a truly broad-spectrum fly, with a natural buggy appearance that can imitate a wide variety of aquatic insect life.

I can remember many years ago when this drab-looking little fly worked a thousand miracles for me on the River Torridge in Devon. It was early autumn, but the leaves on the trees were already changing into their finest red and gold raiment and they stood like sentinels in burnished armour guarding the river. There was no wind to rustle their leaves and they lined the bank as though on some final parade before the cold fingers of winter robbed them of their glory. My old friend Phil Seppings, alas no longer with us, had borrowed a Land Rover so we did not have the usual long walk down to the river. Over the years we had fished most of the Devon rivers and streams together and he taught me much. He showed me the lie of salmon and where big trout were always to be taken. We had fished for seatrout on the Teign and for trout, salmon and grayling on the Exe, and he usually caught bigger fish than I did. When the rivers were out of order we went up onto the Dartmoor and fished Fernworthy Reservoir for browns and rainbows. I have shared so many happy days in his company, fishing the West Country streams, each one a moment to treasure, and I miss him.

On that particular day there was a light rain that hung in the air like a fine mist and did little more than caress and dampen the face; my West Country friends call it a 'mizzle'. The river sparkled and sang despite the lack of sun, as though it was welcoming us to a feast or festival. The air was warm and heavy with scents of autumn and the rooks in the tall trees called noisily at our intrusion. I entered the water carefully, for I had slipped many times in the Torridge; its rocks and stones are far more slippery than those on the Exe and I have had many a wetting to prove it. A fish rose by the far bank and I cast my fly above the sunken log that marked the rise.

My fly dipped just below the surface and the leader uncoiled itself and then straightened as the fish took hard. The finely spotted brown cavorted at the end of my line – a small 10in (25cm) fish that thought itself much bigger. I released the fish into the rippling current and cast again speculatively close to the sunken log. My leader straightened and once more I was into a fish, a carbon copy of the first.

It was one of those days, a day that I shall never forget; in my life I have not had many such days. Oh, I have had bigger fish, and there have been the odd times when I have had more fish, but I cannot say that these occasions matched the mixture of experiences I enjoyed that day: a perfect companion, perfect fishing weather, a river set in perfection, and about 20 small wild trout that refused to ignore my fly. My fly? A size 14 Gold-ribbed Hare's Ear. A traditional fly for a day that set for me a tradition.

The Madison River is a mighty long way from the gentle Torridge, and a much larger river, perhaps three or four times wider, if not more. No autumnal trees here, no soft and gentle rain, but a sun that hangs in the sky line a gigantic orb and a sky that fills the world. A few years ago, in the company of Darrel Martin and our trusty guide Harold Roberts, my wife and I made a memorable float. Drifting down, casting our flies close to the bank and taking, but missing far more of the browns and rainbows for which this Blue Ribbon River is justly famous.

For the drift we used Harold's favourite fly, the H. & L. variant, a small, white-winged dry fly easily seen in the shadow of the bank. Before the actual float, while Harold and Darrel were driving to our departure point, we were left to our own devices for about 45 minutes. Madeleine and I tackled up and, looking at this vast river, I decided to put on the old reliable Gold-ribbed Hare's Ear, size 14. When in doubt, take the Hare's Ear out; it is that sort of fly, a good searching pattern.

I waded out a short way from the bank, not expecting to catch much. I felt sure that every angler who came to this river access must have done the same thing while awaiting the return of his guide. I cast my fly half-heartedly towards a largish boulder that stood out of the water, dry and bold like the back of a hump-backed whale. My fly bounced off the stone and into the hurly-burly of the conflicting currents. I watched my line swing with the flow before taking the path of least resistance and snaking down with the strongest current between two more boulders. I was on the point of lifting the rod to cast once more when the take occurred. An explosive shock-take of a mean and wild fish. A take that almost tore the rod out of my hands such was its ferocity. Don't these sort of things happen when you least expect them?

The fish must have been lying secure between the two rocks in about 2ft (60cm) of water when a little greyish-brown, nondescript insect bobbed into his cone of vision – too tempting to ignore, and possibly the first thing it had seen that day that bore any resemblance of food. From then on it did all the things a brown trout does when hooked. It shot down the river causing my reel to sing. It tried to take the line around rocks. It even jumped out of the water but, in the end, it came to hand, a fine Madison brown with red spots like rubies and black spots of mourning jet. It weighed almost 3lb (1.4kg), a serendipity fish.

BRITISH AND EUROPEAN PATTERNS

According to Courtney Williams in his *Dictionary of Trout Flies*, the Gold-ribbed Hare's Ear was considered in the time of Halford to be probably the most killing fly on the River Test. It was an

infallible pattern when the large dark olive was on the water. It was fished then, as it is today, either just under the surface or in the surface film. It was an emerger if ever there was one but that term had not really entered fishing vocabulary in those days. It was about that time, in order to give it a degree of respectability, that wings were added, perhaps to make it appear more like a dry fly and to satisfy the dry-fly-only dogma that surrounded the followers of Halford. Today most of us who fish this jewel of a fly have long ago shed its wings and, whether we fish on stillwaters or on tumbling rivers, the Gold-ribbed Hare's Ear continues to appeal to both angler and, perhaps what is more important, to fish.

### Gold-ribbed Hare's Ear · UK

| | |
|---|---|
| *Hook* | Mustad 94840, sizes 12–16 |
| *Tail* | Primrose |
| *Tail* | Few fibres of hare fur |
| *Body* | Hare's ear fur |
| *Rib* | Fine flat tinsel |
| *Hackle* | Fur picked out to resemble legs |

Gold-ribbed Hare's Ear (UK)

Many beginners have difficulty in dubbing the short, stiff hair from the ears. If you take a very small amount of underfur from the face of the hare and mix it with the hare's ear fur, so that it acts as a carrier, you will find it dubs more easily. On some British reservoirs it is quite common to fish the Hare's Ear on a bigger longshank hook.

### Long-shanked Hare's Ear

As for Gold-ribbed Hare's Ear except:
*Hook*　Mustad 9672, sizes 8–10

### Pearl-ribbed Hare's Ear

As for Gold-ribbed Hare's Ear except:
*Rib*　Pearl Flashabou

### Green-ribbed hare's Ear

As for Gold-ribbed Hare's Ear except:
| | |
|---|---|
| *Hook* | Longshank or conventional hook |
| *Rib* | Fluorescent green silk |

Stuart Billam, one of the Nottingham stillwater stalwarts and contributor to such magazines as *Trout Fisherman*, created the next pattern.

**Hare's Face Nymph** · Billam · UK
*Hook*       Mustad 9672, sizes 8–10
*Thread*     Black
*Tail*       White cock hackle
*Body*       Fur from the hare's face, ginger and blue dun mixed
*Rib*        Medium copper wire
*Thorax*     As body
*Wing case*  Mottled turkey or similar

The next Hare's Ear is one favoured by John Wilshaw, editor of *Practical Gamefishing*. He has also held the editorships of *Trout & Salmon* and *Trout Fisherman* in past years.

**Hare's Ear Nymph** · Wilshaw · UK
*Hook*       Mustad 94840, sizes 10–14
*Thread*     Black
*Tail*       Ginger hackle fibres
*Body*       Hare fur from face and ear
*Thorax*     As body
*Wing case*  Grey duck feather fibre

The next variation uses bronze mallard for the tail and is a good all-round ephemerid nymph.

**Gold-ribbed Hare's Ear Nymph**
*Hook*       Mustad 94840, sizes 12–16
*Thread*     Brown
*Tail*       Bronze mallard fibres
*Body*       Hare fur from the mask
*Rib*        Fine flat tinsel
*Thorax*     As body
*Wing case*  Cock-pheasant tail fibres
*Legs*       Thorax fur picked out

Peter Cockwill is, without doubt, the master of small-stillwater fishing. He has caught more large fish than any other angler I know. He is equally at home on Hampshire waters, such as Avington Fishery, and on some of the large Alaskan rivers. The results are always the same – big fish. This pattern of Peter's is a shrimp imitation. The type of hook helps to make the pattern shrimp-like.

**Cockwill's Hare's Ear Shrimp** · Cockwill · UK
*Hook*       Mustad 80200BR, sizes 10–14
*Thread*     Brown

*Body*       Hare's mask well picked out over lead wire
*Rib*        Fine oval silver tinsel

Cockwill's Hare's Ear Shrimp

Arthur Cove's Hare Ear Nymph is pretty conventional. The dressing is as follows.

**Cove's Hare's Ear Nymph** · Cove · UK
*Hook*       Mustad 3906, sizes 10–14
*Thread*     Black
*Tail*       Furnace hen hackle fibres
*Body*       Hare's ear
*Legs*       Furnace hen

The final pattern of the British Hare's Ears in this chapter is a reservoir pattern given by Tom Saville. The firm of Tom Saville was, and still is, a byword in quality fly-tying materials. Tom himself, now retired, is one of the most knowledgeable stillwater anglers in the country. He currently writes for the fly-fishing magazine, *Practical Gamefishing*. Tom recommends this pattern for use in May and it can be tied weighted or unweighted.

**Orange Hare's Ear** · Saville · UK
*Hook*       Partridge L2A, sizes 10–12
*Thread*     Orange
*Tail*       Orange fluorescent floss (Glo-Brite 7)
*Body*       Hare's ear mixed with orange seal fur
*Rib*        Oval gold tinsel

The famous French fly-tier, André Ragot, adapted a favourite wet fly of his father, Eugene Ragot, and converted it to a nymph pattern. The fly was called Poil de Lièvre (Hair of the Hare), a fly for the Breton rivers. The original fly had a body of hare fur with a tip of orange silk and a smoky-grey hackle. André Ragot's nymph version is as follows.

**Poil de Lièvre Nymphe** · Ragot · France
*Hook*       Mustad 94840, sizes 10–16
*Thread*     Grey
*Tail*       Grey hackle fibres

*Body*　　Almond-green wool, over copper wire
　　　　　(optional)
*Thorax*　Hare fur
*Hackle*　None

Jean-Paul Pequegnot, in his valuable book *French
Fishing Flies*, mentions another Breton fly, Lièvre
et Perdrix (Hare & Partridge). This fly is reminiscent of some traditional Welsh wet-fly patterns.
A Celtic link perhaps?

### Lièvre et Perdrix · France
*Hook*　　Mustad 94840, sizes 12–16
*Thread*　Brown
*Tail*　　Brown partridge
*Body*　　Buff-yellow wool and hare fur, over
　　　　　copper wire (optional)

In 1993, I had the great pleasure of crossing the
border from Slovenia into Croatia – the quiet part
I might add – to fish with some Croatian fly-
fishers. They introduced me to the lovely small
stream, the Kupiča, a tributary of the Kulpa River,
which forms the new border between the two
countries. One of my Croatian companions was
Mladen Merkas Goranin, an excellent fly-tier and a
very good artist; one of his composite pictures
now hangs on my wall. The following Hare's Ear
is a pattern of his designed for the Kupiča River; it
is intended to be used for the whole season, for
both trout and grayling.

### M.M.G. Hare's Ear · Goranin · Croatia
*Hook*　　　Mustad 94840, sizes 10–22
*Thread*　　Brown
*Tail*　　　Hare fur picked out
*Body*　　　Blended hare fur
*Rib*　　　　Gold wire
*Thorax*　　As body
*Wing case*　Small slip taken from the quill (not
　　　　　　feather fibre) of a goose
*Legs*　　　Thorax fur picked out

The following gold-bead pattern is now used
universally throughout the fly-fishing world, including the USA. The use of gold beads probably
originated in Austria, although small bead-headed
flies were used in northern Italy and also Switzerland. All I can say is that bead-headed flies are
European in origin.

### Gold-head Hare's Ear · Austria
*Hook*　　Mustad 9672, sizes 4–16
*Thread*　Black
*Tail*　　Partridge fibres
*Body*　　Hare's ear
*Rib*　　　Oval gold tinsel
*Legs*　　Hare fur picked out
*Head*　　Gold bead

AMERICAN PATTERNS
There are a number of versions of the Gold-ribbed
Hare's Ear originating in the USA. The first is a
version of the standard pattern.

### Gold-ribbed Hare's Ear · USA
*Hook*　　　Mustad 3906B, sizes 8–16
*Thread*　　Black
*Tail*　　　Guard hairs from the hare's mask
*Body*　　　Hare's ear dubbing
*Rib*　　　　Oval gold tinsel
*Thorax*　　As body
*Wing case*　Mottled turkey
*Legs*　　　Thorax fur picked out

Gold-ribbed Hare's Ear (USA)

### Mono-eyed Hare's Ear · USA
*Hook*　　　Mustad 3906B, sizes 6–12
*Thread*　　Brown
*Tail*　　　Guard hairs from the hare's mask
*Body*　　　Hare's ear dubbing
*Rib*　　　　Flat gold tinsel
*Thorax*　　As body
*Wing case*　Dark turkey
*Eyes*　　　Burnt monofilament

### Flash-back Hare's Ear · USA
*Hook*　　　Mustad 3906B, size 8–18
*Thread*　　Tan
*Tail*　　　Partridge hackle fibres
*Body*　　　Hare's ear dubbing
*Rib*　　　　Fine oval gold tinsel
*Thorax*　　As body
*Wing case*　Pearl Crystal Flash
*Legs*　　　Thorax fur picked out

On a recent visit to Montana, I checked out fly patterns in every fly-shop I went into. Each shop had the following pattern among their large selections.

**Rubber Legs Hare's Ear** · USA
| | |
|---|---|
| *Hook* | Mustad 3906B, sizes 8–14 |
| *Thread* | Brown |
| *Tail* | Two tan rubber hackles |
| *Body* | Hare's ear dubbing over lead wire |
| *Rib* | Fine oval gold tinsel |
| *Thorax* | As body |
| *Wing case* | Dark turkey |
| *Legs* | Two tan rubber hackles either side of the thorax |

In recent years hare's masks have been dyed in a wide variety of natural-looking colours. The following patterns use dyed hare fur.

**Brown Hare's Ear** · USA
| | |
|---|---|
| *Hook* | Mustad 3906B, sizes 4–16 |
| *Thread* | Brown |
| *Tail* | Brown hare fur |
| *Body* | As tail |
| *Rib* | Oval gold tinsel |
| *Thorax* | As body |
| *Wing case* | Brown turkey |
| *Legs* | Thorax fur picked out |

The Yellow and Olive versions use yellow or olive fur.

NEW ZEALAND PATTERNS
The fly-fishermen of New Zealand are no strangers to the Hare's Ear Nymph. They combine this fur with copper wire to create an efficient killing pattern for New Zealand waters. I took some good rainbows out of the Waipunga on this nymph.

**Hare & Copper** · NZ
| | |
|---|---|
| *Hook* | Mustad 94840, sizes 10–14 |
| *Thread* | Brown |
| *Tail* | Guard hairs from the fur |

Hare & Copper

| | |
|---|---|
| *Body* | Dark hare fur |
| *Rib* | Heavy copper wire |
| *Wing* | Short tuft of guard hairs (more of a thorax than a wing) |

Another version of this nymph was tied by J. Morris and was used as a drifting, searching nymph.

**Hare & Copper** · Morris · NZ
| | |
|---|---|
| *Hook* | Mustad 94840, sizes 10–14 |
| *Thread* | Black |
| *Tail* | Guard hairs from the body of the hare |
| *Rib* | Copper wire |

### FISHING THE HARE'S EAR

Like all nymphs of a broad-spectrum nature, the Gold-ribbed Hare's Ear can be fished in many ways because it can imitate so many creatures. Without extra weight it can be fished on or just in the surface film, as a floating nymph or an emerger. It can be fished at any depth and in any of a number of different ways, depending on what creature is being imitated.

## PHEASANT TAILS

The feathers from the centre and side tails of the ring-neck cock pheasant are used for tails, bodies, wing cases, sometimes wings and also for legs in many nymphal patterns. It is possibly one of the most versatile of feathers. The colour of the feather can vary from off-white in albino birds to a darkish grey in the melanistic varieties. In between there is a there is a whole range of shades, from rich chestnut to buff. The most famous of the Pheasant Tail Nymphs must be the fly created by the doyen of post-war nymph-fishing, Frank Sawyer. His simple pattern must have accounted for many thousands of fish throughout the fly-fishing world. There is not a country that does not have a Sawyer's Pheasant Tail amongst its list of flies.

BRITISH AND EUROPEAN PATTERNS

**Sawyer's Pheasant Tail** · Sawyer · UK
| | |
|---|---|
| *Hook* | Mustad 94840, sizes 12–18 |
| *Thread* | Fine copper wire |

| Tail | About four fibres of cock-pheasant tail |
| Body | Cock-pheasant tail |
| Thorax | As body |
| Wing case | As body |
| Hackle | None |

Sawyer's Pheasant Tail

The method Frank Sawyer used in tying the fly was as follows:

*Step 1*  Run the copper wire down the hook shank and form a thicker portion where the thorax is going to be.

*Step 2*  Select about four fibres of cock-pheasant tail and tie them in at the bend hook with the copper wire so that they project about ¼in (5mm) beyond the bend.

*Step 3*  Form a rope with the rest of the pheasant tail and the copper wire and wind up to the eye. Unravel the feather fibres and double them back by tying down with the copper wire. This forms the wing case.

*Step 4*  Double and redouble the feathers to form the hump-like thorax and wing case.

*Step 5*  Remove any surplus feather and tie off the copper wire.

The next Pheasant Tail of note is the fly created by Arthur Cove, the Cove's Pheasant Tail, a fly used mainly on stillwater. Many years ago we used to run residential courses at Grafham Water. Arthur was our expert on tactics and, after instruction hours, we used to fish togeher. I have stood close to him on many occasions as he fished his famous Pheasant Tail Nymph and marvelled as his long leader sailed out. I watched as he retrieved his fly in a figure of 8, so slowly as to be almost static. He just stood there, blended into the waterscape; you would swear he was a heron in human form except for the Woodbine cigarette that rested between his lips.

Later, I tied up a few of his famous nymphs and stepped into the chill water of Grafham and tried to copy his method of fishing this fly. I cast out to where I thought I saw a fish bulge and, hardly

retrieving at all, I let the fly move with the natural drift of the water as Arthur did. The result that evening was a 2lb (0.9kg) and a 3lb (1.4kg) rainbow.

## Cove's Pheasant Tail · Cove · UK

| Hook | Partridge Wide Gape, sizes 8–12 (I would use a Grub Hook) |
| Thread | Black |
| Body | 10–12 cock-pheasant tail fibres |
| Thorax | Blue underfur of a wild rabbit |
| Wing case | Cock-pheasant tail fibres |

Cove's Pheasant Tail

This fly is pupa-shaped and can represent either a chironomid or a hatching caddis. The body feather is taken right around the bend. Arthur also tied colour variants, using dyed swan feather for the body medium in green, grey and black.

I believe it was Bob Church who took Arthur Cove's fly a stage further by tying it up on longshanked hooks and giving it a tail. The fly became more nymphal than Arthur's pupa imitation. The pattern itself has a hundred and one variations by just altering the colour of the thorax.

## Longshanked Pheasant Tail · Church · UK

| Hook | Mustad 79580, sizes 8–14 (or conventional hooks) |
| Thread | Black or brown |
| Tail | Cock-pheasant tail fibres |
| Body | As tail |
| Rib | Fine gold or silver oval |
| Thorax | Hare or any fur dyed in whatever colours you desire, including fluorescent |

Longshanked Pheasant Tail

*Wing case*   As tail
*Legs*        Tips of thorax fibres swept either side
              of the hook (optional)

Alan Pearson's version uses a fluorescent green tail as an attractor feature.

### Twitchitt Nymph · Pearson · UK
*Hook*        Mustad 79580, sizes 8–12
*Thread*      Brown or black
*Tail*        Fluorescent wool or floss ¼in (5mm)
              long
*Body*        Cock-pheasant centre tail
*Rib*         Copper wire
*Thorax*      Pale grey rabbit over copper wire, half
              the length of the hook and tied slim
*Hackle*      Sloping collar hackle of ginger cock

The twice world fly-fishing champion, Brian Leadbetter, created the next pattern, a normal Pheasant Tail Nymph with the addition of a white hackle.

### Leadbetter Pheasant Tail · Leadbetter · UK
*Hook*        Mustad 94840, sizes 10–16
*Thread*      Brown
*Tail*        Cock-pheasant tail fibres
*Body*        Cock-pheasant tail
*Rib*         Final oval gold tinsel
*Thorax*      Green seal fur or substitute
*Wing case*   As body
*Hackle*      Short white hen

The next fly is an excellent pattern. I have caught many fish on this fly both on rivers and stillwater.

### Pearly Pheasant Tail · UK
*Hook*        Mustad 94840, sizes 10–16
*Thread*      Brown
*Tail*        Cock-pheasant tail fibres or a few
              strands of pearl Crystal Hair
*Body*        Cock-pheasant tail
*Rib*         Fine oval gold tinsel
*Thorax*      Pearl tinsel
*Wing case*   As body

Two small tufts of fluorescent floss marks the next Pheasant Tail pattern, a fly devised by John Moore, one of the many excellent fly-fishermen who seek their quarry on the large Midland reservoirs of the UK.

### Green-eared Pheasant Tail · Moore · UK
*Hook*        Mustad 94840, sizes 10–14
*Thread*      Brown
*Tail*        Cock-pheasant tail
*Body*        As tail
*Rib*         Copper wire
*Thorax*      Peacock herl with tufts of fluoresent
              green wool or floss either side
*Wing case*   As tail

Green-eared Pheasant Tail

Cock-pheasant tails are now available in a variety of dyed shades, including black. Nymphs can be tied in a wide range of colours.

### Black Pheasant Tail · UK
*Hook*        Mustad 94840, sizes 10–14
*Thread*      Black
*Tail*        Black cock-pheasant tail fibres
*Body*        Black cock-pheasant tail
*Rib*         Fine oval gold tinsel
*Thorax*      Black seal fur (or substitute)
*Wing case*   As tail

The Pheasant Tail Nymphs have not been ignored when it comes to gold-bead adornment. Over the last 2 years many fly-dressers in the UK have gone gold-bead mad, putting them on all sorts of patterns, the Pheasant Tail included. I find that, if you put a bead on the leader before tying on the fly, the effect is the same, because during fishing it slips down to the eye of the fly and works just as well as a beaded pattern.

### Gold-head Pheasant tail · UK
*Hook*        Mustad 94840, sizes 8–12 (the barb on
              some hooks will need flattening)
*Thread*      Brown
*Tail*        Cock-pheasant tail fibres or ginger
              cock hackle fibres
*Body*        Cock-pheasant tail fibres
*Rib*         Fine oval gold tinsel
*Thorax*      Grey fur or cock-pheasant tail
*Wing case*   Cock-pheasant tail
*Head*        Gold bead

In 1993, while fishing on the Kupica River just over the boder from Slovenia, in the new and troubled Republic of Croatia, I was given the following Pheasant Tail flies by Mladen Merkas Goranin. The following three flies are his. The first is a small ephemerid imitation, an excellent pattern for grayling.

**Pheasant Tail** · Goranin · Croatia

| | |
|---|---|
| *Hook* | Mustad 94840, sizes 14–18 |
| *Thread* | Black or brown |
| *Tail* | Cock-pheasant tail |
| *Body* | Cock-pheasant tail |
| *Rib* | Fine gold wire |
| *Thorax* | Pheasant tail |
| *Wing case* | Grey duck feather fibre |
| *Hackle* | Red game fibres |

The next Merkas Pheasant Tail is a small, cased caddis fly.

**Pheasant Tail Caddis** · Goranin · Croatia

| | |
|---|---|
| *Hook* | Mustad 9671, sizes 14–16 |
| *Thread* | Brown |
| *Tail* | None |
| *Rear hackle* | Few wisps of ginger cock hackle at the bend of the hook |
| *Body* | Cock-pheasant tail over copper wire |
| *Rib* | Fine gold wire |
| *Front hackle* | Few wisps of ginger cock hackle |

The last of the Merkas Pheasant Tail flies appears in his small book of patterns, *Leksikon Ribolovnih Musica* (A Dictionary of Fishing Flies).

**Drazen Mance** · Goranin · Croatia

| | |
|---|---|
| *Hook* | Mustad 94840, sizes 10–20 |
| *Thread* | Black |
| *Tail* | Brown cock hackle fibres |
| *Body* | Cock-pheasant tail fibres |
| *Rib* | Fine gold wire |
| *Thorax* | As body |
| *Wing case* | Yellow foam |

Raymond Rocher, the eminent French writer whose work has often appeared in British magazines, created the next pattern. He has found it very effective on most rivers on the chalkstreams of southern England, as well as on his native rivers.

**Pheasant & Orange** · Rocher · France

| | |
|---|---|
| *Hook* | Mustad 3906B, sizes 8–16 |
| *Thread* | Brown |
| *Tail* | Cock-pheasant tail fibres |
| *Body* | Orange silk over lead wire |
| *Rib* | Fine oval gold tinsel |
| *Back* | As tail |

AMERICAN PATTERNS
There are many Pheasant Tail variations in the USA, and the following are a mere sample.

**Pheasant Tail Nymph** · Troth · USA

| | |
|---|---|
| *Hook* | Mustad 3906, sizes 10–18 |
| *Thread* | Brown |
| *Tail* | Cock-pheasant tail fibres |
| *Body* | As tail |
| *Rib* | Copper wire |
| *Thorax* | Peacock herl |
| *Wing case* | Cock-pheasant tail |
| *Legs* | Tips of wing-case fibres tied either side of the hook |

**Flash-back Pheasant Tail** · USA

| | |
|---|---|
| *Hook* | Mustad 9671, sizes 10–18 |
| *Thread* | Black |
| *Tail* | Cock-pheasant tail fibres |
| *Body* | Cock-pheasant tail |
| *Rib* | Copper wire |
| *Thorax* | Peacock herl |
| *Wing case* | Pearl Flashabou |
| *Legs* | As tail |
| *Head* | As rib |

The Teeny Nymph has the dubious distinction of being one of the few flies, if not the only fly, to hold a patent. I doubt whether this could have happened in the UK. Copyright on pattern names is possible, and at least one has been registered, but to take a patent out on a fly would be extremely difficult and costly and, frankly, if it were possible, it would not be worth the hassle. The fly was the creation of Jim Teeny of Oregon, one of the finest steelhead anglers in the USA. Wings are added to this fly when it is used for steelhead and Pacific salmon.

**Teeny Nymph** · Teeny · USA

| | |
|---|---|
| *Hook* | Musad 9671, sizes 8–14 |
| *Thread* | To match colour of fly |
| *Tail* | None |
| *Body* | Cock-pheasant tail, natural or dyed, divided into two, with the tips forming a double set of legs underneath |

## NEW ZEALAND PATTERNS

Fortune's Creek is a small spring creek that flows into the famous Mataura River in South Island, New Zealand. Three years ago I was lucky enough to have a trip to this part of the world, following in the footsteps of anglers such as Zane Gray, to sample the fabulous fishing in this angler's Eldorado. Harry Rae, who has since died, walked me through a long field of thistles to reach the end of this creek so that we could fish upstream and not spook the fish. Being an ex-patriate Scot, he must have felt at home wading through these thistles. Perhaps that is why we walked that mile or so!

The browns in Fortune's Creek run in from the Mataura and, on occasions, can be quite large; Harry said they seldom take a dry fly on this stream and it is nymph-only. The first fish that I saw, a brown of about 3lb (1.4kg) spotted me first and shot beneath the weed. I was a little luckier with the next fish: it did not see me but saw my fly and completely ignored it. And so it went on. I did not get a response to any nymph I tried. I cast speculative nymphs upstream in the channels, sometimes dropping a nymph on the trouts' very noses, but they either glided beneath the weed or shot upstream like a dose of salts. I turned to Harry, offering him my rod, and suggested that he might do better. All I was doing was scaring fish, and at this I was becoming quite expert. Harry took my rod and began to fish.

It was disappointing yet gratifying, because Harry experienced the same lack of success as I had; the fish just did not want to know and it was not just me. I noticed a number of fish swimming in pairs. 'Are they up here to spawn,' I enquired of Harry. 'No, too early,' he replied, as we approached the last few fishable yards of the stream. Harry went off to answer a call of nature and I looked over the small footbridge. Down in the water, a dozen yards from the bridge, I saw a large, dark tail protruding from the weed. I cast the nymph up into the channel and allowed the nymph to free-drift down close to the weeds. I watched the tail, still sticking out of the weeds; it flickered, I immediately tightened, and the water erupted. I had hooked the only trout that wanted to feed that morning. It turned out to be a magnificent brown of between 4 and 5lb (1.8 and 2.3kg) in full mating colours: A butter-yellow belly diffusing into orange, a back of deepest brown and spots like black and red pennies. Harry was as pleased as I was and said I could have been right; for some

strange reason the fish were up to spawn early. I cut off the nymph and handed it back to him. 'No, you keep it,' he said, 'As a reminder of the only fish you caught on Fortune's Creek.' I placed the small, copper-ribbed Pheasant Tail in my box and walked back to the car a little happier than I had been earlier.

A week before this encounter on Fortune's Creek, I had been fishing with Frank Schlosser on Lake Benmore, at the spot where the Ahuriri River braids through many channels into the lake. An area of about 200 yd (160 m) of flat, shallow water, no deeper than one's thighs, was the place where we waited for the cruising brown trout that had left the depths of the lake to maraud, like saltwater bonefish, up the many arms of the river. In many respects you fish for these trout in much the same way as you do for bonefish on some saltwater flats. You first locate the fish and, keeping a low profile, cast your fly into the path of the approaching fish, allowing it to sink to the bottom. This is what we did.

I spotted the trout nosing its way up towards us and cast the nymph about 10 yd (9 m) ahead of it, so as not to spook it. Half-crouching, I watched the trout approach and then adjusted the position of the fly so that it was more directly in its path. The brown came closer and I was biting hard on the stem of my pipe in anticipation. I lifted the rod and the fly came off the bottom in a little spume of mud. This action prompted the trout to move forward with a shake of its tail and a bristling of fins and I saw the white of its mouth. I tightened and it was on. The reel screamed, the rod arced and my line sped out as the fish made a dash for deep water. Truly it was just like fishing for bones. We netted the fish after a short but fierce fight; it weighed about 4lb (1.8kg). We released it straight away and, with a flick of its powerful tail, it sped back into deep water, leaving a trail of disturbed mud in its wake. I cleaned off the fly and set out once more to ambush another fish. The fly was a size 12 New Zealand Pheasant Tail Nymph, of the same pattern that I was to use later on Fortune's Creek but in a smaller size and fished in a totally different way.

### New Zealand Pheasant Tail · NZ

| | |
|---|---|
| *Hook* | Mustad 94840, sizes 12–16 |
| *Thread* | Black or brown |
| *Tail* | Cock-pheasant tail fibres |
| *Body* | As tail |

| | |
|---|---|
| *Rib* | Medium dark copper wire |
| *Thorax* | Cock-pheasant tail |
| *Wing case* | As thorax |
| *Legs* | Dark brown hen |

New Zealand Pheasant Tail

Other New Zealand Pheasant Tails are virtually the same as those in the UK. Tony Orman's pattern is as follows.

**Orman's Pheasant Tail** · Orman · NZ

| | |
|---|---|
| *Hook* | Mustad 94840, sizes 12–16 |
| *Thread* | Brown |
| *Tail* | Cock-pheasant tail fibres |
| *Body* | Cock-pheasant tail |
| *Rib* | Fine copper or gold wire |
| *Thorax* | Green fur dubbing |
| *Wing case* | As body |

Tail fibres from other breeds of pheasant can also be used to create the same sort of flies. The golden pheasant gives attractive-looking Pheasant Tail Nymphs with a variegated brown-and-black coloration. The Amherst pheasant will give flies with a black-and-white magpie effect.

## FISHING THE PHEASANT TAIL

Fishing Pheasant Tails is very much a case of what you want the nymph to represent. This is the case with all broad-spectrum flies. The smaller ephemerid-imitating flies are effective cast upstream and allowed to free-drift. Raising the rod as the fly drifts down, in what is termed the 'Leisenring Lift', also produces the desired effect. I have already mentioned Arthur Cove's method of allowing the nymph to drift with the natural water movement in the reservoir while retrieving ever so slowly. Some of the longshanked, weighted patterns are good point flies on a team of three when fishing traditional loch-style. The weighted Pheasant Tail takes the dropper flies down to the fish-holding levels and, on the lift, will take fish in its own right, or the trout may be attracted to the dropper flies. Pheasant Tails of whatever type are excellent patterns and should be in the armoury of both the river and stillwater angler.

# CHAPTER SEVENTEEN

# EMERGERS AND FLOATING NYMPHS

Until 10 years ago I doubt whether most fly-fishermen had heard the term 'emerger' or given much thought to patterns that represented the nymph at the point of eclosion in the surface film. Over this period of time, 'emerger' has become the buzz-word in fishing. Nowadays, whether you fish gentle chalkstreams, rough and tumble free-stone rivers, quiet ponds or large reservoirs, 'emerger' patterns are part of our fly-pattern selection. They are now some of the most important flies used and I, for one, am using them increasingly. The reason is simple: I am catching more fish on them.

The first book to deal with emerging-nymph patterns in any detail was the slim volume *The Rough Stream Nymph* by W.H. Lawrie, which was published in 1947. Lawrie himself states that the representation of Ephemeroptera at the time of eclosion had not been dealt with in any previous angling book and he felt that he was breaking new ground with his theories and patterns. He went on to state that the patterns should suggest the emerging dun complete with the shuck and, above all, the 'nymph' should float. He pointed out the different manner in which a hatching dun and a hatched dun floated: the latter with its body clear of the water and the former with its body half-submerged in the surface film. His patterns looked like half-submerged dry flies; he used a double hackle at the front to represent wings and legs, clipping the darker leg hackle at the top. His sunk-nymph flies were very close to the traditional English North Country soft-hackled wet fly.

Another source of potential early-emerger patterns can be found in some of the traditional French flies, patterns used on the Normandy rivers. These are not nymphs but dry flies, such as Pont Audemer, Pont Eveque and President Billard, all of which were tied with forward facing (advanced) wings. It was believed that all such advanced-winged French flies were developed from a pattern called the Mole Fly, a British

French dry fly

pattern named after the River Mole in Surrey. This fly received far more attention and popularity in France than it ever did in England. These Normandy flies were designed to be fished with the hook under water and only the wing, held up by the hackle, showing above the surface. Although these flies have never been described as, or given the appellation, 'emergers', in my opinion they can be nothing else. A case can also be made for some of the traditional British lake and loch patterns, those flies with palmered hackles that are fished on the top dropper. Many believe these flies emulate a hatching insect in the surface because the many hackle points cling to the surface film just like the legs of an insect on the point of hatching.

After Lawrie's book virtually nothing was written about emerging flies until comparatively recently. The dry or nymph patterns tied by Swisher and Richards to represent stillborn or crippled duns, and given in their book *Fly Fishing Strategy*, are similar to the emergers. More recently Swisher and Richards have devoted a whole book to the emerger (*Emergers*, 1991). In *Nymph Fishing for Larger Trout*, Charles E. Brookes gives one of the first floating-nymph patterns, using a ball of polypropylene dubbing retained in a nylon net to provide buoyancy. John Goddard in the UK took this a stage further and used polystyrene or other light foam beads to give extra buoyancy to his Suspender Chironomid Pupa (p. 118)

The recent upsurge of interest in emerger patterns coincides with the use of the wispy feathers surrounding the preen gland of the duck, known as *cul de canard* and abbreviated by American fly-tiers to CDC. These feathers had been in use for over 100 years in Europe but it took the tiers of the UK and USA that long to catch up. There are still some individuals in both countries who believe these feathers to be a new fly-tying medium. The first patterns using CDC. were tied in the Swiss region of the Jura and soon crossed the border into France, whence they spread throughout Europe. I published such patterns in *Fly Patterns, An International Guide* in 1986.

I was first introduced to this feather about 15 years ago when the Dutch angling-writer, Kees Keating, sent me a small dry fly tied with these feathers. At the time I did not pay too much attention, to my lasting regret because I would have caught many more fish if I had. Some 8 years ago I first met my good friend Marjan Fratnik, who introduced me to the many joys of fishing in Slovenia. It was in this country that I first started to use patterns tied with this versatile feather, little dry patterns tied by Marjan and other tiers of the area. A year or so later I was using emerger flies tied by Andrij Urban from Skopje in Macedonia. He told me that flies using CDC had been used for many years in Dalmatia, certainly as long as some of the local anglers could remember. Andrij Urban blends natural and man-made fibres in most of his flies so that they sparkle with in-built life. An example of one his patterns, an Emerging Chironomid is given on p. 118.

In the USA, Rene Harrop and his family have produced many patterns using CDC feathers and most fly-suppliers, such as Orvis, Umpqua Feather Merchants and Spirit River Inc. in the USA, and Fulling Mill Flies in the UK, now have a wide selection of CDC-emerger patterns. Fly-suppliers in Italy, France, Austria, Bavaria and Switzerland have had such flies in their lists for a number of years. They have been selling bead-headed patterns for almost as long but the British and Americans have only just caught up with them.

CDC feathers are now supplied dyed in a variety of colours. I have never been convinced that this is an improvement or enhancement because the prime reason for using this feather is the natural oils that coat it: nature's floatant. Dyeing the feather washes out most if not all of this oil. It is true, however, that the very structure of the feather, with its many small barbules, aids flotation and, in the case of sunken flies, retains bubbles of air. Another material used in modern emerger patterns has recently become the vogue with some American tiers. This is the fur found on the feet of snowshoe rabbits, which has water-repellent properties.

In the past I used to attempt to imitate the shuck of the hatching insect, usually with clear plastic film or a single slim hackle, and sometimes by using a tuft of Antron or polypropylene yarn as a tail. In recent years I have dispensed with this adornment and now use normal tails. The shuck simulation did not appear to make any difference to the effectiveness of the patterns and I catch just as many, if not more, fish using a conventional feather-fibred tail. Many of the patterns tied to imitate the sedge (caddis) pupa are, in effect emerger patterns and a number of examples are given in Chapter 7.

There are one or two patterns tied to represent hatching damsels, the ones that have failed to reach some convenient vegetation in order to crawl out, or those that have become trapped in the film prior to hatching. I have also given a number of floating emerger patterns in Chapter 16; Shipman's Buzzer is an example.

BRITISH AND EUROPEAN PATTERNS

The first flies I describe are basically broad-spectrum emergers converting established well-tried flies by using CDC in a loop over the thorax. I use a short tail of cock-pheasant tail fibres for all my emergers for convenience; cock hackle fibres can be used if desired. The are tied in the style first shown to me by Andrij Urban and are a type of fly I have found most successful.

**Hare's Ear Emerger** · Price · UK

| | |
|---|---|
| *Hook* | Mustad 94840, sizes 12–18 |
| *Thread* | Black or brown |
| *Tail* | Cock-pheasant tail fibres |
| *Body* | Hare's ear dubbing |
| *Rib* | Gold wire |
| *Thorax* | As body but tied a little thicker |
| *Wing case* | Thin black foam (optional) |
| *Wing* | Two CDC feathers looped over the thorax and tied at the head |

**Tups Emerger** · UK

| | |
|---|---|
| *Hook* | Mustad 94840, sizes 12–18 |
| *Thread* | Yellow |
| *Tail* | Cock-pheasant tail fibres |
| *Body* | Creamy-yellow hair and Antron, mixed |
| *Rib* | Fine gold wire |
| *Thorax* | Yellow dubbing mixed with a little red to give an overall pinkish shade |
| *Wing case* | Yellow foam (optional) |
| *Wing* | Two CDC feathers looped over the thorax and tied at the head |

**March Brown Emerger** · UK

| | |
|---|---|
| *Hook* | Mustad 80000BR, sizes 10–12 |
| *Thread* | Brown |
| *Tail* | Cock-pheasant tail fibres |
| *Body* | Hare fur |
| *Rib* | Fine gold wire |
| *Thorax* | Brown fur dubbing |
| *Wing case* | Brown foam (optional) |
| *Wing* | Two CDC feathers and a brown partridge hackle inside, all looped over the thorax and tied down |

I am not a great lover of the smaller put-and-take fisheries, except for Lakedown in Sussex, with its four lakes, set like jewels in a valley and surrounded by wooded hills and soft, rolling pastures. This excellent fishery is owned by pop superstar Roger Daltrey of the Who and it is, to my mind, the best smallwater in the south of England. It is well run and the fish, stocked from its own hatcheries, are always of good quality.

In May 1993 I took an inexperienced friend for a day's fishing. We chose to fish the dry and nymph lake. During the morning a few *Ephemera danica* (or their slightly darker cousins *E. vulgata*) fluttered in the lake margins but the fish did not seem interested in them. We took a trout or two on Mayfly Nymphs and then, as usually happens at lunchtime, things had gone quiet. An occasional fish showed itself from time to time so I decided to put on one of my small emergers, and so did my companion. 'Cast out,' I said, 'and then watch your fly carefully.' One minute his fly was floating in the film on the edge of a slight ripple, and the next minute there was a mighty splash, but he failed to connect. 'See what I mean,' I remarked. 'You have to concentrate really hard when fishing these flies. The take usually comes when you least expect it.' Well, he soon got the hang of it and

landed two fine Lakedown rainbows while I contented myself with an errant brown and another rainbow. The small Olive Emerger proved its worth. I have always had good results on this fly, even with grayling in Slovenia, which can be the most difficult of fish when they are in sulky mood.

**Olive Emerger** · UK

| | |
|---|---|
| *Hook* | Mustad 94840, sizes 12–18 |
| *Thread* | Olive |
| *Tail* | Cock-pheasant tail fibres |
| *Body* | Olive fur dubbing |
| *Rib* | Fine gold wire |
| *Thorax* | Olive-brown fur dubbing |
| *Wing case* | Brown foam (optional) |
| *Wing* | Two CDC feathers looped over thorax |

Light, dark and medium olive flies are shown in the colour photograph.

**Mayfly Emerger** · UK

| | |
|---|---|
| *Hook* | Mustad 9672, sizes 12–14 |
| *Thread* | Brown |
| *Tail* | Cock-pheasant tail fibres |
| *Body* | Yellowish-cream dubbing |
| *Rib* | Brown thread |
| *Thorax* | Yellowish-olive dubbing |
| *Wing case* | Brown foam (optional) |
| *Wing* | Two or three CDC feathers looped over thorax |

**Claret Emerger** · UK

| | |
|---|---|
| *Hook* | Mustad 94840, sizes 12–14 |
| *Thread* | Black or claret |
| *Tail* | Cock-pheasant tail fibres |
| *Body* | Light claret fur dubbing |
| *Rib* | Gold wire |
| *Thorax* | Dark claret or black fur |
| *Wing case* | Black foam (optional) |
| *Wing* | Two CDC feathers looped over thorax |

Claret Emerger

Henry's Fork of the Snake River, on the Idaho/Montana border, was everything I expected it to be: a larger-than-life river, moving at an even flow, and only knee-deep from one bank to the other.

The river of fishing legends. The only disappoint-ment was the weather. Cold winds blew from the direction of the Tetons and the sky was a mass of grey clouds, tumbling and twirling like pewter-coloured duvets. With the wind came a cold rain which dripped down my collar but, in truth, did not dampen my spirits, for it is not every day you get to fish Henry's Fork. Because of the weather, any fish that might have been inclined to show kept their heads well down. Late in the evening, when the wind abated and the cold, wet rain eased, just one or two fish rose furtively here and there across the expanse of river, but they were really spooked, rising perhaps once and moving on.

I noticed a few light-coloured pale morning duns floating on the water, braving the inclement weather and, close to a half-submerged log, a fish rose, not just once but twice. I cast my fly ahead of the rise and, within a second, the fish was on. The current on Henry's Fork, although quite benign, still moves at a fair pace and this fish used every available bit of the faster water to seek its freedom, bending my rod in an arc so that it creaked at every joint. Eventually, with a lot of sweat and not a few prayers, it came to hand, a fine Henry's Fork rainbow not far short of 4lb (1.8kg), deep, bellied, finely spotted and as angry as hell. The fly that fooled this fish, was a utility emerger pattern that I had tied to imitate the lighter-coloured ephemerids, e.g. the pale watery dun in the UK and the pale morning or pale evening duns in these western waters of the USA.

**Pale Emerger** · UK

| | |
|---|---|
| *Hook* | Mustad 94840, sizes 12–16 |
| *Thread* | Yellow |
| *Tail* | Cock-pheasant tail fibres |
| *Body* | Pale yellow dubbing |
| *Rib* | Fine gold wire |
| *Thorax* | As body |
| *Wing case* | Brown foam (optional) |
| *Wing* | Two CDC feathers looped over thorax |

**Grey Emerger** · UK

| | |
|---|---|
| *Hook* | Mustad 94840, sizes 12–16 |
| *Thread* | Grey |
| *Tail* | Cock-pheasant tail fibres |
| *Body* | Dubbed CDC feather fibres |
| *Rib* | Fine silver wire |
| *Thorax* | As body |
| *Wing case* | Fine black foam (optional) |
| *Wing* | Two CDC feathers looped over thorax |

The next four patterns, the creations of Charles Jardine, are British

**Floating Nymph** · Jardine · UK

| | |
|---|---|
| *Hook* | Mustad 94840, size 14 |
| *Thread* | Brown |
| *Tail* | Wood-duck fibres |
| *Body* | Olive Antron |
| *Rib* | White thread |
| *Thorax* | As body |
| *Hackle* | Golden-olive cock parachute hackle |

**Emerger No. 2** · Jardine · UK

| | |
|---|---|
| *Hook* | Mustad 94840, sizes 12–20 |
| *Thread* | Brown |
| *Tail* | Light blue dun |
| *Body* | Olive-brown seal fur (or substitute) |
| *Rib* | None |
| *Hackle* | Light blue dun hen |

**Muskrat Emerger** · Jardine · UK

| | |
|---|---|
| *Hook* | Mustad 94840, sizes 12–14 |
| *Thread* | Brown |
| *Tail* | Honey hackle fibres |
| *Body* | Muskrat fur |
| *Rib* | None |
| *Thorax* | As body |
| *Wing* | CDC feather |
| *Hackle* | None |

In the last of this quartet of Jardine emergers deer hair is used in the style of Roman Moser, who was probably the first to make use of deer hair in a dubbed form for many of his emerger patterns.

**March Brown Emerger** · Jardine · UK

| | |
|---|---|
| *Hook* | Mustad 94840, sizes 12–14 |
| *Thread* | Brown |
| *Tail* | Deer-hair fibres |
| *Body* | Dubbed deer hair |
| *Rib* | Gold wire |
| *Thorax* | As body |
| *Wing* | Antron floss |

The next fly is the Olive Emerger created by Andrij Urban who ties a whole range of emerger patterns, including browns and clarets.

**Olive Emerger** · Urban · Macedonia

| | |
|---|---|
| *Hook* | Mustad 94840, sizes 12–16 |
| *Thread* | Olive or brown |
| *Tail* | Brown partridge hackle fibres |

| | |
|---|---|
| *Body* | Olive dubbing (Andrij mixes his own blends of natural and man-made furs) |
| *Rib* | Brown thread |
| *Thorax* | Olive dubbing and orange Antron fibres, mixed |
| *Wing case* | Fine grey foam |
| *Wing* | CDC feather looped over the thorax and tied down at the head |

One of my favourite emerger patterns for both trout and grayling is an adaptation of Marjan Fratnik's 'F' fly. It is called Muha Reka, which is Slovenian for 'river fly.' This pattern can hardly be called a nymph but it is definitely an emerger.

**Muha Reka** · Slovenia

| | |
|---|---|
| *Hook* | Mustad 94840, sizes 12–14 |
| *Thread* | Black |
| *Tail* | None |
| *Body* | Palmered CDC feather |
| *Wing* | CDC feather |

This pattern is fished right in the surface film and is most effective when tweaked so that it submerges and then pops up by itself; the takes usually occur them.

Another pattern I have received from Slovenia is a small midge emerger which proved highly effective for grayling. This pattern incorporates a small, clear plastic bead at the head. I noticed recently that a number of western American patterns now incorporate the lighter beads in some of the ties. I queried this in one shop and was told that they were used on the Bighorn River and fished close to the surface.

**Clear Bead Emerger** · Slovenia

| | |
|---|---|
| *Hook* | Mustad 80100BR, sizes 12–16 |
| *Thread* | Black |
| *Body* | Fine black dubbing |
| *Thorax* | Tuft of grey CDC feathers |
| *Wing* | As thorax |
| *Head* | Small clear bead |

The next two flies are tied by fellow Vice Presidents of the Fly Dressers Guild. Geoffrey Bucknall and John Goddard both imitate an emerging olive.

**Hatching Olive** · Bucknall · UK

| | |
|---|---|
| *Hook* | Mustad 94840, sizes 12–14 |
| *Thread* | Olive |
| *Tail* | Thin slip of olive light goose |

| | |
|---|---|
| *Body* | Light olive goose herl |
| *Rib* | Fine oval gold tinsel |
| *Thorax* | Olive dubbing |
| *Wing case* | Dark feather fibre |

**Hatching Olive** · Goddard · UK

| | |
|---|---|
| *Hook* | Mustad 94840, sizes 12–16 |
| *Thread* | Brown |
| *Tail* | Tips of green-olive condor substitute |
| *Body* | Green-olive condor substitute |
| *Rib* | Flat, silver Lurex |
| *Overbody* | Olive PVC |
| *Thorax* | Cock-pheasant tail fibres |
| *Wing case* | Cock-pheasant tail fibres doubled and redoubled |
| *Legs* | Honey hen hackle |

In *Fly Patterns, An International Guide*, I gave a number of traditional flies from Italy, from the Piedmont region in the Ossola Valley. They were small flies originally tied on reject sewing needles. Needles were traditionally manufactured for many years in the town of Domobossala in this area. Two of the flies were considered to be emergers.

**Ossolina Emerger No. I** · Italy

| | |
|---|---|
| *Hook* | Mustad 80100BR, sizes 14-18 (originals were tied on bent needles and were barbless) |
| *Thread* | Red |
| *Tail* | None |
| *Body* | Tan silk or cotton |
| *Rib* | Fine flat silver tinsel |
| *Legs* | Wispy ginger cock hackle fibres |

Ossolina Emerger

**Ossolina Emerger No. 2** · Italy

| | |
|---|---|
| *Hook* | Mustad 800100BR, sizes 14–16 |
| *Thread* | Black |
| *Body* | Dirty yellow silk or cotton |
| *Rib* | None |
| *Legs* | Wispy ginger cock hackle fibres |

Robert McHaffie, one of the best fly-tiers working in Northern Ireland, published the following pattern in the magazine *Fly Fishing and Fly Tying*. Robert is not a great lover of *cul de canard* feathers and uses a siliconized polypropylene, supplied by Niche products, instead of the more delicate feather.

**Hatching Buzzer** · McHaffie · UK

| | |
|---|---|
| *Hook* | Partridge L3A, size 16 |
| *Thread* | Black |
| *Tail (shuck)* | Grey polypropylene yarn, melted at the end and moulded into shape |
| *Body* | Black yarn |
| *Thorax* | Peacock herl or dubbing |
| *Wing* | White polypropylene yarn |
| *Breathing filaments* | As wing |

In Chapter 8 I gave a couple of patterns by the German tier, Thomas Wolfle, using materials supplied by Traun River Products. The following two flies are others from this creative tier.

**Olive Loop-wing Emerger** · Wolfle · Germany

| | |
|---|---|
| *Hook* | Mustad 94845, sizes 10–18, front half bent upwards |
| *Thread* | Olive |
| *Tail (shuck)* | Bunch of crinkled synthetic fibre (sold in sheet form; fibres are torn off and used as required) |
| *Body* | Brown-olive synthetic dubbing |
| *Thorax* | As body |
| *Loop wing* | Same as tail, tied up and over the thorax in a loop about ¼in (5mm) high |
| *Legs* | Blue-dun grizzle palmered over the thorax before looping the wing; clipped top and bottom |

Olive Loop-wing Emerger

**Bubble Emerger** · Wolfle · Germany

| | |
|---|---|
| *Hook* | Partridge L3A, sizes 12–18 |
| *Thread* | Olive |
| *Tail* | Brown partridge hackle fibres |
| *Body* | Golden-tan Antron bend |
| *Rib* | Gold wire |
| *Thorax* | As body |
| *Bubble* | Fine, grey foam |
| *Legs* | As tail |

Mention has already been made of the traditional flies of Normandy, which I believe, by the way they are fished, to be emerger flies. The following two French patterns are tied to represent the mayfly *Ephemera danica* on the point of hatching. These nymphs are certainly emergers and were created by André Ragot and named after two Normandy rivers, the Andelle and Levrière. They first saw the light of day way back in 1946, proving that the idea of emerging flies is not new, even though the term 'emerger's is a recent innovation.

**Andelle Nymph** · Ragot · France

| | |
|---|---|
| *Hook* | Mustad 3906, sizes 10–12 |
| *Thread* | Yellow |
| *Tail* | Cock-pheasant tail fibres |
| *Body* | A variety of colours (e.g. orange, yellow, cream), flanked by a grey mallard flank tied down at the tail with yellow thread |
| *Front hackle* | French partridge dyed a yellowish-olive |

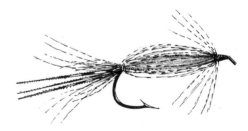

Andelle Nymph

**Levrière Nymph** · Ragot · France
As above except:
*Front hackle*   Grouse hackle

The famous French fly-tier, T. Preskawiec, whose caddis pattern, the Preska Sedge, is known throughout Europe, created a pattern similar to the previous two. He called the fly the Sub-May. This fly is an imitation of a mayfly hatching from its shuck in the surface film.

**Sub-May** · Preskawiec · France
*Hook*     Mustad 9672, sizes 8–10
*Thread*   Olive
*Body*     Condor herl substitute
*Shuck*    Greenish-yellow mallard flank sweeping
           back to surround the body and extend
           approximately ½in (1cm) beyond the
           hook
*Hackle*   Sparse olive cock hackle

AMERICAN PATTERNS
The Natant Nylon Nymph of Charles E. Brookes
was the forerunner of many other similar floating-
nymph patterns tied by other tiers.

**Natant Nylon Nymph** · Brookes · USA
*Hook*     Mustad 9671, sizes 8–16
*Thread*   Brown
*Tail*     Grouse or grizzle hackle fibres
*Body*     Black, brown or tan wool
*Rib*      Gold wire
*Thorax*   Ball of tan or grey polypropylene, encased
           in a net of nylon stocking
*Wing*     As thorax
*Legs*     Beard of grouse or grizzle hackle fibres

The next few patterns are similar to the last
Brookes' pattern.

**Blue-winged Olive Floating Nymph** · USA
*Hook*     Mustad 94840, sizes 20–22
*Thread*   Olive
*Tail*     Medium blue-dun hackle fibres
*Body*     Light olive dubbing
*Thorax*   Medium grey dubbing
*Wing*     As thorax
*Legs*     Beard of blue-dun hackle fibres

The pronounced dubbing hump on these flies is
quite simple to apply. The thread is held vertically
above the hook and the dubbing applied to the
thread. The dubbing is then slid down the hook,
the hackle tied in and a small amount of dubbing
added to the hook. The hump can also be tied
using nylon stocking net if so desired.

**Cream Emerger** · USA
*Hook*     Mustad 94840, sizes 12–18
*Thread*   Cream
*Tail*     Cream hackle fibres
*Body*     Cream dubbing
*Thorax*   Amber dubbing

*Wing*     As thorax
*Legs*     Beard of cream hackle fibres

**Olive Emerger** · USA
*Hook*     Mustad 94840, sizes 14–20
*Thread*   Olive
*Tail*     Olive hackle fibres
*Body*     Medium olive dubbing
*Thorax*   Dark blue-dun dubbing
*Wing*     As thorax
*Legs*     Beard of dark dun hackle fibres

**Brown Floating Nymph** · USA
*Hook*     Mustad 94845, sizes 12–18
*Thread*   Brown
*Tail*     Brown hackle fibres
*Body*     Dark brown synthetic dubbing
*Rib*      Dark brown thread
*Thorax*   Black polypropylene dubbing
*Wing*     As thorax
*Legs*     Brown hackle fibres
*Head*     Dark brown synthetic dubbing

The next pattern is a Gary Borger special.

**Brown Parachute Floating Nymph**
Borger · USA
*Hook*       Mustad 94840, sizes 10–22
*Thread*     Brown
*Tail*       Blue dun hackle fibres
*Body*       Brown dubbing and Antron, mixed
*Thorax*     As body
*Wing hump*  As body
*Legs*       Blue dun parachute hackle wrapped
             around the dubbing hump

Since the properties and versatility of *cul de canard*
feathers have come to be appreciated by American
tiers, a plethora of CDC Emerger patterns have
appeared in various American publications. Articles
by Rene Harrop have played a large part in
educating the tiers of the USA about the value of
these wispy feathers, especially in Emerger flies.
The next two patterns are from his stable.

**Calibaetis Floating Nymph** · Harrop · USA
*Hook*     Mustad 94833, sizes 12–16
*Thread*   Tan
*Tail*     Wood-duck flank fibres
*Body*     Tan rabbit dubbing
*Rib*      Copper wire
*Thorax*   As body

*Wing*     Short clump of white C.D.C. feathers
*Legs*     Brown partridge hackle fibres

### CDC Trico Floating Nymph · Harrop · USA
*Hook*        Mustad 94833, sizes 20–24
*Thread*      Black
*Tail*        Brown partridge hackle fibres
*Body*        Light olive dubbing
*Rib*         Silver wire
*Thorax*      Black rabbit dubbing
*Wing*        Short clump of white CDC feathers
*Legs*        As tail

The next two patterns come from the Spirit River Company.

### Rust-brown CDC Emerger
Spirit River Company · USA
*Hook*        Mustad 80100BR, sizes 14–20
*Thread*      Brown
*Tail*        Cock-pheasant tail fibres
*Body*        Fine dark brown dubbing
*Rib*         Black Crystal Flash
*Thorax*      As body
*Wing case*   Hump of brown CDC feathers
*Legs*        Brown CDC fibres
*Head*        As body

### Sulphur CDC Emerger
Spirit River Company · USA
*Hook*        Mustad 80100BR, sizes 14–20
*Thread*      Cream
*Tail*        Lemon wood-duck fibres
*Body*        Fine cream dubbing
*Rib*         Pearl Crystal Flash
*Thorax*      As body
*Wing case*   Hump of pale yellow CDC
*Legs*        Pale yellow CDC fibres
*Head*        As body

The next pattern, by Farrow Allen, imitates a struggling damsel nymph in the surface film. Many damsel nymphs end up this way for one reason or another and trout, during a hatch of damsels, are always on the look-out for stragglers which represent easy pickings.

### Emergent Damsel Nymphs · Allen · USA
*Hook*        Mustad 79580, sizes 12–14
*Thread*      Primrose
*Tail*        Teased out pale yellow-olive fur
*Body*        Pale yellow-olive dubbed fur
*Rib*         Dark olive tying thread
*Thorax*      As body, teased well out

The final pattern is a fly tied to represent a hatching western green drake and it was created by my good friend Jack Gartside, the only man I know who managed to poach 4 and 5lb (1.8 and 2.3kg) rainbow trout from a moat in the middle of London's West End. I have tied with him on a couple of fly-tying seminars and I can tell you that not only is he a great tier, he is fun to be with. He has produced two small booklets on his flies, *Fly Patterns for the Adventurous Tyer* and *Flies for the 21st Century*. He intimated to me that his next book is possibly *Fly Tying for the Insane*!

### Philo Mayfly Emerger · Gartside · USA
*Hook*        Mustad 94859, sizes 10–12
*Thread*      Black
*Tail*        Brown partridge or grouse hackle fibres
*Body*        Tapered black Antron with a little olive added, tied heavier at the thorax
*Wing*        Black-dyed pheasant aftershaft wound around the hook and clipped on the bottom
*Wing case*   As wing
*Legs*        Brown partridge (or grouse) hackle fibres

In these days, there are many more emerger patterns in the catalogues of the fly suppliers, and in articles and books on the subject. The selection given, however, should be sufficient for the reader to try, if he or she has not yet tasted success with these flies.

# CHAPTER EIGHTEEN

# ADDITIONAL BRITISH NYMPHS

In this chapter is listed a selection of nymphs, some past and some present, all of which have in their time, caught their fair share of fish. And I feel sure many are worth trying again. All types of nymph are represented: searching nymphs, emerging nymphs, crawlers, floaters, attractors, some imitative and some broad-spectrum and others that can only be described as figments of a vivid imagination. Inevitably many flies have been omitted, including some fishermen's favourites, and, by the time this book is published, I have no doubt that many new nymphs will have been created.

## AMBER NYMPH

There are many patterns known as Amber Nymphs but this particular one was given to me by the late Lionel Sweet, the master of the River Usk. In his early days Lionel trained as a sign-writer and, in the design of this fly, he emphasizes the gold rib with another rib of black silk, in much the same way that a sign-writer places shadow behind the letters in order to make them stand out. This is an effective caddis pupa pattern.

**Amber Nymph** · Sweet
| | |
|---|---|
| *Hook* | Mustad 3904A, sizes 10–14 |
| *Thread* | Brown or orange |
| *Body* | Amber floss silk |
| *Rib* | Oval gold tinsel with black silk behind |
| *Hackle* | Light ginger cock |

## ANGORA GRUB

This pattern, devised by Richard Walker for stillwater fishing, is given in his book *Modern Fly Dressings*. It is an excellent searching nymph, imitating nothing in particular but looking like something juicy and trout-tempting. It can be tied in a variety of colours and is also effective tied on smaller shanked hooks. It has a very shrimp-like appearance.

**Angora Grub** · R. Walker
| | |
|---|---|
| *Hook* | Mustad 79850, sizes 8-10 |
| *Thread* | Brown |
| *Body* | Brown angora (also green, olive or amber) |
| *Rib* | Flattened heavy nylon monofilament |
| *Back* | All hair trimmed at the top and given two or three coats of clear varnish |

## ARDLEIGH NYMPH

Bob Church, in *Guide to Trout Flies*, lists this nymph as one of his favourites. It was created by Richard Connell and named after the reservoir which he managed. Bob maintains that this fly is deadly in the evening during a chironomid hatch, and even when sedges are coming off the water. The pattern is an emerger, representing both types of insect.

**Ardleigh Nymph** · Connell
| | |
|---|---|
| *Hook* | Mustad 94840, sizes 10–16 |
| *Thread* | Black |
| *Tail* | Greenwell cock hackle fibres |
| *Body* | Cock-pheasant tail fibres |
| *Rib* | Fine oval gold tinsel |
| *Thorax* | Bronze peacock herl |
| *Hackle* | Small Greenwell hen |

## AYLOTT'S ORANGE

This was created by Richard Aylott, who devised a number of interesting patterns in the 1970s. It works well at dusk during a caddis hatch and will also take fish on rivers, including grayling.

**Aylott's Orange** · Aylott
| | |
|---|---|
| *Hook* | Mustad 94840, sizes 12–14 |
| *Thread* | Black |
| *Body* | Arc chrome fluorescent wool |
| *Hackle* | Light ginger cock |
| *Head* | Peacock herl |

**Aylott's Green** · Aylott
As above except:
*Body*    Signal-green fluorescent wool

## B.W. NYMPH

Although the name of this fly is the same as the initials of its originator, this is mere coincidence. B.W. stands not for Barrie Welham, as some people think, but for 'brown woolly', the body material. It is an excellent pattern during a chironomid rise and works equally well on rivers and stillwater. When I was a professional fly-tier I tied thousands of this pattern.

**B.W. Nymph** · Welham
| | |
|---|---|
| *Hook* | Mustad 94840, sizes 10–16 |
| *Thread* | Black |
| *Tail* | Short tuft of red and yellow fluorescent floss |
| *Body* | Brown wool tied slimly |
| *Rib* | Fine, flat, silver tinsel |
| *Breathing appendages* | Short tuft of white hackle fibres tied over the body |

B.W. Nymph

## BADDOW SPECIAL

Hanningfield Reservoir is one of southern England's most productive fisheries; every year this water seems to produce good, double-figure fish. The Baddow Special was designed by John Poole for fishing at Hanningfield and is best described as a broad-spectrum fly imitating a damsel larva, among other things.

**Baddow Special** · Poole
| | |
|---|---|
| *Hook* | Mustad 79580, sizes 8–10 |
| *Thread* | Black |
| *Tail* | Fluorescent lime wool |
| *Body* | Peacock herl |
| *Rib* | Copper wire (optional) |
| *Hackle* | Sparse long-fibred white cock hackle |

## BARE-HOOK NYMPHS

Along with Frank Sawyer, the late Oliver Kite must be considered as one of the leading exponents of fishing the nymph on southern chalkstreams. This fly was born out of a badly chewed-up Pheasant Tail, which continued to catch fish long after the feathers had fallen off, leaving almost bare copper wire. The fly, like Sawyer's Pheasant Tail, is fished in the manner called the induced take. By casting ahead of a showing fish and raising the rod when the nymph reaches the fish, the nymph will rise, thus inducing the fish to take.

**Bare-hook Nymph** · Kite
| | |
|---|---|
| *Hook* | Mustad 94836, sizes 12–20 |
| *Thread* | None |
| *Body* | Copper wire |
| *Thorax* | Nob of copper wire |

## BARNEY GOOGLE

Richard Walker tied up this fly in the early 1970s. Of course, it imitates nothing and can only be classed as a fantasy fly, but it does catch fish. What the trout see in it heaven only knows; perhaps a form of beetle larva. Richard Walker thought it was effective as a phantom larva, but I have yet to see a phantom midge larva with bloodshot eyes!

**Barney Google** · R. Walker
| | |
|---|---|
| *Hook* | Mustad 94840, sizes 10–14 |
| *Thread* | White |
| *Body* | Clear polythene |
| *Legs* | Grey-partridge hackle fibres |
| *Eyes* | Two red beads |

## BARTON BUG

John Roberts gives this pattern in his *New Illustrated Dictionary of Trout Flies*, attributing it to Roy Darlington. The fly is an emphemerid emerger pattern, fished half in and half out of the water.

**Barton Bug** · Darlington
| | |
|---|---|
| *Hook* | Mustad 94840, sizes 12–16 |
| *Silk* | Primrose |
| *Tail* | Rabbit neck guard hairs |
| *Body* | Hare fur |
| *Rib* | Fine gold wire |
| *Thorax* | As body |
| *Hackle* | Short-fibred blue dun |

## BEWL BEACON

This highly coloured stick-fly pattern was created by my wife, Madeleine, who has caught many fish on it. She first used it on Bewl Water; hence the first part of its name. The second part came from a friend who, on that day, could see the fly as Madeleine cast and called across from his boat 'What the hell have you got on? Looks like a bloody beacon.' It is a good early-season searching nymph. When nothing seems to work it usually tempts a fish or two.

**Bewl Beacon** · Madeleine Price
*Hook*     Mustad 79850, sizes 8–12
*Thread*   Orange
*Tail*      Fluorescent orange wool or silk
*Body*    Fluorescent orange and yellow chenille
*Hackle*   Hot orange

## BEWL GREEN NYMPH

A killing pattern devised by Chris Ogbourn, the English International team member, this fly works well during a hatch of green chironomids. It can be tied weighted or unweighted and fished at all depths. The pattern is very similar to the later nymph of Conrad Voss-Bark in its palmered-hackle conception.

**Bewl Green Nymph** · Ogbourn
*Hook*     Wide Gape, sizes 8–10
*Thread*   Olive
*Tail*      Olive hackle fibres
*Body*    Dark olive seal fur over copper wire if weight is desired
*Legs*     Palmered olive hackle

Bewl Green Nymph

## BILL'S VIVA

The Viva Lure created by Victor Furse is one of the most popular reservoir lures in the UK. It was named after the creator's Vauxhall Viva car. Tom Saville gives a stick-fly/nymph version of this fly in his excellent book *Reservoir Trout Fishing*. The fly relies heavily on the fluorescent green colour which, combined with the black body, proves irresistible to trout.

**Bill's Viva**
*Hook*     Mustad 9672, sizes 8–10
*Thread*   Black
*Tail*      Fluorescent green Glo-Brite floss (shade 12)
*Body*    Dubbed black seal fur or substitute
*Rib*      Silver oval tinsel
*Hackle*   Beard of fluorescent floss as tail

## BLACK BUZZER

This small, heavily weighted chironomid pupa pattern is used by Bill Sibbons to get down to the fish quickly on some of the smaller clearwater fisheries.

**Black Buzzer** · Sibbons
*Hook*     Mustad 94840, size 16
*Thread*   Black
*Tail*      Very short tuft of white marabou
*Body*    Black floss
*Rib*      Fine copper wire
*Thorax*   Lead shot
*Breathing appendages*   Tuft of white deer hair

## BLACK NYMPH

There are many patterns described as Black Nymphs of which the following is one. They can imitate anything from damsel flies to dark mayfly nymphs and, in small sizes, chironomid midge pupa. (See also Kenya Bug, p. 226.)

**Black Nymph**
*Hook*     Mustad 94840 or 79580, sizes 10–14
*Thread*   Black
*Tail*      Black hackle fibres
*Body*    Black seal fur or substitute
*Thorax*   As body
*Wing case*   Black goose feather fibre
*Hackle*   Black hen

## BLUE DAMSEL NYMPH

The first person to produce a blue nymph to imitate a subsurface damsel fly was Geoffrey Bucknall. A number of years ago he produced a blue tube-fly pattern. Bill Sibbons, probably one of the best anglers on the smaller stillwaters of southern England, has taken almost 90 trout of over 10lb (4.5kg) from these fisheries. He believes that trout cannot differentiate between an adult damsel 2in (5cm) above the water and one 2in (5cm) below so he created this pattern for use when the trout are actively feeding on the adults. The fly is fished quickly just under the surface.

**Blue Damsel Nymph** · Sibbons
| | |
|---|---|
| *Hook* | Silver longshank, size 10 |
| *Thread* | Blue |
| *Tail* | Light blue wool |
| *Body* | Light blue ostrich waisted in the middle with blue silk |
| *Hackle* | Swept-back soft blue cock hackle |

## BOOBY NYMPH

We are stretching the term nymph to the nth degree with this fly. It was devised by the Leicestershire tier, Gordon Fraser, as a buoyant pattern for stillwater fishing. The buoyancy is achieved by two polystyrene balls encapsulated in nylon stockings at the front; hence the term 'booby'! The pattern can come in a range of tail and body colour combinations and is so successful that I know of certain stillwater fisheries where it is banned. It is usually fished on a short leader and a sinking line. Gordon told me that he has practically disowned this fly because too many anglers were not fishing it properly. All they were doing was casting out and leaving it as a static fly, hoping a passing fish would pick it up. I felt quite guilty as I agreed with him, for I have done exactly that in the past.

**Booby Nymph** · Fraser
| | |
|---|---|
| *Hook* | Mustad 79580, sizes 6–10 (or a conventional-shanked hook) |
| *Thread* | To match body colour |
| *Tail* | Hackle fibres or marabou in desired colour |
| *Body* | Hare's ear (or any synthetic dubbing) in desired colour |
| *Eyes* | Two polystyrene or other foam beads |

## BOTTOM-SCRATCHER

During a fishing visit to Austria Charles Jardine was influenced by Austrian patterns: flies that use dubbed deer hair and also gold-bead heads. He successfully brings these materials together in this searcher pattern and the marabou tail gives it in-built mobility.

**Bottom-scratcher** · Jardine
| | |
|---|---|
| *Hook* | Mustad 3906, sizes 14–16 |
| *Thread* | Black or yellow |
| *Tail* | Black marabou |
| *Body* | Hare fur |
| *Rib* | None |
| *Thorax* | Dubbed tan deer hair |
| *Head* | Gold bead |

Bottom-scratcher

## BOW-TIE BUZZER

Another development by Frank Sawyer, this fly has a simple pheasant-tail body and a separate piece of white nylon attached to the leader close to the hook, to simulate the breathing appendages. Personally speaking I have not met anyone who uses this pattern these days but I could be wrong.

**Bow-tie Buzzer** · Sawyer
| | |
|---|---|
| *Hook* | Mustad 94840, sizes 12–14 |
| *Thread* | None; use copper wire as in the Pheasant Tail Nymph |
| *Body* | Cock-pheasant tail twisted with copper wire |
| *Breathing appendages* | Separate tuft of white wool |

## BRER RABBIT

A good stalking nymph for clearwater fishing, this should be well weighted to get down fast to the cruising fish.

### Brer Rabbit

| | |
|---|---|
| *Hook* | Mustad 79850, sizes 8–10 |
| *Thread* | Brown |
| *Tail* | Two brown goose biots |
| *Body* | Brown angora wool over lead wire |
| *Rib* | Oval or round gold tinsel |
| *Thorax* | Rabbit fur dubbing |
| *Wing case* | Hen-pheasant centre tail |
| *Leg* | Brown partridge |

## BUFF BUZZER

This a broad-spectrum pattern created by the well-known Nottingham angler and tackle-supplier, Steve Parton. Steve is one of the pioneers of float-tubing in this country. The Buff Buzzer is a pattern that can imitate anything from a hatching, light-coloured chironomid to a small, emergent sedge, or even a *Caenis* nymph.

### Buff Buzzer · Parton

| | |
|---|---|
| *Hook* | Mustad Sproat, sizes 10–16 |
| *Thread* | Black |
| *Body* | Pale beige swan or goose fibre |
| *Rib* | Fine gold wire |
| *Thorax* | Beige seal fur |
| *Wing case* | As body |

## BUG-EYED NYMPH

Many years ago I went through a stage when all my flies had to have eyes and I attached a silver bead chain of various sizes to my nymphs and lures. These silver eyes were quite out of proportion on the smaller nymph patterns and prompted several ribald comments from fellow anglers. I had entered one catch in the club record book and indicated that I had taken the fish on a Bug-Eyed Nymph. The following week I looked in the book and found that a fellow member had crossed out 'Bug-eyed Nymph' and put instead *'Testes argentum'*. The fly still catches fish for me, but don't ask me what it imitates!

### Bug-eyed Nymph · Price

| | |
|---|---|
| *Hook* | Mustad 94840, sizes 10–14 |
| *Thread* | Black |
| *Tail* | Short tuft of black marabou |
| *Body* | Dubbed black seal fur or substitute |
| *Rib* | Fine oval silver tinsel |
| *Hackle* | None |
| *Eyes* | Silver bead chain |

The pattern can be tied in a wide variety of colours: red, brown, olive, green, orange or even white.

## BUTCHER NYMPH

This fancy nymph pattern is a development of the traditional wet-fly pattern. The fly is given a nymphal appearance but the colours of the original fly remain. This also applies to the variant, the Bloody Butcher. I suspect that the fish take these two nymphs as small fish.

### Butcher Nymph

| | |
|---|---|
| *Hook* | Mustad 80000BR, sizes 8–14 |
| *Thread* | Black |
| *Tail* | Scarlet hackle fibres |
| *Body* | Flat, silver tinsel |
| *Rib* | Fine oval silver tinsel |
| *Thorax* | Black dubbing |
| *Wing case* | Blue mallard feather |
| *Hackle* | Black |

Butcher Nymph

### Bloody Butcher Nymph

| | |
|---|---|
| *Hook* | Mustad 80000BR, sizes 8–14 |
| *Thread* | Black |
| *Tail* | Scarlet hackle fibres |
| *Body* | Flat silver tinsel |
| *Rib* | Fine oval silver tinsel |
| *Thorax* | Black dubbing |
| *Wing case* | Blue mallard feather |
| *Hackle* | Scarlet hackle fibres |

## CARROT NYMPH

G.E.M. Skues, father of modern nymph-fishing, did, in fact, have a lighter side. Fishing was not an all-serious affair and the Carrot Nymph was, in fact, a joke pattern. Nevertheless the last laugh is on the originator for the damn thing catches fish. (See also p. 203 for an American version.)

### Carrot Nymph · Skues

| | |
|---|---|
| *Hook* | Mustad 94840, sizes 14–16 |
| *Thread* | Yellow |
| *Tail* | Green parrot feather |

*Body*   Yellow wool (rear third), hot orange wool (middle third), green seal fur (rear third)
*Hackle*   Short-fibred olive-green hen

## CHEW NYMPH

Named after the great West Country reservoir at Chew Valley, this pattern was devised by Thomas Clegg, a tier who pioneered the use of fluorescent materials in fly design in the UK.

**Chew Nymph** · Clegg
*Hook*     Mustad 94840, sizes 8–10
*Thread*   Red
*Tail*     Fluorescent magenta floss silk
*Body*     Mole fur dubbing
*Rib*      As tail
*Back*     Mottled turkey
*Hackle*   Short-fibred brown hen

## CLIPPED COACHMAN

A good searching nymph for both rivers and stillwater, I discovered the effectiveness of this fly many years ago while fishing the River Exe in Devon. The traditional Coachman wet fly was a favourite pattern of mine in those days but, on one particular day, it seemed to have lost its magic. I thought I would amend the dressing slightly by shortening the hackle and clipping the wing to a little white stub. The result was an increased interest in this offering from both trout and grayling. I have taken good rainbows on stillwater during a chironomid hatch using this simple fly.

**Clipped Coachman** · Price
*Hook*     Mustad 94840, sizes 12–16
*Thread*   Black
*Body*     Bronze peacock herl (tied thinner than for the standard wet fly)
*Wing*     Short tuft of white feather fibre or white fluorescent silk
*Hackle*   Sparse brown hen

## COACHMAN NYMPH

This is another amendment to the old standard wet pattern. (See also Lead-wing Coachman Nymph p. 206).

**Coachman Nymph**
*Hook*      Mustad 94840, sizes 10–14
*Thread*    Black
*Tail*      Brown hackle fibres
*Body*      Bronze peacock herl
*Thorax*    As body
*Wing case* White feather fibre
*Legs*      As tail

## COLLYER NYMPHS

This highly successful series of simple all-purpose nymphs, was devised by the late Dave Collyer for both rivers and stillwater.

**Collyer's Black Nymph** · Collyer
*Hook*      Mustad 94840, sizes 10–12
*Thread*    Black
*Tail*      Tip of black swan or goose feather fibre
*Body*      Black goose or swan feather fibre
*Rib*       Fine oval gold tinsel
*Thorax*    Black ostrich herl
*Wing case* As body

**Collyer's Green Nymph** · Collyer
*Hook*      Mustad 94840, sizes 10–12
*Thread*    Brown
*Tail*      Tip of olive swan or goose feather fibre
*Body*      Olive swan or goose
*Rib*       Fine oval gold tinsel
*Thorax*    Olive ostrich herl
*Wing case* As body

**Collyer's Brown Nymph** · Collyer
*Hook*      Mustad 94840, sizes 10–12
*Thread*    Brown
*Tail*      Brown goose or swan feather fibre
*Body*      Brown goose or swan feather fibre, or cock-pheasant tail
*Rib*       Fine oval silver tinsel
*Thorax*    Brown ostrich
*Wing case* As body

**Collyer's Grey Nymph** · Collyer
*Hook*      Mustad 94840, sizes 10–12
*Thread*    Grey
*Tail*      Tip of heron herl (or dyed goose substitute)
*Body*      Heron herl (or substitute)

| | |
|---|---|
| *Rib* | Fine flat silver tinsel |
| *Thorax* | Grey ostrich herl |
| *Wing case* | As body |

## COLONEL'S CREEPERS

This series of flies was devised by Colonel Andy Unwin, who has run the Kenyan fly-tying factory in the Nandi Hills, for Fulling Mill Flies, for more years than I can remember. In more ways than one he has been responsible for the high-quality products supplied by this company. This series consists of excellent searcher nymphs which have proved their worth on a number of clearwater fisheries in the south of England, particularly on the Chalk Springs Fishery in Hampshire. The flies are similar in many respects to large stonefly creepers. They are tied in brown, black, cream, orange and olive, usually with the point of the hook uppermost.

**Colonel's Creeper** · Fulling Mill Flies

| | |
|---|---|
| *Hook* | Mustad 79850, sizes 4–8 |
| *Thread* | To match body |
| *Tail* | Short tuft of hair to match body colour |
| *Body* | Fur dubbing (brown, black, cream, orange-cream, etc.) over lead wire for weight |
| *Rib* | Plastic Larva Lace or similar product |
| *Thorax* | As body |
| *Wing case* | Two slips of feather fibre to match body colour |
| *Legs* | Three pairs of goose biots to match body colour |

## CONRAD VOSS-BARK NYMPH

This palmered nymph was created by Conrad Voss-Bark, the well-known author and broadcaster. He maintains that the double-coloured hackle gives life to the pattern. I can only say that it has worked for me. The fly can be tied weighted or unweighted. In my opinion the fly, tied as it is with palmered hackle, would be better described as a wet fly but Conrad Voss-Bark calls it a nymph, so a nymph it shall be.

**Conrad Voss-Bark Nymph**

| | |
|---|---|
| *Hook* | Mustad 94840, sizes 8–12 |
| *Thread* | Green |
| *Tail* | Golden-pheasant crest |

| | |
|---|---|
| *Body* | Yellow, dark olive and olive seal fur (or substitute), blended and darkening towards the thoracic area |
| *Rib* | Fine gold or silver wire |
| *Body hackles* | Two (natural red and golden olive) |
| *Head hackle* | Natural red-brown cock |

## COPPER CHEAT

This pattern uses red copper wire and, to be truthful, does nothing to advance the art of fly-dressing. Some years ago, while observing small fish in my aquarium, I wrapped a small hook in red-coated copper wire and left two ends dangling either side. I thought that the fish might view it as a small annelid worm. Not only was the lure attacked by small minnows but it also received the attention of the diving beetles. Thus the Copper Cheat was born. On its first outing, it took the limit of fish on our local water. John Kelley, my colleague in the boat on that day, eventually tried the fly under the strictest instructions not to tell anybody in case I was drummed out of the Fly Dressers Guild for doing nothing to promote the gentle art of fly-tying.

**Copper Cheat** · Price

| | |
|---|---|
| *Hook* | Mustad 80000BR, sizes 10–14 |
| *Thread* | None |
| *Body* | Built up of red copper with a strand at the front and at the rear |

## COPPER NYMPH

There are many nymphs of this name but they are all basically the same. All use copper wire as the body to give the pattern weight and a certain amount of flash. This simple nymph I devised as a pupa of some sort, hoping trout would take it either as a chironomid or possibly a caddis pupa.

**Copper Nymph** · Price

| | |
|---|---|
| *Hook* | Mustad 80200BR, sizes 8–18 |
| *Thread* | Fluorescent orange |

Copper Nymph

| | |
|---|---|
| *Body* | Copper wire with a tag of fluorescent green floss |
| *Thorax* | Copper wire |
| *Legs* | Brown partridge, sparse |

## DIAWL BACH

The name of this Welsh pattern means 'little devil'. It became very popular on the reservoirs of Chew and Blagdon and, although originally a wet fly, it is now generally fished as a nymph.

**Diawl Bach**

| | |
|---|---|
| *Hook* | Mustad 94840, sizes 10–14 |
| *Thread* | Brown |
| *Tail* | Brown cock hackle fibres |
| *Body* | Peacock herl (may be wrapped with copper wire for weight and durability) |
| *Legs* | As tail |

Diawl Bach

This pattern has also been tied with a thorax cover of pearl tinsel.

## DOVE BUG

This fly is a fancy grub pattern for grayling devised by that excellent fisherman and author, John Roberts. He is considered by many to be one of the best grayling anglers in the country.

**Dove Bug** · Roberts

| | |
|---|---|
| *Hook* | Mustad 94840, sizes 10–16 |
| *Thread* | Brown |
| *Tail* | Small tuft of red wool |
| *Body* | Orange and pink seal fur |
| *Underbody* | Three layers of copper wire |
| *Thorax* | Orange and brown seal fur |
| *Rib* | Copper or gold wire the length of the body |

## DUBBING-WICK PUPA

Dubbing wicks were first manufactured in the Czech Republic, using different furs twisted with copper wire. They really do make fly-tying easier and certainly quicker because, with one application, we have weight, rib and body all in one fell swoop. I devised the following pattern using such wicks spun about with dyed angora.

**Dubbing-wick Pupa** · Price

| | |
|---|---|
| *Hook* | Mustad 80200BR, sizes 6–10 |
| *Thread* | Brown |
| *Body* | Yellow dubbing wick |
| *Thorax* | Brown dubbing wick |
| *Wing case* | Cock-pheasant tail |
| *Antennae* | As wing case |
| *Legs* | Brown partridge |

## EMERGING CADDIS

Mention has already been made of Davy Wotton and his fly-tying and fishing skills. He is one of the most innovative of fly fishermen and his seal fur substitute (synthetic living fibre or SLF), I would say, is even better than the real thing.

The following pattern of his uses this product to great effect. To achieve translucency in the dubbing, Davy uses a Danville tying thread; he divides this with a fine needle, placing the dubbing between the strands and then spinning the bobbin.

**Emerging Caddis** · Wotton

| | |
|---|---|
| *Hook* | Partridge SH2 or similar, sizes 10–14 |
| *Thread* | Danville yellow |
| *Body* | Orange SLF |
| *Thorax* | Amber SLF |
| *Wing* | Treated Raffene |
| *Legs* | Light ginger cock hackle |

## EYEBROOK NYMPH

This nymph is named after the Eyebrook Reservoir. It owes a lot in its design to Tom Ivens' flies, his Brown & Green Nymph in particular. It is probably taken as a sedge pupa.

**Eyebrook Nymph**

| | |
|---|---|
| *Hook* | Mustad 94840, sizes 8–14 |
| *Thread* | Black |
| *Tail* | Peacock herl |
| *Back* | As tail |
| *Body* | Amber seal fur (or substitute) |
| *Rib* | Oval gold tinsel |
| *Head* | As tail |

## FLUFFY FOAM PUPA

Fluffy foam is a plastic foam with a flock of soft fibres either side and is excellent for tying all types of fly. I have used it to create a very effective sedge pupa pattern.

**F.F. Pupa** · Price
*Hook*      Mustad 37160, sizes 10–12
*Thread*    Black or brown
*Body*      Fluffy foam (orange, green, olive, brown or grey)
*Thorax*    Brown dubbing over lead wire
*Wings*     Starling body feather
*Wing case* Cock-pheasant centre tail
*Legs*      Brown partridge
*Head*      Black or brown dubbing
*Antennae*  Cock-pheasant tail fibres
*Eyes*      Black plastic bead chain or burnt nylon monofilament

## FRASER NYMPHS

Gordon Fraser is a professional fly-tier and author of the excellent book *Mastering the Nymph*. Mention has already been made of his Booby Nymph (p. 185) but his more conventional nymphs are just as effective. They can be tied on long-shanked or normal-shanked hooks.

**Fraser Nymph** · Fraser
*Hook*      Mustad 9672, size 10
*Thread*    Fawn
*Tail*      Hen-pheasant tail fibres
*Body*      As tail
*Rib*       Fawn polyester thread
*Thorax*    Beige blended fur dubbing
*Wing case* As tail
*Legs*      Tips of the wing-case fibres swept backwards either side of the thorax

**Fraser Nymph (Olive)** · Fraser
*Hook*      Mustad 9672, size 10
*Thread*    Fawn
*Tail*      Hen-pheasant tail fibres
*Body*      As tail
*Rib*       Green polyester thread
*Thorax*    Pale olive dubbing
*Wing case* As tail
*Legs*      Tips of the wing-case fibres swept backwards either side of the thorax

Another of the Gordon Fraser specials, the Fourwater Nymph can be tied with or without a gold-bead head.

**Fourwater Nymph** · Fraser
*Hook*      Mustad 94840, sizes 10–14
*Thread*    Brown
*Tail*      Brown rabbit fur
*Body*      Hare fur well picked out
*Rib*       Fine oval gold tinsel

## FRESHWATER SHRIMP

This pattern has been reserved for this chapter because it really deserves to stand on its own. I consider it to be one of the best. I have watched its creator, Oliver Edwards, tie this fly on a number of occasions and never cease to marvel at his exquisite tying. Oliver uses the Darrel Martin Dubbing Whirl to dub the fur and feather onto the hook.

**Freshwater Shrimp** · Edwards
*Hook*      Straight shank, wide gape, sizes 10–14
*Thread*    Olive
*Body*      Brown partridge hackle fibres, pale olive hare's belly fur over lead wire
*Back*      Olive polythene
*Rib*       Clear monofilament approx 4lb (1.8kg) BS
*Legs*      Few fibres of olive partridge, tied under the hook and for one third of the body length; a few tied projecting over the eye
*Antennae*  Natural or olive partridge hackle fibres

## FULLING MILL FLIES

Fulling Mill Flies sells a wide range of bead-headed flies, and the following two flies are from its extensive list.

**Golden Nugget Orange Tag** · Fulling Mill Flies
*Hook*      Scorpion 31150, sizes 10–12
*Thread*    Black
*Tail*      Fluorescent floss, orange
*Body*      Peacock herl
*Hackle*    Light red or ginger
*Head*      Gold bead

**Golden Nugget Stick Fly** · Fulling Mill Flies

| | |
|---|---|
| *Hook* | Scorpion 31150, sizes 10–12 |
| *Thread* | Black |
| *Tag* | Fluorescent floss, green, red or orange |
| *Body* | Peacock herl |
| *Head* | Gold bead |

## GERROFF NYMPH

Small but often deadly, this nymph comes from the vice of John Goddard. It was originally devised as a slow-sinking shrimp pattern. According to Kenneth Robson, the fly was given its name by Brian Clarke. When he first used the fly he was plagued by a number of small fish and, while he was attempting to snatch the fly from their mouth he kept crying, 'Get off.' This became somewhat corrupted to the fly's present name.

**Gerroff Nymph** · Goddard

| | |
|---|---|
| *Hook* | Mustad 9672, sizes 14–16 |
| *Thread* | Brown |
| *Body* | Brown-olive seal fur (three parts) and fluorescent seal fur (one part), mixed and tied to take up half the shank space |
| *Back* | Clear PVC strip or latex |

## GREEN D.F. PARTRIDGE

Another of Richard Walker's flies, this is a general searching pattern that can be fished weighted or unweighted. Like the Gerroff Nymph of Goddard's, this too is an abbreviated dressing. Walker also tied a 'dressed short' Partridge & Orange.

**Green D.F. Partridge** · R. Walker

| | |
|---|---|
| *Hook* | Mustad 94840, sizes 8–10 |
| *Thread* | Black |
| *Body* | Bulky, fluorescent lime-green wool |
| *Rib* | Fine, silver wire |
| *Hackle* | Brown partridge |

## GREEN PEA NYMPH

Some years ago, on the Oxfordshire reservoir, Farmoor, this nymph proved very killing indeed. I was shown it at the height of its fame and could not believe how it could prove so attractive to trout, Arthur Cove recommends the fly in his book *My Way with Trout*. The fly was given to Cove by Arthur Smith of Oxford, a regular at Farmoor.

**Green Pea Nymph** · Smith

| | |
|---|---|
| *Hook* | Mustad 9671, sizes 10–12 |
| *Thread* | Green |
| *Tail* | None |
| *Body* | Green ostrich herl with a fluorescent red wool centre |

## GREEN PEARL

Tied by Glyn Hopper of Kent, this fancy pattern uses pearl tinsel. The green effect is rendered by tying pearl tinsel over the varnished black tying thread.

**Green Pearl** · Hopper

| | |
|---|---|
| *Hook* | Kamasan B175, sizes 12–16 |
| *Thread* | Black then olive |
| *Tail* | Golden-pheasant tippets dyed fluorescent green |
| *Body* | Black tying thread, varnished, with pearl tinsel tied over while the varnish is still wet; when complete change the tying thread to olive |
| *Rib* | Green wire |
| *Thorax* | Peacock herl |
| *Wing case* | Olive goose fibres |

## GREEN RABBITS

A natural-looking broad-spectrum pattern devised by Richard Walker, this is a good river fly for trout and grayling in small sizes. When tied on long-shanked hooks, it makes a fair representation of a damsel nymph. The longshanked version is weighted with lead.

**Green Rabbits** · R. Walker

| | |
|---|---|
| *Hook* | Mustad 94840, sizes 10–14, and 79580, sizes 8–10 |
| *Thread* | Light olive |
| *Tail* | Brown cock hackle fibres |
| *Body* | Fluorescent lime wool (one part) and wild rabbit back (two parts), chopped up, mixed well and dubbed onto the thread |
| *Rib* | Fine oval gold tinsel |
| *Hackle* | Brown partridge |

## GREEN SEDGE PUPA

Another Arthur Cove special for reservoir trout, this fly was obtained from Peter Grundell, who worked at the well-known London tackle-shop, Don's of Edmonton.

**Green Sedge Pupa** · Grundell

| | |
|---|---|
| *Hook* | Partridge Wide Gape, sizes 10–14 |
| *Thread* | Green |
| *Body* | Pale green seal fur (or substitute) |
| *Back* | Pheasant-tail fibres |
| *Thorax* | Rabbit underfur |

## GREEN SQUIRREL NYMPH

This Charles Jardine creation imitates a number of olive nymphs. He recommends that it be fished in an upstream dead drift.

**Green Squirrel** · Jardine

| | |
|---|---|
| *Hook* | Mustad 94840, sizes 12–14 |
| *Thread* | Olive |
| *Tail* | Brown feather fibres |
| *Body* | Grey-squirrel fur dyed olive or treated with picric acid |
| *Rib* | None |
| *Thorax* | As body |
| *Wing case* | Cock-pheasant tail |

## GREENWELL NYMPH

This is the nymph version of the traditional dry fly, Greenwell's Glory, named after Canon William Greenwell of Durham. The original fly was tied by James Wright of Tweedside. The nymph version is a broad-spectrum pattern to imitate a wide number of olive nymphs.

**Greenwell Nymph** · Greenwell/Wright

| | |
|---|---|
| *Hook* | Mustad 94840, sizes 12–14 |
| *Thread* | Primrose |
| *Tail* | Few fibres of light furnace cock hackle |
| *Body* | Yellow-olive silk |
| *Rib* | Gold wire |
| *Thorax* | Grey mole or similar |
| *Wing case* | Grey feather fibre |
| *Legs* | Few fibres of light furnace cock hackle tied beard fashion |

## GRENADIER NYMPH

Sometimes referred to as just the Grenadier, this nymph is an early stillwater pattern of Dr Bell, of Blagdon fame. I have seen this pattern used successfully when fish were feeding on daphnia. It

works well at dusk during a rise to caddis and has also proved its worth when red midges were emerging.

**Grenadier Nymph** · Dr Bell

| | |
|---|---|
| *Hook* | Mustad 94840, sizes 12–14 |
| *Thread* | Orange |
| *Body* | Hot orange seal fur |
| *Rib* | Fine oval gold tinsel |
| *Hackle* | Soft light furnace cock hackle, two turns |

## GREY-GOOSE NYMPH

This pattern is one of the Sawyer series of nymphs, the most popular being, of course, the Sawyer's Pheasant Tail. It was used by Sawyer when he required a pattern to represent the nymphs of mayflies such as the pale watery. Although primarily a river pattern, it works well during a hatch of pond olives on stillwater.

**Grey-goose Nymph** · Sawyer

| | |
|---|---|
| *Hook* | Mustad 94840, sizes 12–16 |
| *Thread* | None; like the Pheasant Tail, copper wire is used as the tying medium and also provides the weight |
| *Tail* | Grey goose fibres |
| *Body* | Grey goose |
| *Thorax* | As body |

Grey-goose Nymph

## HOPPER'S COPPER

Another Glyn Hopper fancy nymph, this is similar to the Green Pearl given earlier.

**Hopper's Copper** · Hopper

| | |
|---|---|
| *Hook* | Kamasan B200, sizes 12–16 |
| *Thread* | Brown |
| *Tail* | Fluorescent orange golden-pheasant tippet |
| *Body* | Copper Lurex tinsel |
| *Rib* | Copper wire |
| *Thorax* | Peacock herl |
| *Wing case* | Orange cock-pheasant tail |

## INTERNATIONAL SHRIMP

I tied up this shrimp pattern on a video produced by Gary Brooker and Pete Cockwill. I called it International because of the materials used in its make up. The antennae came from Spanish *coq de léon* feathers, the body fur from the tail of a Slovenian edible dormouse, the nylon was of German origin, and the back was from a sheet material called Spectraflash, from Traun River Products. I think the lead underbody was possibly of British manufacture. The use of Spectraflash as a shell back was pioneered by Roman Moser, an Austrian, making the fly truly international. The strange thing is that, since the production of the video, many other shrimp patterns have been created using reflective back materials but, although many have been similar to my International Shrimp, nobody has used quite the same ingredients.

**International Shrimp** · Price
| | |
|---|---|
| *Hook* | Mustad 80200BR, sizes 8–12 |
| *Antennae* | Bunch of mottled grizzle hackle fibres |
| *Eyes* | Bead chain or burnt monofilament |
| *Body* | Grey dormouse tail fur over lead wire |
| *Back* | Spectraflash (a reflective pearl sheet material) |
| *Rib* | Clear monofilament nylon |

## IVENS' NYMPHS

The late Tom Ivens was a pioneer of post-war reservoir fishing, along with the likes of Richard Walker and Cyril Inwood. He transformed fly-fishing into the sport for all that we enjoy today. In his book *Stillwater Trout Fishing* he outlined his methods and gave a number of subsurface flies which are still fished today. Perhaps his best-known fly is the small lure, the Jersey Herd.

**Ivens' Brown & Green Nymph** · Ivens
| | |
|---|---|
| *Hook* | Mustad 9672, sizes 6–10 |
| *Thread* | Brown |
| *Tail* | Four strands of peacock herl tips |

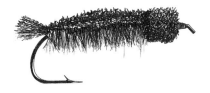

Ivens' Brown & Green Nymph

| | |
|---|---|
| *Body* | Green and brown ostrich twisted together |
| *Back* | Rest of peacock herl that was used for tail |
| *Head* | Four strands of peacock wound into a ball-type head |

**Ivens' Brown Nymph** · Ivens
| | |
|---|---|
| *Hook* | Mustad 94840, sizes 8–12 |
| *Thread* | Brown |
| *Body* | Brown ostrich |
| *Rib* | Oval gold tinsel |
| *Back* | Green ostrich herl |
| *Head* | Peacock herl two strands, with the ends as stubby antennae |

**Ivens' Green Nymph** · Ivens
| | |
|---|---|
| *Hook* | Mustad 94840, sizes 8–12 |
| *Thread* | Green |
| *Body* | Pale green nylon over white floss |
| *Hackle* | Sparse brown partridge |
| *Head* | Peacock herl |

**Ivens' Green & Yellow Nymph** · Ivens
| | |
|---|---|
| *Hook* | Mustad 94840, sizes 10–14 |
| *Thread* | Green |
| *Body* | Green swan or goose herl (rear half) and yellow swan or goose herl (front half) |
| *Head* | Peacock herl |

## KILLER BUG

Apart from his Pheasant Tail, this simple bug is perhaps Frank Sawyer's most famous fly and it is considered to be one of the most killing flies for grayling on the southern chalkstreams. The only problem these days in getting the right shade of wool for the body. The original wool, Chadwick's 477 darning wool, was a subtle blend of grey, fawn and pink, giving an overall beige shade. The fly itself can represent a freshwater shrimp or even a small pupa of sorts.

**Killer Bug** · Sawyer
| | |
|---|---|
| *Hook* | Mustad 94840, sizes 10–16 |
| *Thread* | None (copper wire is used) |
| *Body* | Beige-fawn wool over copper wire |

## LARGE RED MITE

Most water mites are tiny almost insignificant creatures which dance about in the water close to the weed-beds. They are found in a variety of colours but the most prolific species appear to be red. Their very size makes them difficult to imitate, most being less than ¹⁄₁₆in (1mm) long. Do the trout take them? I have often found them in the stomach contents of caught fish, but whether the trout take them by design or by accident I cannot say. Richard Walker gave a pattern for the largest of them, so I will give the dressing. A number of years ago I attempted to get over the size problem by tying a number of mites on a single hook but, to be absolutely honest with you, I cannot say that it was very successful.

**Large Red Mite** · R. Walker
*Hook*     Mustad 9672, sizes 16–18
*Thread*   Red (Walker suggests vermilion)
*Body*     Ball of red feather fibre
*Hackle*   Short red hen feather

## LEAD BUG

I have watched Pete Cockwill, using this very fly, stalk and land more double-figure rainbows than I care to remember. He usually spots the fish and lands them before I have had time to put a fly on my leader. This ugly little pattern is all weight and no finesse, exactly what you need to get down to the fish quickly. Yellow is used so that you can see the fly in the water at a reasonable depth and follow its progress as you retrieve; then, with any luck, you will see it vanishing into the white maw of some gigantic rainbow. Bill Sibbons also ties similar brown and olive versions of this fly.

**Lead Bug** · Cockwill
*Hook*     Mustad 94840, sizes 8–12
*Thread*   Yellow
*Tail*     Yellow fluorescent floss
*Body*     Varnished lead wire
*Thorax*   Fluorescent yellow chenille
*Hackle*   Short tuft of fluorescent yellow floss

Lead Bug (Cockwill)

## MONTANA NYMPH

I have included this American pattern here because I believe that the fly is probably used more in the UK than in the USA. The creature started life as the Montana Stone, a pattern to imitate the nymph of some of the larger stoneflies found on the Blue Ribbon streams of the western USA. In the UK the pattern is fished exclusively on stillwaters, in habitats that have never seen stoneflies. Since its introduction to the British scene there have been a number of variations, all potential fish-takers on their day.

**Montana Nymph**
*Hook*       Mustad 79580, sizes 6–12
*Thread*     Black
*Tail*       Black cock hackle tips (black marabou is also now used)
*Body*       Black chenille
*Thorax*     Yellow chenille
*Wing case*  As body
*Hackle*     Palmered black cock wound through the thorax

**Montana Nymph (Cream)**
As Montana Nymph except:
*Tail*     Brown cock hackle fibre
*Thorax*   Fluorescent cream yarn
*Hackle*   As tail

**Montana Nymph (Green)**
As Montana Nymph except:
*Thorax*   Fluorescent green chenille

**Montana Nymph (Orange)**
As Montana Nymph except:
*Thorax*   Fluorescent orange chenille

**Montana Nymph (Red)**
As Montana Nymph except:
*Thorax*   Fluorescent red chenille

**Montana Nymph Cat's Whisker**
*Hook*       Mustad 9672, sizes 8–10
*Thread*     Red
*Tail*       Green fluorescent marabou
*Body*       White chenille
*Thorax*     Fluorescent green chenille
*Wing case*  Black chenille
*Hackle*     Black

**Montana Bead Eye**
As Montana Nymph except:
*Tail*   Black marabou
*Rib*    Silver (optional)

*Wing case*   None
*Hackle*   None
*Eyes*   Silver beads

I would consider this version to be almost certainly a lure and not a nymph, but include it nevertheless.

## Montana Wasp Nymph
As Montana Nymph except:
*Tail*   Fluorescent yellow or orange
*Body*   Banded yellow and black chenille

## MURK-MEISTER

It is hard to decide whether this is a lure or a searcher nymph but as I have already given dressings of much larger patterns and called them nymphs I will include this pattern because the fly is used to search out fish and is also fished in a nymph-like manner. The fly is reputed to be a good pattern in cloudy water conditions (hence its name) and also during algal blooms. The pattern was conceived by Richard Aylott.

**Murk-meister** · Aylott
*Hook*   Mustad 79580, sizes 6–10
*Thread*   Orange
*Tail*   White fluorescent wool
*Body*   Chrome fluorescent wool over lead wire, divided into two and separated by a hackle
*Hackles*   Ginger cock hackles, one at the head and one in the middle

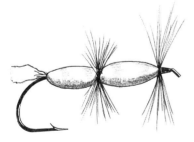

Murk-meister

## OLIVE SUN NYMPH

This Richard Aylott pattern is for fishing on calm days. The fly should be retrieved just under the surface.

**Olive Sun Nymph** · Aylott
*Hook*   Mustad 94840, sizes 12–14
*Thread*   Pale green
*Tail*   Golden-pheasant topping
*Body*   Thin body of greenish-yellow fluorescent floss
*Rib*   Fine gold thread
*Head*   Peacock herl

## OMBUDSMAN

Brian Clarke devised this fly to be all things to all fish, a broad-spectrum pattern to search out the lake bottom. It can act as a damsel or dragonfly nymph, an alder larva or even an aquatic beetle larva.

**Ombudsman** · Clarke
*Hook*   Mustad 79580, sizes 8–12
*Thread*   Black
*Tail*   None
*Body*   Peacock herl over lead or copper wire
*Wing*   Roof of any mottled feather
*Hackle*   Soft brown hen
*Head*   Elongated head of tying thread

## ORANGE EMERGER

This is another of my wife's favourite patterns when the red or orange midges are abroad. She catches many good-quality rainbows on the small fishery at Penshurst Place, formerly managed by John Veniard. The syndicate fishery was created from the medieval fishponds used by the manor house, a perfect setting in the heart of Kent. Penshurst Place was the home of Sir Philip Sidney, the Elizabethan courtier, poet and soldier, who died at the battle of Zutphen in Holland.

**Orange Emerger** · M. Price
*Hook*   Mustad 80100BR, sizes 12–16
*Thread*   Orange
*Body*   Fluorescent orange marabou, dubbed

Orange Emerger

| | |
|---|---|
| *Rib* | Gold or silver wire |
| *Thorax* | Peacock herl with CDC plume tied over |
| *Breathing appendages* | Ends of CDC feather projecting over the eye |

## ORANGE SEAL'S FUR NYMPH

Another of Arthur Cove's classics, this is a good pattern to use during the time of the caddis. Arthur recommends fishing this pattern in the evening with a slow recovery but occasional tweaks.

**Orange Seal's fur Nymph** · Cove

| | |
|---|---|
| *Hook* | Mustad 9672, sizes 10–12 |
| *Thread* | Orange |
| *Body* | Hot orange seal fur |
| *Rib* | Flat, silver tinsel |
| *Thorax* | As body |
| *Wing case* | Cock-pheasant tail fibres |

## PERSUADER

A John Goddard fancy sedge pupa pattern, this works well in the evening even though it is of a colour that hardly matches any caddis pupa I have seen. I have had a lot of fish on this fly.

**Persuader** · Goddard

| | |
|---|---|
| *Hook* | Mustad 9672, sizes 8–10 |
| *Thread* | Orange |
| *Body* | White ostrich herl |
| *Thorax* | Orange seal fur |
| *Wing case* | Cock-pheasant tail fibres |

Persuader

## PINK NYMPH

This Tom Saville special is recommended for the month of May, especially during the chironomid hatches. I am not sure why the colour pink sometimes works but work it does.

**Pink Nymph** · Saville

| | |
|---|---|
| *Hook* | Partridge L2A, sizes 12–14 |
| *Thread* | Black |
| *Tail* | Fluorescent pink Glo-Brite |
| *Body* | As tail |
| *Rib* | Gold wire |
| *Thorax* | Peacock herl |
| *Hackle* | Blue dun hen |

## POACHER NYMPH

A nymph version of the Scottish hackled wet fly, this is a good attractor pattern.

**Poacher Nymph**

| | |
|---|---|
| *Hook* | Mustad 9672, sizes 10–14 |
| *Thread* | Black |
| *Tail* | Red golden-pheasant body feather |
| *Body* | Orange fluorescent silk (rear third), bronze peacock herl (remaining two thirds) |
| *Rib* | Oval gold tinsel |
| *Hackle* | Dark furnace tied small and sparse |

## POND OLIVE NYMPH

This pattern is additional to those given in Chapter 5. It was devised by Brian Harris, an expert on bank-fishing stillwaters. Brian was once editor of *Angling* and, later, of *International Fly Fisher*.

**Pond Olive Nymph** · Harris

| | |
|---|---|
| *Hook* | Partridge Limerick, sizes 12–14 |
| *Thread* | Olive |
| *Tail* | Tips of dark olive goose fibres; the rest is used as body |
| *Body* | Dark olive goose herl |
| *Rib* | Fine, gold wire |
| *Thorax* | Olive rabbit |
| *Wing case* | Dark feather fibre |

## S.S. NYMPH

The final nymph in the Sawyer's series, the S.S., standing for Sawyer's Swedish, is supposed to imitate one of the summer dun nymphs. It is tied up in the same way as the standard Sawyer patterns.

**S.S. Nymph**

| | |
|---|---|
| *Hook* | Mustad 94840, sizes 12–14 |
| *Thread* | None (copper wire) |
| *Tail* | Dark grey goose |
| *Body* | As tail |
| *Thorax* | As tail |

## SHARPE'S FAVOURITE

A pattern that is still fished from time to time, this dates back to the 1960s. Apparently it was used frequently by the pioneers of reservoir fishing at that time, namely the late Cyril Inwood and the late Jim Sharpe. I believe it was Bob Carnill who gave the fly its present name. The pattern imitates a hatching sedge but, in its garish colour combination, it represents no living sedge that I have seen. So perhaps we should call it a fancy sedge attractor.

**Sharpe's Favourite** · Sharpe/Carnill

| | |
|---|---|
| *Hook* | Mustad 9578A, sizes 10–18, or a sedge-type hook |
| *Thread* | Olive |
| *Body* | Brick-red seal fur (or substitute) |
| *Rib* | Gold wire (or oval gold on larger sizes) |
| *Thorax* | Insect-green seal fur (or substitute) |
| *Wing case* | Grey mallard feather |
| *Legs* | Hot orange hackle fibres |

## STICK FLIES

I have already mentioned this type of fly in Chapter 7 but this kind of pattern also works well in smaller sizes during a hatch of midge. The following pattern, from Brian Harris, works well in such circumstances and is often unweighted.

**Stick Fly** · Harris

| | |
|---|---|
| *Hook* | Mustad 9672, sizes 10–12 |
| *Thread* | Brown or buff |
| *Body* | Light brown turkey (original called for condor herl) |
| *Rib* | Oval gold tinsel |
| *Thorax* | Amber dubbing |
| *Hackle* | Short-fibred medium red cock, two turns |

Stick Fly (Harris)

Brian Harris also has another version with a mobile marabou tail. Some stick flies are given a tail and have no thorax colour. One such pattern, by Chris Ogbourn, is usually tied on smaller hooks so that they fall into the size limits imposed for international competitions. When tied on such hooks I would consider them to be almost hackled wet flies, not nymphs, but as others would disagree I include one here.

**Stick Fly** · Ogbourn

| | |
|---|---|
| *Hook* | Wide Gape, sizes 10–16 |
| *Thread* | Brown |
| *Tail* | Fluorescent green wool or silk; this can also be tied as a tag if so desired |
| *Body* | Cock-pheasant tail fibres |
| *Rib* | Gold wire |
| *Hackle* | Brown cock hackle |

Short Green Stick Fly

## TIGER NYMPH

One of Bob Church's favourite patterns, this is used mainly during the summer months and works when more conventional buzzer-type flies have failed.

**Tiger Nymph** · Church

| | |
|---|---|
| *Hook* | Mustad 9672, sizes 10–14 |
| *Thread* | Black |
| *Tail* | Few white cock hackle fibres |
| *Body* | Bronze peacock herl fibres |
| *Thorax* | Bronze peacock herl tied fatter than the body |
| *Wing case* | Grey feather fibre |
| *Hackle* | Brown partridge |

## TUP'S NYMPH

This nymph version of the famous R.S. Austin dry or wet fly is effective when pale wateries are hatching.

**Tup's Nymph**

| | |
|---|---|
| *Hook* | Mustad 94840, sizes 12–16 |
| *Thread* | Primrose |
| *Tail* | Blue dun hackle fibres (some tiers use honey) |

| | |
|---|---|
| *Body* | Yellow silk |
| *Rib* | Gold wire |
| *Thorax* | Yellow, cream and red seal fur (or substitute) mixed to give pinkish colour |
| *Wing case* | Grey feather fibre |
| *Hackle* | Short-fibred, grey or honey hen |

### TWINKLE NYMPHS

This series of attractor nymphs was created by that fine tier, Sid Knight, of Bridgenorth, in the county of Shropshire. These nymphs of Sid's have been responsible for the capture of record-breaking rainbow and brown trout. Twinkle is a polyester yarn combined with metallic tinsels, which gives a fly-tying product with plenty of flash and glitter.

**Twinkle Damsel** · Knight

| | |
|---|---|
| *Hook* | Mustad 79580, sizes 8–10 |
| *Thread* | To match body colour |
| *Tail* | Marabou to match body colour with two strands of pearl Twinkle or Flashabou-type material incorporated in the tail |
| *Body* | Seal fur substitute (black, brown, light olive, golden olive) |
| *Rib* | Ultra Lace or Larva Lace |
| *Thorax* | As body, over lead wire |
| *Wing case* | Cock-pheasant tail fibres |
| *Legs* | Dyed mallard breast feather (to match body colour) |
| *Head* | Dubbed fur as body |
| *Eyes* | Plastic bead eyes |

**Twinkle Damsel Mark 2** · Knight

| | |
|---|---|
| *Hook* | Mustad 79580, size 8 |
| *Thread* | Olive |
| *Tail* | Cock-pheasant tail fibres |
| *Body* | Seal fur substitute (olive with other colours mixed in to give a natural effect) |
| *Back* | Two strands of Twinkle |
| *Rib* | Fine gold wire |
| *Thorax* | As body |
| *Wing case* | Cock-pheasant tail fibres |
| *Legs* | Brown partridge hackle |

Sid ties very similar patterns using Twinkle yarn as the body. Fulling Mill Flies also produce a series of flies using woven Twinkle yarn bodies.

### WESTWARD BUG

This nymph became popular a few years ago on such waters as Avington in Hampshire. Like most flies used on that water, the fly is heavily weighted. The fly was created by Bob Church.

**Westward Bug** · Church

| | |
|---|---|
| *Hook* | Mustad 79580, sizes 8–10 (or normal-shanked hooks) |
| *Thread* | Brown |
| *Body* | Dubbed brown marabou herl |
| *Rib* | Orange floss |
| *Back* | Cock-pheasant tail fibres |
| *Hackle* | Sparse honey hen hackle fibres at the throat |

Westward Bug

### WINTERSHALL NYMPH

This pattern is a black version of the Arthofer Nymph (see p. 213). I christened this nymph after the fishery at Wintershall in Surrey, a syndicate water managed by Pete Cockwill. We first used it on this water and it took a number of 4lb (1.8kg) browns. I have to admit that it has not worked as well since, but I live in hope.

**Wintershall Nymph**

| | |
|---|---|
| *Hook* | Mustad 9672, sizes 8–12 |
| *Thread* | Black |
| *Tail* | Three strands of black ostrich herl |
| *Body* | Black ostrich herl |
| *Thorax* | Bronze Fingerling over lead wire (original uses copper wire only for the thorax) |
| *Wing case* | Cock-pheasant tail fibres |
| *Hackle* | Beard of guinea-fowl or partridge |

### WONDERBUGS

This series of heavy, large searcher nymphs was devised by Alan Pearson for clearwater fishing. There are a number of colour versions – black, brown, cream and orange – and all are heavily weighted. I shall give the brown version here.

**Wonderbug** · Pearson

| | |
|---|---|
| *Hook* | Mustad 79850, sizes 6–10 |
| *Thread* | Brown or black |
| *Tail* | Brown hackle fibres or teased-out body dubbing |
| *Body* | Brown floss or yarn (rear third), yellow wool or yarn (remaining two thirds) |
| *Thorax* | Lighter yellow wool |
| *Wing case* | Cock-pheasant tail |
| *Hackle* | Reddish-brown hen tied sloping back between the body and the thorax |

Substitute other colours for the brown to create the other variations.

## WOVEN CORIXA

This final pattern is an attractive creation by Davy Wotton. In this fly he has woven brown yarn and oval silver tinsel to create the brown back and the silver breast of a diving *Corixa*.

**Woven Corixa** · Wotton

| | |
|---|---|
| *Hook* | Partridge SH1 or similar, sizes 10–12 |
| *Thread* | Brown or red |
| *Body* | Woven from brown thread and oval silver tinsel |
| *Paddles* | Grey duck slips |

# CHAPTER NINETEEN

# ADDITIONAL NORTH AMERICAN NYMPHS

In this chapter I shall give patterns that I have used both in the UK and in the USA, as well as patterns that have crossed the Atlantic and found themselves in the British angler's fly-box. I have also included some flies that are of historical value and flies that have appealed to me personally for some reason. A more comprehensive coverage of American nymphs can be found in books such as *Fly Tyer's Nymph Manual*, by Randolph Kaufmann, and *Flies for Trout*, by Dick Stewart and Farrow Allen.

In providing this list I have tried to give as diverse selection as possible in order to show the great breadth and scope of American nymph patterns. I have bought most of these flies at one time or another during my visits to the USA. I am a compulsive buyer of flies and cannot resist going into fly-shops. I always end up buying patterns to bring home to try on our waters in Britain and Europe. Although some of the patterns are for steelhead or bass, I have found that many of them work well for browns and rainbows on British waters. Many of the flies which I have selected are broad-spectrum flies, although there are one or two tied with specific insects in mind.

## ALL-PURPOSE NYMPHS

This is a group of nymphs from the Orvis range of flies. They are broad-spectrum flies in a variety of colours to imitate a wide selection of natural insects.

### All-purpose Nymph (Dark) · Orvis
*Hook*  Mustad 9671, sizes 8–18
*Thread*  Black
*Tail*  Cock-pheasant tail fibres
*Body*  Dark brown beaver dubbing
*Rib*  Gold wire
*Thorax*  As body
*Wing case*  Turkey tail segment
*Legs*  Black hen either side of the thorax

### All-purpose Nymph (Light) · Orvis
*Hook*  Mustad 9671 sizes 8–16
*Thread*  Brown
*Tail*  Wood-duck flank fibres
*Body*  Cream fur dubbing (or synthetic)
*Rib*  Brown silk
*Thorax*  As body
*Wing case*  Cock-pheasant tail fibres
*Legs*  Light ginger or honey hen, tied either side of the thorax

### All-purpose Nymph (Medium) · Orvis
*Hook*  Mustad 9671, sizes 8–18
*Thread*  Brown
*Tail*  Cock-pheasant tail fibres
*Body*  Greyish-brown fur dubbing
*Rib*  Gold wire
*Thorax*  As body
*Wing case*  Turkey tail segment
*Legs*  Brown hen either side of the thorax

## ATHERTON NYMPHS

This nymph series is similar in intent to the All-Purpose Nymphs, in as much as they can represent a number of different mayfly nymphs. The unusual thing about them is the bright blue wing cases. The flies were created by John Atherton.

### Atherton Nymph (Dark) · Atherton
*Hook*  Mustad 9671, sizes 10–14
*Thread*  Black
*Tail*  Brown partridge hackle fibres
*Body*  Claret dubbing mixed with grey muskrat
*Rib*  Fine oval gold tinsel
*Thorax*  As body
*Wing case*  Kingfisher or blue goose feather
*Legs*  Dark furnace-cock hackle

### Atherton Nymph (Light) · Atherton

| | |
|---|---|
| *Hook* | Mustad 9671, sizes 10–14 |
| *Thread* | Yellow |
| *Tail* | Wood-duck fibres |
| *Body* | Cream dubbing |
| *Rib* | Fine oval gold tinsel |
| *Thorax* | As body |
| *Wing case* | Two tiny jungle-cock feathers tied flat on top |
| *Legs* | Grey-partridge fibres |

### Atherton Nymph (Medium) · Atherton

| | |
|---|---|
| *Hook* | Mustad 9671, sizes 10–14 |
| *Thread* | Black |
| *Tail* | Dark furnace cock hackle fibres |
| *Body* | Hare's ear |
| *Rib* | Fine oval gold tinsel |
| *Thorax* | As body |
| *Wing case* | Kingfisher or blue goose feather |
| *Legs* | Brown partridge |

## BEAVER NYMPH

A long-time traditional favourite of many fly fishermen, this simple nymph still catches its fair share of fish.

### Beaver Nymph

| | |
|---|---|
| *Hook* | Mustad 9671, sizes 10–16 |
| *Thread* | Brown |
| *Tail* | Grey-partridge fibres or wood-duck flank |
| *Body* | Beaver fur dubbing |
| *Rib* | Gold or silver wire |
| *Thorax* | As body (tied fatter) |
| *Wing case* | None |
| *Legs* | Beard hackle of grey or brown partridge |

Beaver Nymph

## BIG HOLE DEMON

A fancy searcher nymph named after the Big Hole River in Montana, this is a Dan Bailey pattern.

### Big Hole Demon · Bailey

| | |
|---|---|
| *Hook* | Mustad 9671, sizes 2–10 |
| *Thread* | Black |
| *Tail* | Badger hackle fibres |
| *Body* | Flat silver tinsel |
| *Thorax* | Black chenille |
| *Hackle* | Badger, palmered through the thorax |

## BITCH CREEK

A fantasy stonefly-type nymph complete with mobile rubber appendages, this is named after the small river, Bitch Creek, that runs into the Teton River. I suppose it would be classed as a searcher nymph.

### Bitch Creek Nymph

| | |
|---|---|
| *Hook* | Mustad 79580, sizes 4–10, sometimes bent |
| *Thread* | Black |
| *Tail* | Two white rubber hackles |
| *Body* | Woven black and orange chenille over lead wire |
| *Thorax* | Black chenille |
| *Legs* | Natural red cock hackle palmered through the thorax |
| *Antennae* | Two white rubber hackles |

Bitch Creek Nymph

## BLACK MARTINEZ

A standard long-time favourite, going back to the 1930s, this was a popular pattern on the rivers of Montana but found favour throughout the USA. It was created by Don Martinez of California.

### Black Martinez · Martinez

| | |
|---|---|
| *Hook* | Mustad 9671 |
| *Thread* | Black |
| *Tail* | Guinea-fowl fibres |

| | |
|---|---|
| *Body* | Black seal fur dubbing (or rabbit) |
| *Rib* | Silver, copper or gold wire |
| *Thorax* | As body (some dressings call for black chenille) |
| *Wing case* | Green Raffene (Swiss Straw) |
| *Legs* | Long-fibred grey partridge |

## BLONDE BURLAP

One of Polly Rosborough's classic nymphs, this is simple yet effective. (See also Burlap Nymph.) Burlap is the American equivalent of jute or hemp sacking material.

**Blonde Burlap** · Rosborough
| | |
|---|---|
| *Hook* | Mustad 9672, sizes 4–10 |
| *Thread* | Tan |
| *Tail* | Honey hen hackle fibres |
| *Body* | Light tan burlap |
| *Legs* | Honey hen hackle |

## BUCKSKIN CADDIS

This caddis pattern from the Umpqua Feather Merchants' list is included in this compilation for the simple reason that it is almost identical to the fly mentioned by Colonel Robert Venables way back in the seventeenth century. If nothing else it proves that little is ever new in fly tying; the wheel is often reinvented.

**Buckskin Caddis** · Umpqua Feather Merchants
| | |
|---|---|
| *Hook* | Mustad 80050BR, sizes 10–14 |
| *Thread* | Black |
| *Body* | Tan deer hide |
| *Head* | Peacock herl |

## BURKE NYMPH

A traditional dark-coloured nymph created by Ed Burke.

**Burke Nymph** · Burke
| | |
|---|---|
| *Hook* | Mustad 3906B, size 8–12 |
| *Thread* | Black |
| *Tag* | Flat, gold tinsel |
| *Tail* | Black cock hackle fibres |
| *Body* | Dubbed black rabbit fur |
| *Rib* | Fine flat gold tinsel |
| *Thorax* | As body |
| *Wing case* | Hen-pheasant wing slip |
| *Legs* | Black hen hackle fibres |

Burke Nymph

## BURLAP NYMPH

A fly that has been around since the early 1970s, in larger sizes this has proved to be a good pattern for steelhead and, in smaller sizes, an excellent pattern for Arctic grayling.

**Burlap Nymph**
| | |
|---|---|
| *Hook* | Mustad 3906, sizes 6–14 |
| *Thread* | Brown |
| *Tail* | None (some variations give a tail) |
| *Body* | Natural burlap |
| *Rib* | Black thread (optional) |
| *Hackle* | Soft brown hackle |
| *Head* | Peacock herl (optional) |

Burlap Nymph

## BURLAP CADDIS

A more modern variation of the Burlap Nymph, this is a popular steelhead fly in Northern California.

**Burlap Caddis**
| | |
|---|---|
| *Hook* | Mustad 36890, sizes 4–8 |
| *Thread* | Black or brown |
| *Body* | Natural burlap |

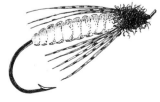

Burlap Caddis

| | |
|---|---|
| *Rib* | Gold wire |
| *Hackle* | Cock-pheasant rump |
| *Head* | Dubbed black marabou |

## CARROT NYMPH

An old pattern first tied by Rube Cross, I include this as a comparison with the Skues' pattern given in Chapter 18.

**Carrot Nymph** · Cross
| | |
|---|---|
| *Hook* | Mustad 9671, sizes 12–18 |
| *Thread* | Orange |
| *Tail* | Black hackle fibres |
| *Body* | Orange rabbit dubbing |
| *Thorax* | Black rabbit dubbing |
| *Legs* | Black hen hackle |

## CASUAL DRESS

This is perhaps the best known of Polly Rosborough's patterns. A couple of years ago I asked him why the name 'Casual Dress'? He said that, after tying the flies, he happened to glance at a newspaper and the main item was the wedding of Bing Crosby. Now, Polly thought, there's a guy who dresses kind of casual. And that is how the fly obtained its name. I have taken good fish on this pattern whenever I have fished with it. It is generally accepted that it represents a caddis pupa. I have found it is best fished in a dead drift.

**Casual Dress** · Rosborough
| | |
|---|---|
| *Hook* | Mustad 9672, sizes 4–12 |
| *Thread* | Black |
| *Tail* | Muskrat fur |
| *Body* | Dubbed muskrat wound with a segmented effect |
| *Collar* | Muskrat fur teased out to provide the collar |
| *Head* | Black ostrich herl |

Casual Dress

## COOPER BUG

This type of nymph has proved very successful on stillwaters, Henry's Lake, at the source of the famous Henry's Fork, is one such water where this pattern has been used. (See Henry's Lake Nymph, p. 205.) Without weight the pattern can be fished as a dry fly. A close variation is called the Devil Bug; this has a red body.

**Cooper Bug** · Cooper
| | |
|---|---|
| *Hook* | Mustad 3906B, sizes 12–16 |
| *Thread* | Black |
| *Tail &* *back* | Deer hair |
| *Body* | Black chenille over lead wire |
| *Head* | Butt ends of the deer hair back |

Cooper Bug

## DETTE'S ISONYCHIA

This fly imitates a common mayfly of eastern America, *Isonychia bicolor*. The pattern is one of the flies from the famous fly-tying family headed by the late Walt Dette, a name synonymous with all that is best in American fly-tying.

**Dette's Isonychia Nymph** · Dette
| | |
|---|---|
| *Hook* | Mustad 9762, sizes 10–12 |
| *Thread* | White |
| *Tail* | Cock-pheasant tail fibres |
| *Body* | Grey ostrich herl over a mixture of muskrat fur and red wool; lead wire underneath |
| *Thorax* | Grey muskrat fur |
| *Wing case* | Grey duck quill |
| *Legs* | Brown partridge |
| *Head* | Brown varnish |

There is a certain similarity between this pattern and the Austrian Arthofer Nymph (see p. 213).

## DOC SPRATELY

A pattern from the northwest, and popular in British Columbia, this fly was brought over to the UK and met with a degree of popularity in south Wales. It works well as a dragonfly larva imitation or as a large caddis pupa.

**Doc Sprately** · Prankard
*Hook*     Mustad 9672, sizes 6–10
*Thread*   Black
*Tail*     Guinea-fowl hackle fibres
*Body*     Black wool
*Rib*      Fine flat silver tinsel
*Legs*     Grizzle-hen hackle fibres
*Wing*     Bunch of cock-pheasant tail fibres across the back
*Head*     Peacock herl

Doc Sprately

## DREDGEBUG

A general dragonfly nymph pattern created by Dick Stewart, this pattern is a popular nymph for large- and small-mouth bass.

**Dredgebug** · Stewart
*Hook*     Mustad 79580, sizes 4–10
*Thread*   Brown
*Body*     Bronze peacock herl or brown wool over lead wire, tied full
*Legs*     Grouse hackle
*Wing*     Brown mallard flank tied flat over the body
*Head*     Brown chenille
*Eyes*     Dumb-bell eyes (optional)

Dredgebug

## FLEDERMOUSE

This is sometimes spelt Fledermaus (the Bat). I have had many quiet and informative discussions with Polly Rosborough at various conclaves of the Federation of Fly Fishers and I include his flies in this list out of respect for him and his work. He describes this pattern as a good, all-purpose nymph and one not to be confused with Snyder's Fledermouse, which was supposed to emulate a bat.

**Fledermouse** · Rosborough
*Hook*     Mustad 79580, sizes 8–12
*Thread*   Brown
*Body*     Mink fur (two parts), muskrat (two parts) and rabbit (one part), with guard hairs removed, blended and applied as a noodle of fur to the hook
*Collar*   Opossum (Australian)
*Wing*     Teal fibres over bronze mallard extending over the body

## FREESTONE CADDIS

It is not often that I get a chance to fish for steelhead, the last occasion being on the Kalama River on the borders of Washington and Oregon. While I was there, I noticed that many of the local fishermen were using insect-imitating patterns rather than some of the garish flies associated with this fish. The Freestone Caddis tied by Wayne Orzell at the local fly-shop, Pritchard's Western Angler, is a larger-than-life caddis larva or pupa for the Kalama steelhead. I include it here simply because I enjoyed my time on the 'river of the beautiful maiden', the Kalama.

**Freestone Caddis** · Orzell
*Hook*     Mustad 36890, sizes 8–10
*Thread*   Black
*Body*     Fluorescent pink chenille
*Hackle*   Sparse black hackle
*Head*     Black chenille

Freestone Caddis

## FULL-BACK NYMPH

This popular pattern, along with its brother, the Half-back Nymph, has crossed all borders and even oceans. It is as popular in New Zealand as it is in the USA and Canada.

### Full-back Nymph
| | |
|---|---|
| *Hook* | Mustad 9672, sizes 8–12 |
| *Thread* | Black |
| *Tail* | Cock-pheasant tail fibres |
| *Body* | Peacock herl |
| *Rib* | Black thread |
| *Thorax* | As body but tied fuller |
| *Back* | As tail |
| *Legs* | Tips of the wingcase tied back |
| *Wing case* | As tail |

Full-back Nymph

## GIRDLE BUG

A popular nymph for all freshwater game-fish, this is a searcher nymph with plenty of action from the white rubber legs.

### Girdle Bug
| | |
|---|---|
| *Hook* | Mustad 79580, sizes 4–10 |
| *Thread* | Black |
| *Tail* | Two white rubber hackles |
| *Body* | Black chenille |
| *Legs* | Three sets of white rubber hackles spread evenly along the body |
| *Antennae* | Two more white rubber hackles |

Girdle Bug

## HALF-BACK NYMPH

There are a number of different recipes for this popular fly and I shall give two here. The flies are very similar to the traditional Welsh pattern, the Diawl Bach (see p. 189).

### Half-back Nymph
| | |
|---|---|
| *Hook* | Mustad 9672, sizes 8–14 |
| *Thread* | Black |
| *Tail* | Brown hackle fibres |
| *Body* | Peacock herl |
| *Thorax* | Peacock herl, just a slight thickening of the body |
| *Wing case* | Brown mallard flank |
| *Legs* | Beard of brown hackle fibres |

Half-back Nymph

### Half-back Nymph No. 2
| | |
|---|---|
| *Hook* | Mustad 9672, sizes 2–10 |
| *Thread* | Black |
| *Tail* | Cock-pheasant tail fibres |
| *Body* | Peacock herl |
| *Wing case* | Cock-pheasant tail fibres, over the body but not the thorax |
| *Thorax* | As body |
| *Legs* | Palmered brown saddle, through the thorax area, clipped top and bottom |

Half-back Nymph No. 2

## HENRY'S LAKE NYMPH

Named after the famous lake, this pattern is similar in style to the Cooper Bug.

**Henry's Lake Nymph**

| | |
|---|---|
| *Hook* | Mustad 9672, sizes 6–14 |
| *Thread* | Grey |
| *Tail* | Grey-squirrel tail |
| *Back* | As tail |
| *Body* | Yellow chenille over lead wire |
| *Antennae* | Forward tuft of grey squirrel |

## HEXAGENIA NYMPH

There are a number of dressings tied to imitate this large, burrowing nymph. One of the best is by Oscar Feliu. I met him at the 1993 Federation of Fly Fishers' Conclave at Livingstone in Montana and watched him tie at the demonstrations.

**Hexagenia Nymph** · Feliu

| | |
|---|---|
| *Hook* | Mustad 79580 or similar, sizes 6–10 |
| *Thread* | Orange |
| *Tail* | Cock-pheasant tail fibres and a short tuft of soft hen hackle fibres |
| *Body* | Cream sparkle yarn |
| *Underbody* | Dental floss |
| *Breathing appendages* | Filoplume tied flat across the back and tapered |
| *Back* | Dark turkey tail, lacquered |
| *Thorax* | Orange sparkle yarn |
| *Legs* | Palmered brown cock hackle, trimmed on the top |
| *Wing case* | As body |
| *Head* | Orange tying thread |
| *Eyes* | Burnt monofilament |

## IDA MAY

A large, broad-spectrum pattern by Charles E. Brookes, this imitates a number of large mayfly nymphs (*Ephemerella* spp).

**Ida May** · Brookes

| | |
|---|---|
| *Hook* | Mustad 9671, sizes 8–10 |
| *Thread* | Brown |
| *Tail* | Dark green grizzle hackle fibres |

Ida May

| | |
|---|---|
| *Body* | Black wool |
| *Rib* | Two: peacock herl then gold wire wrapped in the opposite direction |
| *Hackle* | Dark green soft grizzle hackle swept backwards |

## JIM'S DAMSEL

I include this pattern in memory of a good day's fishing on the Deschutes in Oregon in the company of the fly's originator, Jim Schollmeyer. Jim is one of the best angling photographers working today and his pictures grace the pages of many publications, including Dave Hughes' excellent book on the River Deschutes.

**Jim's Damsel** · Schollmeyer

| | |
|---|---|
| *Hook* | Mustad 9672, sizes 8–12 |
| *Thread* | Olive |
| *Tail* | Short tuft of olive marabou and olive Crystal Flash |
| *Body* | Olive marabou |
| *Rib* | Olive Crystal Flash |
| *Legs* | Cock-pheasant back feather fibres |
| *Eyes* | Olive-green beads |
| *Head* | As body |

## LEAD-WING COACHMAN NYMPH

This is a nymph version of the grey-winged Coachman wet fly. Sometimes the wing case is applied in the conventional manner; on other dressings it is left as a small, stunted wing.

**Lead-wing Coachman Nymph**

| | |
|---|---|
| *Hook* | Mustad 9671, sizes 8–12 |
| *Thread* | Black |
| *Tail* | Brown hackle fibres (some dressings call for brown-speckled mallard) |
| *Body* | Peacock herl |
| *Thorax* | Slight thickening of the body |
| *Wing case* | Grey duck quill |
| *Legs* | Beard of brown hackle |

## LIEB'S BUG

This simple nymph seems to be a darker version of the popular Prince Nymph.

**Lieb's Bug** · Lieb

| | |
|---|---|
| *Hook* | Mustad 9671, sizes 8–14 |
| *Thread* | Black |

| Tail | Two brown goose biots |
| Body | Peacock herl |
| Rib | Gold wire |
| Hackle | Palmered brown cock hackle |
| Legs | Two brown goose biots pointing backwards at the sides of the fly |

## LINGREN'S OLIVE

A general nymph pattern to imitate a variety of olive nymphs.

**Lingren's Olive** · Lingren

| Hook | Mustad 9671, sizes 14–18 |
| Thread | Black |
| Tail | Black hackle fibres |
| Body | Dubbed olive marabou |
| Rib | Fine gold wire |
| Thorax | Peacock herl |
| Legs | Black hackle clipped top and bottom |

## LONG-TAILED MARCH BROWN

This is a popular pattern in most fishing states, including Alaska.

**Long-tailed March Brown**

| Hook | Mustad 3906, sizes 10–16 |
| Thread | Black |
| Tail | Wood-duck or brown mallard feather fibres |
| Body | Dubbed rabbit or hare fur |
| Rib | Yellow thread |
| Shell back | Cock-pheasant tail fibres or mottled turkey |
| Legs | Brown partridge |

## MAGGOT

There are a number of patterns tied to imitate this rather unappetizing creature. This type of fly has proved very effective on Alaskan waters where trout feed on similar maggots as they are washed out of the many salmon carcases left after spawning. If a slight revulsion is felt at the thought of this, what about those flies that are now tied to represent bits of rotting salmon flesh!

**Maggot**

| Hook | Mustad 9671, sizes 12–14 |
| Thread | Black |
| Body | Creamy-white synthetic dubbing or rabbit fur |

There is another slight variation on the same theme called the Swannundaze Maggot. The dressing is as follows.

**Maggot-Swannundaze**

| Hook | Mustad 80200BR, sizes 10–14 |
| Thread | White |
| Body | White chenille |
| Rib | White Swannundaze |
| Thorax | Dubbed white rabbit fur |

Maggot-Swannundaze

## MATT'S FUR

A broad-spectrum pattern that, by altering the dressing slightly and by using different-shaped hooks, can represent anything from a damsel nymph to a stonefly creeper. The fly was created by Matt Lavell and is found in many fly catalogues and fly-tying books.

**Matt's Fur** · Lavell

| Hook | Mustad 9672, sizes 8–12 |
| Thread | Brown |
| Tail | Wood-duck flank fibres |
| Body | Blended dubbing of otter and cream angora |
| Rib | Oval gold tinsel |
| Thorax | As body |
| Wing case | Wood-duck flank feather |
| Legs | Tips of the wing-case feather pulled down either side of the thorax |

## MESS

An emerger pattern or an imitation of a trapped mayfly nymph in the surface film, this was created by the innovative author and fly-tier Gary LaFontaine.

**Mess** · LaFontaine

| Hook | Mustad 3399A, sizes 6–12 |
| Thread | Cream |
| Tail | Brown hackle fibres divided in two |

*Body*      Brown SLF
*Back*      Jiffy or Cellaire packaging foam, marked with waterproof ink (optional)
*Legs*      Brown cock hackle with grey mallard curving over the eye
*Head*      As body

## NEAR ENOUGH

Another of the Polly Rosborough 'Fuzzy' nymphs, this is tied to represent a variety of creatures in what Polly calls the 'grey spectrum'.

**Near Enough** · Rosborough
*Hook*      Mustad 38941, sizes 8–16
*Thread*    Pale grey
*Tail*      Tan mallard
*Body*      Grey fox underfur with no guard hairs
*Thorax*    As body
*Wing case* Tan mallard
*Legs*      Tan mallard, short fibres

## NONDESCRIPT

This is yet another of the Rosborough classic flies.

**Nondescript** · Rosborough
*Hook*      Mustad 9672, sizes 8–16
*Thread*    Brown
*Tail*      Short tuft of fiery-brown marabou
*Body*      Fiery-brown fuzzy yarn
*Rib*       Bright yellow thread
*Hackle*    Brown saddle hackle palmered down the body and clipped

## PEACOCK DAMSEL NYMPH

A simple but effective imitation of a damsel, this nymph uses peacock herl for the body. Apparently this is a good pattern for some of the Alaskan lakes.

**Peacock Damsel Nymph**
*Hook*      Mustad 9671, sizes 6–10
*Thread*    Black
*Tail*      Peacock sword
*Body*      Bronze peacock herl
*Thorax*    Light olive synthetic dubbing
*Wing case* Cock-pheasant tail fibres
*Legs*      Black cock palmered through the thorax

Peacock Damsel Nymph

## PEACOCK DRAGON

A similar pattern to the last but this time tied to imitate the larger dragonfly nymph.

**Peacock Dragon**
*Hook*      Mustad 79580, sizes 6–8
*Thread*    Black
*Tail*      Cock-pheasant back feather fibres
*Body*      Peacock herl over a tapered underbody of olive wool or floss
*Thorax*    Muskrat, well picked-out
*Wing case* Cock-pheasant tail fibres
*Head*      Peacock herl
*Eyes*      Burnt nylon monofilament

## PICKET PIN

This has been a long-time favourite of mine. Some people would consider it a wet fly, or even a lure, but I find it works well as a caddis pupa imitation and also as a dragonfly larva.

**Picket Pin**
*Hook*      Mustad 9672, sizes 6–10
*Thread*    Black
*Tail*      Brown hackle fibres
*Body*      Peacock herl
*Hackle*    Palmered brown cock hackle
*Wing*      Grey-squirrel tail
*Head*      As body

Picket Pin

## PRINCE NYMPH

A popular nymph pattern that has crossed the Atlantic, this has become a firm favourite with many British anglers. It works well on the Madison River in the Yellowstone National Park, especially in the fall when the large trout are on the move.

**Prince Nymph** · Prince
| | |
|---|---|
| *Hook* | Mustad 9672, sizes 10–14 |
| *Thread* | Black |
| *Tail* | Two brown goose biots in a fork |
| *Body* | Peacock herl |
| *Rib* | Fine, flat, gold tinsel |
| *Hackle* | Brown cock hackle |
| *Wings* | Two white goose biots |

Prince Nymph

## RENEGADE NYMPH

This is a nymph version of the famous Fore-and aft dry fly.

**Renegade Nymph**
| | |
|---|---|
| *Hook* | Mustad 9671, sizes 8–14 |
| *Thread* | Brown |
| *Tag* | Fine, flat, gold tinsel |
| *Tail* | None |
| *Rear hackle* | White cock hackle |
| *Body* | Peacock herl, over lead or copper wire |
| *Front hackle* | Brown cock hackle |
| *Shell back* | Cock-pheasant tail fibres, taken over both hackles as well as the body |

## RUBBER LEGS

Another bottom-searcher nymph with plenty of wiggle and movement from the rubber legs, this is usually tied in black but other colours are sometimes used, e.g. orange, brown, yellow or orange.

**Rubber Legs**
| | |
|---|---|
| *Hook* | Mustad 79580, sizes 2–10 |
| *Thread* | Black |

| | |
|---|---|
| *Tail* | Two white rubber hackles |
| *Body* | Black chenille (may be weighted) |
| *Legs* | Three pairs of white rubber hackles evenly spaced along the body |
| *Antennae* | Two white rubber hackles (optional) |

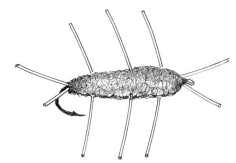

Rubber Legs

## SERENDIPITY

This simple fly comes from the vices of Blue Ribbon Flies, an excellent fly-shop at West Yellowstone. I noticed most shops in the area had examples of this fly tied up in a variety of colours. It is a pattern that can represent hatching chironomids or even hatching caddis and is popular on the Madison and its sister rivers.

**Serendipity (Red)** · Matthews
| | |
|---|---|
| *Hook* | Mustad 80200BR, sizes 8–16 |
| *Thread* | Black or red |
| *Body* | Red Z-lon wound on like floss |
| *Head* | Natural deer hair spun and clipped |

The Black, Olive and Orange versions of the Serendipity are tied in a similar fashion but the appropriately coloured Z-lon is used. These Serendipity flies are very similar to a number of British hatching-chironomid patterns.

## SKINNY MINNIE

This fly started life in British Columbia but has proved successful in northern Montana on waters such as Duck Lake. It is a broad-spectrum pattern that can imitate anything from a large ephemerid nymph to a damselfly nymph.

**Skinny Minnie**
| | |
|---|---|
| *Hook* | Mustad 79580, sizes 8–12 |
| *Thread* | Brown |
| *Tail* | Brown partridge hackle fibres |

| | |
|---|---|
| *Body* | Fine olive dubbing |
| *Back* | Cock-pheasant tail fibres |
| *Rib* | Gold wire |
| *Thorax* | As body |
| *Wing case* | As back |
| *Legs* | Beard of cock-pheasant tail fibres |
| *Head* | Peacock herl |
| *Eyes* | Burnt monofilament |

## SPARROW NYMPH

Jack Gartside specializes in the use of aftershafts and grizzle marabou in many of his flies. These feathers have a delicate mobility in the water and this fly can be tied up in a number of different colours. Jack maintains that it can be fished as a nymph or a small baitfish.

**Sparrow Nymph** · Gartside

| | |
|---|---|
| *Hook* | Mustad 9671, sizes 6–14 |
| *Thread* | Olive |
| *Tail* | Short tuft of olive grizzle marabou |
| *Body* | Squirrel, rabbit and olive Antron dubbing, mixed |
| *Hackle* | Pheasant rump tied full and sweeping back to the end of the tail |
| *Head* | Pheasant aftershave feather wound around the shank |

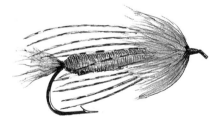

Sparrow Nymph

## SQUIRREL NYMPH

I think that the body fur from most squirrels is one of the finest dubbing materials you can use for both nymphs and dry flies. The first pattern uses grey squirrel.

**Squirrel Nymph (Grey)**

| | |
|---|---|
| *Hook* | Mustad 9672, sizes 8–16 |
| *Thread* | Grey |
| *Tail* | Grey-squirrel, guard hairs or grey-partridge |

| | |
|---|---|
| *Body* | Grey-squirrel body hair (can be weighted) |
| *Rib* | Oval silver tinsel |
| *Thorax* | As body |
| *Wing case* | Dark turkey, lacquered with vinyl cement |
| *Legs* | Guard hairs picked out |

**Squirrel Nymph (Red)** · Whitlock

| | |
|---|---|
| *Hook* | Mustad 9672, sizes 8–16 |
| *Thread* | Black |
| *Tail* | Red-squirrel fur |
| *Body* | Red-squirrel body fur |
| *Rib* | Fine oval gold tinsel |
| *Thorax* | Red-squirrel back fur and Antron, mixed |
| *Wing case* | Dark turkey feather (optional) |
| *Legs* | Grouse hackle or speckled hen |

This fly is sometimes given additional rubber legs and is then often used for large- or small-mouthed bass.

## STRIP NYMPH

This is a highly mobile pattern devised by Gary Borger.

**Strip Nymph** · Borger

| | |
|---|---|
| *Hook* | Mustad 94840, sizes 6–12 |
| *Thread* | Tan |
| *Tail* | Strip of tan rabbit fur |
| *Body* | As tail |
| *Thorax* | Tan rabbit underfur over lead wire |
| *Legs* | Rabbit guard hairs spun in a dubbing loop |
| *Wing case* | Peacock herl |

## TED'S STONEFLY

A brown version of the well-known Montana Stone, which was originally tied by Ted Trueblood.

**Ted's Stonefly** · Trueblood

| | |
|---|---|
| *Hook* | Mustad 9672, sizes 6–10 |
| *Thread* | Brown |
| *Tail* | Brown goose biots in a V-shape |
| *Body* | Brown chenille |
| *Thorax* | Orange chenille |
| *Wing case* | As body |
| *Legs* | Black saddle hackle palmered through the thorax |

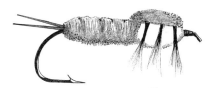

Ted's Stonefly

## TELLICO

Another of the American classic nymphs that has travelled well and has become popular with fly-fishermen in most countries. It is usually fished in the dead-drift manner and is sometimes weighted.

**Tellico**
| | |
|---|---|
| *Hook* | Mustad 3906, sizes 10–16 |
| *Thread* | Black |
| *Tail* | Guinea-fowl hackle fibres |
| *Body* | Yellow floss |
| *Rib* | Peacock herl |
| *Shell back* | Cock-pheasant tail fibres |
| *Hackle* | Sparse furnace cock |

Tellico

## TERRIBLE TROTH

As its name indicates, this is one of Al Troth's patterns, tied to imitate the nymph of the large western stonefly.

**Terrible Troth** · Troth
| | |
|---|---|
| *Hook* | Mustad 79580, sizes 2–6 |
| *Thread* | Black |
| *Tail* | Black goose biots |
| *Body* | Black and brown mixed dubbing over black or brown chenille which in turn is over lead wire; dubbing is well picked out |
| *Legs* | Six hackles stalks bent and glued, with feather barbs trimmed close to the stalk |
| *Antennae* | As tail |

## TIMBERLINE

A Randall Kaufmann nymph, this was developed for use on lakes high above the timberline. He also ties an emerger pattern called the Timberline Emerger.

**Timberline** · Kaufmann
| | |
|---|---|
| *Hook* | Mustad 3906B, sizes 12–18 |
| *Thread* | Light brown |
| *Tail* | Cock-pheasant tail fibres |
| *Body* | Beaver and hare's ear blended in equal proportions |
| *Rib* | Copper wire |
| *Thorax* | As body |
| *Wing case* | As tail |
| *Legs* | Tips of the wing case swept back |

## WHITE CADDIS

This pattern is used in Alaska for cut-throat trout. White, grub-like flies are often very attractive to all game-fish; the Maggot flies already mentioned (p. 207) and John Goddard's Persuader (p. 196) are such patterns.

**White Caddis**
| | |
|---|---|
| *Hook* | Partridge K2B Sedge Hook, sizes 8–10 |
| *Thread* | Black |
| *Body* | White floss overwrapped with clear Swannundaze or similar product |
| *Thorax* | Black ostrich |
| *Legs* | Black hackle |

White Caddis

## YUK BUG

A rubber-legged fly from the Al Troth stable, this can be either black or brown, the version given is the brown one.

**Yuk Bug** · Troth
| | |
|---|---|
| *Hook* | Mustad 79580, sizes 2–8 |
| *Thread* | Brown |
| *Tail* | Grey squirrel |
| *Body* | Brown chenille over lead wire |

*Hackle*　Grizzle palmered cock
*Legs*　White rubber hackles, four either side

Yuk Bug

A recent innovation and variation on the Yuk Bug, this comes from Wyoming.

### Yuk Bug Pepperoni
*Hook*　Mustad 79580, sizes 2–8
*Thread*　Black
*Tail*　Grey squirrel
*Body*　Black chenille (half) followed by orange chenille (half) over lead wire
*Hackle*　Brown cock palmered through the orange chenille
*Legs*　White rubber hackles, four either side

## ZUG BUG

A very popular pattern on both sides of the Atlantic, this attractor nymph accounts for many fish in the rivers of the USA and in the stillwaters of the UK. It was first tied by Cliff Zug.

**Zug Bug** · Zug
*Hook*　Mustad 3906B, sizes 8–12
*Thread*　Black
*Tail*　Peacock sword
*Body*　Peacock herl over lead or copper wire
*Legs*　Beard of brown hackle
*Wing case*　Short tuft of wood-duck flank

Zug Bug

# CHAPTER TWENTY

# NYMPHS FROM AROUND THE WORLD

In this selection of nymphs you will find patterns from all corners of the fly-fishing world, showing the diversity of styles and materials used in their make-up. I am always amazed at the ingenuity of my fellow fly-dressers. Fly-tying has become an international craft that has developed into an art form. It is true to say that styles from some countries will influence others but the flow of information these days is never one way.

In times past, most countries used British flies. This was the case even in the USA where, in the early days of fly-fishing, there was nothing else available; since then a school of tying has developed and patterns have been created that are entirely American. This has also been the experience of such places as New Zealand, South Africa and many parts of Europe.

It is a different story today as the nymphs in the following list will show only too well. By placing them alphabetically the list becomes a veritable United Nations as patterns from different countries rub shoulders with each other and lie hugger-mugger on the page.

## ALLETSON'S BROWN NYMPH

This simple brown fly was devised by Jake Alletson. We spent 14 days wandering around South Africa, fishing and watching the wildlife in Kruger National Park. The drought meant that we caught few fish but the 'crack' more than made up for it; and the wildlife, as you would expect, was magnificent.

**Alletson's Brown Nymph** · Alletson · S. Africa
| | |
|---|---|
| *Hook* | Mustad 3906, sizes 8–10 |
| *Thread* | Yellow |
| *Tail* | Small piece of brown Raffene |
| *Body* | Brown tinsel chenille (chenille with in-built tinsel rib) |
| *Thorax* | Fiery-brown seal fur (or substitute) |
| *Wing case* | Brown Raffene |

## ARTHOFER NYMPH

I based the Wintershall Nymph (see p. 198) on this searcher-type nymph created by the late Louis Arthofer. It is used both on rivers and stillwater.

**Arthofer Nymph** · Arthofer · Austria
| | |
|---|---|
| *Hook* | Mustad 9671, sizes 8–12 |
| *Thread* | Brown |
| *Tail* | Three tips of fine brown ostrich |
| *Body* | Brown ostrich herl |
| *Thorax* | Copper wire |
| *Wing case* | Hen-pheasant wing fibres |
| *Legs* | Guinea-fowl or brown partridge clipped short |

## B.G. SEDGE PUPAE

The B.G. nymphs were created by Henning von Monteton of Frankfurt. The initials come from the materials used in the construction of the flies: Burzelfeder (CDC) and Gamshaar (chamois).

**B.G. Deep Pupa** · von Monteton · Germany
| | |
|---|---|
| *Hook* | Kamasan 420, sizes 8–12 |
| *Thread* | Black |
| *Underbody* | Pearly green Glitterbody (a tinsellated yarn) or yellow Polyfloss, over copper wire |
| *Overbody* | Magic Glass (clear PVC body material) |
| *Thorax* | Rabbit dubbing |
| *Legs* | Two turns of chamois dubbing spun in a dubbing loop, the hair is then clipped on the top and sides |
| *Wing* | Two sparse bunches of CDC feathers tied in both sides of the thorax |

The B.G. Emergent Pupa is tied in the same way but with no copper wire and the chamois is left unclipped.

## BANDIT

A New Zealand pattern, this represents a caddis pupa and has a woven body. The pattern was devised by Keith Collins.

**Bandit** · Collins · NZ
| | |
|---|---|
| *Hook* | Partridge K2B, sizes 8–12 |
| *Thread* | Brown |
| *Body* | Woven with brown and olive acetate floss, brown on top, olive below |
| *Thorax* | Hare fur with guard hairs removed |
| *Wing case* | Hen-pheasant tail |
| *Legs* | Hen-mallard breast-feather fibres |

## BIGGS' SMALBLAAR NYMPH

Tony Biggs is one of the best fly-fishers in South Africa. This fly is very unusual and is used on the clearwater streams of the western Cape where the fish are easily spooked. There is another version, the Golden Heron Nymph, which Jack Blackman gives in his book, *Flies and Fly Fishing in South Africa*; this has a thin, peacock herl body and a blue-dun tail but is otherwise the same.

**Biggs' Smalblaar Nymph** · Biggs · S. Africa
| | |
|---|---|
| *Hook* | Mustad 9671, sizes 12–16 |
| *Thread* | Red |
| *Body* | Red tying silk |
| *Legs* | Palmered golden-pheasant crest |

Bigg's Smallblaar Nymph

## BLACK & SILVER NYMPH

I do not think there is a European country that has not adopted the gold or silver bead-headed flies and Holland is no exception. This pattern is one of many fishing-catching flies devised by Hans van Klinken.

**Black & Silver Nymph** · van Klinken · Holland
| | |
|---|---|
| *Hook* | Partridge CS20, sizes 10–12 |
| *Thread* | Black |
| *Tail* | Black cock-pheasant tail |
| *Body* | Black pheasant tail |
| *Thorax* | Black sparkle yarn and Spectraflash mixed, dubbed, then well picked out |
| *Head* | Silver bead |

Black & Silver Nymph

## BLACK CREEPER

Throughout the world there are many black nymphs. This Japanese version has a flattened, almost square body.

**Black Creeper** · Japan
| | |
|---|---|
| *Hook* | Mustad 3906B, sizes 8–10 |
| *Thread* | Black |
| *Tail* | Black hackle fibres |
| *Body* | Black silk over lead wire, the lead is flattened before winding on the floss |
| *Rib* | Flat gold tinsel |
| *Legs* | Short tufts of black hackle fibres at the sides only |

## BLACK SPIDER

There are many Black Spider patterns and the following minute fly was created by Lars Olson from Sweden. This fly imitates a wide range of small black creatures found in rivers, e.g. *Simulium* midge larvae or drowned adults.

**Black Spider** · Olson · Sweden
| | |
|---|---|
| *Hook* | Mustad 80100BR, sizes 18–26 |
| *Thread* | Black |
| *Body* | Small button of black dubbing |
| *Hackle* | Black (small hen, crow or similar) hackle |

Black Spider

## BREATHING NYMPH

The German fly-company Traun River Products sells a number of excellent nymph patterns. This fly has plenty of movement with the hackles projecting from the side. A broad-spectrum pattern, it imitates a wide number of large nymphs.

**Breathing Nymph**
Traun River Products · Germany

| | |
|---|---|
| *Hook* | Mustad 798509, sizes 6–10 |
| *Thread* | Black |
| *Tail* | Soft grizzle hackle fibres |
| *Body* | Brown synthetic dubbing |
| *Breathers* | Soft grizzle laid flat across the body |
| *Back* | Yellow furry foam |
| *Rib* | Fine pearl tinsel |
| *Thorax* | Brown synthetic dubbing |
| *Head* | As thorax |

## BROWN CADDIS PUPA

This is another of Lars Olson's patterns. Lars works the summer months in Gimdalen, Sweden, as a guide and instructor. For the rest of the time he does the same thing, working out of Bozeman, Montana. Lars was instrumental in setting up the first catch-and-release river in Sweden on the River Idsojöströmmen, part of the Gim River.

**Brown Caddis Pupa** · Olson · Sweden

| | |
|---|---|
| *Hook* | Partridge K2B, or similar, sizes 10–14 |
| *Thread* | Brown |
| *Body* | Hare fur or similar over dubbed black fur |
| *Rib* | Copper wire |

Brown Caddis Pupa

| | |
|---|---|
| *Thorax* | As body |
| *Legs* | Grouse hackle fibres or brown partridge |

## CDC MAGIC

Gerhard Laible was one of the many European tiers who provided patterns for my last book *The Angler's Sedge*. The CDC Magic is one of his emerger patterns. He has recently produced a book devoted to CDC flies.

**CDC Magic** · Laible · Germany

| | |
|---|---|
| *Hook* | Mustad 94840 or similar, sizes 10–14 |
| *Thread* | To match body colour |
| *Tail* | Brown cock hackle fibres |
| *Body* | Synthetic dubbing (yellow, black, etc) |
| *Wing* | Double tuft of CDC feathers; the rear tuft clipped, the front tuft unclipped |

CDC Magic

## CADDIS NYMPH

The caddis is an important item of diet in the trout of Australia. In *Fly Fishing in Australia and New Zealand*, M.E. McCausland gives some autopsy results on caught fish; the largest item of diet was the caddis (in a ratio of 525 caddis larvae to 195 ephemerid nymphs).

The following Australian pattern was given by John Veniard in *A Further Guide to Fly Dressing*. For the record, brown trout were first introduced into Australian waters in 1865, from eggs taken from fish in the River Itchen, UK.

**Caddis Nymph** · Australia

| | |
|---|---|
| *Hook* | Mustad 94840, sizes 10–14 |
| *Thread* | Black |
| *Body* | Black hackle quill protruding ¼in (6mm) beyond the bend then wrapped with green raffia (I would varnish after wrapping) |
| *Legs* | Black cock hackle, one turn |

## CAMOLE NYMPHS

In Chapter 17 I gave some examples of early emerger patterns from Italy, the Ossolina Emergers. The Camole series of flies are similar traditional patterns from northern Italy, many adorned with tiny, clear-glass beads and all originally tied on blind hooks direct to nylon or, in the old days, gut. The following are just three patterns from a large number of variants.

**Camole Red** · Italy

| | |
|---|---|
| *Hook* | Mustad 80250BR, sizes 18–20 |
| *Thread* | Black |
| *Body* | Red silk |
| *Rib* | Flat, gold tinsel |

**Camole Black** · Italy

| | |
|---|---|
| *Hook* | Mustad 80250BR, sizes 18–20 |
| *Thread* | Red |
| *Body* | Black silk |
| *Rib* | Flat gold tinsel |
| *Head* | Clear glass bead |

**Camole Brown** · Italy

| | |
|---|---|
| *Hook* | Mustad 80250, sizes 18–20 |
| *Thread* | Brown |
| *Body* | Brown silk |
| *Thorax* | Peacock herl |
| *Hackle* | Sparse ginger cock hackle |
| *Head* | Clear glass beads |

Camole Brown

## CATFISH NYMPHS

Earlier (p. 148) I gave a shrimp pattern from Slovenia using eel skin as the back. This pattern, created by Hans Nischkauer from Austria, uses the skin of the catfish in the same way. The skin must be wetted before application. The first of these fish-skin flies is a caddis and the second a shrimp.

**Caseless Catfish Caddis** · Nischkauer · Austria

| | |
|---|---|
| *Hook* | Tiemco TMC900BL, sizes 12–16 |
| *Thread* | Brown |
| *Underbody* | Two or three layers of silver tinsel |
| *Body* | Catfish skin treated with picric acid, wound up the body |
| *Back* | As body |
| *Rib* | Silver wire |
| *Thorax* | Hare's mask over lead wire |

**Catfish Shrimp** · Nischkauer · Austria

| | |
|---|---|
| *Hook* | Tiemco TMC900 BL, sizes 10–16 |
| *Thread* | Grey |
| *Underbody* | Lead wire |
| *Body* | Self-made dubbing wick of silver wire twisted with hare's ear |
| *Rib* | Silver, gold or copper wire |
| *Back* | Catfish skin treated with picric acid |
| *Head* | End of catfish back material over the eye |
| *Antennae* | Brown partridge hackle |

Catfish Shrimp

## CHESTNUT-BROWN NYMPH

A Norman Marsh pattern, this imitates the nymph of the New Zealand mayfly, *Zephlebia dentata*.

**Chestnut-brown Nymph** · Marsh · NZ

| | |
|---|---|
| *Hook* | Mustad 9671, sizes 14–16 |
| *Thread* | Black |
| *Tail* | Brown hen hackle fibres |
| *Body* | Dark brown wool |
| *Rib* | Black tying thread |
| *Thorax* | As body |
| *Wing case* | Peacock herl |
| *Legs* | Beard of brown hen hackle fibres |

## CHILEAN NYMPHS

I am indebted to Luis Antunez of Madrid for the next three patterns, which are used for the fighting rainbows and browns of Chile. Brown trout were introduced to Chile in the early 1900s and, like the rainbows, they have thrived.

**Chilean Nymph No. 1** · Antunez · Chile
| | |
|---|---|
| *Hook* | Mustad 79580, sizes 2–8 |
| *Thread* | Black |
| *Tail & back* | Dark grey feather fibre |
| *Body* | Medium grey chenille |

This fly is similar to the Richard Walker pattern, the Angora Grub (p. 182).

**Chilean Nymph No. 2** · Antunez · Chile
| | |
|---|---|
| *Hook* | Mustad 79580, sizes 2–8 |
| *Thread* | About ten strands of pearl Crystal Hair as long as the body |
| *Body* | Yellow chenille |
| *Hackle* | Palmered badger cock hackle |

This fly is a variation on the Woolly Worm theme.

**Chilean Nymph No. 3** · Antunez · Chile
| | |
|---|---|
| *Hook* | Mustad 79580, sizes 2–8 |
| *Thread* | Black |
| *Tail* | Few strands of pinkish-red Crystal Hair and a few strands of cock-pheasant tail |
| *Body* | Reddish-brown Antron or similar dubbing |
| *Side whiskers* | Three or four strands of cock-pheasant tail either side of the body |
| *Thorax* | Yellow Antron or similar dubbing |
| *Wing case* | Grey chenille |
| *Hackle* | Dark grey soft hen collar |
| *Throat* | Two or three strands of pearl Crystal Hair extending to the end of the tail |

## CLARET NYMPH

This is just one of many nymphs sent to me by Andrij Urban of Skopje in Macedonia. This pattern is designed to float in the surface film.

**Claret Nymph** · Urban · Macedonia
| | |
|---|---|
| *Hook* | Mustad 94840 or similar, sizes 10–14 |
| *Thread* | Black |
| *Tail* | Cock-pheasant tail fibres |
| *Body* | Claret dubbing (Andrij mixes his own dubbings and uses natural furs such as seal, rabbit, hare and dormouse with modern, man-made fibres to achieve an overall colour effect) |
| *Thorax* | As body |
| *Wing case* | Black foam |
| *Legs* | Thorax fur picked out |

## CLEAR-WATER BEAD MIDGE PUPA

Another von Monteton pattern from Germany, this is fished upstream and across, close to the surface. It is just one of a number of bead-head patterns tied by this excellent tier.

**Clear-water Bead Midge Pupa** · von Monteton · Germany
| | |
|---|---|
| *Hook* | Kamatsu B160, sizes 12–16 |
| *Thread* | Black |
| *Body* | Black rabbit underfur |
| *Rib* | Black Fashabou |
| *Thorax* | Black rabbit with plenty of guard hairs |
| *Head* | Pearlescent black handicraft bead |

Clear-water Bead Midge Pupa

## CLEAR-WATER NYMPH

This is one of a number of flies specially tied for O. Mustad & Son of Norway, the world's leading hook-manufacturer, to promote its 80000 range of hooks. This fly was created by Laurie Matcham of Australia.

**Clear-water Nymph** · Matcham · Australia
| | |
|---|---|
| *Hook* | Mustad 80000, sizes 10–14 |
| *Thread* | Brown or black |
| *Tail* | Black cock hackle fibres |
| *Body* | Black fur dubbing |
| *Rib* | Blue metallic thread |
| *Thorax* | As body |
| *Wing case* | Black crow feather fibre |
| *Legs* | Thorax fur picked out |

## COACHMAN NYMPH

This New Zealand pattern differs enough from the Coachman Nymph given in Chapter 18 to be included here. This version has a shell back.

**Coachman Nymph** · NZ

| | |
|---|---|
| *Hook* | Mustad 94840, sizes 10–18 |
| *Thread* | Black |
| *Body* | Bronze peacock herl tied slim |
| *Shell back* | White duck or goose |
| *Legs* | Brown hen hackle fibres |

## COPPER-RIBBED HARE'S EAR

This pattern from Sweden, devised by Lars Olson, is very similar to patterns using exactly the same materials found in New Zealand.

**Copper-ribbed Hare's Ear** · Olson · Sweden

| | |
|---|---|
| *Hook* | Mustad 80050BR, sizes 8–14 |
| *Thread* | Burnt orange |
| *Body* | Dark hare's ear, well picked out |
| *Rib* | Copper wire |

## CROCHETED NYMPH

There are many ways to tie a fly and the methods devised by Toril Kolbu of Norway are unique in the world of fly-tying. She skilfully uses a crochet needle to weave intricate bodies on her patterns. The resulting flies are perfect examples of the fly-tier's art. The following are just five of her many patterns.

**Crocheted Damsel Nymph** · Kolbu · Norway

| | |
|---|---|
| *Hook* | Mustad 80150BL, sizes 8–14 |
| *Thread* | Black |
| *Underbody* | Lead wire |
| *Tail* | Olive-dyed Arctic fox |
| *Body* | One length each of green-Highlander and medium olive Antron yarn crocheted together |
| *Rib* | Olive ostrich herl |
| *Gills* | Two small bunches of olive fox hair either side of the body |
| *Wing case* | Green-Highlander Antron yarn |
| *Head* | Olive Arctic fox dubbing |
| *Eyes* | Burnt monofilament |

**Crocheted Dragonfly Nymph** · Kolbu · Norway

| | |
|---|---|
| *Hook* | Mustad 80050BL, sizes 6–10 |
| *Thread* | Olive |
| *Underbody* | Lead wire, with a shaped body of hot glue melt |
| *Body* | Two shades of olive Antron yarn crocheted together |
| *Legs* | Six goose biots |
| *Thorax* | Olive dubbing |
| *Wing case* | Green Raffene |
| *Antennae* | Olive goose biots |
| *Head* | Olive tying thread |
| *Eyes* | Burnt monofilament |

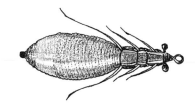

Crocheted Dragonfly Nymph

**Crocheted Corixa** · Kolbu · Norway

| | |
|---|---|
| *Hook* | Mustad 3906B, sizes 10–14 |
| *Thread* | Black |
| *Underbody* | Lead wire with shaped hot-glue melt over |
| *Body* | Light brown Antron with 10 or 12 strands of dark Antron (top) and two strands of Cream Crystal Flash (belly), all crocheted together |
| *Thorax* | Brown dubbing |
| *Paddles* | Two hen hackles stripped with the ends cut to shape |

**Crocheted Stonefly Nymph** · Kolbu · Norway

| | |
|---|---|
| *Hook* | Mustad 80050BL or 9672, sizes 6–8 |
| *Thread* | Black |
| *Underbody* | Lead wire with shaped hot-glue melt over |
| *Tail* | Two striped cock hackles |
| *Body* | One length each of brown black and ginger Antron yarn crocheted together |
| *Legs* | Six brown goose biots |
| *Thorax* | Brown fox dubbing |

| | |
|---|---|
| *Wing case* | Pre-printed fabric (Fantastic Wing) cut to shape, over golden-pheasant tail fibres |
| *Antennae* | Stripped cock hackles |

**Crocheted Water Beetle** · Kolbu · Norway

| | |
|---|---|
| *Hook* | Mustad 3906B, sizes 10–14 |
| *Thread* | Black |
| *Underbody* | Lead wire and shaped hot-glue melt |
| *Body* | Two lengths of black Antron yarn crocheted together |
| *Back stripe* | Cream Crystal Flash |
| *Legs* | Four black goose biots |
| *Thorax* | Black dubbing |
| *Antennae* | Black goose biots |

## DENDIF NYMPH

This pattern was given to me by Dik Hooimeijer of the Dutch company Paho Fly Fishers; he said that the pattern was popular in Germany.

**Dendif Nymph** · Paho Fly Fishers · Germany

| | |
|---|---|
| *Hook* | Mustad 94840, sizes 8–12 |
| *Thread* | Black |
| *Tail* | Grey mallard flank |
| *Body* | Bronze peacock herl |
| *Thorax* | White synthetic yarn |
| *Wing case* | Light brown Raffene |
| *Legs* | Mallard flank swept either side of the thorax |

Dendif Nymph

## DENNY CADDIS

This pattern is named after Lake Denny in South Island, New Zealand. It is a pupal pattern.

**Denny Caddis** · Wright · NZ

| | |
|---|---|
| *Hook* | Partridge K2B, sizes 8–12 |
| *Thread* | Black |
| *Body* | Peacock herl |
| *Thorax* | Opossum fur |
| *Wing case* | Turkey feather fibre |
| *Legs* | Guard hairs picked out |

## DORMOUSE NYMPH

The European edible dormouse figures highly in the culture of Slovenia. The creature is a pest of the fruit crops in that country and many are trapped each year. In fact, the trapping of the dormouse can be quite a social event, with fair quantities of alcohol being consumed while everyone waits for the dormice to enter the traps. Marjan Fratnik, from the village of Most na Soči on the fabulous River Soča, tied this nymph using the fur from the tail of such a dormouse. The fur is used extensively throughout the Balkans for many patterns.

**Dormouse Nymph** · Fratnik · Slovenia

| | |
|---|---|
| *Hook* | Mustad 9671, sizes 8–12 |
| *Thread* | Black or grey |
| *Tail* | Dormouse tail fibres |
| *Body* | Dubbed dormouse tail fur |
| *Rib* | Fine oval tinsel |
| *Thorax* | As body; over lead wire if weight is desired |
| *Wing case* | Brown feather fibre |

Dormouse Nymph

## DUTCH GOLD-HEAD

Another of Hans van Klinken's bead-headed flies, this is used mainly for grayling, although it is just as enticing for trout on stillwater. Holland is not very well served when it comes to game-fish so it comes as no surprise that most of Hans' flies take their fair share of coarse fish: bream, rudd, perch and roach.

**Dutch Gold-head** · van Klinken · Holland

| | |
|---|---|
| *Hook* | Partridge CS20, sizes 10–12 |
| *Thread* | Brown |
| *Tag* | Fluorescent green floss, two or three turns |
| *Body* | Rabbit fur well picked out |
| *Hackle* | Brown partridge, wound just after the tag |
| *Head* | Gold bead |

Dutch Gold-head

## EILDON SHRIMP

There are shrimp species other than *Gammarus* in some Australian waters, and this fly is a broad-spectrum nymph pattern.

**Eildon Shrimp** · Australia
| | |
|---|---|
| *Hook* | Mustad 94840, sizes 8–12 |
| *Thread* | Brown |
| *Body* | Flat gold tinsel (rear half), plump claret wool (front half) |
| *Legs* | Palmered brown cock over the gold tinsel followed by a black cock hackle tied in just before the claret body |

Eildon Shrimp

## ELEPHANT-TUSK CADDIS

This imitation by Ed Herbst is tied to represent the larva of the African caddis *Hydrosalpinx sericea*, a species that used to be common in the waters of the Cape. Ed tells me the insect is still common on the Witte River at Bains Kloof in the western Cape. The name *Hydrosalpinx* is derived from the Greek and means 'water trumpet'. The pattern is very similar to the New Zealand pattern the Horn Cased Caddis. Ed Herbst is a leading fly-tier and fisherman in Cape Town, as well as being a television journalist.

**Elephant-tusk Caddis** · Herbs · S. Africa
| | |
|---|---|
| *Hook* | Mustad 80050BR, sizes 10–14 |
| *Thread* | Spiderweb |

| | |
|---|---|
| *Underbody* | Cone shaped of copper wire |
| *Body (case)* | Black Flashabou under brown raffia |
| *Body (larva)* | Dubbed yellow mole and fluff from the base of a wood-duck flank feather with a few hare-fur guard hairs to imitate legs |

## EXOTIC NYMPH

This pattern is best described as a fancy stonefly imitation. Mladen Merkas Goranin maintains it is an excellent pattern for trout throughout the season, especially at twilight. In smaller sizes, it is a good nymph for grayling.

**Exotic Nymph** · Goranin · Croatia
| | |
|---|---|
| *Hook* | Mustad 9672, sizes 8–18, the shank bent slightly |
| *Thread* | Black |
| *Tail* | Golden-pheasant tippets |
| *Body* | Capercaillie tail feather fibre |
| *Rib* | Gold wire |
| *Thorax* | As body |
| *Wing case* | Two short jungle cock feathers |
| *Legs* | Badger hackle fibres |

Exotic Nymph

## FLAT-BODY NYMPH

Another Hare's Ear/Pheasant Tail variation, this pattern is by Hans Nischkauer of Austria.

**Flat-body Nymph** · Nischkauer · Austria
| | |
|---|---|
| *Hook* | Tiemco TMC900, sizes 14–16 |
| *Thread* | Brown |
| *Tail* | Cock- or golden-pheasant tail fibres |
| *Body* | Cock-pheasant tail over lead strips which are applied to the sides of the hook in order to give a flat, tapered underbody |
| *Thorax* | Hare's back with plenty of guard hairs |
| *Wing case* | Brown or black feather fibre |
| *Head* | Hare's fur but with next to no guard hairs |

## G.P.W. PATTERNS

The Crayfish pattern and the following two flies were created by the German tier Gerd-Peter Weiditz. The crayfish is based on Whitlock's Crayfish pattern with slight amendments.

### G.P.W. Crayfish · Weiditz · Germany

| | |
|---|---|
| *Hook* | Mustad Keel Hook, sizes 2–6 |
| *Thread* | Black |
| *Weight* | Confined to front third of hook |
| *Long antennae* | Wild boar bristle |
| *Short antennae* | Golden-pheasant tippets |
| *Claws* | Cock-pheasant breast cut to shape |
| *Eyes* | Black beads |
| *Body* | Brown chenille |
| *Thorax* | As body |
| *Legs* | Brown cock hackle |
| *Back* | Brown Raffene |
| *Rib* | Brass wire |
| *Tail* | As back, cut to shape |
| *Egg sack* | Burnt nylon monofilament |

G.P.W. Crayfish

Others colours include black to almost white (to imitate the crayfish after it has moulted).

### G.P.W. Nymph · Weiditz · Germany

| | |
|---|---|
| *Hook* | Swimming-nymph hook, size 10 |
| *Thread* | Black |
| *Tail* | Cock-pheasant tail fibres |
| *Body* | Glass beads (red, green, etc) |
| *Thorax* | Black mohair |
| *Legs* | Black grizzle cock hackle |
| *Wing case* | Green peacock sword fibres |
| *Head* | Gold bead |

This pattern looks extremely attractive, bedecked as it is with coloured glass beads and a golden head.

### G.P.W. Emerger · Weiditz · Germany

| | |
|---|---|
| *Hook* | Swimming-nymph hook, size 12 |
| *Thread* | Black |
| *Tail* | Cock-pheasant tail fibres |
| *Body* | Glass beads (red, green, clear, etc) |
| *Thorax* | Black mohair |
| *Legs* | Cock hackle |
| *Wings* | Two cock hackles tied 'wonder-wing' style |
| *Wing case* | CDC feather tied in a loop between the wings |
| *Head* | Black glass bead |

G.P.W. Emerger

## GAČKA NYMPH

The Gačka River in Croatia is one of the most prolific rivers in Europe, if not the world. A trout can put on about 2lb (1kg) in weight in a year on natural insect food. The river is deep and slow-flowing and in many ways can almost be termed a chalkstream. The large trout that live in this lush stream are both very finicky and spooky; small flies are the order of the day. There are a number of nymphs called Gačka Nymphs, of which this is one. I am indebted to Mladen Merkas Goranin for the pattern, and to my friend Borut Jerse of Ljubljana who translated the dressing from Croatian for me. The current war in the Balkans has devastated this river which is now in the Serbian enclave. The river is poached out and the fishing hotel burnt down.

### Gačka Nymph · Croatia

| | |
|---|---|
| *Hook* | Mustad 94840, sizes 12–22 |
| *Thread* | Dark cream |
| *Body* | Light yellow seal fur and yellow rabbit, mixed and tied in a cigar-shaped and weighted with copper wire beneath |
| *Rib* | Gold wire |

## GOLDEN DIVER

Hans van Klinken maintains that this type of fly was used extensively in Sweden in the early 1950s and was introduced into Holland by Theo Bakelaar. He reckons that Theo has the largest collection of bead-head flies anywhere in the world. The next two patterns are both excellent for trout and grayling.

**Golden Diver** · van Klinken · Holland

| | |
|---|---|
| *Hook* | Partridge CS20, sizes 10–12 |
| *Thread* | Grey |
| *Body* | Yellow furry foam |
| *Rib* | Copper wire |
| *Wing* | Tuft of white Antron fibres |
| *Thorax* | Grey hare and Antron mix dubbed over green fur dubbing |
| *Head* | Gold bead |

**Golden Spider** · van Klinken · Holland

| | |
|---|---|
| *Hook* | Partridge CS20, sizes 10–12 |
| *Thread* | Black |
| *Body* | Pearl Crystal Flash, wound on to form a tapered body then lacquered |
| *Hackle* | Brown partridge collar hackle |
| *Thorax* | Peacock herl |
| *Head* | Gold bead |

## GOVERNOR NYMPH

A fancy nymph pattern from New Zealand this was derived from an earlier conventional fly from the UK called the Governor. This was adapted in New Zealand to become the Red-tipped Governor, from which this nymph pattern was conceived.

**Governor Nymph** · NZ

| | |
|---|---|
| *Hook* | Mustad 94840, sizes 8–12 |
| *Thread* | Black |
| *Tail* | Brown hackle fibres |
| *Body* | Red silk (in the normal pattern this was just a tip, for the nymph it forms the abdomen) |
| *Thorax* | Peacock herl |
| *Legs* | Throat hackle of brown cock hackle fibres |

## GRASSINGTON SILVER

Another of Hans van Klinken's bead-head flies, this was named after the Grassington Club water on the River Wharfe in Yorkshire, UK.

**Grassington Silver** · van Klinken · Holland

| | |
|---|---|
| *Hook* | Partridge CS20, sizes 10–12 |
| *Thread* | Grey |
| *Tail* | Brown partridge hackle fibres |
| *Body* | Bluish-grey wool |
| *Rib* | Fine gold wire |
| *Hackle* | Sparse brown partridge collar hackle |
| *Thorax* | Grey ostrich herl |
| *Head* | Silver bead |

## GRAYLING GRUBS

The city of Ljubljana is the capital of the Republic of Slovenia. It is a beautiful city combining the old with the new. There is an excellent exhibition centre with an annual fishing fair. About 50yd (45m) from this centre there are a number of small kiosks, one of which houses a fishing-tackle shop, Riks & Sluga. It must be one of the smallest tackle-shops anywhere and I bought the following grub-type flies there a few years ago.

**Grayling Grub (Pink)** · Riks & Sluga · Slovenia

| | |
|---|---|
| *Hook* | Mustad 94840, sizes 14–16 |
| *Thread* | Black |
| *Body* | Pink floss over lead wire |
| *Rib* | Silver wire |

**Grayling Grub (Yellow)**

| | |
|---|---|
| *Hook* | Mustad 94840, sizes 14–16 |
| *Thread* | Red |
| *Body* | Yellow silk over lead wire |
| *Rib* | Red thread |

**Grayling Grub (Olive)**

| | |
|---|---|
| *Hook* | Mustad 94840, sizes 14–16 |
| *Thread* | Olive |
| *Body* | Olive wool over lead wire |
| *Head* | Green-glass bead |

## GREEN CADDIS LARVA

This is Lars Olson's interpretation of the *Rhyacophila* caddis larva.

**Green Caddis Larva** · Olson · Sweden

| | |
|---|---|
| *Hook* | Mustad 80200BR, sizes 8–14 |
| *Thread* | Olive |
| *Body* | Tight olive dubbing |
| *Back* | Over the thorax area, dark feather fibres segmented with olive thread |
| *Legs* | None |

## GREEN CADDIS PUPA

This pattern was picked up in a fine tackle shop in Lucerne, Switzerland. Like many continental patterns, it is adorned with a gold bead. The beads on the Swiss flies are generally much smaller than those used in other countries.

**Green Caddis Pupa** · Switzerland

| | |
|---|---|
| *Hook* | Partridge Caddis Hook, size 10 |
| *Thread* | Dark olive |
| *Body* | Dark olive PVC (or fine Swannundaze) |
| *Rib* | Peacock herl |
| *Antennae* | Two cock-pheasant tail fibres, swept back |
| *Head* | Tiny gold bead |

## GREEN GIM RIVER NYMPH

This is a broad-spectrum pattern to imitate a number of *Baetis* nymphs. Lars Olson has checked the stomach contents of fish for over 20 years as well as installing a light trap to determine the indigenous insects of his rivers in Sweden. This Gim River nymph is just one of the patterns he has devised from his observations. He has also tied a floating version of this nymph.

**Green Gim River Nymph** · Olson · Sweden

| | |
|---|---|
| *Hook* | Mustad 80000BR, sizes 12–18 |
| *Thread* | Olive |
| *Tail* | Bronze mallard flank fibres |
| *Body* | Fine olive dubbing |
| *Rib* | Pale yellow silk |
| *Thorax* | As body |
| *Wing case* | Pheasant-tail fibres or any dark brown feather fibre |
| *Legs* | Brown partridge hackle fibres either side of the thorax |

## GREEN XMAS TREE

A fly does not have to be pretty to catch fish; neither does it have to be realistic. If this were the case, then this rather garish concoction would never leave the fly-box. I was given it by my good friend Bill Mincher who apologized when he gave it to me but swore it did catch fish.

**Green Xmas Tree** · Mincher · S. Africa

| | |
|---|---|
| *Hook* | Mustad 9671, sizes 8–12 |
| *Thread* | Red |
| *Tail* | Few strands of green crystal chenille (sometimes called cactus or Kactus chenille) |
| *Body* | Green crystal chenille |

## GREY-BROWN EMERGER

Another of Henri Hosinger's simple but effective patterns, this is used for trout and grayling.

**Grey-brown Emerger** · Hosinger · Luxembourg

| | |
|---|---|
| *Hook* | Mustad 94840 or Partridge L2A, sizes 10–14 |
| *Thread* | Black |
| *Tail* | Dark cock-pheasant or cock hackle fibres |
| *Body* | Grey rabbit dubbing |
| *Rib* | Brown thread (optional) |
| *Thorax* | Hare's mask |
| *Wing case* | Short tuft of grey mallard breast |

## GREY GOLD-HEAD

This is yet another Gold-head variation by Henri Hosinger.

**Grey Gold-head** · Hosinger · Luxembourg

| | |
|---|---|
| *Hook* | Mustad 94840, sizes 12–16 (or similar) |
| *Thread* | Black |
| *Tail* | French-partridge hackle fibres |
| *Body* | Grey rabbit dubbing |
| *Rib* | Brown thread |
| *Thorax* | Brown Antron |
| *Head* | Gold bead |

Grey Gold-head

## GREY NYMPH

Most countries have a Grey Nymph of sorts, this one was created by Henri Hosinger of Luxembourg. It is a very simple, plain, no-nonsense kind of nymph which takes trout, grayling, roach, chub, bream and even barbel.

**Grey Nymph** · Hosinger · Luxembourg
*Hook*          Mustad 94840 or Partridge L2A, sizes 10–14
*Thread*        Black
*Tail*          Dark cock-pheasant tail fibres or cock hackle fibres
*Underbody*     Copper wire, one layer on body two layers on thorax areas
*Body*          Grey chenille
*Thorax*        As body
*Wing case*     Black Raffene or feather fibre

This Croatian pattern is a variant on the Pheasant Tail theme but, instead of the normal ringneck pheasant tail, Mladen Merkas Goranin uses the fibres from a Lady Amherst's pheasant. He uses this fly early in the season and right at the tail end.

**Grey Nymph** · Goranin · Croatia
*Hook*          Mustad 9672, sizes 10–18
*Thread*        Black
*Tail*          Guinea-fowl hackle fibres
*Body*          Lady Amherst-pheasant tail fibres
*Rib*           Gold wire
*Wing case*     Guinea-fowl
*Legs*          Guinea-fowl hackle fibres

## HANNA'S NYMPH

This nymph was devised by Thomas Hanna from Monneymore, Co. Londonderry.

**Hanna's Nymph** · Hanna · Ireland
*Hook*          Mustad 9671, sizes 10–12
*Thread*        Olive
*Tail*          Cock-pheasant tail fibres
*Body*          Yellow balloon rubber
*Rib*           Gold wire
*Thorax*        Blue hare underfur
*Legs*          Partridge hackle dyed olive

## HARE'S-EAR NYMPH

This is one of a number of Irish Hare's Ear Nymphs, many of which incorporate some claret colour into the dubbing.

**Hare's Ear Nymph** · Ireland
*Hook*          Mustad 9671, size 14
*Thread*        Brown
*Tail*          Bronze mallard fibres
*Body*          Hare's ear

*Thorax*        Hare's ear and claret seal fur in equal proportions
*Wing case*     Dark grouse
*Legs*          Dark furnace-cock hackle, two turns

## HAIR NYMPHS

The following patterns are Australian nymphs from the 1960s.

**Hair Fibre Nymph** · Australia
*Hook*          Mustad 94840, sizes 8–14
*Thread*        Brown
*Body*          Blue-grey rabbit underfur lightly dubbed
*Rib*           Oval silver tinsel
*Thorax*        Hare fur
*Wing case*     Speckled brown partridge tail
*Legs*          Thorax fur well picked out

**Hair Silver Nymph**
*Hook*          Mustad 94840, sizes 8–12
*Thread*        Brown
*Tail*          Brown partridge hackle
*Body*          Silver twist tinsel
*Thorax*        Hare fur
*Wing case*     Speckled brown partridge tail
*Legs*          Brown partridge

## HORVATOVA NIMFA

Horvat's Nymph is the creation of Professor Miroslav Horvat of Banja Luka in Bosnia. Professor Horvat is an expert on the flies and traditions of Bosnia and, some years ago, sent me some of the historical flies of that area, flies similar to, if not the same as, those seen by Skues when he visited the area in the 1890s. This pattern is used for trout and grayling.

Bosnia is the only home of the rare soft-mouthed trout (*Salmotymallus*), an Ice-Age relict. It is similar to a brown trout but with a head resembling that of a grayling.

**Horvatova Nimfa** · Horvat · Bosnia
*Hook*          Mustad 94840, size 16
*Thread*        Grey
*Tail*          Brown hackle fibres
*Body*          Olive thread or silk, lacquered
*Rib*           Black thread
*Legs*          As tail
*Wing*          Short tuft of grey feather fibre

## HOT CAT

A good, searching nymph pattern, this was tied by my good friend Jack Blackman from South Africa.

**Hot Cat** · Blackman · S. Africa
| | |
|---|---|
| *Hook* | Mustad 79580, sizes 6–10 |
| *Thread* | Brown |
| *Tail* | Red-squirrel tail fibres |
| *Body* | Rabbit or hare fur over lead wire (well picked out to give a good shaggy effect) |
| *Rib* | Oval gold tinsel |
| *Hackle* | Sparse orange cock hackle |

**Hydropsyche (Polish)** · Poland
| | |
|---|---|
| *Hook* | Mustad 79671, sizes 10–14 |
| *Thread* | Black |
| *Body* | Cream chenille |
| *Back* | Clear polythene |
| *Rib* | Clear monofilament or cream thread |
| *Thorax* | Black dubbing |
| *Wing case* | As back |
| *Legs* | Thorax fur picked out |

## ITALIAN SEDGE PUPA

This simple pattern is very similar in design to the famous Spanish Pallaretta fly except that it is hairier and lacks the smooth lacquered finish.

**Italian Sedge Pupa** · Italy
| | |
|---|---|
| *Hook* | Mustad 94840, sizes 8–12 |
| *Thread* | Black |
| *Body* | Cream wool or fur dubbing |
| *Rib* | Silver wire |
| *Hackle* | Grey cock hackle tied in the Spanish style (the fibres are stiff and swept back) |

There is a yellow version with a brown rib.

## J.J. RED-TAIL PUPA

This is a Longhorn type of caddis pupa from Finland. Quite often, added touches of bright colour act as a hot-spot for the fish to concentrate on.

**J.J. Red-tail Pupa** · Finland
| | |
|---|---|
| *Hook* | Mustad 94840, sizes 6–10 |
| *Thread* | Black |
| *Tail* | Red yarn |
| *Body* | Peacock herl |

| | |
|---|---|
| *Thorax* | Grey Antron dubbing |
| *Legs* | Black hackle fibres |
| *Antennae* | Cock-pheasant tail fibres, swept backwards |

## J.R. SPECIAL

A simple dragonfly imitation from South Africa, this is attributed to John Robinson.

**J.R. Special** · Robinson · S. Africa
| | |
|---|---|
| *Hook* | Mustad 79580, sizes 6–12 |
| *Thread* | Black |
| *Tail* | Short tuft of black cock hackle fibres |
| *Body* | Green peacock herl |
| *Rib* | Oval gold tinsel |
| *Thorax* | Black chenille |
| *Hackle* | Short black cock or hen hackle |

## JANSSEN NYMPH

This fly is the creation of Frans Janssen of Holland. He uses it for roach as well as for stillwater trout.

**Janssen Nymph** · Janssen · Holland
| | |
|---|---|
| *Hook* | Partridge L2A, sizes 10–12 |
| *Thread* | Black |
| *Tail* | Cock-pheasant tail or short tuft of Crystal Hair |
| *Body* | Peacock herl over lead wire |
| *Rib* | Fine oval gold tinsel |
| *Eyes* | Two split shot tied on with figure-of-8 tyings |

## JAPANESE NYMPHS

The following Japanese nymphs were given to me by Barry Unwin of Fulling Mill Flies; they are just three patterns that he ties for that country.

**Japanese Nymph (Higenga Tobikera)** · Japan
| | |
|---|---|
| *Hook* | Mustad 3906 or similar, sizes 10–14 |
| *Thread* | Brown |
| *Tail* | Golden-pheasant tail, long fibres |
| *Body* | Brown synthetic dubbing |
| *Back stripe* | Single strand of white floss (this also goes over the wing case) |
| *Rib* | Brass wire |
| *Thorax* | As body |
| *Wing case* | Brown synthetic yarn |
| *Legs* | Brown partridge |

### Japanese Nymph (Himefutao Kagero) · Japan

| | |
|---|---|
| *Hook* | Mustad 3906 or similar, sizes 8–14 |
| *Thread* | Grey |
| *Tail* | Black-and-white silver-pheasant, long fibres |
| *Body* | Grey synthetic dubbing |
| *Rib* | Brass wire |
| *Thorax* | As body |
| *Wing case* | Grey synthetic yarn |
| *Legs* | Grey-partridge hackle fibres |

### Japanese Emerger Nymph

| | |
|---|---|
| *Hook* | Mustad 94840 or similar, sizes 10–14 |
| *Thread* | Black |
| *Tail* | Brown partridge hackle fibres |
| *Body* | Light brown synthetic dubbing |
| *Thorax* | As body |
| *Legs* | Brown partridge hackle |
| *Wings* | Piece of white polyethylene foam tied on top of the thorax |

## JIG NYMPHS

This type of nymph is popular with many European anglers. They are very effective for many species of fish, especially grayling that lie in deep pools. The first examples come from Traun River Products of Germany.

### Jig Nymph No. 1
Traun River Products · Germany

| | |
|---|---|
| *Hook* | Jig Hook, sizes 10–12 |
| *Thread* | Brown |
| *Tail* | Short tuft of pearl Crystal Hair |
| *Body* | Grey synthetic dubbing with plenty of sparkle (Antron fibres are ideal) |
| *Collar* | Hare's ear |
| *Head* | Gold bead |

Jig Nymph No.1

### Jig Nymph No. 2

| | |
|---|---|
| *Hook* | Jig Hook, sizes 14–16 |
| *Thread* | Brown or black |
| *Tail* | Short tuft of pearl Crystal Hair |

| | |
|---|---|
| *Body* | Peacock herl |
| *Collar* | Hare's ear |
| *Head* | Gold bead |

**Jig Nymph No. 3** is tied in the same way as No. 1 but brown fur is used instead of grey.

Ernest Loidle of Gmunden in Austria also sent me some similar patterns.

### Jig Nymph No. 4 · Loidle · Austria

| | |
|---|---|
| *Hook* | Jig Hook, size 12 |
| *Thread* | Brown |
| *Body* | Brown Larva Lace or similar plastic body medium |
| *Collar* | Grey fur well picked out |
| *Head* | Gold bead |

**Jig Nymph No. 5** is the same as No. 4 except the brown fur thorax/collar is well picked out.

## KAKAHI QUEEN

This New Zealand pattern is the nymph version of the well-known dry fly of that name. The artificials are intended to imitate the indigenous mayfly *Coloburiscus humeralis*.

### Kakahi Nymph · NZ

| | |
|---|---|
| *Hook* | Mustad 3666, sizes 12–14 |
| *Thread* | Brown |
| *Tail* | Brown hen hackle fibres |
| *Body* | Bronze peacock herl |
| *Thorax* | Rich brown silk |
| *Wing case* | Grey mallard feathers |
| *Legs* | Brown hen hackle fibres |

## KENYA BUG

This pattern goes back a long way; John Veniard gives a dressing for it in *A Further Guide to Fly Dressing*. It is used throughout southern Africa and still catches fish. My first trout in New Zealand came to a Kenya Bug. I was fishing the Waipunga River in North Island, a fast-flowing stream that has carved its way through the volcanic rock to form a steep-sided valley. The banks were covered with *toi toi*, the feathery plants that held a fatal attraction for my flies. I had not had much success with a dry fly so I reverted to a nymph and chose a Kenya Bug that had rested in my fly-box unused for years. Why I chose this fly I do not know. I suppose it was a case of one fly is as good as another when you haven't a clue what to use. But it worked, this little international combination of a Welshman using an African fly on a New Zealand river, and that is what fishing is all about.

### Kenya Bug · Kenya

| | |
|---|---|
| *Hook* | Mustad 94840, sizes 8–12 |
| *Thread* | Black |
| *Tail* | Black cock hackle fibres (or guinea-fowl) |
| *Body* | Plump body of black wool |
| *Rib* | Flat silver tinsel |
| *Hackle* | Long-fibred black cock hackle |

## KEVENNAN SPECIAL

A Swedish pattern given to me by Hans van Klinken of Holland, this is an excellent pattern for large grayling.

### Kevennan Special · van Klinken · Sweden

| | |
|---|---|
| *Hook* | Partridge H1A, sizes 10–12 |
| *Thread* | Black |
| *Underbody* | Two layers of lead wire |
| *Tail* | Wild boar hair |
| *Body* | Flyrite polypropylene dubbing No. 8 and No. 3, mixed in equal proportions |
| *Rib* | Fine gold wire |
| *Body hackle* | Olive grizzle saddle |
| *Thorax* | Beaver underfur |

## KUPIČA NYMPH

The River Kupiča is a small stream that flows into the much larger Kupa River in Croatia. It is a pretty stream of clear sparkling water, fast runs and deep pools. In some of the pools the *Huchen* sometimes lie like dark shadows on the bottom. Grayling and brown trout are found in the same pools, feeding in the faster, shallower riffles. The river winds its way through leafy woods and, altogether, is a delightful stream to fish. Mladen Merkas Goranin was our guide on the day we fished this stream and he named the Kupiča series of nymphs after that Croatian jewel of a river.

### Kupiča Nymph (Natural) · Goranin · Croatia

| | |
|---|---|
| *Hook* | Mustad 94840, sizes 12–22 |
| *Thread* | Dark brown |
| *Tail* | Hare's ear fibres |
| *Body* | Stripped peacock fibres |

| | |
|---|---|
| *Thorax* | Hare's ear |
| *Wing case* | Jay wing quill section |
| *Legs* | Sparse brown hen hackle |

The other nymphs in the series are: Black, with tail and hackle in black and thorax of black seal fur; Copper, with tail and hackle in brown and thorax of copper wire; White, with tail and hackle in cream and thorax of white seal fur; and Brown, Claret, Olive, Orange and Yellow, all with tail and hackle in brown and with thorax in the appropriately coloured seal fur.

## LA MUE

A pattern from the famous French tackle-company of Guy Plas, this fly represents a stillborn insect with its wing still caught up in the shuck. It is a fly that works well on rivers and stillwater.

### La Mue · Guy Plas · France

| | |
|---|---|
| *Hook* | Mustad 9672, sizes 10–16 |
| *Thread* | Brown |
| *Body* | Light olive silk |
| *Rib* | Brown silk |
| *Hackle* | Short brown cock hackle fibres, one side only |
| *Thorax* | Cock-pheasant tail fibres |
| *Wing* | Grey hackle fibres on one side, one only. |

## LARGE DARK OLIVE NYMPH

This is one of Thomas Hanna's patterns, many of which were way ahead of his time.

### Large Dark Olive Nymph · Hanna · Ireland

| | |
|---|---|
| *Hook* | Mustad 9671, size 14 |
| *Thread* | Brown |
| *Tail* | Dark olive cock hackle fibres |
| *Body* | Dark olive floss |
| *Rib* | Palmered brown cock hackle clipped short |
| *Thorax* | Dark olive seal fur (or substitute) |
| *Wing case* | Cock-pheasant tail fibres |
| *Legs* | Brown-olive hen hackle |

## LATEX PUPA

The next three patterns were tied by Ernest Loidle of Austria. Though I have called them pupae, the first makes an excellent non-case-making caddis larva pattern.

**Latex Pupa** · Loidle · Austria
| | |
|---|---|
| *Hook* | Mustad 80200BR, sizes 8–12 |
| *Thread* | Dark olive |
| *Tail* | Short tuft of white fluorescent floss |
| *Body* | Dark olive or plain hare fur |
| *Back* | Dark olive latex |
| *Rib* | Clear monofilament |
| *Thorax* | Hare's ear |
| *Legs* | Thorax hair well picked out |

**Latex Emerging Pupa** · Loidle · Austria
| | |
|---|---|
| *Hook* | Mustad 80200BR, sizes 8–12 |
| *Thread* | Dark olive |
| *Body* | Dark olive hare's ear |
| *Rib* | Clear monofilament |
| *Pupal sheath* | White Antron, tied in at the tail, taken over the body and tied at the thorax |
| *Thorax* | Hare's ear and brown synthetic dubbing, mixed, with a few fibres of pearl Flashabou or similar iridescent fibres |
| *Legs* | Thorax fur well picked out |

**Latex Gold-head pupa** · Loidle · Austria
| | |
|---|---|
| *Hook* | Mustad 80200BR, sizes 8–12 |
| *Thread* | Dark olive |
| *Body* | Dark olive hare fur |
| *Back* | Olive latex |
| *Rib* | Clear monofilament |
| *Thorax* | Hare fur |
| *Legs* | Thorax fur well picked out |
| *Head* | Gold bead |

### LEAD-HEAD JIGS

These flies from Riks & Sluga, Slovenia, are used when extra weight is needed to get down to the fish in fast-flowing alpine rivers.

**Lead-head Jig No. 1** · Riks & Sluga · Slovenia
| | |
|---|---|
| *Hook* | Mustad 94840, sizes 8–10 |
| *Thread* | Black |
| *Tail* | Peacock herl |
| *Tip* | Red silk |
| *Body* | As tail |
| *Head* | Pre-formed lead weight |

**Lead-head Jig No. 2** · Riks & Sluga · Slovenia
| | |
|---|---|
| *Hook* | Mustad 94840, sizes 8–10 |
| *Thread* | Olive |
| *Body* | Olive dubbing |

| | |
|---|---|
| *Rib* | Flat multi-coloured tinsel |
| *Head* | Lead shot |

### LERCH'S PHEASANT TAIL

This fly was sent to me by Gerhard Lerch, a friend I meet every year on one river or another in Slovenia. Gerhard takes fishing courses there every year, bringing his students from all over Europe to fish the pristine rivers of this country. He also has the finest vodka that I have ever got tight on.

**Lerch's Pheasant Tail** · Lerch · Germany
| | |
|---|---|
| *Hook* | Mustad 94840, sizes 12–14 |
| *Thread* | Black or brown |
| *Tail* | Cock-pheasant tail fibres |
| *Body* | Cock-pheasant tail |
| *Rib* | Gold wire |
| *Thorax* | Orange dubbing and gold bead |
| *Wing case* | As body |

### LITTLE BLACK

This tiny nymph is excellent for difficult trout and grayling. Henri Hosinger took ten Nase (a European coarse fish, *Chondostomus nasus*) in an hour. This fish is difficult to catch on maggots let alone an artificial fly. The pattern probably imitates a small chironomid pupa or perhaps a *Simulium* larva.

**Little Black** · Hosinger · Luxembourg
| | |
|---|---|
| *Hook* | Partridge Midge or Mustad 80100BR, sizes 16–18 |
| *Thread* | Black |
| *Tail* | Black feather fibre |
| *Body* | Crow or similar feather fibre, over lead wire |
| *Wing* | Tuft of light-coloured Antron |

Little Black

### M.A.D. NYMPHS

The following three patterns are from the vice of Henning von Monteton of Frankfurt. The name 'M.A.D.' comes from the initials of the dubbing used in the construction: Monteton's Abfall Dubbing (*abfall* is German for 'waste'). Henning saves all the waste from his tying and every so often blends this mixture in a coffee grinder. The dubbing contains three parts soft feather (e.g. marabou), three parts soft fur (e.g. rabbit), one part synthetic fibres (e.g. Antron), one part feather fibres (e.g. partridge without stalks), one part coarse hair (e.g. squirrel or badger) and one part chamois, deer, etc.

### M.A.D. Emerger · von Monteton · Germany

| | |
|---|---|
| *Hook* | Partridge E3AY, sizes 10–16 |
| *Thread* | Black |
| *Pupal Shuck* | Bunch of grey mallard flank |
| *Body* | M.A.D. dubbing, grey or brown |
| *Thorax* | As body but wound with a dubbing loop |
| *Wing* | Grey mallard fibres sloping backwards |

### M.A.D. Brown Nymph

| | |
|---|---|
| *Hook* | Partridge E3AY, sizes 10–16 |
| *Thread* | Black |
| *Tail* | Cock-pheasant tail fibres |
| *Body* | Brown M.A.D dubbing over copper wire, weighted |
| *Thorax* | As body |
| *Wing case* | Hen saddle hackle |
| *Legs* | Brown partridge hackle |

The M.A.D. Grey Nymph follows the same pattern as the Brown but grey M.A.D dubbing is used and the legs of grey partridge.

### M.A.D. Suspender Nymph

| | |
|---|---|
| *Hook* | Partridge E3AY, sizes 10–16 |
| *Thread* | Black |
| *Tail* | Cock-pheasant tail fibres |
| *Body* | M.A.D. dubbing (grey or brown) |
| *Suspender ball* | Polystyrene in nylon stocking material |
| *Thorax* | M.A.D dubbing looped once around the hook shank and twice around the suspender ball, like a parachute hackle |

M.A.D. Suspender Nymph

### M.M.G. FAVOURITE NYMPH

Mladen Merkas Goranin's favourite nymph, this pattern consistently takes the largest grayling out of the Kupa and Kupiča Rivers.

### M.M.G. Favourite Nymph · Goranin · Croatia

| | |
|---|---|
| *Hook* | Mustad 94840, sizes 12–22 |
| *Thread* | Brown |
| *Tail* | Brown hackle fibres |
| *Body* | Stripped peacock quill |
| *Wing case* | Small strip of goose quill from the stem and not feather fibre |
| *Legs* | Brown hackle, two turns |

The M.M.G. Favourite Floating Nymph is the same as the sunk pattern but with CDC added to the wing case.

### M.M. NYMPH

This pattern was given in the excellent book *Stalking Trout* by Les Hill and Graham Marshall. M.M. stands for 'Marshall's Monstrosity'. It is a broad-spectrum nymph.

### M.M. Nymph · Marshall · NZ

| | |
|---|---|
| *Hook* | Mustad 94840, sizes 10–16 |
| *Thread* | Black |
| *Tail* | Golden-pheasant tippet fibres |
| *Body* | Green seal fur or substitute |
| *Rib* | Gold wire (optional) |
| *Thorax* | Dark reddish-brown opossum fur |
| *Wing case* | Peacock herl |

### MALCOLM'S JOSEPH

This fly of Malcolm Meintjies of South Africa obtains its name from the multi-coloured body of the pattern.

### Malcolm's Joseph · Meintjies · S. Africa

| | |
|---|---|
| *Hook* | Mustad 3906, sizes 8–12 |
| *Thread* | Olive |
| *Tail* | Sparse olive marabou |
| *Body* | Fur dubbing, light olive followed by darker olive, then amber, orange and, finally, fiery brown |

## MATCHAM'S DAMSEL NYMPH

This damselfly imitation is tied upside down, in a similar way to the other patterns given in Chapter 8. Damsel nymphs are important flies 'down under'.

**Matcham's Damsel**

**Nymph** · Matcham · Australia

| | |
|---|---|
| *Hook* | Mustad 80150BR, sizes 8–10 |
| *Thread* | Brown monofilament |
| *Tail* | Strands of green ostrich herl |
| *Body* | Green Antron dubbing |
| *Rib* | Peacock herl |
| *Thorax* | As body |
| *Wing case* | Brown Raffene |
| *Legs* | Black fox fur |

## MAYFLY NYMPH

I received the following pattern from an Italian fly fisherman on the banks of the River Soča in Slovenia. I noticed afterwards that it appears in the catalogue of Francesco Palu of Udine. The fly itself bears a strong similarity to some of the traditional nymphs from the Province of Léon in Spain.

**Mayfly Nymph** · Palu · Italy

| | |
|---|---|
| *Hook* | Mustad 9672, sizes 8–12 |
| *Thread* | Brown |
| *Tail* | Cock-pheasant tail fibres |
| *Body* | White rabbit or synthetic dubbing (rear half), amber dubbing (front half) |
| *Rib* | Brown thread |
| *Thorax* | Brown dubbing |
| *Hackles* | Grey partridge on top of the hook over the white part of the body, brown partridge over the amber, and grouse hackle fibres over the thorax |

The next three patterns come from Finland and are broad-spectrum mayfly nymphs tied by Veli Autti.

**Mayfly Nymph No. I** · Autti · Finland

| | |
|---|---|
| *Hook* | Mustad 9672, sizes 12–14 |
| *Thread* | Brown |
| *Tail* | Three cock-pheasant tail fibres |
| *Body* | Yellow fur dubbing |
| *Back* | Cock-pheasant tail fibres |
| *Rib* | Gold wire |
| *Thorax* | Brown fur |
| *Wing case* | As back |
| *Legs* | Brown partridge |

**Mayfly Nymph No. 2** · Autti · Finland

| | |
|---|---|
| *Hook* | Mustad 9672, sizes 12–14 |
| *Thread* | Brown |
| *Tail* | Three cock-pheasant tail fibres |
| *Body* | Filoplume |
| *Back* | Cock-pheasant tail |
| *Rib* | Clear monofilament |
| *Thorax* | Hare fur |
| *Wing case* | As back |
| *Legs* | Guard hairs picked out |

**Mayfly Nymph No. 3** · Autti · Finland

| | |
|---|---|
| *Hook* | Mustad 9672, sizes 12–14 |
| *Thread* | Brown |
| *Tail* | Cock-pheasant tail |
| *Body* | Filoplume |
| *Back* | As tail |
| *Rib* | Fine wire |
| *Thorax* | Grey dubbing |
| *Wing case* | As tail |
| *Legs* | Golden-pheasant tail fibres |

## MIDGE

Among some of the patterns sent to me from New Zealand was a simple midge pattern tied by Bill McLay of Dunedin, the fly is used in slow-moving pools.

**Midge** · McLay · NZ

| | |
|---|---|
| *Hook* | Mustad 80250BR, sizes 10–14 |
| *Thread* | Black |
| *Body* | Black Swannundaze |
| *Thorax* | Black ostrich herl |
| *Breathing appendages* | White polypropylene fibres |

## MONTANA RABBIT

This pattern was published in the French magazine *La Pêche Mouche*, in an article by Thierry Cloux. As its name suggests, this pattern is a variation on the Montana Stone, but instead of using chenille this fly uses rabbit fur.

**Montana Rabbit** · France

| | |
|---|---|
| *Hook* | Mustad 79580, sizes 6–10 |
| *Thread* | Black |
| *Tail* | Two strands of black rubber hackle |
| *Body* | Black rabbit fur, dubbed |
| *Thorax* | Yellow rabbit fur |
| *Wing case* | Black rabbit fur |
| *Legs* | Six black rubber hackles |

## MORTON'S CREEPER

Among the many patterns sent to me from New Zealand by Brian and Nancy Tichborne was a creeper pattern devised by John Morton. He describes the body of this nymph as a button of dubbing placed on top of the hook and, in his words, 'readers will wonder how the hell I get this effect, if it ever gets into print'. Well, it has made it into print, so readers start wondering! The fly is generally fished unweighted as a spider-type fly. It is a very good pattern on the Ahuriri River in South Island, New Zealand.

**Morton's Creeper** · Morton · NZ

| | |
|---|---|
| *Hook* | Mustad 94840, sizes 8–10 |
| *Thread* | Olive or brown |
| *Tail* | Long cock-pheasant tail fibres |
| *Body* | Olive dubbing tied on top of the hook shank, giving a rather bulbous shape to the abdomen |
| *Thorax* | Peacock herl |
| *Side antennae* | Cock-pheasant tail fibres tied between the body and thorax |
| *Wing case* | Dark feather fibre |
| *Legs* | Cock-pheasant tail fibres clipped short |

## MOSER STONEFLY NYMPH

This is yet another pattern from one of Europe's foremost innovative tiers, Roman Moser of Gmunden in Austria.

**Moser Stonefly Nymph** · Moser · Austria

| | |
|---|---|
| *Hook* | Partridge H1A, sizes 8–12 |
| *Thread* | Black |
| *Tail* | Two goose biots |
| *Body* | Multi-coloured synthetic dubbing mix with an overall light brown hue but containing yellow, red and brown-amber highlights |
| *Back* | Treated light brown Raffene (Moser has a secret recipe, I tend to use a flexible cement) mottled with waterproof ink |
| *Rib* | Nylon monofilament |
| *Thorax* | As body |
| *Wing pads* | As back |
| *Legs* | Sparse ginger hackle |

## NYMPHE MOUSSE

I found this pattern in the French magazine *La Pêche Mouche*, in an article by Victor Borandelli. The fly is a nymph pattern devised to catch barbel.

**Nymph Mousse** · France

| | |
|---|---|
| *Hook* | Mustad 94840, sizes 10–14 |
| *Thread* | Brown or black |
| *Underbody* | Double layer of copper wire |
| *Body* | Olive-brown polypropylene yarn |
| *Wing* | Sparse olive-brown marabou |

## OLIVE NYMPH

This pattern was created by the well-known Danish fly-tier, Preben Torp Jacobsen. His full-time occupation was as a veterinary surgeon.

**Olive Nymph** · Jacobsen · Denmark

| | |
|---|---|
| *Hook* | Mustad 3904A, sizes 12–16 |
| *Thread* | Primrose |
| *Tail* | Plain guinea-fowl hackle fibres dyed olive |
| *Body* | Mole fur treated with picric acid to give an olive shade |
| *Rib* | Fluorescent green nylon filament |
| *Thorax* | Dark red cow's hair |

## PALLARETTA

This is a traditional Spanish pupa pattern that is used in many other European countries. The feathers for the hackles come from the fabled *coq de léon*, especially bred cockerels that have provided feathers for Spanish fly-dressers for about four centuries. The feather on the pattern given below is a steely-grey colour, called in Spanish *indio acerado*.

**Pallaretta** · Spain

| | |
|---|---|
| *Hook* | Mustad 94840, sizes 8–12 |
| *Body* | Off white-cream silk |
| *Rib* | Fine black silk (body and rib heavily lacquered) |
| *Hackle* | Dark grey hackle fibres swept back |

Pallaretta

There is also a green version of this fly; just substitute green silk for the white.

## PALLARETTA VARIANT

This pattern was given to me by Luis Antunez of Madrid. In this version the body is very bulbous at the tail end and tapers towards the head. The hackle is mottled or, in Spanish, *pardo flor de escoba* (the colour of the flower of the mountain broom).

**Pallaretta Variant** · Antunez · Spain
| | |
|---|---|
| Hook | Mustad 94840, sizes 6–10 |
| Thread | Black |
| Body | Orange silk (rear half), tapered white silk (front half) |
| Rib | Black silk (body and rib heavily lacquered) |
| Hackle | Mottled hackle fibres |

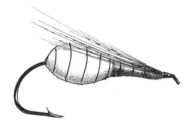

Pallaretta Variant

## PEARL SHRIMP

This simple design by Laurie Matcham uses modern materials. There are a number of pearl tinsels on the market suitable for this pattern.

**Pearl Shrimp** · Matcham · Australia
| | |
|---|---|
| Hook | Mustad 80200BR, sizes 8–12 |
| Thread | Brown monofilament |
| Weight | Lead wire |
| Body | Green Antron dubbing |
| Back | Pearl Lureflash |
| Rib | Copper wire |

## PERLODES BICOLOR

This stonefly pattern by Henning von Monteton is a fine example of woven-body application. The pattern comes in various colour combinations: Black & Red, Black & Yellow, Black & Cream for dark water; Brown & Yellow, Brown & Cream, Dark Grey & Light Grey and Grey & Cream for clear water.

**Perlodes bicolor** · von Monteton · Germany
| | |
|---|---|
| Hook | Partridge Z11, sizes 4–10 |
| Thread | Black Superfine |
| Weight | Copper wire |
| Tails | Black or brown goose biots |
| Body | Woven polyamide knitting yarn (dark back, light belly) |
| Thorax | Rabbit dubbing |
| Wing case | Black or brown Raffene |
| Legs | Brown or grey partridge hackle |

## PFANDL NYMPH

Traun River Products sell a number of flies to catch the shy carp. They have patterns to imitate such mundane items as floating breadcrust. This is a small nymph pattern devised to tempt the carp that is feeding on insects.

**Pfandl Nymph** · Pfandl · Germany
| | |
|---|---|
| Hook | Mustad 80000, sizes 12–16 |
| Thread | Black |
| Tail | Cock-pheasant tail fibres |
| Body | Fluoresent green silk |
| Rib | Black thread |
| Thorax | Peacock herl |
| Wing case | Dark feather fibre |
| Legs | Brown cock hackle fibres |

Pfandl Nymph

## PIKA NYMPH

A Marjan Fratnik special, this uses gold beads as the thorax and not, as is more usual, the head.

**Pika Nymph** · Fratnik · Slovenia
| | |
|---|---|
| Hook | Mustad 94840, size 6 |
| Tail | Cock-pheasant tail fibres, tied short |
| Body | Greyish-brown natural fur dubbing |
| Thorax | Two gold beads |
| Wing case | Black Raffene lacquered at least twice |

Pika Nymph

## PLECIONKA

There are many fine fly-tiers and fishermen in Poland. Adam Skrechota who provided me with examples of Polish nymphs maintains that the most effective pattern is the Plecionka, a woven-bodied fly used for both trout and grayling. It represents a small caddis pupa.

**Plecionka Olive** · Skrechota · Poland
| | |
|---|---|
| *Hook* | Partridge K4, sizes 8–16 |
| *Thread* | Black |
| *Weight* | Lead wire |
| *Body* | Golden-yellow floss |
| *Back* | Woven olive yarn and yellow thread |

**Plecionka Tan**
As above, except:
| | |
|---|---|
| *Body* | Tan thread |
| *Back* | Fluorescent lime |

## POLIFEITUS NYMPH

A pattern from the Italian/Slovenian border, this is tied by Branko Gasparin from Nova Goriča. Branko ties many interesting patterns.

**Polifeitus Nymph** · Gasparin · Slovenia
| | |
|---|---|
| *Hook* | Mustad 79850, sizes 8–12 |
| *Thread* | Brown |
| *Tail* | Brown partridge or other game-bird feather |
| *Body* | Light olive fur dubbing |
| *Rib* | Gold wire |
| *Thorax* | Brown fur dubbing and a gold bead (put on with a small pin before the other materials) |
| *Legs* | Brown partridge or other game-bird feather |

## POLISH SHRIMPS

Like most countries, Poland has a number of freshwater shrimp imitations. The following were

sent to me by Adam Skrechota of Sanok on the edge of the Carpathian Mountains.

**Polish Shrimp (Cream)** · Poland
| | |
|---|---|
| *Hook* | Partridge K4A, sizes 8–14 |
| *Thread* | Olive |
| *Body* | Cream chenille |
| *Back* | Clear polythene |
| *Rib* | Copper wire |

**Polish Shrimp (Brown)** · Poland
| | |
|---|---|
| *Hook* | Partridge K4, sizes 8–14 |
| *Thread* | Olive or brown |
| *Body* | Light brown synthetic dubbing |
| *Back* | Clear polythene |
| *Rib* | Clear nylon monofilament |

## POOKELI

This is a simple fly from Finland, combining modern and traditional materials with an added touch of fluorescents.

**Pookeli** · Finland
| | |
|---|---|
| *Hook* | Partridge GRS2A, size 12 |
| *Thread* | Black |
| *Tail* | Short tuft of pearl Flashabou |
| *Body* | Bronze peacock herl |
| *Rib* | Fluorescent green silk |
| *Legs* | Dark grey cock hackle fibres or black hackle fibres |

## PRECIEUSE

This fly comes from the French fishing company Guy Plas, based in the Limoges region of France. This area is famous for its cockerels, which are bred, just like those in the Province of Léon in Spain, for their fine glass-like feathers. This pattern comes in a variety of body colours and hackle shades. The nymph is best described as a broad-spectrum pattern and is used to imitate a number of different ephemerid species.

**Precieuse** · Guy Plas · France
| | |
|---|---|
| *Hook* | Mustad 7780C or similar, sizes 12–18 |
| *Thread* | Grey or black |
| *Tail* | Ash-grey hackle fibres |
| *Body* | Light grey polypropylene dubbing |
| *Rib* | Fine, silver tinsel |
| *Thorax* | Dark grey polypropylene dubbing |
| *Hackle* | Short-fibred ash grey |

## QUIVER NYMPH

This is another innovation by Roman Moser of Gmunden in Austria. Roman introduces concave sequins at the head of the fly in order to activate the pattern in fast water. The sequin is held in place by a small glass bead in the front and by a build-up of tying thread behind. The tails of the flies vibrate and quiver when the pattern is retrieved. There are many colour and material variations.

**Quiver Nymph** · Moser · Austria

| | |
|---|---|
| *Hook* | Partridge RMCS29, sizes 8–12 |
| *Thread* | Black |
| *Tail* | Marabou, Flashabou, or even Crystal Hair |
| *Body* | Dubbed fur (e.g. SLF) |
| *Thorax* | Contrasting dubbed fur |
| *Front* | Sequin with a diameter less than the hook gape; small glass bead in front |

Quiver Nymph

## RED-BACK NYMPH

This fancy stonefly nymph is for deep-water fishing in fast-flowing, deep rivers.

**Red-back Nymph** · Italy

| | |
|---|---|
| *Hook* | Mustad 94840, sizes 6–10 |
| *Thread* | Black |
| *Tail* | Cock-pheasant tail fibres |
| *Body* | Yellow polypropylene yarn |
| *Rib* | Clipped palmered dark furnace hackle |
| *Back* | Red polypropylene yarn |
| *Thorax* | Brown polypropylene yarn |
| *Wing case* | As body |
| *Legs* | Grouse or brown partridge hackle fibres |

## RUBBER LEGS

This nymph came in a selection sent to me by Richardt Jensen of Denmark. It is a strange pattern with dumb-bell eyes tied in at the bend and rubber hackles at the head.

**Rubber Legs** · Jensen · Denmark

| | |
|---|---|
| *Hook* | Mustad 79580, sizes 6–12 |
| *Thread* | Black |
| *Weight* | Dumb-bell tied on top of the hook at the bend |
| *Body* | Black fur and copper wire dubbing wick |
| *Legs* | Four white rubber hackles over the eye of the hook |

## SMALL'S GREEN NYMPH

A pattern from South Africa, this has now been around for sometime.

**Small's Green Nymph** · Small · S. Africa

| | |
|---|---|
| *Hook* | Mustad 9671, sizes 8–12 |
| *Thread* | Olive |
| *Tail* | Few strands of partridge hackle |
| *Body* | Tapered green wool |
| *Rib* | Oval gold tinsel |
| *Legs* | Sparse brown hackle |

## STONEFLY CREEPER

This is a semi-realistic stonefly creeper from Spain which uses modern materials.

**Stonefly Creeper** · Spain

| | |
|---|---|
| *Hook* | Mustad 79580, sizes 8–12 |
| *Thread* | Black goose biots |
| *Body* | Brown transparent Swannundaze marked with black waterproof ink top and bottom |
| *Thorax* | Brown dubbing |
| *Legs* | Black hen hackle, palmered through the thorax |
| *Wing pads* | Brown latex cut to shape and marked with black waterproof ink |
| *Head* | As body |
| *Eyes* | Burnt monofilament |
| *Antennae* | Cock hackle stems |

## STONEFLY NYMPH

A semi-realistic pattern from Australia, this was tied by one of that country's leading tiers, Laurie Matcham.

**Stonefly Nymph** · Matcham · Australia

| | |
|---|---|
| *Hook* | Mustad 80050BR, sizes 8–10 |
| *Thread* | Brown monofilament |
| *Tail* | Brown goose biots |

| | |
|---|---|
| *Body* | Black fur dubbing |
| *Thorax* | As body |
| *Back & wing cases* | Brown Raffene |
| *Side flashes* | Red mohair wool |
| *Legs* | Thorax fur picked out |
| *Antennae* | Two cock hackle stalks |

### T.V.N. NYMPH

The small-mouthed yellowfish (*Barbus holubi*) is indigenous to the Orange and Vaal River systems in South Africa. When mature it can exceed 15¾lb (7kg) in weight and is a pale golden-olive in colour with yellow fins, except for the anal fin which is orange. Many South Africans now fish for this splendid creature with the fly. The diet of the fish is made up of insect food, daphnia and molluscs. The T.V.N. nymph is the creation of Theo van Niekierk and is tied to represent a small freshwater mussel.

**T.V.N. Nymph** · van Niekierk · S. Africa

| | |
|---|---|
| *Hook* | Mustad 94840, sizes 6–10 |
| *Thread* | Black |
| *Underbody* | Lead wire |
| *Body* | Peacock herl |
| *Rib* | Copper wire |
| *Head* | White clipped deer hair |

T.V.N. Nymph

Sometimes this pattern is given a tail.

### THEO'S BEAD-HEAD

Another bead-head fly from Holland, this one comes from the vice of Theo Bakelaar. Hans van Klinken credits Theo with introducing bead-headed flies to Holland.

**Theo's Bead-head** · Bakelaar · Holland

| | |
|---|---|
| *Hook* | Partridge L2A or similar, sizes 8–16 |
| *Thread* | Brown |
| *Tail* | Reddish-brown hackle fibres |
| *Body* | Reddish-brown dubbing |

| | |
|---|---|
| *Rib* | Gold wire |
| *Thorax* | Peacock herl |
| *Collar* | CDC feather |
| *Head* | Gold bead |

### TUMBLING STONE

This is a searcher-nymph pattern for heavy water and is heavily weighted.

**Tumbling Stone** · Austria

| | |
|---|---|
| *Hook* | Mustad 94840, sizes 4–6 |
| *Thread* | Brown |
| *Tail* | Two brown goose biots |
| *Body* | Brown synthetic dubbing over a number of lead layers |
| *Back* | Spectraflash sheet |
| *Rib* | Silver and copper tinsel |
| *Collar* | Heavy brown hackle |
| *Head* | As body |

Tumbling Stone

### UNUSUAL

Hans Nischkauer credits this fly to the American tier, Art Lee. It is based on an earlier pattern by Francis Betters called the 'Usual'. Hans maintains that this fly, although little known in Europe, is one of the finest emerger patterns he has used so, although this should appear be in the American section, I include it here.

**Unusual** · Lee · Austria via USA

| | |
|---|---|
| *Hook* | Tiemco 900BL |
| *Thread* | Black |
| *Tail* | Three strands cock-pheasant tail |
| *Body* | Cock-pheasant tail |
| *Rib* | Silver wire |
| *Thorax* | Hare's mask |
| *Wing case* | Black feather fibre |
| *Wing* | Tuft of hair from a hare's hind leg sticking out between the wing case |
| *Head* | As body |

## URBAN SEDGE PUPA

This simple, orange caddis pupa comes from Andrij Urban of Skopje in Macedonia.

**Urban Sedge Pupa** · Urban · Macedonia
*Hook*     Mustad 94840, sizes 8–12
*Body*     Orange fur mix dubbing
*Thorax*   Hare's ear mix dubbing
*Legs*     Sparse partridge hackle
*Wings*   Two grey feather slips either side of the body.

## WALKER'S NYMPHS

This pattern usually comes in either green yellow or red. Lionel Walker who created these nymphs is perhaps most famous for the South African fly to end all flies, Walker's Killer. This pattern is used all over South Africa and some anglers use it in the UK as a reservoir lure. In fact, in devising his 'Killer', Lionel had a large nymph in mind. The Walker's nymphs are much smaller patterns.

**Walker's Green Nymph** · L. Walker · S. Africa
*Hook*     Mustad 94840, sizes 8–12
*Thread*   Green
*Tail*     Bunch of black cock hackle fibres or black squirrel hair
*Body*     Green chenille
*Rib*      Flat gold tinsel
*Wing pads*  Striped partridge shoulder feathers either side of the body

Walker's Green Nymph

## WOVEN RHYACOPHILA

This Polish pattern is a stretched out version of the Plecionka nymph.

**Woven Rhyacophila** · Skrechota · Poland
*Hook*      Mustad 79671, sizes 10–14
*Thread*    Black
*Body*      Green fluorescent wool
*Back*      Woven olive yarn and yellow thread
*Thorax*    Black dubbing
*Wing case*  Clear PVC or polythene
*Legs*      Fur picked out

# LIST OF COUNTRIES PROVIDING PATTERNS

| | | | |
|---|---|---|---|
| Australia | Denmark | Japan | Slovenia |
| Austria | Finland | Kenya | South Africa |
| Bosnia | France | Luxembourg | Spain |
| Canada | Germany | Macedonia | Sweden |
| Croatia | Holland | New Zealand | Switzerland |
| Chile | Ireland | Norway | United Kingdom |
| Czech Republic | Italy | Poland | United States of America |

# USEFUL ADDRESSES

## WHOLESALE FLY-TYING MATERIALS

**Lureflash Products Ltd**
Victoria Street
Kilnhurst
Nr Rotherham
South Yorkshire S62 5SQ
UK

**Medway Feather Company**
Brasenose Road
Gillingham
Kent
UK

**Raymond C. Rumpf & Son**
PO Box 319
Sellersville
Pennsylvania 18960
USA

**Rocky Mountain Dubbing Co.**
PO Box 1478
Lander
Wyoming 82520
USA

**E. Veniard Ltd**
138 Northwood Road
Thornton Heath
Surrey CR4 8YG
UK

## WHOLESALE FLY SUPPLIERS

**Fulling Mill Flies Ltd**
5/46 Croydon Road
Reigate
Surrey RH2 0NH
UK

**Graham Trout Flies Ltd**
Eastcombe
Garway
Herefordshire HR2 8RE
UK

**Mouche Devaux**
10 rue de Pont de l'Epée
39300 Champagnole
France

**Umpqua Feather Merchants**
PO Box 700
Glide
Oregon 97443
USA

### RETAIL AND MAIL ORDER

**Blue Ribbon Flies**
PO Box 1037
West Yellowstone
Montana 59758
USA

**Dan Bailey's Fly Shop**
209 West Park Street
Livingstone
Montana 59047
USA

**Francesco Palu**
33030 Campoformido
via Silvio Pellico 44
Udine
Italy

**Guy Plas**
19320 Marcillac-La-Croisille
France

**Kaufmann's Streamborn Flies**
PO Box 23032
Portland
Oregon 97223
USA

**Marryat Interfly**
Postfach 8031
Gasometerstrase 23
CH-8005 Zurich
Switzerland

**Orvis Company**
Manchester
Vermont 05254
USA

**Orvis Company**
Nether Wallop Mill
Nether Wallop
Hampshire
UK

**Roman Moser**
Kuferzeile 129
A-4810 Gmunden
Austria

**Salmo**
Apartado De Correos 53206
Madrid
Spain

**Sportfish**
Lion Street
Hay-on-Wye
Herefordshire HR3 5AD
UK

**Steff's Fluebinding**
Skjolevaenget 14
83100 Tranbjerg
Denmark

**Traun River Products**
Haupstrasse 6
D-8227 Siegsdorf
Germany

NATURAL HISTORY EQUIPMENT
SUPPLIERS

**Watkins & Doncaster Ltd**
Four Throws
Hawkhurst
Kent
UK

ANGLING-BOOK SUPPLIERS

**Coch y Bonddu Books**
Penegoes
Machynlleth
Powys SY20 8NN
Wales
UK

**John & Judith Head**
The Barn Book Supply
88 Crane Street
Salisbury
Wiltshire SP1 2QD
UK

HOOK MANUFACTURERS

**O. Mustad & Son**
PO Box 41
N-2801 Gjøvik
Norway

**Partridge of Redditch Ltd**
Mount Pleasant
Redditch
Worcestershire B97 4JE
UK

# HOOK CHARTS

The following hook charts are of hooks that I use from the following hook manufacturers:

**O. Mustad & Son**
PO Box 41
N-2801 Gjøvik
Norway

**Partridge of Redditch Ltd**
Mount Pleasant
Redditch
Worcestershire B97 4JE
UK

## MUSTAD HOOKS

**94840 FLY HOOK**
Forged, straight, round bend,
turned down tapered eye,
bronzed, extra fine wire.

**AC94840**
Accu-Point Knife Edge.

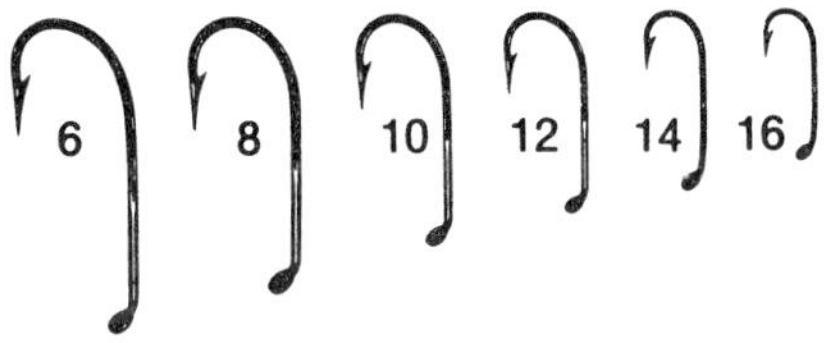

**94841 HOLLOW POINT VIKING**
Forged, straight, turned down
eye, chemically polished, fine
wire, bronzed.

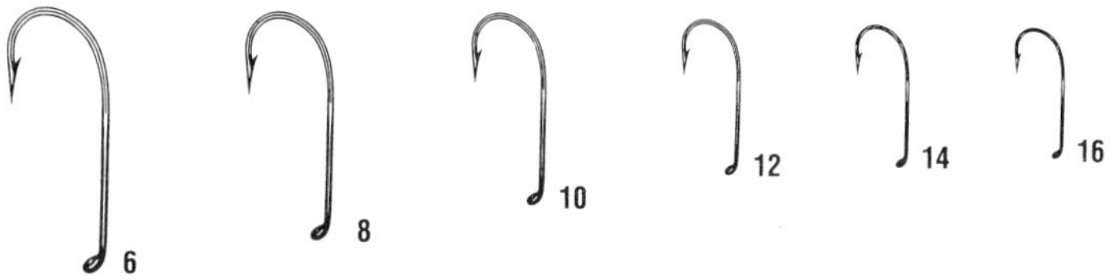

**94845 HOLLOW POINT VIKING**
Forged, straight, turned down
eye, chemically polished, extra
fine wire, bronzed.
**Barbless**

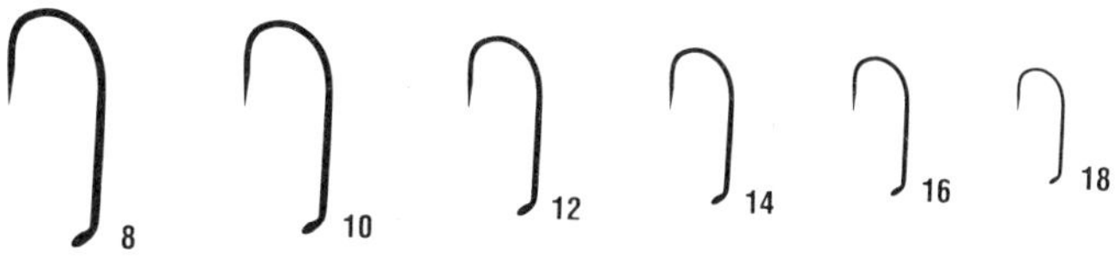

**94838 HOLLOW POINT VIKING**
Forged, straight, turned down
eye, extra fine wire, extra short
shank, chemically polished.

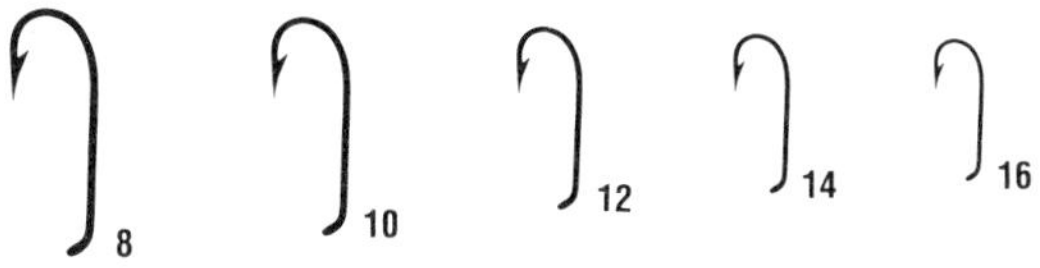

**3904A SPROAT WET**
Hollow Point, special sproat,
turned down eye, slightly
reversed, chemically polished,
wide gape, bronzed.

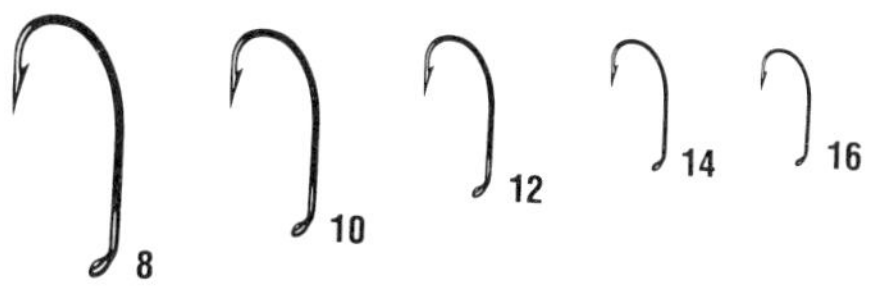

**7780C WET FORGED**
Superior Point, round bend,
forged, reversed, turned down
eye, chemically polished,
bronzed.

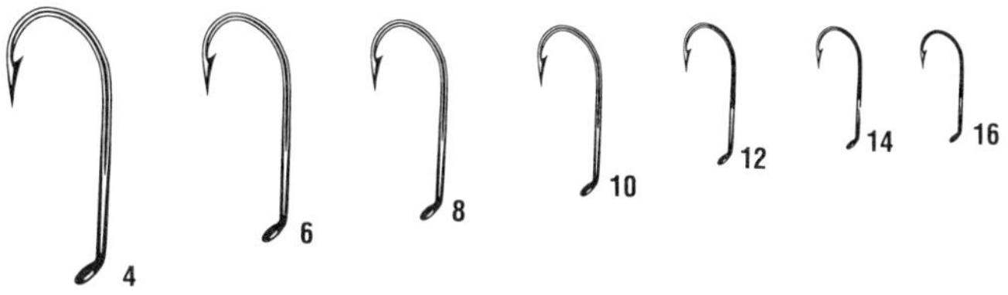

**7948A HOLLOW POINT VIKING**
Forged, straight, turned down
eye, chemically polished,
bronzed.

**79672 VIKING**
Forged, straight, fine wire,
turned down small eye,
chemically polished, bronzed.
**Micro Barb.**

**79703 WET VIKING EXTRA FINE**
Hollow Point, viking, forged,
straight, turned down eye,
chemically polished, extra fine
wire, bronzed.

**9578A HOLLOW/SHORT POINT
SPECIAL LIMERICK**
Slightly reserved, turned down
eye, chemically polished,
bronzed.

**9671 ROUND BEND FLY HOOK**
Forged, straight, round bend,
turned down tapered eye,
Bronzed, 2 extra long shank.

**AC9671**
Accu-Point Knife Edge.

**79580 LURE 4 EXTRA LONG**
Hollow Point, viking, forged,
straight, turned down eye,
bronzed, chemically polished, 4
extra long shank.

**79706 LURE 3 EXTRA LONG**
Hollow Point, viking, forged,
straight, turned down eye,
bronzed, chemically polished, 3
extra long shank.

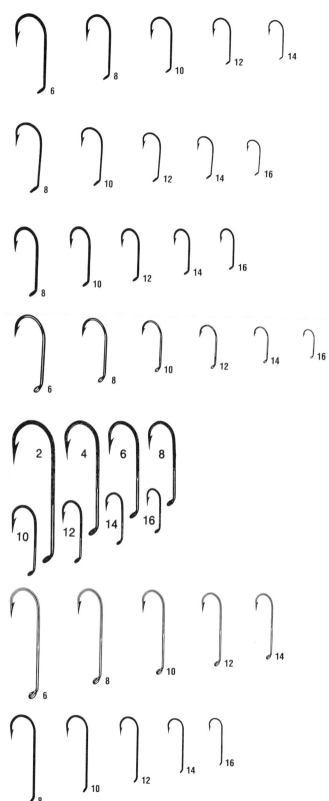

**79717 BARBLESS LURE**
Short Point, viking, forged, straight, chemically polished, turned down eye, 4 extra long shank, bronzed.
**Barbless.**

**79671 VIKING**
Forged, straight, turned down small eye, 4 extra long shank, bronzed, chemically polished.
**Micro Barb.**

**AC80000BR**
Accu-Point Knife Edge Fly Hooks, straight, forged, turned down 30 degree, extra small ball-eye, bronzed, small barb, dry fly hook

**AC80100BR**
Accu-Point Knife Edge Fly Hooks, reversed 10 degree, forged, turn down 30 degree, extra small ball-eye, bronzed, small barb, dry fly hook

**AC80050BR**
Accu-Point Knife Edge Fly Hooks, straight, forged, extra small ball-eye, bronzed, small barb, dry fly hook

**AC80150BR**
Accu-Point Knife Edge Fly Hooks, straight, slightly forged, ringed bronzed, shank bent up 40 degree, small barb swimming nymph hook

**AC80200BR**
Accu-Point Knife Edge Fly Hooks, reversed 15 degree, turn down 30 degree, extra small ball-eye, bronzed, 2 extra strong, small barb, Shrimp/Caddis Pupae Hook

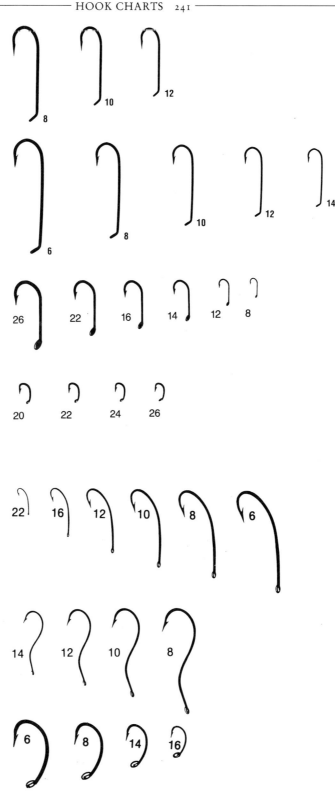

**AC80250BR**
Accu-Point Knife Edge Fly Hooks, forged, reversed 15 degree, turn down 30 degree, extra small ball-eye, bronzed, small barb Shrimp/Caddis Pupae Hook

12    14    16    18

**11871  CARP BOILIE**
Hollow Point, forged, reversed, turned up, ball eye, black.

4    6    8    10

**37160  HOLLOW POINT**
Wide gape, slightly reversed, turned up ball eye, chemically polished, bronzed.

8    10    12    14    16    18    20

**9479  HOLLOW POINT VIKING**
Forged, reversed, turned down eye, 5 extra short shank, extra fine wire, chemically polished, bronzed.

4    6    8    10    12    14    16

**3257B  FLY HOOK**
Turned down tapered eye, sproat bend, bronzed, kink instead of barb.

8    10    12

**32760**
Eyed, bronzed, extra short shank bent down, extra strong.

**32762**
Eyed, gold-plated, extra short shank bent down, extra strong.

2    4    6    8    10    12

**79666**
Hollow point, Mustad Viking Keel Hook forged, ringed, bronzed, straight.

4    6    8    10

# PARTRIDGE HOOKS

**STRONGHOLD WET FLY HOOKS**
Made out of heavy wire. For very
strong wet flies (and nymphs).
Grey Shadow finish. (Size 10 is
within the limit for international
competitions.)

8    10    12    14    16

**STRONGHOLD NYMPH HOOKS**
For most nymph patterns. Grey
Shadow finish. (Size 12 is within
the limit for international
competitions.)

8    10    12    14    16

**STRONGHOLD LONG SHANK
HOOKS**
For longer flies – streamer and
long nymphs. Grey Shadow finish.
(Size 14 is within the limit for
international competitions.)

8    10    12    14

16

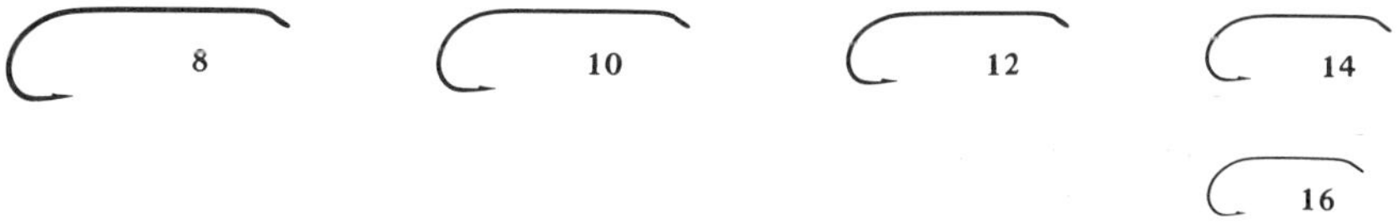

**PARTRIDGE STRAIGHT EYE
STREAMER HOOKS**
These were originally designed
for attractor flies but have been
used by many tiers in the smaller
sizes for nymph patterns. Straight
eye. Bronze finish.

10    12    14

**PARTRIDGE BUCKTAIL/
STREAMER HOOKS**
Another hook developed for
streamer flies but now used
widely for longer shank nymphs
in these smaller sizes. Down eye.
Bronze finish.

10    12    14

**BOB CHURCH GOLDHEAD
HOOKS**
Wide gape wet fly hooks which
can take the gold (or silver)
beads which are now popular as
the heads on wet fly patterns.
Forged bend. Bronze finish.

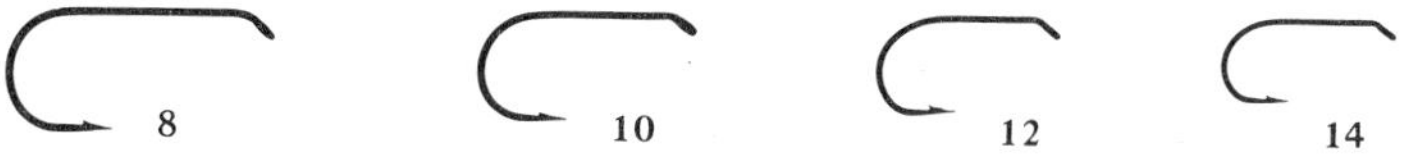

8    10    12    14

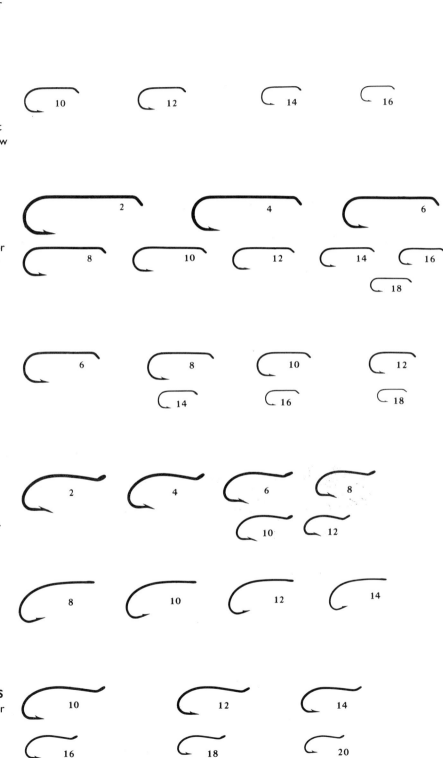

**L/S 4X FINE DRY FLY HOOKS**
A lightweight, slightly longer than standard hook which is ideal for emerger patterns such as buzzers. Forged bend. Bronze finish.

**GREY SHADOW CAPTAIN HAMILTON WET FLY HOOKS**
The L2A Captain Hamilton wet fly hook but with a Grey Shadow finish.

**CAPTAIN HAMILTON NYMPH HOOKS**
The basic nymph hook – about 2X long shank. (Also suitable for shorter streamer and attractor flies and for some larger dries.) Forged bend. Bronze finish.

**CAPTAIN HAMILTON WET FLY HOOKS**
The ideal hook for all types of wet fly (and nymphs). Forged Hamilton bend. Bronze finish. (Also in Grey Shadow finish as GRS2A.)

**McHAFFIE MASTERS WET FLY HOOKS**
For traditional wet trout flies. Special Dublin point and up eye. Black finish.

**GREY SHADOW EMERGER/ NYMPH HOOKS**
The K12ST long shank Sedge/ Caddis hooks with a Grey Shadow finish.

**JARDINE LIVING NYMPH HOOKS**
A graceful and effective hook for all curved body imitations. Turned up eye. Grey Shadow finish.

**YORKSHIRE SEDGE/CADDIS HOOKS**

Superb hook for all types of curved body insect imitations. Bronze finish.

8  10  12  14

16  18

**TAFF PRICE SWIMMING NYMPH HOOKS**

A longer shank used to imitate swimming nymphs with shape to add movement to the fly on the retrieve. Straight eye. Bronze finish.

8  10  12  14

**LONG SHANK SEDGE/CADDIS HOOKS**

Sweeping bend for flies like caddis and emerger patterns. Straight eye. Bronze finish. (Also in Grey Shadow finish GRS12ST.)

8  10  12  14

16  18  20  22

**ROMAN MOSER BARBLESS NYMPH HOOKS**

A medium shank and middleweight wire for wet flies and nymphs. Grey Shadow finish.

8  10  12  14

**JOHN VENIARD GRUB/SHRIMP HOOKS**

A special hook for all types of grub and shrimp, curved body and some emerger patterns. Offset bend. Bronze finish.

8  10  12  14  16  18

**OLIVER EDWARDS NYMPH/ EMERGER HOOKS**

Designed for small nymph and emerger patterns, these hooks are also good for dry flies. Silver finish.

16  18  20

**DRAPER FLAT-BODIED NYMPH HOOKS**

A speical hook at a base for all types of flat broad bodied nymph patterns. Straight eye. Bronze finish.

6  8  10

12  14  16

# BIBLIOGRAPHY

Anon., *Patterns of the Masters*, Federation of Fly
  Fishers, 1990
Bergera, *Manuscrito de Astorga*, 1624
Bergman, *Trout*, Knopf, 1938
Berners, 'Treatyse of fysshynge with an angle,'
  *Boke of St Albans*, Westminster, 1496
Blackman, *Flies and Fly Fishing in South Africa*,
  Accucut Books, 1985
Blades, *Fishing Flies and Fly Tying*, Stackpole,
  1951
Borger, *Designing Trout Flies*, Tomorrow River,
  1991
Boyle & Whitlock, *Fly Tyers*, Almanac, Crown,
  1975
Boyle & Whitlock, *Second Fly Tyer's, Almanac*,
  Lippincott, 1978
Brookes, *Nymph Fishing for Larger Trout*,
  Crown, 1976
Bruce & Hobart, 'Biology of the larvae of the
  Chironomidae', *Entomology Gazette*, 1972
Carpenter, *Life in Inland Waters*, Sidgwick &
  Jackson, 1928
Church, *Guide to Trout Flies*, Crowood, 1987
Clegg, *Freshwater Life*, Warne, 1965
Cockwill, *Big Trout Fishing*, Hamlyn, 1987
Collyer & Hammond, *Flies of the British Isles*,
  Warne, 1951
Costen, 'Beneath the surface', *Country Life*, 1938
Cove, *My Way with Trout*, Crowood, 1986
Crass, *Trout in South Africa*, Macmillan, 1986
del Poso Obese, *Moscas para La Pesca*, Everest,
  1987
Dereksen (ed.), *Fly Patterns of Alaska*, Frank
  Amato Press, 1993
Diez, *Pesca de la Trucha*, Pethe, 1978
Draper, *Trout Flies in New Zealand*, Reed, 1971
Dulude, 'Ephemères du pecheur Quebecois',
  *L'Homme*, 1992
Fogg, *The Art of the Wet Fly*, A. & C. Black
Francis, *Book of Angling*, Jenkins, 1867
Fraser, *Mastering the Nymph*
Gartside, *Flies for the 21st Century*, Gartside, 1993

Gartside, *Fly Patterns for the Adventurous Tyer*,
  Gartside, 1993
Gilbert, *Hover Flies*, Cambridge University Press,
  1986
Goddard, *Trout Fly Recognition*, A. & C. Black,
  1966
Goddard, *Trout Flies of Stillwater*, A. & C. Black,
  1969
Goddard, *Trout Flies of Britain and Europe*, A. &
  C. Black, 1991
Gordon, *How to Fish from Top to Bottom*,
  Stackpole, 1952
Hafele & Hughes, *Western Hatches*, Frank Amato
  Press, 1986
Hammond, *Dragonflies of the British Isles and
  Ireland*, Curwen, 1977
Hammond, *New Zealand Encyclopedia of Fly
  Fishing*, Halcyon, 1988
Hanna, *Fly Fishing in Ireland*, 1993
Hellekson, *Popular Fly Patterns*, Peregrine Smith,
  1984
Hickin, *Caddis Larvae*, Hutchinson, 1967
Hill & Marshall, *Stalking Trout*, SeTo/Halcyon,
  1985
Hughes, *Living Insects*, Collins, 1974
Hynes, 'A key to the adults and nymphs of the
  British stoneflies', *Freshwater Biological
  Association Publications* No. 17, 1967
Ivens, *Stillwater Trout Fishing*, Deutsch, 1952
Jacques, *Development of Modern Stillwater
  Fishing*, A. & C. Black, 1974
Jardine, *Sotheby's Guide to Fly Fishing*, Dorling
  Kindersley, 1981
Jennings, *A Book of Trout Flies*, Derrydale, 1935
Kaufmann, *American Nymph Manual*, S.T.S.,
  1975
Kaufmann, *Fly Tyer's Nymph Manual*, Western
  Fisherman's Press, 1986
Kimmins, 'Keys to the British species of
  Megaloptera and Neuroptera', *Freshwater
  Biological Association Publications* No. 8, 1962
Koch, *Fishing the Midge*, Freshet Press, 1970

LaFontaine, *Caddis Flies*, Winchester, 1981

Laible, *CDC Flies*, Traun River, 1993

Lane, *Lake and Loch Fishing*, Seeley Service, 1955

Lawrie, *The Rough Stream Nymph*, Oliver & Boyd, 1947

Lawrie, *Scottish Trout Flies*, Muller, 1966

Lawrie, *Reference Book of English Trout Flies*, Pelham, 1967

Lawrie, *International Trout Flies*, Muller, 1969

Leiser, *The Book of Fly Patterns*, Knopf, 1987

Leonard, *Flies*, Barnes, 1972

Linsenmaier, *Insects of the World*, McGraw Hill, 1972

Linssen, *Beetles of the British Isles*, Warne, 1959

Macan, 'Revised key to the British water bugs', *Freshwater Biological Assocation Publications* No. 16, 1965

Macan, 'A key to the nymphs of the British Ephemeroptera', *Freshwater Biological Association Publications* No. 20, 1970

McCafferty, *Aquatic Entomology*, Scientific Books, 1981

McCausland, *Fly Fishing in Australia and New Zealand*, Lothian, 1967

McLachlan, *Trichoptera of European Fauna*, Classey, 1968

Malone, *Irish Trout and Salmon Flies*, Colin Smythe, 1984

Mann, 'Key to the British freshwater leeches', *Freshwater Biological Association Publications* No. 14, 1964

Marsh, *Trout Stream Insects of New Zealand*, Millwood, 1983

Martin, *Fly Dressing Methods*, Nick Lyons, 1987

Matthews & Juracek, *Fly Patterns of the Yellowstone*, Blue Ribbon, 1987

Merkas, *Leksikon Ribolovnih Musica (A Dictionary of Fishing Flies)*, Merkas, 1990

Metz, Kretschner & Rubel, *Zwanzig Fliegenmuster Reicham Aus*, Schuck, 1977

Miall, *Aquatic Insects*, Macmillan, 1992

Migel & Wright Jr (eds), *Masters of the Nymph*, Nick Lyons, 1979

Morgan, *Fly Patterns for Wales*, Gomer, 1984

Mottram, *Fly Fishing: Some New Arts and Mysteries*, A. & C. Black, 1914

Norman, *Fresh and Saltwater Fly Fishing in South Africa*, Van Rensberg, 1987

Orman, *Trout with the Nymph*, Hodder & Stoughton, 1974

Pennel, *Fishing*, Longman, 1970

Pequenot, *French Fishing Flies*, Nick Lyons, 1987

Pethe, *Traité Pratique des Mouches*, Pethe, 1957

Price, *Fly Patterns, an International Guide*, Ward Lock, 1986

Price, *Rough Stream Trout Flies*, A. & C. Black, 1976

Price, *Stillwater Flies*, vols 1–3, Benn, 1979

Price, *Fly Patterns*, Ward Lock, 1986

Price, *Tying and Fishing the Sedge*, Blandford, 1994

Reid, *Clyde Style Flies*, David & Charles, 1971

Ritz, *A Fly Fisher's Life*, Rheinhardt, 1959

Roberts, *The Grayling Angler*, Witherby, 1982

Roberts, *A New Illustrated Dictionary of Trout Flies*, Allen & Unwin, 1986

Robson, *Robson's Guide*, Beekay, 1985

Rosborough, *Tying and Fishing the Fuzzy Nymphs*, Stackpole, 1965

Roskelly, *Flies of the North West*, Frank Amato Press, 1979

Saloman, *Freshwater Fishing in South Africa*, Van Rensberg, 1976

Saville, *Reservoir Trout Fishing with Tom Saville*, Witherby, 1991

Schwiebert, *Nymphs*, Winchester, 1973

Sharp, *Insects*, vols 1 & 2, Macmillan, 1909

Skues, *Way of a Trout with a Fly*, A. & C. Black, 1921

Solomon & Leiser, *Caddis and the Angler*, Stackpole, 1977

Southwood & Leston, *Land and Water Bugs of the British Isles*, Warne, 1959

Stetzer, *Flies (The Best One Thousand)*, Frank Amato Press, 1992

Stewart & Allen, *Flies for Bass and Panfish*, Mountain Pond, 1992

Stewart & Allen, *Flies for Trout*, Mountain Pond, 1993

Swain, *Guide to North American Insects*, Doubleday, 1962

Swisher & Richards, *Fly Fishing Strategy*, Crown, 1975

Swisher & Richards, *Emergers*, Lyons Burford, 1991

Swisher, Richards & Arbona, *Stoneflies*, Nick Lyons, 1980

Tashiro, [*The Tashiro Nymphs and Naturals*], in Japanese, 1981

Tashiro, [*The World of Tashiro Nymphs*], in Japanese, 1986

Venables, *The Experienced Angler*, London, 1662

Veniard, *Fly Dresser's Guide*, A. & C. Black, 1952

Veniard, *A Further Guide to Fly Dressing*, A. & C. Black, 1964

Veniard, *Reservoir and Lake Flies*, A. & C. Black, 1970

Walker, C.F., *Chalk Stream Trout Flies*, A. & C. Black, 1949

Walker, C.F., *Lake Flies and Their Imitation*, Jenkins, 1960

Walker, R. Fly Dressing Innovations, Benn, 1974

Walker, R.*Modern Fly Dressings*, Benn, 1980

Walton, *Compleat Angler*, 1663

Ward & Whipple, *Freshwater Biology*, Wiley, 1945

Whitlock, *Guide to Aquatic Trout Food*, Nick Lyons, 1982

Williams, *Dictionary of Trout Flies*, A. & C. Black, 1949

Wolfle & Heger, *Modernes und Enfaches Fliegenbinden*, Traun River, 1993

# INDEX OF
# FLY PATTERNS

# INDEX OF NAMES